CORRECTION SYMBOLS

(**Boldface** numbers refer to sections in the *Handbook*.)

ab	abbreviation **41**	**num**	number **42**
ack	acknowledging sources	**p**	punctuation error **28-41**
	MLA style **50,**	◊	apostrophe **38**
	APA style **51**	**[ ]**	brackets **34**
adj/adv	adjective/adverb **9d–e,**	**:**	colon **31**
	19a–d	⌄	comma **29**
agr	agreement **16, 17**		no comma needed **29e**
appr	inappropriate language **24**	**—**	dash **32**
art	article **9d, 17a, 23c**	**. . .**	ellipsis points **36**
awk	awkward construction **23**	**. ? !**	end punctuation **28**
bias	biased language **25b**	**( )**	parentheses **33**
cap	capital letter **46**	**" "**	quotation marks **35**
case	error in case **18**	**;**	semicolon **30**
cl	cliché **26g**	**par, ¶**	start new paragraph **5d**
coh	coherence **3d, 5**	**//**	faulty parallelism **23c**
comp	comparison **20**	**pass**	passive voice **9b**
con	connotation **26c**	**ref**	pronoun reference **17b**
coord	coordination **9g, 11a**	**rep**	repetition **26d**
cs	comma splice **14a**	**rev**	revise **3**
dev	inadequate development	**sexist**	sexist language **25a**
	2d, 3a	**shift**	unnecessary shift **21**
div	faulty word division **39e**	**sl**	slang **24a**
dm	dangling modifier **23d**	**sp**	misspelled word **44**
exact	exactness **26, 27**	**ss**	faulty sentence
fl	flowery language **26e**		structure **23**
frag	fragment **13**	**sub**	subordination **9g, 11b**
fs	fused sentence **14b**	**t**	verb tense **9b**
gr	grammatical error **8-12**	**trans**	transition needed **5d, 43d**
hyph	incorrect use of	**var**	lack of variety in sentence
	hyphen **39**		structure **6a**
inc	incomplete	**vag**	vague word **26b**
	construction **23**	**vb**	verb form **15**
ital	italics (underlining) **37**	**w**	wordy **26d**
jg	jargon **24c**	**ww**	wrong word **26a-b, 27**
lc	lowercase letter **46**	⌒	close up space
log	faulty logic **7a, b, c**	ℒ	delete
mixed	mixed construction **23a, b**	**x**	error
mm	misplaced modifier **23e**	**∧**	insert
mood	error in mood **9b, 21e**	**#**	insert space
ms	manuscript form **43**	∪	transpose

To my parents, Frank O'Hare
and Theresa Sutherland O'Hare,
for their encouragement and support
and for their love

To my wife, Marge,
and our daughters, Judith and Maureen,
for their love, patience,
encouragement, and support

THIRD EDITION

THE MODERN WRITER'S HANDBOOK

Frank O'Hare
THE OHIO STATE UNIVERSITY

Edward A. Kline
UNIVERSITY OF NOTRE DAME

Macmillan Publishing Company
NEW YORK
Maxwell Macmillan Canada
TORONTO
Maxwell Macmillan International
NEW YORK   OXFORD   SINGAPORE   SYDNEY

Editor: Barbara A. Heinssen
Development Editor: Sharon Balbos
Production Supervisor: Katherine Mara Evancie
Production Manager: Valerie Sawyer and Susan Levine
Text Designer: Natasha Sylvester
Cover photo: Slide Graphics of New England, Inc.

This book was set in Garamond and Slimbach by V & M Graphics, Inc.
and was printed and bound by R. R. Donnelley & Sons Company/Crawfordsville.
The cover was printed by New England Book Components.

Macmillan Publishing Company
A Simon & Schuster Company
Needham Heights, MA 02194

Library of Congress Cataloging-in-Publication Data
O'Hare, Frank.
   The modern writer's handbook.—3rd ed.
Frank O'Hare, Edward A. Kline
     p. cm.
  Includes index.
  ISBN 0-02-389170-X (paper)
  1. English language—Rhetoric—Handbooks, manuals, etc.
  2. English language—Grammar—1950– —Handbooks, manuals, etc.
  I. Kline, Edward A. II. Title.
PE1408.037 1993
808' .042—dc20   91-46727
              CIP

Printing: 5 6 7   Year: 5 6 7 8 9

PREFACE

To the Instructor

The third edition of *The Modern Writer's Handbook* is up to date, complete, user friendly, and of value not only in composition classes but also in writing across the curriculum courses. New chapters and sections have been added, including two chapters on writing in the disciplines and chapters on avoiding sexist language, writing with computers, and writing essay examinations. To help students find information quickly and work with the handbook on their own, we have included a full system of cross-referencing, added seven completely new examples of student writing (essays and research papers), most of which are annotated, and introduced useful checklists and a new look. These improvements are designed to build on the strengths of the successful second edition.

New Chapters on Writing Across the Curriculum

This edition of the handbook provides valuable information on writing in the disciplines. Two new chapters make this handbook easily adaptable for use in Writing Across the Curriculum programs.

"Writing in the Humanities and About Literature" (Chapter 53) explains how to write reaction, interpretation, review, and analysis papers and provides a complete guide to writing about literature. The chapter concludes with an annotated, student-authored example of literary analysis.

"Writing in the Social, Natural, and Applied Sciences" (Chapter 54) covers writing and documenting field research, lab reports, and technical reports, with student samples of each.

Additional New Chapters

In response to reviewer requests, four additional new chapters appear in this edition. The inclusion of these chapters ensures that the handbook is current and complete.

"Writing with a Computer" (Chapter 4) covers the entire process of writing with a computer, from prewriting through printing the essay. It includes a brief dictionary of important computer terms and focuses on helping students feel confident using a computer.

"Sexist and Other Biased Language" Chapter 25) has been expanded into a full chapter based on the second edition's successful section on sexist language. This chapter offers one of the most comprehensive handbook guides to the issue of sexist and biased language and gives students the means to avoid sexism and bias in their writing.

"The Slash" (Chapter 40) has been added to the part on punctuation marks.

"Writing Essay Examinations" (Chapter 55) offers step-by-step guidelines on preparing for and writing essay examinations. An annotated sample student response concludes the chapter.

New Sections and Expanded Coverage

The important new sections in the third edition include the following:

New coverage of collaborative writing and peer critiques, Section 3a.

New detailed treatment of writing arguments, Section 7d, which concludes the chapter on critical thinking (Chapter 7) by showing students how to construct an effective argument.

New coverage on using computerized research sources such as computerized catalogs and databases, Section 48a.

Subject areas expanded in this edition: ways to find a topic; the pentad as a discovery technique; audience and tone; thesis statement; working and formal outlines; manuscript form for computer-generated papers; MLA and APA in-text and end-of-text sample entries to include non-library sources; listing of general reference tools to include agriculture, biological and life sciences, engineering and technology, environment and ecology, mathematics and physics; and plagiarism.

"Glossary of Usage" and the **"Glossary of Grammatical Terms"** have also been expanded and updated.

New Pedagogy

New Student Models and Examples. This edition contains **seven new samples of student writing** including a student's essay in different drafts, two new model research papers, one in MLA style, the other in APA style, and a sample literary analysis. **All of these models are annotated to help the student understand how a piece of writing develops and what decisions a writer needs to make.** Also included are excerpts of student papers for courses in the social, natural, and applied sciences.

In addition, hundreds of examples appear throughout the text to illustrate the various principles of grammar and usage.

Nearly fifty paragraphs by professional and student writers serve as examples of writing or appear in exercises.

New Checklists. Thirteen checklists appear at critical points in the text to serve as efficient summary references for student writers. Complete listings of these checklists appear on the inside front cover of the handbook and after the table of contents.

New Exercises. All exercises in this edition have new content and reflect the diversity of today's student body. Many of the exercises consist of related sentences to simulate proofreading and editing in paragraph form.

ESL Index. An ESL index has been added to enhance the accessibility of the handbook for all students. It follows the general index and includes a comprehensive listing of topics most often referred to by speakers of English as a second language.

Organizational Improvements

The basic organization of the second edition has been retained but improved. The handbook begins with the stages in the process of writing, from prewriting through drafting, revision, and proofreading and editing to final product. It then treats the grammar of the sentence, punctuation and mechanics, spelling, the research paper, and then academic and business writing. Each of the handbook's eight parts subdivides into chapters and then further subdivides into sections that contain a rule followed by examples, cross-referenced to appropriate sections in the handbook. Exercises that allow for practical applications of the subject matter appear throughout.

Organizational improvements include

Earlier coverage of style and diction (Part IV).
Separate chapters for MLA and APA documentation styles (Chapters 50 and 51).

Supplements

This new edition of *The Modern Writer's Handbook* is accompanied by a comprehensive supplementary package. An ***Instructor's Annotated Edition*** includes all of the answers to the exercises found in the handbook. A new tool has been added to this edition, the ***Guide to Teaching Writing***, which provides both theoretical and practical information for composition instructors. Much of the information is cross-referenced to the handbook. The ***Guide to Teaching Writing*** emphasizes important topics—ESL-related concerns, writing across the curriculum, collaborative writing, and avoiding biased language. ***The Modern Writer's Workbook***, second edition (with accompanying answer key), by Marie-Louise Nickerson of Bronx Community College, offers additional exercises, tabs that correspond to those found in the handbook, and a cross-referencing index on the front endpapers that allows for easy integration of the handbook and workbook. The ***Test Item File*** by Marie-Louise Nickerson includes diagnostic and achievement tests and a comprehensive test. It is available in printed form as an 8½"×11" booklet with perforated pages and as ***The Professor's Assistant*™ *software program*** for both the IBM and Macintosh computer. Software for both the IBM and Macintosh computers is also available.

Acknowledgments

We are deeply grateful to all who helped make this third edition possible, especially the freshman composition students at the University of Notre Dame with whom portions of this book were tested. We especially thank student authors Brian Liptak, John Michael Jansen, Eileen B. Biagi, Jennifer M. Neidenbach, and Colleen Templin for permission to use their essays and papers as models.

Thanks must also be extended to faculty colleagues at the University of Notre Dame: Peri Arnold, Willis Bartlett, James P.

Dougherty, Jeremiah Freeman, Sandra Chrystal Hayes, Eugene W. Henry, Judith Heyhoe, C. Lincoln Johnson, Naomi M. Meara, Leda McIntyre-Hall, Rev. Joseph L. Walter, C.S.C., James H. Walton, and Thomas Werge. Grateful appreciation is expressed to Douglas Archer and Thomas J. Cashore of the Hesburgh Memorial Library Bibliographic Services; Georgeanna Caldwell and Lois VanTornhout for advice on facsimile transactions; and Fay Boulton, Noelle Werge Barton, Margaret Jasiewicz, and Janet Kay Wheeler for manuscript preparation. Thanks is also expressed to the reviewers whose advice proved most helpful in preparing this edition:

Victoria Aarons, *Trinity University*
Deborah C. Andrews, *University of Delaware*
Arthur W. Biddle, *University of Vermont*
Tim Crusius, *Southern Methodist University*
Linda J. Daigle, *Houston Community College*
Susan Dean Jacobs, *DePaul University*
Paula Gillespie, *Marquette University*
Patricia H. Graves, *Georgia State University*
Ruth Greenberg, *Jefferson Community College*
Dana Gulling Mead, *Elizabethtown College*
Dona J. Hickey, *University of Richmond*
Francis A. Hubbard, *Marquette University*
Christine Hult, *Utah State University*
Grace Ioppolo, *University of California, Los Angeles*
Archibald E. Irwin, *Indiana University Southeast*
Janet W. Jones, *Middlesex Community College*
Jane G. Jordan (late), *University of Richmond*
Russ Larson, *Eastern Michigan University*
Anne Lesse, *Lord Fairfax Community College*
Helane Levine-Keating, *Pace University*
Diane Martin, *Eastfield College*
Gloria Mason Henderson, *Gordon College*
Mary E. McGann, *University of Indianapolis*

Robert Moore, *State University of New York–Oswego*
Alleen Pace Nilsen, *Arizona State University*
Marcia Peoples Halio, *University of Delaware*
Phil Sittnick, *Northern Essex Community College*
John W. Taylor, *South Dakota State University*
Christopher J. Thaiss, *George Mason University*
Arthur A. Wagner, *Macomb Community College*
Leslie J. West, *Houston Community College*
Elizabeth Goodridge Westgard, *Saint Mary-of-the-Woods College*
Betty Anne Younglove, *Houston Community College System*
Barbara Zapffe Vielma, *University of Texas–Pan American*

For the guidance and encouragement received from the Macmillan staff, we remain indebted and flattered: Sharon Balbos, Development Editor, especially for her kind manner, wise judgments, diplomatic criticisms, and appropriate, firm reminders that helped us shape the text and who became a good friend in the process; Ellie Eisenstat, Assistant Editor; Katherine Evancie, Senior Production Supervisor; and Barbara A. Heinssen, Senior English Editor, who initiated this project and encouraged us with intelligence, grace, and good humor.

Frank O'Hare   Edward A. Kline
Ohio State University   *University of Notre Dame*

To the Student

How to Use This Book

This book will help you develop and refine your writing skills. It does not provide you with a foolproof formula for writing an essay or a quick answer on how to avoid all errors. No such shortcuts exist. *The Modern Writer's Handbook* does provide you with a plan for good writing that begins by illustrating general writing strategies and proceeds to help you work through planning, prewriting, drafting, revising, and proofreading. The book offers you options, not laws. It is not wrong, for example, to compose a first draft without writing a formal outline first, but because some people find outlining helpful, we describe strategies for outlining in Section 2c.

How to Find the Information You Need

This handbook has been designed to help you locate information quickly. It is a good idea to spend a few minutes familiarizing yourself with how the book works, especially with the devices that will help you find the information you need.

Red Tabs at the top of each page in the handbook contain particular chapter numbers, section letters, and chapter symbols (these symbols are shorthand for the chapter title and correspond to the correction symbols listed on the front endpapers). The tabs can help you find information by thumbing through the book. Note also that at the top of every page, **chapter titles** appear in full on left-hand pages and **section titles** appear on right-hand pages to give you more specific guidance.

Checklists (boxed and tinted red) appear throughout the handbook and provide you with convenient summaries of the handbook's guidelines on writing and revising. A

To the Student **xiii**

list of all the handbook's checklists appears on the inside front cover of the text. **Numerous lists** appear throughout the text to assist you with your writing. A listing of every list and checklist in the handbook follows the table of contents.

Endpapers (the inside front and back covers and facing pages) contain important information:

1. A list of all the handbook's checklists appears on the inside front cover.

2. A list of correction symbols, which your instructor may use in correcting your essays and papers, appears on the endpaper facing the inside front cover. If your instructor marks the symbol *dm* in the margin of your paper, you can consult the correction symbol list and note that the abbreviation means dangling modifier. You can then consult the section number indicated (23d) for more information.

3. On the back endpapers, you will find an overview of the handbook's contents. Glance at it to get a sense of how the handbook is structured.

The **Glossary of Usage** and the **Glossary of Grammatical Terms** provide you with accessible and brief explanations of what words to use in certain situations. For example, use the Glossary of Usage to determine whether the word *who* or *whom* is appropriate. Use the Glossary of Grammatical Terms to find the definitions of basic grammatical terms like *case* or *pronoun*. Entries are arranged alphabetically in both glossaries.

The general **Index** contains a complete listing of all topics covered in the handbook along with page references. The index has been designed for easy access. It is followed by the **ESL Index,** which lists topics often referred to by speakers of English as a second language.

Organization

This book first presents a general view of the writing process: planning, drafting, and revising your essay. It then considers the surface features of the language, emphasizing the important conventions that educated readers expect to encounter when they read your writing. The handbook concludes by introducing you to the specialized writing tasks you will encounter in your various college courses and in the business world.

- □ **Part I offers advice about the writing process:** preparation for writing, producing a first draft, revising (re-seeing) the draft, and proofreading and editing it. Detailed coverage on writing with a computer follows. Next the parts of an essay including paragraph development, transitions within and between paragraphs, and sentences with suggestions for combining, variety in structure, clarity, and effective emphasis are discussed. Part I concludes with a consideration of critical thinking and faulty reasoning and a new section on writing arguments.

- □ **Parts II through VI examine the principles of grammar, sentence form, diction and style, punctuation and mechanics, and spelling.** You will use these parts of the book as reference if you are already familiar with grammatical principles and the terms and conventions of usage. If your familiarity with this material is limited, you can use these sections to help you master the conventions of grammar and usage.

- □ **Part VII explains and illustrates how to write a research paper:** how to select and limit a topic; how to plan, research, and write the paper; and then how to document it according to the styles recommended by the Modern Language Association (MLA) and the American Psychological Association (APA). Two complete annotated sample research papers demonstrate each style. Refer to these samples for guidance as you write your own papers.

☐ **Part VIII explains and illustrates the types of writing you will be called on to do in your different college courses** whether in the humanities, literary analysis, or in social, natural, and applied sciences and in the business world with examples of each type of writing. You may also find the new chapter on preparing for and writing essay examinations (Chapter 55) useful.

The handbook is divided into parts, then into chapters and sections. Each chapter contains sections that explore in detail the subject matter at hand. For instance, Part IV, "Diction and Style," contains the following subdivisions: Chapter 24, "Appropriate Word Choice"; Chapter 25, "Sexist and Other Biased Language"; and Chapter 26, "Exact Word Choice." Each of these chapters is further subdivided into sections. Thus, Chapter 24 covers the following: 24a on slang, 24b on colloquialisms, 24c on jargon, and 24d on gobbledygook. Each of these sections provides you with advice to follow, examples for clarification, and practice exercises.

You learn to write better only by writing often. *The Modern Writer's Handbook* serves as a guide to all steps in the writing process and with continued use will help you grow in competence and confidence. Paradoxically, the more diligently you use this handbook, the less you will need it.

Edward Kline
University of Notre Dame

CONTENTS

PART II
GRAMMAR

PART III
SENTENCE FORM

PART IV
DICTION AND STYLE

PART V
PUNCTUATION AND MECHANICS

PART VI
SPELLING

PART VII
THE RESEARCH PAPER

CHECKLISTS FOR WRITERS

(**Boldface** numbers refer to sections in the *Handbook*; page numbers appear in *italics* within parentheses.)

Other Helpful Lists in the *Handbook*

PART I

THE PROCESS OF WRITING

1   Preparation for Writing

Some people can pick up a tennis racket for the first time and hit a perfect serve across the net without thinking. Such competence among athletes is rare, however, and the same is true among writers. Like the tennis serve, writing requires a combination of skills perfected over time. It requires coordination of thought, language, and hand, and most of us are no more naturally adept at making the three work together than we are at making our arm muscles, our eyesight, and a racket put a tennis ball where we want it. So, like the tennis player, we must discover the strategies for learning to write and then practice. Writing strategies include prewriting, drafting, and revising, and each strategy involves a series of steps.

Critical thinking is an important component of these writing strategies. When we think critically, we analyze and evaluate information to arrive at understanding or insight. As you will see, thinking critically about drafting and the revision process will help you write well. But when preparing to write, three activities are especially useful: keeping a journal, reading, and writing letters.

1a Keeping a Journal

A journal differs from a diary because it goes beyond recounting the events of the writer's day to recording what the writer *thought* about the events or about some information. The following is an example of a diary entry:

May 17
Met Juanita at the ice cream parlor yesterday p.m. She had a bandaged knee from falling off her bicycle and couldn't keep our

date for the dance. Ralph's girlfriend offered to call a friend of hers for me, but I stayed with Juanita and went with her to a movie and Burger King instead.

A journal entry, on the other hand, might read like this:

> Juanita had to break our dance date the other night because she had damaged her knee in falling off her bike. She piled up, of course, because she was riding no-hands the way she always does on her heavy class days. Nothing I say seems to convince her that a backpack would be much better for hauling her books around than four texts under each arm and a prayer that God will steer and brake for her. She says the backpack would look sloppy, and I have to admit she dresses well. But why wear a boutique on your shoulders and live dangerously? I suppose there is something to be said for going in style, but she ought to realize as well that pride goeth before a fall.

You need not keep a journal on a daily basis, but you should keep it with some regularity if you are to gain any benefit from it. The journal gives regular practice in coordinating thought, language, and hand; it also provides a reservoir of ideas for future writing. In the preceding sample entry, there is an abundance of raw material to develop into an essay: the sacrifice of safety and practicality to appearance, the futility of arguing for a change in a person's basic values, the theme of pride leading to a fall. That great authors like Jane Austen, F. Scott Fitzgerald, Henry James, George Sand, and many, many others kept journals is no accident. The practice of thinking things out in a journal can be invaluable preparation for writing.

1b Reading and Being a Critical Reader

Travel with a book. When you are held up in traffic, waiting for a bus, or standing in line at the bank or the supermarket, read everything—books, newspapers, magazines, poems, billboards. Learn through reading what others have experienced and learned. What you read becomes part of your own experience for later use.

As you read, do more than absorb information; think about the way the author writes, about the turns of phrase, about the rhythm of sentences, and how the author avoids—or fails to avoid—a monotonous delivery. Try to store up particularly effective passages as models for your own prose. Read critically. Learn to argue with the printed word. A disagreement with another's point of view can be a potential starting point for an essay. Read looking for grammatical mistakes and errors of punctuation. If you can spot the faults of others, you will proofread your own work more accurately. Read to discover the author's tone and purpose and the ways they complement each other. Use your journal to record what you think about what you read.

1c Writing Letters

Writing letters to friends and relatives constitutes excellent writing practice because the recipient of a letter provides a clearly defined audience for the writer. We usually adjust our letters consciously or unconsciously to the likes and dislikes of the person to whom we are writing. Think of the adjustments you find yourself making in such letters. Ask yourself why you wrote to Great Uncle Herman about the "minor automobile accident" that prevented you from attending your cousin's wedding, and why you described the same event as "a stupid fender-bender" to your best friend. Work at making your letters entertaining. Invent new ways of communicating that "nothing much has happened here"—and remember, something always has.

1d Using Observation

Critical thinking underlies our preparation for writing, and it evolves from careful observation and our perceptions or insights into what we see. Can you make any connections between what you saw on the evening television news and some incident you saw today on campus? Practice looking at things with an eye to detail: the colors of automobiles, the shoe styles nonstudents wear, the varying textures of coats hanging on a rack, the shapes of cereal boxes on a supermarket shelf. Then move your body a few feet to your left or right. Does this new point of view alter your perception of the cars, shoes, coats, cereals? Does color alone differentiate the cars? What qualities other than shape distinguish the cereal boxes? How do these properties relate to the functions of the products, if at all? You can record those and similar results from careful observing and perceiving in your journal, in book margins, in your letters, or you can simply store them in your memory for use at another time.

EXERCISE 1-1

Set yourself the goal of writing at least 150 words a day for a month. The writing can be of any type as long as it is not required academically or professionally. Count personal letters, journal entries, and any personal observations as part of the exercise. Write more than 150 words if you wish, but do not write 1,000 words on Tuesday evening and call it a week's work. Instead, write every day so that you will sharpen your writing and thinking skills.

EXERCISE 1-2

Keep a record of everything you read for one week. (Do not count advertisements and notices.) At the end of the week, review your record and select the one piece of reading that you remember most clearly. Write a brief discussion of your choice, explaining why you remember it so well. Look at what you have written and evaluate how you did it. Did the author write something that makes the piece memorable for you? Did the author use observation in any way?

2 The Process of Writing: First Draft

The finished essay is the product of the writer's work, and that product results from interrelated and interwoven actions that are collectively called a *process*. It is a complex process whose parts are unpredictable, because writers tend to develop their own distinct processes as they grow in experience. And it is a process that shapes itself as it goes.

If you set out to make a box, you begin with a clear mental picture of what a box is and can easily follow a simple process of construction that will give you a product with a bottom, four sides, and a lid connected at right angles. But when you decide to write, your image of the product is either vague or nonexistent. You might, for example, begin with the idea of writing something about air pollution and find yourself discussing alternative forms of energy production, only to discover that what you really feel strongly about is the possible danger of nuclear reactors. The process of writing often produces such discoveries.

In addition, the process may loop back on itself or even change direction altogether, and so it is partly misleading to present it as a series of steps that one completes and cements in place one on top of another. But familiarity with the various steps in the writing process will help you understand the process as a whole and give you freedom to apply it as you find best in your case. The actions most writers find necessary in the process of writing are *prewriting, drafting, revising,* and *proofreading.*

2a Prewriting

When people think about writing a paper, they usually think in terms of the finished product. They envision a paper that is correct in terms of both *form* and *content.* In truth, however, a successful draft stems from planning, which with writing is called **prewriting.** This stage of the writing process involves various activities that enable you to focus on a specific subject and generate examples, illustrations, and details to support and explain that subject. This stage also includes identifying and addressing other elements of writing that affect the effectiveness of your paper, such as its purpose, audience, and tone. But the emphasis at this point in the writing process is on content—on developing ideas—rather than on form.

On the following pages, you will find a number of suggestions for prewriting. Experiment with these strategies until you find the practices that work for *you.* If some do not help, do not frustrate yourself by following them.

Freewriting

If you are at a loss for an idea, try **freewriting.** Set yourself a time limit of, say, ten minutes, and write down anything that comes to mind during that time. No restrictions apply as far as content is concerned. Don't worry about misspelling words or using incorrect grammar or about your writing digressing from the subject or even making sense. The only rule is that your pen or pencil must keep moving on the page for those ten minutes. This is a sample of one writer's freewriting:

Well here I go again trying my hand at freewriting. Ten minutes seems like a lot of time. Sometimes it goes fast when I'm writing. I can't think of anything to write. But I'll keep on trying. It is rainy and dark out today. It's been raining heavily for three days now. On the way to class today I saw water flooding the streets. One car was stuck in a puddle of water that reached up past the floor of the car. A man and woman sat there with their flasher lights on. Funny, no one stopped to see if they needed help. I didn't stop because I might be late for class. One car drove by real fast and splashed a ton of water all over the stopped car. I wasn't late for class.

I wonder if the motor died because the battery got wet or something like that. Maybe I should've called the police or a tow truck for those people. Well anyhow, I didn't. Here I am in class and we begin with freewriting again. Ten minutes isn't up yet and I can't think of more to write about. Wonder what I'll have for lunch today. I'm tired of pizza.

In this example of freewriting, the writer begins with a preoccupation with the process itself and a concern for time. Recalling the observation of events earlier in the day, the writer develops a focus with a few descriptive, supporting details. The writer mentions time again and then returns to the previous focus by adding some new concerns, but then looks ahead to the lunch hour. As you can see, not all the writing produced in this process will be useful. Such excess of material is another characteristic of freewriting. Sometimes a random observation of things around you will lead you to a specific focus. With freewriting, as you will discover, almost any subject will lead you in some direction. At first glance, this freewriting might not seem to hold much promise. However, this writer has found two or three openings for an essay: inconveniences and difficulties caused by heavy rain storms, the indifference of some people to others who are in distress, and the author's obvious feelings of guilt for not trying to help the couple in the car.

Brainstorming

Another prewriting technique is **brainstorming.** Freewriting is designed so that a writer generates information with the intent of discovering a specific focus in the random material, but brainstorming is a far more deliberate, purposeful attempt to develop a specific list of information. You can brainstorm alone or in a group. Obviously, the results of a group's brainstorming will be more diverse than the products of a single imagination, but the object in either case is the same: to generate as many topics as possible for exploration. The first stage of brainstorming is topic selection. During the interplay of observation, perception, memory, and critical thinking, keep the topics to simple nouns and noun phrases. Set a goal of ten different topics for a start, such as the following:

gun control	new roles for women
television cartoons	the ideal marriage

newspaper cartoons   vocational training
drunken driving   environmental pollution
military conscription   drug abuse

Any of these topics would be worthy of your attention; sometimes you might consider combining two or more of the topics. Unless for some reason you must write on a specific topic, choose a subject from the list that you already know about or are interested in pursuing. The less you know about a subject or the less interested you are in finding out about it, the more difficult you will find writing about that topic.

Once you have completed the first part of brainstorming, move to the next step, and write down as much as you can about the topic selected. The following is a sample of brainstorming on the topic "television cartoons."

So I have to write a 3-4 page paper on anything I want. Great. What do I like? friends, girl friends, food, entertainment, family, children. Disneyland. My goal is to work there, love what they do. Especially the Disney cartoon characters— Donald Duck, Mickey, Goofy, Pluto. What's so great about Disney animation? Realistic emotions in a fresh and humorous way. Provoke feelings that make me laugh, make me feel sad, deeper than people think. I remember Flintstones, Jetsons, Speed buggy, Daffy Duck, Yosemite Sam, Mickey and the gang. what's on TV now? G I Joe, Masters of the Universe and other dull stuff. Remember how angry and frustrated how loving and caring Donald Duck could be — just like the all-American father. My dad likes watching old cartoons too. Cartoons today are real violent, over involved with technology. Are they for adults? But the Smurfs ones seem to be on the right track. Could they take a clue from them? Cartoons now are about machines that act like real people. They're not as funny anymore. I can't get as excited about a robot like I did about Wyle E. Coyote.

Note that this example of brainstorming includes a mixture of sentences and fragments—that's all right for now. The goal here is to generate as much writing as you can about the topic you selected. If your brainstorming does not result in an adequate range of thoughts or does not appear to be leading toward a topic, try it again in ten or fifteen minutes. Or, try another topic.

Clustering

A variation of brainstorming is **clustering.** Write your topic in the middle of a piece of paper or on your computer monitor. As ideas related to the topic occur to you, place them randomly around the topic. Let one subject lead you to another. Try to visualize your ideas as rays of light streaming out from the central topic. Then examine the related ideas and see what kinds of connections you can find among them. Draw

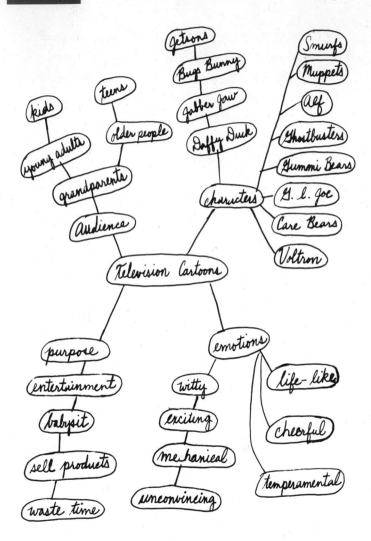

lines between the connected ideas. If you find that this all becomes too messy, write the topic on another page and arrange the potentially related ideas in clusters around it. Your purpose is not only to generate more ideas about your topic but also to discover relationships that might exist between the ideas. See p. 12 for an example of clustering around the topic of television cartoons.

Other ways to find a topic

If freewriting, brainstorming, and clustering fail to produce a workable topic for an unspecified essay, try these other approaches.

1. If you keep a journal, page through it for a thought or an impression you can enlarge.

2. Open a newspaper or magazine at random and read the first piece or article you see. Keep trying until something inspires you to state an opinion about it.

3. Open a magazine and look only at the ads until you find one that leads you to generate a topic.

4. Walk through a crowded area (the mall, the student union) or sit in a busy place (the cafeteria, the library), anyplace where many people congregate. Then, with notepad in hand, simply observe and take notes on what you see. Chances are you will see something that will interest you enough for you to explore it through writing.

5. Go through your class notes and see if these will jog your memory or imagination.

6. Leaf through the last book you read and look for any marginal notations you may have made. Do any of these lead you toward a topic?

7. Think of your conversations with friends, family, fellow students. Would any of these topics be appropriate for your paper?

EXERCISE 2–1

Select two of the following topics. Using prewriting techniques of your choice, narrow each to a topic suitable for an essay. Then generate a list of twelve subtopics from each of your two choices.

recycling household wastes
verbal harassment
exercising
evening television programs
drinking and driving
space travel
advances in technology
the joys of giving
balancing school and
    work obligations
doing household repairs

smoking cigarettes
rock groups
keeping a pet
saving money
caring for others
preparing meals
parental obligations
your favorite hobby
women in politics
homeless people

Finding a purpose: The preliminary thesis

The **purpose** of an essay is not the same as the reason for writing an essay. An error in your telephone bill gives you a reason to write to the telephone company—the motivation—but the purpose of your letter is to *inform* the company it has made a mistake and to *persuade* it to make a correction in your favor. Once you have found a topic, a preliminary decision on your purpose in writing about that topic will help you shape your essay. The essay's **preliminary or tentative thesis** is a sentence that summarizes the point that your essay will make. At this time in the writing process, as you discover a purpose for your essay, you will want to posit a preliminary thesis that will help you to organize the materials you have generated from freewriting, brainstorming, and clustering. You can, of course, change your preliminary thesis while you are discovering a purpose as well as after you have determined a purpose. The preliminary thesis should evolve from your writings and thoughts and not serve as a mold into which your writings and thoughts must be forced. In finding a purpose and stating a preliminary thesis, you may choose to inform or to persuade or to argue or to do any of the following:

- **To record** your thoughts on a topic. Some journal entries are written to record, as are your class notes.
- **To entertain** an audience. In entertaining essays the writer embellishes the topic with wit, humor, word play, and action. A writer can entertain a reader without humor, though: a good tragedy entertains, as does a good horror story or a gripping first-person presentation of a near-drowning. Entertaining in these cases means satisfying a reader's interest.
- **To instruct.** You might tell someone, for example, how to connect a printer to a Macintosh or IBM computer. Such essays are often called process papers because they describe a process.
- **To analyze** a topic, that is, to examine the parts of the topic and the way they relate to one another. Essays about literary works are often analytical; they probe the author's performance to understand its effect.
- **To argue** a point and express an opinion. Such an essay must take both sides of an issue into account while favoring one of them.
- **To reveal the writer.** A job application letter is written not only to describe the applicant's qualifications but also to reveal the applicant's character through the manner of its describing.
- **To evaluate** a work or item. Criticism is a way to evaluate a drama, novel, story, or poem.

This list is not exhaustive, but it includes the primary purposes. Two or more purposes may characterize the same essay: for example, an argumentative essay may be entertaining, and an evaluation paper may include the writer's expression of opinion and an analysis of the topic. You will probably find it most helpful to decide on a single purpose and let it serve as the preliminary thesis while you work on developing your first draft.

Reviewing freewriting, brainstorming, and clustering

As an aid in finding a purpose for your topic, study your prewriting. You will usually find a variety of possibilities for development. The freewriting, brainstorming, and clustering on television cartoons, for instance, hint at the following ideas:

1. Today's cartoons are noisy but are different from old cartoons.

2. The characters aren't animals or humans but machines and dolls.

3. Plot lines are predictable.

4. The cartoons are not as funny.

5. The audience seems limited to youngsters.

6. Is their real purpose to sell things?

7. Can't identify with the characters.

All of the information concerning these subtopics is interesting and potentially useful, but the writer must identify the purpose of the writing before deciding which information to include and which to discard, at least for now.

The basic purpose formula

You may be ab to establish a preliminary purpose by filling out the following formula:

In this essay I will _____.

> Fill in the blank with statements such as *record my impressions of* (the topic); *express my opinion that* (the topic) *is or is not* _____; *argue that* (the topic) *should or should not be approved; analyze* (the topic) *to show that* _____; *instruct my audience how to* _____. You need not use exactly these phrases, but do give yourself something specific to achieve in the essay.

The pentad

As a way of discovering what you know about your topic (or need to know) in order to state a purpose, you can use the **pentad.** Adapted from the writings of Kenneth Burke, the pentad (which means "five") views events from five perspectives:

1. **Action.** What action took place? Was it physical or mental? Was it planned or accidental?

2. **Agent.** Was the actor human or nonhuman (a force of nature or technology)?

3. **Scene.** When did the action occur, in the past or the present? What year, month, day, time? Where did it occur—in the world of the mind or in the physical world? What country, state, or city?

4. **Agency.** How was the action accomplished (planned, accidental, spontaneous)?

5. **Purpose.** Why was the action done (an immediate or simple result, a complex, broader result)?

By asking these questions about your topic you can generate much writing. You can also consider the *ratios,* or the results of various combinations of the pentad: action-scene, agent-purpose, scene-agency, and so on. For example, here is how the pentad might be applied to the topic of the changing nature of television cartoons:

- Action—cartoons have undergone a planned change
- Agent—production studios and merchandisers
- Scene—during the past ten years
- Agency—a change designed to capitalize on new merchandise and technology
- Purpose—to sell products

By considering these perspectives singly and in combination, you can use them to focus in on your purpose. If you discover that you are drawn to the perspective of agency, you can apply the pentad to that particular action and generate additional supporting material. The more often you can use the perspectives of the pentad, the more specific the information you produce will be. Many consider the pentad to be similar to **the journalist's formula,** which is a method of discovery based on the questions who, what, when, where, why, and how.

Using your audience to guide you

One of the best ways to help you establish a purpose in your writing is to consider the needs and interests of your audience. Therefore, writing successfully means providing a focus and supporting information that will communicate your ideas to those for whom you are writing.

The first step in communicating your ideas is to identify your audience. Sometimes doing so seems too simple; if you are writing a paper in your writing class, then the audience would logically seem to be your instructor. But it isn't always that simple. If you write your paper with the idea that your writing teacher alone will read it, then you are preparing the paper to fit the special, idiosyncratic needs of a single person whom you have gradually come to know better day by day in class. As a result, you begin to get a sense of what that instructor knows and does not know about a variety of subjects, and you begin to make subtle adjustments in your presentation. In other words, as you develop a sense of your shared information, you leave out material that you feel reasonably sure your instructor knows.

But imagine for a moment that one of the papers you prepare for this instructor is somehow sent to another instructor for evaluation. If you have written about baseball, for example, and you have talked about the infield fly rule and suicide squeeze because you knew your own instructor understands baseball, you will be in trouble if the instructor who actually does evaluate your paper does not share the same level of knowledge about baseball. Therefore, except under certain circumstances (e.g., specific directions of your instructor to do so) you should not consider your instructor your reader.

Focusing on the general reader

Successful newspaper columnists Andy Rooney and Erma Bombeck, along with thousands of their colleagues nationwide, reach millions of readers every day. They do so by providing the types of information that most people would need in order to understand the points they are presenting. In writing terms, they focus on the general reader, the average individual who knows a little about many things but lacks the specific information on the subject the writer wants to present. The general reader knows what an opera generally is but not the specific details about a specific opera; the general reader knows that blood carries nourishment throughout the body but not the specific role that red blood cells, white blood cells, and platelets play in this process. And the general reader may know that more working mothers means a greater need for child care but not that there are not nearly enough reliable, inexpensive child-care centers available.

Likewise, the general reader has a variety of interests. This variety works to your benefit as the writer. As you gauge the material you have produced through your freewriting, brainstorming, or clustering and try to decide on a focus, consider the interests of the average person. Think, for example, of those specific subjects you like and of how your interests developed. Certainly, you did not awake one day with the level of enthusiasm you possess today about any subject—and you cannot expect that your reader is automatically going to have such a deep interest either. Therefore, focus on some aspect that you feel will lead that average reader to develop an interest, much as it gradually led to a greater interest on your own part. Considering the needs of the general reader will ease your job of choosing a focus for your writing.

Of course, you will occasionally want to write to a more expert audience. If you are preparing a lab report for chemistry, you will probably be writing to readers at least as knowledgeable about chemistry as you. If you are writing an article for a running magazine, you will be writing to a group of running enthusiasts who share a great amount of technical information about running. You will not need to gear down your presentation for these audiences. Likewise, if you are preparing a pamphlet on human conception for an elementary school student audience, you would also adjust your presentation, this time to a far simpler level than you would for the general reader.

As with any writing assignment, the whole context—the subject, reader, purpose, and so on—must be considered. If you take some time to consider these elements, especially the most important element in the writing process—your reader—you will be more likely to develop an effective focus. That is the first step toward writing a successful paper.

Setting a tone

Tone cannot be determined by completing a formula; sometimes it cannot be determined until the first or even the third draft of the essay is complete. But making a decision on tone before the writing begins will help you keep a consistent delivery and find the right tone for the finished essay.

Tone results from word choice based on attitude—on how the writer feels about the subject, on how the writer feels about the audience, and on how the writer wants the audience to feel about the writer and the subject. The writer's purpose will influence decisions on all three points, but especially on the last.

Consider the different ways two writers handled the same subject in the following sentences:

> The city planning board has apparently surpassed its usual high standard of idiocy and irresolution by willfully ignoring the menace of increased and uncontrolled heavy vehicle traffic on Prospect Avenue.

> The city planning board may have shown poor judgment in making no plans for controlling the number of trucks using Prospect Avenue.

Both sentences say essentially the same thing. The second, however, has a more neutral tone. We cannot say much about how the author sounds, except to say she sounds concerned. Her audience could be anyone she does not want to offend, her subject is of minor importance to her and her audience, and her purpose is to call attention gently to a situation that may need correction at some time in the distant future.

The tone of the first sentence, on the other hand, is full of sounds. We might even call it strident. The author has loaded the statement with scorn (*apparently surpassed*), sarcasm (*high standard of idiocy*), accusation (*willfully ignoring*), foreboding (*menace*), and—overall—anger. But the author is doing more than venting wrath at the city planners. For that effect she might have written the following:

> Those lunkheads on the planning board really loused up when they forgot to put a "No Trucks" sign on Prospect.

But if she had written that, she would have written without considering her audience. (Are we moved by someone who writes "lunkheads"?) She would also have written without considering her purpose. (The tone calls attention to the writer, not to how the writer wants us to respond.) Instead, the writer chose an almost literary tone. She determined that this subject and her feelings called for formal language (*irresolution, vehicle, increased and uncontrolled*) and stylistic devices (scorn and sarcasm) to show that she was angry at the city planners and that her intelligent readers would agree with her. The choices may not be entirely successful, but we can see that they were made consciously.

Tone is like fire: a good servant and a bad master. To control it, the writer must have a good sense of subject and purpose and must keep a constant vision of audience in mind. To make a preliminary choice of tone, try to answer the following questions.

QUESTIONS ON AUDIENCE AND TONE

1. What is my attitude to my topic? (Am I enthusiastic? Am I bitter? Am I cynical? Am I concerned? Many other attitudes are possible.)
2. How deeply do I feel this attitude?
3. How do I want my audience to perceive my attitude?
4. How closely do I want my audience to feel my presence as writer? (Talking directly, individual to individual? Talking from the front of the room to a group? Talking from a distance via radio?)
5. What response do I want from my audience? (Amusement? Agreement? Action?)

Remember that the audience senses the writer through tone. Writers must learn to hear themselves if they want to sound natural, for although writing and speaking differ, the essay tone of an experienced writer reflects rhythms and word choices of the writer's speaking habits. Such a tone reads more naturally than an assumed or forced one does. As you write, ask yourself, *"Would I say that if I were talking?"* If, in all honesty, you doubt that you would, consider carefully whether you want to keep the construction you have used or to replace it with a more familiar expression.

2b Stating a Thesis

Before starting your draft, you may want to summarize how your prewriting to this point led to your preliminary thesis. Then state a **thesis,** which is a complete sentence, before beginning the draft. The thesis should encapsulate the point the essay will make. As you think of a thesis statement, keep two things in mind.

1. Do not at this time try to put your thesis statement into words appropriate to the style and tone of your finished essay. Good writing does not happen on the first try. Make the plainest possible declaration of what you want to achieve. A thesis almost always includes a value judgment. One good formula to begin with is the following:

   I think __(topic)__ is _____
                 shows _____
                 should or should not _____
   because _____

2. Do not assume your thesis statement is a fixture. If work on your essay proves that the thesis statement is

indefensible or that some other aspect of your topic is more appealing, more interesting, or more controversial, *restate your thesis to meet the new developments.* Remember you are experimenting with an idea in the rough. You have several drafts in which to test the idea for validity.

If you use the formula recommended, take the product another step before beginning to write. *Make sure that your thesis statement does more than merely announce your topic.*

TOPIC:	A Brooklyn neighborhood
FORMULA:	I think my Brooklyn neighborhood is unique because diverse cultures form a unique identity.
THESIS STATEMENT:	My own neighborhood, Bay Ridge, shows how diverse ethnic cultures combine to give the area a unique identity.

The preceding statement not only announces the topic but also restricts it, moving from the general concept, *a Brooklyn neighborhood*, to a specific one, *Bay Ridge*.

Build on the formula to include specific words. The more precise you are, the more guidance you will have in writing your essay.

TOPIC:	Drivers' responsibilities
FORMULA:	I think young drivers are unaware of the responsibility involved in driving.
THESIS STATEMENT:	A person of seventeen seldom fully appreciates the responsibility of driving.

Be certain that the formula results in a thesis that is *unified*, that is, concerned with one main idea. Ideas of secondary importance may appear in a subordinate clause, but be certain that your main point is expressed in the main clause.

TOPIC:	Underage drinking
FORMULA:	I think teenage drinking is a real problem in our school.
THESIS STATEMENT:	Many teenagers begin drinking due to peer pressure; however, parental example and anxiety often play a role as well.

Most often the first attempt to produce a thesis statement results in one that is too broad to suit the task at hand. For example,

> Agricultural subsidies have major disadvantages.

This thesis is so broad that a book could be written about it. You will want either to limit the topic to suit the average length of an essay assigned in your course or abandon it and search for a new topic. Less often, the first attempt will result in a thesis statement that is too narrow, one that cannot be developed sufficiently to meet the needs of the assignment. For example,

> Reading history books is boring.

This thesis is such a vague and narrow generality that developing it into an essay would be quite problematic. Sometimes you do not know if your thesis statement is too broad or too narrow until you begin to develop it. If you discover it to be either of these, brainstorm or cluster on the topic again in an attempt to discover a remedy, or try priming writing (see p. 26).

A thesis statement should make a *vigorous* statement; it should assert the topic in a context that demands explanation, expansion, analysis, or defense.

BLAND:	Those who argue for abortion on demand sometimes also argue against capital punishment.
VIGOROUS:	Those who argue for abortion on demand are inconsistent when they also argue against capital punishment.

A good test of a thesis statement is to ask: Could I state the opposite and make a case for that point of view? If you can answer yes, you probably have a workable thesis statement.

The thesis statement will usually emerge in the finished essay as a thesis sentence, but let the essay's development determine how and where the thesis sentence appears.

EXERCISE 2–2

Comment on each thesis and explain what content you would expect to find in the essay.

1. Our student council has major organizational flaws and can't seem to succeed in planning successful events.

2. The interesting and colorful professor of economics succeeds in making us want to study the subject.

3. At least five important reasons exist to convince students to pursue a liberal arts major in college.

4. Fast food restaurants no longer provide fast service.

5. The campus bookstore charges too much money for everything in an attempt to exploit a captive market.

EXERCISE 2–3

Write thesis statements for the topics you narrowed in Exercise 2–1, p. 14

Priming writing

Sometimes you work and think, but you simply cannot seem to develop a thesis statement. If this happens, begin to write by brainstorming and clustering again on the topic. This technique is called **priming writing,** and it is easy to master. First, set a goal of 150 to 200 words, and start writing sentences about the topic from an approach as if you were brainstorming or clustering. But try to produce connected sentences with details or subordinate points to support generalizations without worrying about style. The purpose of this writing is to prime the pump, to get your mind and fingers working with your topic and in the mood to write.

The following is an example of priming writing on the topic of television cartoons.

Kids in the last 20 years jumped out of bed on Saturday mornings and sat glued to the TV for about four hours to watch the cartoons. Do kids still do so today with the same excitement and anticipation that I experienced. Did my parents look down on the cartoons I watched the same way I look down on the ones I see today like Voltron? When I was a kid cartoons had a magic about them. The characters were funny and were like real people. They laughed, cried, got scared, were happy, had joy and contentment. They got themselves into some awful and silly situations where one idiotic thing led to another. But everything always worked out okay. The stories held my interest. Today's cartoons feature robots and dolls not animals and humans. It's hard for me to identify with machine-like characters. These characters are special, based on ones from science fiction movies and dolls they sell in the K-Mart. It appears as if the manufacturers of the dolls got the studios to invent characters that try to make the dolls human.

Although the writing resulting from the priming contains no specific preliminary thesis yet, it does express some of the writer's feelings and attitudes about television cartoons: the cartoons are different today because their main characters are hard to identify with and story lines are not as interesting. As a result, the writer has a more specific direction and can develop a tentative thesis statement.

I think the nature of television cartoons has changed and the change is dictated by a desire to sell merchandise.

A more explicit statement derived from the formula might be the following:

The nature of television cartoons has changed in the past ten years with a desire to sell merchandise taking precedence over enchantment, originality, and humor.

2c Outlining

An outline provides a framework or model for a first draft. It can help you shape and organize your thoughts and impressions and keep you from making organizational blunders. An **informal outline** is especially practical for those times when you are struggling to establish a preliminary thesis, plan your first draft, and organize your ideas. An informal outline can take the form of a **scratch outline** in which you use words and phrases and sometimes even symbols to sketch out your ideas either on paper or on the computer. Because this type of outline is primarily for your own use, you do not need to be overly concerned with format. The following example illustrates a typical scratch outline.

TV cartoons

Saturdays, a.m. noon

Animal types

Robot/outerspace types

Fun and games

Commercial interests

No fun!

Formal outlines, as you might guess, have more structure and detail than informal outlines. Formal outlines are especially valuable for keeping your thoughts on a topic organized, and some instructors require the submission of formal outlines along with the essay. If a formal outline is required, you might opt for the **sentence outline,** in which each subordinate topic of the thesis appears as a sentence and the sentences follow the order of development that the essay will follow. Usually, but not always, each sentence in the outline serves as a topic sentence for a paragraph in the essay. Consider the following example of a sentence outline:

SENTENCE OUTLINE

Thesis: The nature of television cartoons has changed in the past ten years with a desire to sell merchandise taking precedence over enchantment, originality, and humor.

1. The joy of watching television cartoons in the past has been replaced by a stupor brought about by today's cartoons, which lack enchantment, originality, and humor.
2. There is something magical about yesterday's cartoons.
3. Today's cartoons are based on successful television programs, movies, and store products.
4. The animation has changed because the characters, no longer humans or animals, are now robots and dolls.
5. The purpose of these cartoons appears to be to sell a product based on the cartoon character.
6. Some exceptions do exist on ABC and cable networks.
7. The destructive robots are taking over.

Another type of formal outline is the **topic outline.** Whereas the sentence outline includes only paragraph topic sentences, the topic outline lists topics, rather than complete sentences, and usually includes the details that will appear within each paragraph. When the topic outline is completed, the first draft is not far off. The most common type of formal topic outline uses a combination of roman numerals, capital letters, arabic numbers, lowercase letters, and lowercase roman numerals to indicate the various divisions of a subject. The largest divisions are indicated by roman numerals, each of which is subdivided into sections signified by capital letters. If further subdivision of these sections is required, it is signified by arabic numbers, and so on. One traditional rule to remember with the formal outline is that any topic you divide must be

separated into at least *two* portions—logically, one apple cannot be divided into one piece. In other words, there must be a
subtopic B if there is a subtopic A, a subtopic 2 if there is a
subtopic 1, and so on. The following example shows the arrangement of part of a typical formal topic outline:

FORMAL TOPIC OUTLINE

Thesis: The nature of television cartoons has
changed in the past ten years with a desire to
sell merchandise taking precedence over
enchantment, originality, and humor.

Roman numeral	I. Cartoons and Enchantment
Capital letter	A. Characters Yesterday
Arabic number	1. Animals
	a. Bugs Bunny
Lowercase letter	b. Donald Duck
	c. Woody Woodpecker
	2. Human Beings
	a. Flintstones
	b. Jetsons
	B. Characters Today
	1. Robots
	a. Voltron
	b. Transformers
	2. Dolls
	a. G.I. Joe
	b. Care Bears
	c. Muppets

    II. Cartoons and Originality
       A. Plots Yesterday
          1. Not predictable
          2. Exciting
       B. Plots Today
          1. Repeats of movies
             a. Muppets
             b. Ghostbusters
          2. Repeats of TV programs
             a. Alf
             b. Voltron

As you can see, the writer who chooses a formal topic outline as a start must think the topic through completely and develop working notes *before* trying to write a formal outline. (The scratch outline can usually serve this purpose.) The formal topic outline is equally effective for short essays and research papers. In addition, it can be valuable in *revising* papers. Once you have a suitable draft, you can plot your ideas into the framework of an outline and be certain that every part of your draft is relevant and connected.

EXERCISE 2–4

Develop a sentence outline or a topic outline for one of the topics that you narrowed down in Exercise 2–1, p. 14.

2d Writing the First Draft

Having selected a topic using the various prewriting techniques, settled on a purpose by positing a tentative thesis, decided on audience and tone, and planned your essay's organization through outlining, you are ready to write a first draft.

But take a breather for a moment. All those prewriting steps, or some of them, may well help you get started; however, there is such a thing as getting bogged down in the preliminaries. Another way of getting started is to write the first draft without making any of the preparatory efforts. It is not a crime to plunge straight in and see what happens. *But to plunge in under the impression that the first draft will become the final draft with only a bit of light tinkering is foolhardy.*

Whether you make a careful prewriting preparation or let the essay happen as it may from your pen, you *must* regard your first draft as a throwaway—as something that will be only vaguely related to the finished essay. Always think of it as something to be broken down and rearranged, as prose to be thoroughly rewritten until it is right, as something far beneath your potential. In short, your first draft is a starting point *only*.

Keeping in mind that the first draft is only the first stage of an essay, follow these strategies when writing the draft.

EXERCISE 2–5

From the list of topics in Exercise 2–1 on p. 14, select a topic that you have not written about or work with topics provided by your instructor. Using prewriting techniques, arrive at a preliminary thesis and then construct a scratch outline. Develop the scratch outline into a formal outline and write a first draft of the essay. When you submit this essay, also submit your prewriting and outlines.

DRAFTING STRATEGIES

1. Write the first draft well before the finished essay is due. A week in advance is desirable; a twenty-four-hour lead is essential. *Don't wait until the last minute—ever.*

2. Write the first draft as rapidly as possible. You want to capture ideas rather than form.

3. Ignore spelling and punctuation problems. If you are uncertain of one or the other at any point, mark the place and write on. Do not stop to look things up until the first draft is complete.

4. Write double or triple space. Leave room to insert.

5. Cross out; do not erase. And when you cross out, let what you have crossed out show through. You might want to go back to that wording later.

6. Be sloppy! Discourage yourself from even *thinking* of the draft as finished work.

7. Write the draft where you are comfortable. You want a free, sequential flow of ideas.

8. Do not worry about intriguing openings and watertight conclusions. Keep your mind on your thesis, the main points supporting it, and the details that support the main points. Lay a foundation and leave architectural refinements for later.

9. If your first draft wanders from your thesis or suggests more interesting developments, stop. Weigh the merits of starting over to return to the thesis against the possible value of letting the paper lead you to a thesis. *At this stage nothing is permanent.*

10. If you are preparing a first draft on the computer, be certain to consult Chapter 4.

3   The Process of Writing: Revision

The process of writing does not consist of a series of finite steps, that is, of stages that have defined beginnings and ends. Once you have stated your thesis, you are not finished with that thesis. The first draft and subsequent revisions of it may substantially alter your thesis as you discover more about your relation to your topic while you write about it. You may also find that your purpose, audience, and tone change as you work. You will probably find yourself going back to the prewriting activities after a first draft—or even after a second or third one—because you have found a new topic or a radically different aspect of the original one during the process of writing. You must not, therefore, think that the separation of first draft and revision shown here represents a true sequence of events. It is true only insofar as revision, by definition, follows a first attempt.

3a Revision Is Re-Vision

The purpose of **revision** is to change your draft in such a way that it better communicates what it is you are writing about. This is a very important step in the writing process that cannot be eliminated, because very few writers produce a polished, finished essay on their first attempt. In fact, almost all successful writers revise a draft two, three, or even more times. Revising a draft is a matter of seeing again the topic, purpose, audience, and tone, and it should not be confused with proofreading (reviewing the paper to correct surface errors such as misspellings). To revise you must probe to discover possible new insights and overlooked opportunities, and you must critically test what you have written to be sure it properly communicates what you want to write. Revision, or re-seeing, requires detachment, critical thinking and analytic attention, the generation of new ideas, ruthlessness, and, possibly, a reconsideration of the thesis. It can also involve collaborative efforts and some degree of self-discipline.

Detachment

The effort of writing leaves most of us too closely involved with what we have written to judge the result immediately; therefore, put distance between you and your work. Wait several hours or a few days before revising. The difference between an impression of a draft on its completion and the impression of it a week later is often startling. You might consider asking someone who will be honest to read it; other people are generally more objective about your writing than you are. (See the section on collaboration and peer critiques on p. 39.)

Critical thinking and analytic attention

Revision is a search for a way to express a point better, but it is also a search for the best possible point. The critical thinking question is not "Could I have put that better?" but "Does my writing truly reflect what I think *now* about my topic?" The analytic revision question is not "Do my sentences and paragraphs flow smoothly from my thesis to my conclusion?" but "Can I disprove or refute anything I have said?" Here are some other questions to ask yourself when revising critically and analytically:

QUESTIONS TO HELP YOU REVISE CRITICALLY AND ANALYTICALLY

- Who is my audience? How will he or she respond to my points?
- If someone else had written this, what would my impression be of that person and his or her opinions?
- Can I make a topic outline of this draft in which all the main ideas are consistent and related?
- Do the thesis and the conclusion match? If they do not, which should I choose to guide my revision?
- Does everything in the draft relate to my thesis and my conclusion? Is each point a development toward the conclusion or a digression?
- Is each generalization developed with adequate specific facts, illustrations, or examples? Can I think of exceptions to my generalizations that I have not anticipated in my argument?
- If I were to start this paper over from scratch, what would I do differently?

Generating new ideas

Revision should not be restricted to what is in the draft. It should include all aspects of the topic treated—even if these aspects did not occur to you in the first trial. If a review of your draft suggests new departures, explore them. Do not abandon new ideas because the first set is on paper and the new ones are not. The more you work with a topic, the more thoughts on the topic you will gather. Let those thoughts occur to you; seek them out; brainstorm again while revising.

Ruthlessness

Cross out and rewrite freely. If the change you have in mind will not fit in the space available, cut the draft apart with scissors and tape it back together with the addition inserted. *Assume from the start that the draft has promise but needs additional work to fulfill that promise.* But do not throw away what is good. Critical revision should discover merits as well as faults in a draft.

Reconsidering the thesis

Up to this point in the writing process, you have formulated a preliminary thesis that has helped you get started. It is all right to leave your preliminary thesis as it is until after you complete writing the first draft; however, while writing the first draft try not to lose track of your thesis. Many difficulties that arise when writing a first draft can stem from a thesis that is too broad (contains a generality), is too narrow or specific, is imprecise in wording (contains words that are ambiguous), or is noncommittal (doesn't contain a judgment). Reconsidering the thesis in light of the writing you generate will usually help to solve these problems. Remember that your preliminary thesis can evolve and change during the drafting process. In the student-authored essay that follows, the preliminary thesis statement was

Today's cartoons just aren't the same as when I was a kid.

After writing the first draft of the essay, the author realized that what "wasn't the same" about cartoons (a generality) was that lack of enchantment, originality, and even humor in today's cartoons compared to those of his childhood. He then reconsidered his preliminary thesis and added these three specific points to replace the generality; hence, the actual act of writing a draft can help you refine your preliminary thesis.

Collaboration and peer critiques

Seeing your writing as others see it is an invaluable guide when revising. Assuming your teacher has no objections, ask someone else to read your draft and give you an opinion. What you have written may be clear to you but unintelligible to someone else, and a collaborative effort could help you see the need to express yourself better. Be sure, however, to ask someone who will be honest with you. A reader who tells you that your paper is good because that person does not want to offend you is not helping you.

Many teachers have formalized this shared evaluation process as **collaborative writing,** or **peer critiques.** In class, students are usually paired, read one another's drafts, and mark them, use them as a basis for dialogue, or do both. At other times students join in groups of three or four to read the drafts and discuss them, mark them, or both. Regardless of the type of grouping, you can gain much if you are prepared to ask questions about the parts of your essay that trouble you (such as tone, audience, coherence, transitions, and ambiguities) and can receive and use constructive criticism. You can help others and yourself by asking questions that require more than a "yes" or "no" response. If these groupings are to work properly, the students involved must read one another's essays in an honest, fair, critical way and be prepared to point out strengths as well as weaknesses. For an example of a peer critique, see p. 46.

GUIDELINES FOR COLLABORATION AND PEER CRITIQUES

1. What is the essay's purpose?
2. Are the topic sentences related to the preliminary thesis?
3. Do any paragraphs require more development?
4. Can you notice any development patterns? Are they appropriate for the subject matter?
5. Do transitions appear to help the flow of the content?
6. Does the essay include examples or need them? If examples appear, are they appropriate and convincing?
7. Is the tone appropriate? If not, how could it be changed?
8. What is the most positive comment you can make about the essay?

Self-discipline

However you revise, do not be lazy. Revision is a crucial part of the creative process. As you've seen, it deserves at least as much effort and time as a first draft—usually more. Revision is the time to test the essay for coherence and to refine your tone so that revision serves the content instead of directing it. Revision is the time to suit your diction to your topic, purpose, and audience. As with peer critiques, it is not the time to be overly concerned about comma splices or pronoun references, which are editing rather than revision concerns.

3b Sample First Draft

Brian Liptak, the student writer whose first draft of an essay appears here, began, as most of us do, without an idea for a topic. As shown in Chapter 2, by using the various prewriting strategies of freewriting and brainstorming, he arrived at the possible topic of television cartoons, developed and explored that topic through clustering, posited a purpose and tone, and after additional prewriting and critical analysis of his work, arrived at a preliminary thesis: I think today's cartoons just aren't the same as when I was a kid. Outlining helped Brian structure and organize his ideas. He then produced the following first draft.

FIRST DRAFT

Cartoons

1   What kid in the past twenty-five years hasn't rolled out of bed Saturday morning to watch the TV? There are probably very few who miss this habits. Watching cartoons is a part of growing up in America. The morning began with "The Jetsons," Speedbuggy, and "Jabber Jaw." I remember waking up and rushing to the television ready for four hours of entertainment. As morning went on, I changed the television to The Flintstones, "Hong Kong Phooey," and "Scooby Doo." At the end—I would watch the Looney Tunes hour with Daffy Duck, the Road Runner, Tweety Bird, and Bugs Bunny. Recently, at thome on saturday I was surprised to see new cartoons. What a difference. Could it be that I am getting older, wiser and outgrowing the pleasures of watching cartoons? The old gang was gone, replaced by Kissyfur, Gummi Bears, Care Bears, Transformer, Voltron, Thundercats, Silverhawks, and the Snorks. Who are all of these colorful animals

and robotic superheroes? Did my parents look down on Bugs Bunny? I do not like Voltron! Today's cartoons just aren't the same as when I was a kid.

2   There was magic with yesteryear's cartoons. The creators have given them human emotions and characteristics like pride, humor, revenge, wit. This combination of characteristics provided a funny crazy escape from busy and stressful lives. This may be the reason I still enjoy watching Bugs Bunny, the Road Runner, and my personal favorite, Donald Duck. They also maybe have an unrealistic resistance to pain and appear real tough. For example, Wyle E. Coyote is able to survive being run over by a truck, falling off a cliff,and being blown within one episode. My roommates rarely miss an episode of Woody Woodpecker. My dad always gets a good laugh from Yosemite Sam. All kinds of people seem to enjoy the wonders of Warner Bros., Hanna Barbera, and Walt Disney Productions whodo this stuff. These studios are to animation what Hemingway is to literature and Pavarotti is to music.

3   Today's cartoons are boring stuff. A large number of the cartoons on television noware take-offs on good television programs and movies such as "The Muppets," Alf, Voltron, and "Ghostbusters." Others are on popular store products such as Gummi Bear candy, G.I. Joe's, Transformer and Care Bear dolls. Some use the popularity of new stars to market a cartoon to kids. The character of Ed Grimley, (Marty Short), from "Saturday Night Live" has been made into a Saturday morning mockery. Rather than being original, they are signs of success by copying new entertainers.

4   These are boring and many cartoons aren't funny. The
fun spirit of cartoons which has in the past provided us with
so much enjoyment. Our modern world today places great
stock in technology. "Thundercats," "The Transformer,"
and "Silverhawks,"are cartoons of science fiction with stray
from a happy Mickey Mouse, crabby Daffy Duck, and clever
Bugs Bunny. Modern cartoons aren't funny. They don't provide
any escape.

5   However, it is unlikely that programs such as "Ghostbusters"
and "Thundercats" will have the same impact on today's kids like
the cartoons had on our generation. In this sense, such cartoons
will be soon forgotten, are failures. Modern cartoons do have a
purpose as is seen in those based on store products, which have
advertising value.

6   There's is still hope for Saturday mornings. ABC presently
has an hour saved for "The Bugs and Tweety Hour." Cable
stations still run the Hanna Barbera and Disney classics.
Animators are always creating new characters who may become
long-lasting favorites. A few years back, Hanna Barbera Studios
introduced a new group of characters. They immediately worked
themselves into many young hearts—The Smurfs. The Smurfs
were new and, funny.They were like other traditional cartoons.
They portrayed human qualities which added the necessary
sincerity for success. Once in awhile, then among all of today's
second-rate cartoons, new characters appear worthy to be called
"cartoons" in the traditional sense. No, I'm not outgrowing the
pleasures of watching cartoons. My roommates and Dad likes
them too.

7   I still enjoy my old favorites. I search among a new age of
cartoons to find characters that fit in with the ones I remember.
Some of our favorite characters have been lumped into a herd of
robots and things. A great tradition of cartoons is faded as a
result of the Transformer. These destructive robots are here. A
new era has arrived.

Critical analysis of the first draft

Returning to the draft after a few days had passed, Brian
tried to think critically about what he had written using the critical analysis checklist on p. 37. He realized coherence, tone,
and audience considerations would require some degree of
change. (See also pp. 117–130 on Thinking Critically.) Here is
how he reacted to each of the paragraphs in his first draft.

Paragraph 1. Maybe I ask too many questions in the opening
paragraph. One or two might serve for variety. I think my
preliminary thesis fits nicely at the end of the paragraph but
maybe I could place it at the beginning. What advantage would I
gain? Perhaps I mention too many kinds of cartoons here. Do I
need to be this specific in the introduction? Maybe I can group
them into classes—animals and machines—and make it easier for
the reader. I'll need to check my conclusion paragraph to make
sure it harmonizes with the introduction. But I worry about my
preliminary thesis; maybe it's still too general.

Paragraph 2. I must be sure that I'm communicating my ideas
to my reader. I enjoy writing about this subject because I have

fond memories of it. But I need to remember that not everyone
remembers as much about these cartoons as I do. They probably
don't share my enthusiasm either. So I'll have to select my
examples carefully. Should it be Donald Duck or Wyle E. Coyote?
Does Woody Woodpecker really belong here? How much detail
will I need to get the reader's attention and interest? Maybe my
last sentence is too grandiose. Will my readers know who
Pavarotti is? Does it make my tone too stuffy? Does it look like
I'm showing off?

Paragraph 3. I'm not certain this paragraph convinces the
reader that today's cartoons are boring. Maybe I am listing too
many cartoons again. I could shorten the list or group the
cartoons into classes for brevity. I really need to stress *why* they
are boring because not all imitations are boring. I better limit all
these examples: enough is enough!

Paragraph 4. This paragraph needs focus: it jumps around
between "funny" and "technology" and I don't really provide any
support for the topic sentence. I do like my transition from
paragraph 3 to paragraph 4.

Paragraph 5. This paragraph doesn't seem to belong here
because it almost reads like a conclusion. Maybe I need to think
of reorganizing here, perhaps combining paragraphs 3 and 4 to
combine the business of lack of humor and interest. Paragraphs 4
and 5 can't combine; both are on really different things.

Paragraph 6. I'll need a transition word or phrase here. Focus
is a problem again: the paragraph jumps around and doesn't
really center in on what I want to write: that the Smurfs are an

example of a new cartoon that preserves the best qualities of the older traditional cartoons. My last sentence appears to be an afterthought. Maybe I'll drop it or relocate the idea to the beginning of the paragraph. Will my readers know who the Smurfs are or do I need a more familiar example?

Paragraph 7. I don't like this concluding paragraph. It has no sentence variety, and it doesn't really reinforce my thesis in the introduction. I'll need to reassess my tone for the entire essay. I sound folksy in the opening but get preachy in paragraph 6. I think I can prove all the points made in my thesis. I noted some typo and grammatical errors in my draft but now is not the time to worry about them: I'll do that when editing. Right now I need to get the overall structure to support my purpose and arrange my details to support the topic sentences.

Peer critique

Brian submitted his first draft to some friends in his class for peer critique. A sampling of the commentary he received follows:

1. You seem to be trying to say that you like the older cartoons better than the newer ones.

2. You have *lots* of examples. Do you need so many? Pick the well-known examples that clearly relate to your points.

3. I wonder if your thesis is precise enough. Shouldn't it indicate what isn't the same about the cartoons?

4. Your tone is appealing because you sound like a college student. That Hemingway and Pavarotti reference just doesn't fit in with your relaxed but serious tone.

5. Do you need to mention what cartoons your roommates and dad like? It's interesting but this essay is about what you like. You can't speak for them.

6. Your essay has real possibilities because it's interesting. I never thought about these things before. But you need to get it organized and make sure your transitions make the paragraphs flow together.

7. Can you do more with the Smurfs? You mention them in paragraph 6 but don't really make your point. It's all choppy!

EXERCISE 3-1

Select any two adjoining paragraphs in Brian's first draft (or paragraphs designated by your instructor) on pp. 41–44. How would you revise these two paragraphs?

Revising the first draft

Taking into consideration this critical analysis of the first draft and comments from his classmates, Brian was able to see his essay anew. He kept some of his own ideas and those of his peers and rejected some as well. Brian revised his first draft extensively and then proceeded through several additional drafts. Many writers find it useful to produce multiple drafts. Through each draft they can work toward expressing their ideas more clearly and directly. The result of multiple drafts and thoughtful revision is often a more effective essay. The excerpt on page 48, showing the second paragraph of the first draft, illustrates some of Brian's revisions. In this paragraph, he revises to communicate his ideas with clarity and show greater sensitivity to his audience.

EXAMPLE OF REVISION

~~There~~ *Something magical* ~~was magic in~~ yesteryear's cartoons. The creators have given them emotions and characteristics ~~like~~ *such as* pride, humor, revenge, ~~wit~~ *and* This combination of ~~living~~ *animate* and ~~nonliving~~ *inanimate* characteristics provides a light humored ~~crazy escape~~ *even childlike* escape from busy and stressful lives. This may be the reason ~~I still~~ *that young adults* enjoy watching Bugs Bunny, the Road Runner, ~~and my personal favorite,~~ *Woody Woodpecker, and* Donald Duck. They also ~~have~~ *had* an unrealistic resistance to pain. For example, Wyle E. Coyote ~~is able to~~ survive being run over by a truck, falling off a cliff, ~~and being blown~~ *a dynamite explosion, all* within one episode. My roommates rarely miss an episode of Woody Woodpecker. My *While* *comd* father always gets a good laugh from Yosemite Sam. ~~All kinds of~~ *People of all ages and backgrounds* people seem to enjoy the wonders of Warner Bros., Hanna Barbera, and Walt Disney Productions ~~who~~ *which* bring their art to life. *omit* ~~These studios are to animation what Hemingway is to literature and Pavarotti is to music.~~

EXERCISE 3-2

Revise and rewrite the following paragraph, which is from the first draft of a student's essay. You may wish to rearrange the order of the sentences or combine sentences to achieve organization, structure, emphasis, tone, and so on.

I spent much of my childhood doing one of two things. As a young child, solitude was my savior. I would take long walks through nearby woods. I would relax in a swing attached to a tremendous oak tree. This was peaceful. It was also refreshing for me. I enjoyed my solitude. There are other pleasant things I associate with solitude. I connect the word with personal reflection serenity peaceful quietness and reflection. I imagine the warm silence of a monastery. Solitude is growth, also, in a comic way, I pictured the famous Calgon commercial. After a hectic day a woman sits in her bubble bath. She is in her solitude. She is content.

3c The Final Draft

Brian revised his paper extensively and wrote additional drafts before proofreading and editing his work (see pp. 59–60 on proofreading and editing). The result of his endeavors is the final draft reproduced here.

FINAL DRAFT

Title		Back Up, Bugs
Rhetorical question stimulates interest	1	What child in the past twenty-five years has not scurried out of bed on Saturday morning to watch the cartoons? Probably very few have missed this ritual since watching cartoons has become a part of growing up in America: four uninterrupted hours of entertainment. The
Examples help author illustrate the four hours of cartoons		morning would begin with "The Jetsons," "Speedbuggy," and "Jabber Jaw." As the sun continued to rise, the television schedule moved onto "The Flintstones," "Hong Kong Phooey," and "Scooby Doo." In the final stretch of the morning entertainment would appear the Looney Tunes hour with Daffy Duck, the Road Runner, Tweety Bird, and Bugs Bunny. Recently, a new cast of characters has appeared on the morning cartoons. The old neighborhood is gone, replaced

Examples

Thesis

by Kissyfur, Gummi Bears, Care Bears, Transformers, Voltron, Thundercats, Silverhawks, and the Snorks. These colorful animals and robotic superheroes do not have the same effect on viewers that cartoon characters used to have because today's cartoons lack enchantment, originality, and humor.

Support for first part of thesis

2   Something magical surrounded yesteryear's cartoon characters. Their creators gave them human emotions and characteristics such as pride, humor, and wit. They also had an unrealistic resistance to pain. For example, Wyle

Example and details

E. Coyote survives being run over by a truck, falling off a cliff, a dynamite explosion, all within one episode. This combination of animate and inanimate characteristics provides a light-humored, even slightly crazy escape from busy

Support for topic sentence

and stressful lives. This may be the reason that young adults still enjoy watching Bugs Bunny, the Road Runner, Donald Duck, and Woody Woodpecker, while even my father always gets a

Restatement of topic sentence

good laugh from Yosemite Sam. People of all ages and backgrounds seem to enjoy the wonders of Warner Bros., Hanna Barbera, and Walt Disney Productions, which bring their art to life.

Support for second part of thesis

3   Besides lacking enchantment, today's cartoons primarily lack originality. A large

percentage of the current cartoons are derivative and modeled on successful television programs and movies such as The Muppets, Alf, Voltron, and Ghostbusters. Other cartoons are based on popular store products such as Gummi Bear candy, G.I. Joes, and Care Bear dolls. Some programs abuse the popularity of new celebrities to market a cartoon to younger audiences. For example, the character of Ed Grimley (Marty Short) from Saturday Night Live has been made into a Saturday morning mockery. Thus, rather than displaying originality, cartoons have deteriorated into success gauges for new entertainers.

4   In addition to lacking originality, many cartoons lack humor and the fun-loving spirit of animation that used to provide us with so much enjoyment. "Thundercats," "The Transformers," and "Silverhawks," forms of animated science fiction influenced by technology, have strayed far from a cheerful Mickey Mouse, temperamental Daffy Duck, and witty Bugs Bunny, representations of the traditions of older cartoons. Contemporary cartoons rarely show humor and appear incapable of providing a light-humored escape through fantasy because viewers find it more difficult to identify with robots with the possible exception of R2D2 than the personified

Examples for illustration

Support for topic sentence

Transitional phrase opens paragraph

Support for second part of thesis continues

Examples

Support for topic sentence

animals of yesterday. Instead of humor, modern cartoons stress merchandise by modeling characters on products, thus giving themselves significant advertising value. However, it is unlikely that programs such as "Ghostbusters" and "Thundercats" will have the same endearing and enduring impact on youth today as the classic cartoons did in the past. Instead of living in our memories because they excited our imaginations, the newer cartoons will be soon forgotten. Designed to send us running into the stores, their resultant pleasures will not survive the test of time.

Transitional sentence

5   Is there still hope for Saturday mornings? ABC presently has an hour reserved for The Bugs and Tweety Hour and many cable stations continue to show the Hanna Barbera and Disney classics. In addition, animators continue to create new characters who may become long-lasting favorites. A few years ago, as Saturday mornings became dull, Hanna Barbera Studios introduced a new group of characters who immediately worked themselves into many young hearts—The Smurfs. The Smurfs were original, funny, and like other traditional cartoons, portrayed exceptional human qualities, which added the necessary sincerity for success even though the Smurf products were heavily marketed. Thus,

Question

Author's response

Sustained example to support opening question in paragraph

occasionally, among all of today's second-rate cartoons, new characters emerge from the drawing board worthy to be called "cartoons" in the traditional sense of the word.

Conclusion   6   Do we outgrow the pleasures of watching cartoons? Do we still enjoy our old favorites as we search in a new age of cartoons to find original characters that fit with the classics? Final sentence looks back to thesis and title   Some of our favorite characters have been overtaken by a herd of robots and imitators almost bringing a great tradition of cartoons to an end. These destructive robots are here, so back up, Bugs. A new era has arrived.

3d Components of the Essay

During the process of writing, you should be concerned primarily with generating ideas and shaping them for expression. The "form" of the essay should develop naturally during this process, and worrying about parts of the form in isolation is often counterproductive. Toward the end of the composing process, however, an awareness of the parts of the essay may help in revising and polishing. The parts that most often come under consideration are the *title,* the *thesis sentence*, the *introduction*, the *body*, and the *conclusion.*

Title

It is a good idea to wait until the essay is almost complete before selecting a **title.** When you do choose a title, search for a word or phrase—the briefer, the better is the rule—that suggests the topic, the tone, and perhaps the purpose of the essay. Alternatively, you may want to use a title that does none of these things but that challenges interpretation. This is what Brian did with his essay, "Back Up, Bugs." At first glance the meaning of the title is not evident, but after reading the essay its multiple meanings become clear. Make sure, however, that you do not rely on your title to direct your reader; your thesis should do that. Remember—a good title caps off a good paper, but it does not make a weak paper any better. Therefore, choose your title carefully, but recognize its limitations, too.

Thesis sentence

Much has been written about the **thesis.** As a safe rule of thumb, the more complex the topic is and the more serious the discussions of it is, the more value a thesis will have. The lighter the topic and treatment, the less significant a *detailed* thesis will be.

The most obvious place to insert your thesis sentence is in the first paragraph—in your introduction—but it can be the first sentence in the introduction or the last sentence. Placing the thesis in the middle of the introduction is rarely effective. In "Back Up, Bugs," for example, the thesis is the last sentence of the first paragraph. It serves as a fine lead-in to the remainder of the essay for the reader.

The most effective thesis sentences tend to be simple or complex sentences. Compound sentences rarely succeed as thesis sentences because by their very nature, they result in two thesis sentences of equal importance. A simple thesis sentence avoids ambiguity. When the thesis is a complex sentence, the main clause usually indicates the material that is stressed, and the subordinate clause may indicate what role the supporting material will play.

Introduction

In most essays, the **introduction** is usually restricted to the first paragraph. The introduction is important because it shapes the reader's first impression and often serves as a deciding factor in whether the reader goes beyond it. The introduction sets the tone of the essay, establishes the writer's relation to the reader, and indicates the direction the essay will take. Introductions can take many forms to achieve a variety of effects. An introduction can be a straight piece of narrative that sets the scene for the reader and gives information necessary to an understanding of the essay's thesis. Brian did this in "Back Up, Bugs." It can be a personal anecdote or invented piece of fiction to arouse the reader's interest or entertain as a way of leading to the thesis sentence or a joke or an inflated treatment of a minor issue to amuse the reader; however, it should always be in good taste and done with sensitivity. The introduction may begin with a paradoxical statement, one that seems to contradict itself: "Most law-abiding citizens break at least three laws a day." Or the writer may use the opening to take a position toward the subject that is the opposite of the position to be developed in the essay. Such openings surprise readers or intrigue them. The introduction may begin with a contradiction of a popular assumption as a challenge to the reader: "Cats and dogs are by nature affectionately drawn to each other. Unfortunately, dogs like playing tag and cats don't." It may employ a famous quotation or a piece of dialogue as a means of leading up to the thesis sentence.

An introduction can also, of course, simply identify the topic to be addressed, as in the case of the following introduction for a paper on young drivers:

When we obtained our first driver's licenses at sixteen, seventeen, or eighteen, few of us paused before hitting the accelerator to think that we were about to solo in a machine with the destructive power of four sticks of dynamite and a record for manslaughter three times greater than that of the notorious handgun.

Or an opening may be a focus of inquiry. An essay on legalized abortion, for example, might begin with an explanation of the views in opposition over the topic.

Avoid attempts at perfecting the introduction in your first draft. You cannot expect to do your best writing the first time. Refine your introduction and thesis as you work through multiple drafts. In other words, shape the final introduction against the structure, intent, and tone of the essay.

Body

The **body** of an essay consists of everything between the introduction and the conclusion. In the body, the writer develops the thesis with facts, examples, and specific points so that the reader can fully understand or accept the writer's position. Every part of the body must not only relate to the essay's thesis but also increase readers' understanding of the problem being explored or their appreciation of the thesis.

A finished essay should balance generalization and specific information. The thesis of the essay is a statement that includes all conditions or circumstances indicated by a given set of evidence. You, the writer, have arrived at your thesis by considering the evidence. In the body of your essay, you must retrace your steps to your thesis to demonstrate the truth of it to your reader. In most essays, this demonstration follows a pattern of a thesis supported by a series of narrower generalizations that are supported in turn by reference to facts, examples, specific details, or other information that confirms or strongly suggests the truth of the thesis. This pattern of generalization, narrower generalization, and specific detail need not emerge in the finished essay as a rigid A-because-B-because-C formula, but the principle of it should influence the overall content of the essay.

Consider the final draft of the sample essay, "Back Up, Bugs" (see p. 49). The final thesis of the essay is "These colorful animals and robotic superheroes do not have the same effect on viewers that cartoon characters used to have because today's cartoons lack enchantment, originality, and humor." The writer's obligation to the reader is to show that old cartoons produced each of the attributes listed—enchantment, originality, and humor—and had an effect on the viewers.

Paragraphs 2, 3, and 4 therefore specifically address these attributes and feature examples of cartoons to support the topic sentence of each paragraph. The result, when these three paragraphs are taken together, provides support for the essay's thesis.

Paragraph 5 concerns itself with the one exception that the writer wishes to stress among the changing nature of television cartoons—the Smurfs. This paragraph does not contradict the thesis; in fact, it emphasizes it by showing that cartoons incorporating enchantment, originality, and humor are still being produced.

Coherence

The essence of the body of the essay is **coherence**, from the Latin word *cohaerere*, which means "to cling together." Coherence is that quality of writing concerned with the flow and connection of all the elements in any text. This quality depends not only on the relevance of detail and use of transitions, but also on an agreement of tone, subject, purpose, and audience. All the parts of the essay should have meaning within the context of the essay. Through the various drafts of "Back Up, Bugs," the supporting examples have been revised and organized in different ways, each time improving upon the first draft. As a result, the various examples are more obviously connected to one another, and the final draft flows better than the earlier drafts. In a coherent essay, the reader should be able to follow the writer's thoughts without having to ask, "Why is that here?" or "How is one idea connected to the rest?" In the final draft of "Back Up, Bugs," both the rationale behind the examples and the connections between them become obvious to the reader. In short, then, the essay is coherent. (See also Section 5d on transitions.)

Conclusion

The Latin word *concludere,* from which **conclusion** is derived, means "to shut up closely." An essay should not just stop; it should conclude—that is, it should end by emphasizing the point the writer has made.

The thesis should therefore be reflected in some way in the conclusion. In paragraph 6 of "Back Up, Bugs," Brian makes the point once again that current cartoons have lost the unique appeal that they used to have, threatening the loved tradition they established. Although the conclusion is not a word-for-word repetition of the thesis (in fact, the words from the original thesis, *enchantment, originality,* and *humor,* do not even appear), it is clearly, as it should be, a reaffirmation of that main idea.

When writing a conclusion then, remember to look back. The final paragraph or final sentence should not contain arguments, perceptions, expansions, or ideas that do not already exist within the essay. Such new ideas belong in the body of the paper where they can receive explanation and support. Although a conclusion may contain a prediction for the future or a suggestion for future action, it should include such an element only if the preceding content of the essay clearly establishes the ground for it. In other words, the conclusion should refer to "what I have written" rather than to "what I can write next."

As a general rule, avoid phrases such as "in sum," "in summary," "to conclude," and "in conclusion" when ending your essay. A good conclusion does not need to be announced.

3e Proofreading and Editing

You **proofread** your writing to edit out errors in spelling, grammar, punctuation diction, and problems in the mechanics of the essay (pagination, margins). This is the last stage of the writing process. This final check may be a noncreative, mechanical duty, but it is certainly *not* an optional part of the writing process. You have no choice about proofreading. Spell "receive" as "recieve" and your paper will strike someone as flawed, however ingeniously it is constructed.

When proofreading and editing, look up in this handbook or a dictionary every point in your essay that you have marked for spelling, grammar, or punctuation. The checklist on p. 60 can help as you proofread and edit.

After making all editorial changes, carefully proofread your essay one last time to be certain that you have not inadvertently created new problems in eliminating the older ones. The main point to remember about proofreading is that it is vitally important. Readers generally notice mistakes in form first; therefore, if you know you are weak in punctuation or spelling, proofread with special attention to these issues or persuade someone who is knowledgeable in these areas to proofread with you. After being corrected half a dozen times, you will catch on.

Most important of all, if an essay is returned to you by your instructor or a peer editor with mistakes marked, go through it and correct each mistake. Look up the rule that refers to each error in this handbook, and be sure you understand it. If you do not understand the error, ask someone to

CHECKLIST FOR PROOFREADING
AND EDITING

- Read your final draft backward, from last word to first word. You may find spelling errors you miss reading from beginning to end.
- Check each pronoun carefully. Does it have an antecedent? Can it possibly refer to the wrong antecedent?
- Read each sentence critically. Begin by locating the verb. Have you by chance used a singular verb form with a plural subject, or vice versa?
- Read your essay aloud. Where you make pauses in reading to make the sense clear, have you used the appropriate punctuation mark?
- Be careful of possessives. Have you included all the apostrophes you should?
- Check the format of your paper. Have you observed the expectations of manuscript mechanics that your teacher requires?
- If there is time, put your paper aside for twenty-four hours and return to it with fresh and objective insights.

explain it. Try writing out misspelled words twenty times, using the correct spelling, or keeping a list of words that you have misspelled to consult when you proofread. Remember that the coordination of language, hand, and thought builds and reinforces good writing habits. Also, be sure to consult Chapter 43 for guidelines on manuscript form.

4   Writing with a Computer

The computer is a valuable writing tool that can help you with every stage of the writing process. Imagine no more crossing out, erasing, drawing arrows, writing in margins, cutting and pasting, and whiting-out as you revise; instead, you hit a few keys and the computer handles these mechanical tasks.

With a computer you can save material from each of your writing sessions on a floppy disk (a piece of plastic 3½″ or 5¼″ on which the computer records and stores information) or on the machine's hard drive (the computer's internal storage compartment). You can then retrieve it whenever you wish to make insertions and deletions, reorganize paragraphs and sentences, or generate multiple versions of your draft. You may also have access to many automated editing aids, such as spelling and style checkers, on-line dictionaries, thesauri, and footnote and bibliography compilers. Of course, your personal writing habits, the accessibility of machines, and the particular project will determine how you will use the computer. Some people prefer to use pen and paper to write. Others use the computer for parts or all of the writing process. If you do have access to a computer, this chapter will help you recognize how the computer can assist you with the mechanical tasks of writing and how useful it is when drafting and revising. Keep in mind, however, that as useful as the computer is, it cannot write for you or do your thinking. It is merely a machine.

4a Overcoming Computer Phobia

You need not fear using a computer. Learning to use the machine will make the entire process of writing easier. Getting practice and experience on the computer are the first steps.

Although facility in typing is an advantage, you do not need to know how to type proficiently in order to write with a computer. The "hunt and peck" system will work fine. Regardless of the computer's make (IBM and Macintosh are the two most commonly used in college computing labs), you should first familiarize yourself with the keyboard: the locations of the alphabet characters and numerals, the punctuation and special signs keys, the backspace key, the shift key, the return key, the cursor and, very importantly, the "save" key. You may have heard stories of people who lost entire essays while working on a computer. You can avoid this mishap by locating and using the save function.

If you have never used a computer before, seek help from the computer lab personnel at your school or from a fellow student familiar with computers. First, be sure to read the materials available in the computer lab for new users. Then practice turning the machine off and on, learn how to prepare or format a disk and compose at the terminal. Learn how to make corrections, insertions, deletions, and block moves. Investigate the functions for preparing to print a paper in accordance with your instructor's format requirements. The more practice you get, the easier these manipulations will become.

Perhaps the greatest obstacle for new users is the terminology associated with computers. The best way to master this terminology is to use it. The following list includes some basic terms you should know:

> **Hardware.** The actual computer equipment, its central processing unit, or "brain," the keyboard, monitor, and printer.
>
> **Software.** The programs that tell the hardware what to do.
>
> **On-line.** The state of being connected to a computer and to off-campus computer sources (e.g., library data banks, sending and receiving messages on computerized bulletin boards) as in "I'm on line."

Monitor. The screen on which your writing appears.

Cursor. A flashing blip that always appears on the computer's monitor; it shows your location on the screen at any point.

Mouse. A device that allows you to move the cursor on the monitor to accomplish various functions such as inserting and deleting letters and words.

Shift Key. The key that allows you to capitalize letters; also used in combination with other keys to perform various functions such as saving your writing.

Document File/File Name. The writing you prepare on the computer (the document), which is saved either on a floppy disk or on the computer's hard drive. Assign a file name before saving a document. For example, if you prewrite on two separate occasions, designate filenames such as *prewrite 1* and *prewrite 2*. It is a good idea to keep a written record of document file names in a notebook, even though most systems can print this out for you.

Backup System. A safety system for preserving your work. It is a good idea to make copies of your writing on a separate floppy disk and to keep the hardcopy (the actual printed-out version) of your day's writing as well, in case you lose or damage a disk.

Database. A program that organizes specialized information in information banks, such as bibliographies and indexes to government documents. (See Section 48a for a list of specialized data bases, pp. 440-441.)

Network. Connected computer systems that allow users to access one another's files.

LAN (local area network). A network limited in geographical area, usually to one campus.

WAN (wide area network). A network wider in scope than a LAN, usually involving more than one campus. Such networks can link computers across the world via Bitnet or Internet.

    Hypertext or Hypercard. A program that links together texts creating ease of access to huge quantities of information.

    Hypermedia. An environment that links together a computer, a videodisk player, a compact disk player, speakers and other types of peripherals, to create an environment that combines sight, sound, and text.

4b Prewriting

Many of the prewriting techniques discussed in Section 2 can be done on the computer. When you work through the prewriting stage, concentrate on entering your ideas without concern for surface errors of spelling, grammar, or punctuation. For example, when you do freewriting, type words and ideas as fast as you are able. If you can, turn down the contrast on the monitor to write without seeing the screen, or turn the monitor off. It is important to generate as much writing as possible. You will be surprised at how much faster and, in most cases, how much more material you can generate on the computer compared to writing by hand. The versatility of the computer also makes it useful for brainstorming and outlining. When finished, you can review your freewriting electronically or, even better, obtain a printout of it and begin to rough out your ideas.

4c Drafting

With a computer you can write a draft of your paper, save it or print it and delete it, quickly devise another draft, compare different versions, and make changes to words or to entire blocks of the draft with ease. Some computers are even outfitted with programs that enable you to review several drafts of your paper simultaneously.

Use your prewriting to produce the first draft. Use the computer to write, and do not concern yourself with grammar, punctuation, and format at this early stage. Remember, with the computer you can easily rearrange your draft and make changes. Think, instead, about your thesis, audience, and tone. Repeat prewriting techniques, if you need to, right at the terminal. As you work on the first draft, remember to save it as you write. Use different file names for each of your drafts; read your drafts over and evaluate them. It is always a good idea to work with the hardcopy of your drafts as well.

4d Revising

Computers and revision were made for each other. The computer makes revising easy because you can insert, delete, and rearrange words, sentences, and paragraphs with a few keys strokes or clicks of a mouse. The drudgery of having to recopy or retype your revisions is eliminated. The principles of revision as re-seeing, discussed in Chapter 3, apply when writing with a computer. Be sure not to confuse re-seeing with editing. When you revise, clarify your purpose and ideas, probe for new insights, and produce drafts (see Section 3c) for further revision. Some writers prefer to revise on their hardcopy (printed draft), away from the computer, and then enter a revised draft onto the disk. The approach you use depends on your preferences. But it is a good idea to distance yourself from your work. Evaluating your hardcopy will give you a chance to view your writing a little more objectively.

Remember to save all the revisions you make; otherwise, your hardcopy will not contain the changes. Create separate files for each of your revisions in case you decide later that you prefer an earlier version of the paper.

If your personal computer or workstation is networked and your instructor allows it, you can use peer critique and collaboration to help with revisions. Other students would then have access to your file, read your essay, and leave messages for you concerning its strengths and weaknesses. You might even write some questions at the end of your essay to elicit specific responses if you know you need help with certain problems: Do you think my thesis works? Is the tone of the second paragraph suitable? Do you detect any ambiguities? (See Section 3a for more on peer critiques.)

4e Editing and Formatting

Before generating a final draft, you will need to edit your work. Although editing functions vary among different makes of computers, every computer can delete and add letters, punctuation marks, and words, making it easy to implement those final corrections in grammar, punctuation, and spelling. Many computers have a search function that allows you to search for a word that appears frequently in your paper and replace it or respell it with one simple command. Functions that enable the computer to check spelling and style are often available. Use these spelling and style checkers if your computer is equipped with them, but be aware of their limitations. You might use the wrong word and spell it correctly—*to* instead of *too*, for instance—but the spelling checker does not have the capability to recognize the mistake. Often, because style checkers are designed for business use, the programs will suggest changes, in sentence length perhaps, which your instructor has been encouraging you *not* to do. Whatever changes you make when editing and formatting, be certain to save them. It is also a good idea to perform a close edit of the hardcopy of your paper. Errors that you miss on the screen may be more obvious on the printed page.

Most computers offer an array of options for formatting. As a result, your computer-generated paper will be more professional looking than a handwritten version. After you have edited your text, you will need to format it before printing.

Type font

Select a type font from among those available on the computer. Most teachers will not want you to use the font called *script*, which looks like handwriting. As a general rule, avoid fonts that are very large or very small. Select near-letter quality for your final draft, not the fonts labeled "draft" or "utility," which will produce an inferior print quality.

Justifying margins

You are probably used to producing essays that have left-justified margins (flush left). But computers give you the option of justifying the right-side margin as well, producing a page that resembles a printed-book page. However, almost all computers that justify the right margin insert three, four, or even five spaces between words, resulting in unusual spacing. Unless your teacher specifies otherwise, do not use the right-justified margin option.

Page previewing

Most computers have a page preview option that allows you to see, in miniature, how your text will appear on the printed page. Use it if it is available, and make whatever formatting changes are needed. Be certain to check for page numbers, paragraph indentations, double spacing, centering the title, and whether any peculiar line or page breaks occur. (Also see Section 43b, pp. 407–408, for specific information on formatting a computer-generated paper.)

4f Printing

You are ready to print the essay stored on your disk after you have completed editing and formatting. If your computer is connected to a printer, you can print directly from your workstation. Otherwise, you will have to take your disk to a site where a printer is available. Insert your disk into the computer at the printing site, and type the appropriate instructions. Once you have the printed copy, proofread it carefully. If any changes are necessary, make them on your file, save them, and print the revision. Be certain that your essay is printed on a quality of paper acceptable to your instructor. If it has left- and right-perforated roller holes, carefully remove these so your paper will measure the standard 8½ by 11 inches.

5   Writing Coherent Paragraphs

A **paragraph** is a group of sentences that develops an idea about a topic. The word *paragraph* comes from an ancient Greek word referring to the short horizontal line that the Greeks placed beneath the start of a line of prose in manuscripts to indicate a break in thought or a change in speaker. This convention of marking the places in a written work where the sense or the speaker changed was followed by medieval monks, who used a red or blue symbol much like our modern paragraph symbol (¶) in their manuscripts. Today, we indicate such a change in thought by indenting the first line of each new paragraph.

Although a paragraph is usually self-contained, at the same time it is usually part of a larger work, such as an essay or a research paper, and depends on the paragraphs before and after it. For example, look at the following four paragraphs.

Modern American Indian women, like their non-Indian sisters, are deeply engaged in the struggle to redefine themselves. In their struggle they must reconcile traditional tribal definitions of women with industrial and postindustrial non-Indian definitions. Yet while these definitions seem to be more or less mutually exclusive, Indian women must somehow harmonize and integrate both in their own lives.

An American Indian woman is primarily defined by her tribal identity. In her eyes, her destiny is necessarily that of her people, and her sense of herself as a woman is first and foremost prescribed by her tribe. The definitions of woman's roles are as diverse as tribal cultures in the Americas. In some she is devalued, in others she wields considerable power. In some she is a familial/clan adjunct, in some she is as close to autonomous as her economic circumstances and psychological traits permit. But in no tribal definitions is she perceived in the same way as are women in western industrial and postindustrial cultures.

In the west, few images of women form part of the cultural mythos, and these are largely sexually charged. Among Christians, the madonna is the female prototype, and she is portrayed as essentially passive: her contribution is simply that of birthing. Little else is attributed to her and she certainly possesses few of the characteristics that are attributed to mythic figures among Indian tribes. This image is countered (rather than balanced) by the witch-goddess/whore characteristics designed to reinforce cultural beliefs about women, as well as western adversarial and dualistic perceptions of reality.

The tribes see women variously, but they do not question the power of femininity. Sometimes they see women as fearful, sometimes peaceful, sometimes omnipotent and omniscient, but they never portray women as mindless, helpless, simple, or oppressed. And while the women in a given tribe, clan, or band may be all those things, the individual woman is provided with a variety of images of women for the interconnected supernatural, natural, and social worlds she lives in.

Paula Gunn Allen
from *The Sacred Hoop*

Each of these paragraphs develops its own point. This point, which guides the paragraph, is often referred to as the **controlling idea** and is usually expressed in a topic sentence. The controlling idea of the first paragraph is that American Indian women, like other women in our society, are struggling to define their identities. The idea is made more specific by the sentences that follow. The controlling idea of the second paragraph is that the identity of American Indian women is closely allied to tribal customs and beliefs. This idea is supported by examples of such customs and beliefs. The controlling idea of the third paragraph is that, in contrast, the identity of women outside American Indian culture is easier to define and appears more restricted. This idea is supported by showing that such identities can be summarized as the madonna/goddess figure versus the witch/whore figure. The controlling idea of the fourth paragraph is that American Indian cultures view women in a less restrictive way but still acknowledge the power of femininity. This idea is supported by concrete, specific examples.

Although each of the four paragraphs is controlled by its own idea, the four also work together. The second continues the general subjects discussed in the first paragraph but focuses on American Indian tribal cultures. The first paragraph presents a general controlling idea and makes it narrower. The second paragraph specifically informs the reader of the diverse forms that women's identities assume among various American Indian tribes, which differ greatly from non-American Indian conceptions. The third paragraph then discusses the controlling idea in the non-American Indian culture, and the fourth paragraph clarifies how women are viewed in American Indian cultures. Therefore, we can say that although a paragraph is largely self-contained, its general subject and controlling idea must conform to the objectives of the larger work of which it is a part.

A paragraph is composed of individual sentences, but these sentences must cohere in order to result in effective communication. Paragraphs too must contribute to the coherence of the paper as a whole by providing unity, a consistent recognizable method of development, and clear transition from one idea to another.

5a Unity

Unity in a paragraph results when all the sentences in the paragraph relate to and develop the controlling idea. In other words, no sentences digress, or go off the track. Unity evolves from the use of a topic sentence and of relevant support.

The topic sentence

A paragraph develops a controlling, or main, idea, which is stated in a **topic sentence.** Functioning in a paragraph as a thesis statement functions in an essay, a topic sentence establishes the direction for the paragraph, with all the other sentences in the paragraph supporting and developing it.

Although a topic sentence often appears at the beginning of a paragraph, it may also be placed in the middle or at the end. When it is placed at the beginning of the paragraph, the rest of the sentences support the topic sentence, and the paragraph is developed deductively. In other words, the main idea appears first, and then the information supporting this idea follows. For example, the following paragraph concerns the British composer Peter Maxwell Davies. The controlling idea, or the idea to be developed, is that he had a difficult time winning recognition both at home and abroad.

> **For Davies, winning recognition wasn't easy, at home or abroad.** He was born near Manchester, a grim industrial city. The son of working-class parents, he taught himself composition by studying scores in the library. When he asked to study music at his grammar school, in preparation for the O-level exams given all British students, the headmaster scoffed. The faculty at the Royal Manchester College of Music and at Manchester University, where Davies subsequently studied, proved to be hardly more enlightened. It was the mid-fifties, and the Austrian moderns—Mahler and Bruckner—were still highly suspect. So, in fact, was anyone but such homegrown products as Sir Edward Elgar, Ralph Vaughan Williams, and Charles Villiers Stanford. Davies wanted none of it. Along with a group of other students, including Harrison Birtwistle, who were eager to hear the new European music, he began listening to Stravinsky and Schoenberg.
>
> Annalyn Swan
> "A Visionary Composer"

Sometimes the topic sentence appears in the form of a question. When this occurs, the rest of the paragraph answers the question. For example, the following paragraph details, through support of the initial topic sentence, how individuals must be allowed to mature at their own rate and in their own way.

> Why should we be in such desperate haste to succeed and in such desperate enterprises? If a man does not keep pace with his companions, perhaps it is because he hears a different drummer. Let him step to the music which he hears, however measured or far away. It is not important that he should mature as soon as an apple-tree or an oak. Shall he turn his spring into summer? If the condition of things which we were made for is not yet, what were any reality which we can substitute? We will not be shipwrecked on a vain reality.

Shall we with pains erect a heaven of blue glass over ourselves, though when it is done we shall be sure to gaze still at
the true ethereal heaven far above, as if the former were not?

Henry David Thoreau
Walden

A paragraph that begins with a topic sentence sometimes
ends with a concluding statement that restates the controlling
idea, or summarizes or comments on the information in the
paragraph. For example, the following paragraph is about
wolves. The controlling idea is that they are Holarctic. The
topic sentence is printed in **boldface** and the concluding statement is in *italics*.

> **Wolves, twenty or thirty subspecies of them, are
> Holarctic—that is, they once roamed most of the
> Northern Hemisphere above thirty degrees north lati-
> tude.** They were found throughout Europe, from the Zezere
> River Valley of Portugal north to Finland and south to the
> Mediterranean. They roamed eastern Europe, the Balkans, and
> the Near and Middle East south into Arabia. They were found
> in Afghanistan and northern India, throughout Russia north
> into Siberia, south again as far as China, and east into the
> islands of Japan. In North America the wolf reached a south-
> ern limit north of Mexico City and ranged north as far as Cape
> Morris Jesup, Greenland, less than four hundred miles from
> the North Pole. *Outside of Iceland and North Africa, and such
> places as the Gobi Desert, wolves—if you imagine the differ-
> ences in geography it seems astonishing—had adapted to vir-
> tually every habitat available to them.*

Barry Holstun Lopez
Of Wolves and Men

Sometimes the topic sentence occurs at the end of the
paragraph. When this is the case, the topic sentence provides
the focus for the sentences that lead up to it. The paragraph is

developed inductively; that is, the evidence is given first and then the conclusion derived from this evidence is given. For example, the following paragraph is about the Hill country in Texas. The controlling idea, or the idea that the rest of the sentences lead up to, is that to the early settlers, this country seemed like a paradise.

> And the streams, these men discovered, were full of fish. The hills were full of game. There were, to their experienced eyes, all the signs of bear, and you didn't need signs to know about the deer—they were so numerous that when riders crested a hill, a whole herd might leap away in the valley below, white tails flashing. There were other white tails, too: rabbits in abundance. And as the men sat their horses, staring, flocks of wild turkeys strutted in silhouette along the ridges. Honeybees buzzed in the glades, and honey hung in the trees for the taking. Wild mustang grapes, plump and purple, hung down for making wine. **Wrote one of the first men to come to the Hill Country: "It is a Paradise."**
>
> Robert A. Caro
> *The Path to Power*

This type of topic sentence often appears in opening paragraphs where it acts as a lead-in to the body of the paper.

Sometimes the topic sentence is delayed until the middle or near the middle of the paragraph. When this is the case, the topic sentence serves as a bridge, or transition, between the information in the first part of the paragraph and the information in the second. The following paragraph is about King Richard III of England. The controlling idea of this paragraph is that the traditional view of Richard III has been obstinately opposed over the years.

> History is always written by the victors. The basic Tudor picture of Richard as a bloodthirsty tyrant was handed down through the standard histories of England and the school text-

books for five centuries. **There has been an obstinate opposition, however.** Beginning with Sir George Buck in the 17th century, a series of writers and historians have insisted that Richard was not getting a fair break, that the Tudor version was largely fabrication: far from being a monster Richard was a noble, upright, courageous, tenderhearted and most conscientious king. This anti-Tudor version reached its definitive statement in the work of Sir Clements Markham, a 19th-century eccentric who spent years of passionate research trying to prove that crimes attributed to Richard were either outright libels by, or the actual work of, a pack of villains, most notably including Cardinal Morton and Henry VII.

Robert Wernick
"After 500 Years, Old Crookback
Can Still Kick Up a Fuss"

Support

Support your controlling idea with specific information—facts, statistics, details, examples, illustrations, anecdotes—that provides proof for your idea. Consider the following paragraph.

Oranges and orange blossoms have long been symbols of love. Boccaccio's *Decameron*, written in the fourteenth century, is redolent with the scent of oranges and orange blossoms, with lovers who wash in orange-flower water, a courtesan who sprinkles her sheets with orange perfume, and the mournful Isabella, who cuts off the head of her dead lover, buries it in an ample pot, plants basil above it, and irrigates the herbs exclusively with rosewater, orange-flower water, and tears. In the fifteenth century, the Countess Mathilda of Württemberg received from her impassioned admirer, Dr. Heinrich Steinbowel, a declaration of love in the form of a gift of two dozen oranges. Before long, titled German girls were throwing oranges down from their balconies in the way that girls in Italy or Spain were dropping handkerchiefs. After Francis I dramatically saved Marseilles from a Spanish siege, a great feast was held for him at the city's harborside, and Marseillaise ladies, in token of their love and gratitude, pelted him with oranges. Even Nostradamus was sufficiently impressed with the sensual power of oranges to publish, in 1556, a book on how to prepare various cosmetics from oranges and orange blossoms. Limes were also used cosmetically, by ladies of the French court in the seventeenth century, who kept them on their person and bit into them from time to time in order to redden their lips. In the nineteenth century, orange blossoms were regularly shipped to Paris in salted barrels from Provence, for no French bride wanted to be married without wearing or holding them.

John McPhee
"Oranges"

The controlling idea of this paragraph is contained in the first sentence. Notice all the details McPhee gives to support his controlling idea. First he tells us about oranges and orange blossoms in Boccaccio's *Decameron*. Then he tells us about Countess Mathilda in the fifteenth century and how the gift of oranges from her admirer led to the custom of German girls throwing oranges from their balconies. Next he tells us how Francis I was pelted with oranges as a token of love, and how Nostradamus published a book on how to prepare cosmetics from oranges and orange blossoms. Finally, he tells us that in the nineteenth century a French bride would not want to be married without holding or wearing orange blossoms. Notice how fully he treats these details. He tells you not only that Boccaccio wrote about oranges and orange blossoms in the *Decameron* but also what he said about them—the lovers, the courtesan, the mournful Isabella.

Notice all the supporting details Peter Steinhart uses to develop his controlling idea in the following paragraph.

Adobe is an ancient material. Peruvians and Mesopotamians knew at least 3,000 years ago how to mix adobe—three parts sandy soil to one part clay soil—and box-mold it into bricks. The Walls of Jericho, the Tower of Babel, Egyptian pyramids, and sections of China's Great Wall are adobes. So are more modern structures like Spain's Alhambra, the great mosques of Fez and Marrakesh, and the royal palace at Riyadh.

Peter Steinhart
"Dirt Chic"

Not only must a paragraph contain support for its controlling idea, but this support must be relevant. Consider the following paragraph:

Several writers have used San Francisco as a backdrop for their novels. Kathryn Forbes's novel *Mama's Bank Account,* on which the movie *I Remember Mama* was based, is set in San Francisco. The immigrant family lives on Steiner Street, in a big house in the middle of the city that Mama loved so well. Jack London's novel *The Sea Wolf* is enriched by its vivid depiction of San Francisco, the city in which London grew up. London set what is perhaps his most famous novel, *The Call of the Wild,* in the Klondike, however. Dashiell Hammett's detective, Sam Spade, lives and works in San Francisco. As he solves his cases, Spade reveals to us the seamy underbelly of the city, which challenges his ideals and forces him to develop a mask of cynicism. Other writers reveal to us the corrupt side of city life, too. For example, in his short novel *Maggie: A Girl of the Streets,* Stephen Crane shows us the lower depths of New York's Bowery and the effects of this environment on the destiny of a young girl, Maggie Johnson.

This paragraph lacks unity. The controlling idea is that several writers have used San Francisco as a backdrop for their novels. However, the paragraph contains three sentences that do not relate to this main idea. The fifth sentence is a digression because it does not develop the idea of novels set in San Francisco. The last two sentences also digress. The next-to-last sentence is not limited to San Francisco, and the last is concerned with New York City.

Digressions weaken your paragraphs. Eliminate or rewrite any sentences that do not develop the controlling idea. Notice how the sample paragraph is improved by removing the digressions.

> Several writers have used San Francisco as a backdrop for their novels. Kathryn Forbes's novel *Mama's Bank Account*, on which the movie *I Remember Mama* was based, is set in San Francisco. The immigrant family lives on Steiner Street, in a big house in the middle of the city that Mama loved so well. Jack London's novel *The Sea Wolf* is enriched by its vivid depiction of San Francisco, the city in which London grew up. Dashiell Hammett's detective, Sam Spade, lives and works in San Francisco. As he solves his cases, Spade reveals to us the seamy underbelly of the city, which challenges his ideals and forces him to develop a mask of cynicism.

5b Organizational Strategies

A paragraph should be developed and organized in a purposeful way to assist the reader in following your argument or line of reasoning. The paragraph's organization should depend on your overall aim in the particular section of your essay. Sometimes a method of development will come to you naturally, without thought; at other times you will have to choose deliberately from a variety of options in order to fulfill your purpose. These options include some organization strategies as well as some more specific techniques commonly called the patterns, or modes, of development.

You have a variety of organization strategies available to arrange your paragraphs. The following represent the most common types.

General to specific

Arrange your information from **general to specific** when you want to present a general idea first and then supply specific examples, details, or reasons to support your idea. The following paragraph is organized in a general to specific pattern. Notice how the information in it becomes more and more specific.

> As of now, the biological productivity of the lower Hudson is staggering. Fishes are there by the millions, with marine and freshwater species often side by side in the same patch of water. All told, the population of fishes utilizing the lower Hudson for spawning, nursery or feeding grounds comprises the greatest single wildlife resource in New York State. It is also the most neglected resource; at this writing, not one state conservation department biologist is to be found studying it regularly. Besides sea sturgeon, the river is aswarm year-round or seasonally with striped bass, white perch, bluefish, shad, herring, largemouth bass, carp, needlefish, yellow perch, menhaden, golden shiners, darters, tomcod, and sunfish, to cite only some. There is the short-nosed and round-nosed sturgeon, officially classified by the Department of the Interior as "endangered," or close to extinct, in the United States. Perhaps it is extinct elsewhere along the Atlantic Coast, but not only is the fish present in the Hudson, but occasional specimens exceed the published record size in the scientific literature. The lower Hudson also receives an interesting infusion of so-called tropical or subtropic fishes, such as the jack crevalle and the mullet, both originally associated with Florida waters.

> Robert H. Boyle
> *The Hudson River*

Specific to general

Arrange your information from specific to general when you want to present specific details first and then lead up to a generalization about them. The following narrative paragraph uses a specific to general pattern. The paragraph starts with a specific description of the birds' behavior, which leads up to a generalization about their behavior: they were anting, or deliberately covering themselves with ants.

> As he walked in an orange grove behind Trinidad's Asa Wright Nature Centre, Ray Mendez noticed a pair of birds that were behaving strangely. The birds—violaceous trogons, judging from the ring of bright orange around their eyes—were preoccupied with something, so preoccupied that they seemed to have lost their usual bird sense. They appeared fascinated, expectant, oblivious. Mendez drew close and watched. Suddenly one of the trogons broke from its perch and flew a hard flat line at an ants' nest hanging from a tree branch. The bird crashed into the nest, held on, and then shoved itself in headfirst, allowing *Azteca* ants to cover its body. It flittered its wings a moment and the *Azteca* boarded them too. Then the trogon flew back to a safe perch, and Mendez, entranced by the mystery of these events, suddenly saw the simple answer. The trogons were anting.
>
> David Weinberg
> "Ant Acid Spells Relief"

The following paragraph is also organized in a specific to general pattern. The author first gives evidence supporting his argument and then concludes the paragraph with a general statement of his position.

> American workers understand that the manufacturers of arms have been the bulwark of the capitalist system in the United States, as well as of the communist Soviet Union. In their bones these workers sense that what financial security they have—little enough—is tied to the billions of dollars invested in the arms race. Where would America's "free enterprise" be without that ongoing safety net? Some of us—the more privileged—can afford not to wonder. But most cannot. It wouldn't hurt the peace movement if we found a better way to reach out to this less affluent majority, if we coupled our

opposition to nuclear weapons with a clear and compelling program for economic reform.

Robert Coles
"The Doomsayers:
Class Politics and the Nuclear Freeze"

Climactic order

Arrange your information in **climactic order,** or by order of importance with the most important last, when you want to begin by supporting your generalization with the least important information and build up to the most important. The following paragraph is organized in climactic order. It starts with the least important criterion for judging a behavior as conscious and builds up to the most important.

What criteria lead us to judge that a particular behavior is conscious? What is the difference between the eight-month baby who clumsily knocks over its milk, and the two-year-old who obviously does it on purpose? Several things incline us to judge that another being is acting consciously: if it studies its goal before acting, if it chooses one of a very flexible set of behaviors, or even a novel behavior with detours to reach the goal. Conscious purpose seems especially likely if some learned symbol like "No! Naughty!" communicates the situation to the aggravated parents. Finally, if there is misdirection—hiding or lying—it seems likely that the creature has formed some conception of other animals' intentions and awareness.

Alison Jolly
"A New Science That Sees Animals
as Conscious Beings"

Time order

Arrange your information in **time order** when you want to explain a sequence of events or tell a story. The details in the following expository paragraph are organized according to time order.

Jesuit missionaries stationed in China were probably the first voyagers to bring soybeans to Europe, in the seventeen-thirties, and there, like potatoes before them, the beans were considered a horticultural curiosity. Specimens were planted at the Jardin des Plantes, in Paris, in 1739, and in London's Kew Gardens—these probably from India—in 1790. (As early as 1712, a German botanist, Engelbert Kämpfer, who had visited Japan in the sixteen-nineties, published a recipe for soy sauce; that may have been the first time any Europeans were informed that the bean was in any respect edible.)

E. J. Kahn, Jr.
"Soybeans"

Spatial order

Arrange your information in **spatial order** when you want to explain or describe the relative physical positions of people or objects. The details in the following descriptive paragraph are organized according to spatial order.

Greenwich Village is a mass of "little twisted streets that crossed and recrossed each other and never seemed to get anywhere. . . ." In its center is Washington Square, a stretch of green, bordered by a number of park benches, where one can sit and read, talk, or do nothing at all. In the background of Washington Square looms New York University. Before Washington Square became a park in 1827, it had been "in successive decades Potter's Field, parade grounds, place of executions. . . ." During Millay's time, little delicatessens and coffee shops helped to create an old English atmosphere in the Village.

Anne Cheney
Millay in Greenwich Village

5c Patterns of Development

Numerous other techniques are available in addition to the general techniques for arranging your paragraphs. The **patterns of development,** for instance, enable you to explain information in specific ways as dictated by your purpose and can even be used to develop entire essays, not just paragraphs. These patterns can be used alone in a paragraph or essay or can be used together to suit your writing needs. The following represent the most commonly used of the patterns or modes of development.

Description

Develop your paragraph through **description** when you wish to provide specific details that accurately paint a picture of your topic in the reader's imagination (objective description) or that recreate an impression you have of your topic (subjective description). Be certain to report your point of view, the real or imaginary point from which you are viewing the thing described. If the point of view changes during the description, indicate that for your reader. Following is an example of a subjective description. Note that not all descriptive details are visual.

> Stand on a hilltop in late September, and you can see October coming. Not October only, but all of autumn, which flows like a tide across this land of ours. It creeps down from the mountaintops in a haze of leaf color. It strides across the meadows in a foam of final blossom. It rustles through the marsh-grass at the foot of the shore's dunes, whispers down the valleys in a southward rush of wings, tangs the evening air with wood smoke. Not only can you see autumn; you can hear it, you can feel it in the air upon your cheek, you can smell its pungence.
>
> Hal Borland
> "Autumn in America"

Definition

Develop your paragraph through **definition** when you want to clarify how you are using a term, to assign a particular meaning to a word, or to discuss an abstract concept from a special or unusual point of view. If you think your reader will not know or understand how you are using a term, be safe and define it; however, remember to include in the paragraph *why* a definition is necessary.

> What is war? It is not weapons or warheads or even military force itself; these are only "the *means* of war." According to Clausewitz, war is simply "an act of force to compel our enemy to do our will." That is precisely what the Vietnamese are attempting to do to the Cambodians, what Iraq tried to do to Iran, what Somalia is striving to do with Ethiopia, what Israel attempted to do in Lebanon, and why Soviet troops are in Afghanistan.
>
> Colonel Harry G. Summers, Jr.
> "What Is War?"

Classification

Develop your paragraph through **classification** when you wish to group information into types or classes in order to find or to explain patterns of *similarities*. The following paragraph classifies ranks within a troop of rhesus monkeys.

> The core of the troop's structure is a series of matriarchies. A mother ranks above her own daughters until she becomes very, very old. She supports them in fights, so her offspring rank just below her and thus above all the other matriarchies that she can dominate. Young males commonly migrate to other troops. A male's adult rank depends on his own fighting prowess and on his charm—much of his status depends on whether the females of his new troop back him up. A female, on the other hand, is usually locked for life into the nepotistic matrix of her kin. Her adult rank is roughly predictable the day she is born. But female status changes do occasionally happen, and it is worth a young female's while to test the system. In the wild, predation and disease knock out relatives at random, so there is more flexibility than we see in

our well-tended captive colonies. Wild or captive, kinship is still the major fact of female social life. A baby learns early those situations when its relatives will come and help—and when they won't.

Alison Jolly
"A New Science That Sees Animals
as Conscious Beings"

Comparison and Contrast

Develop your paragraph through **comparison and contrast** when you want to show the similarities and/or differences between two or more things. You have several options in presenting the information. One way is to present the items being compared and contrasted one at a time; the result is called the **block pattern** exemplified in the following excerpt:

Villamuelas, Spain—Soldiers don't start out as generals nor politicians as presidents. In business, managers work their way up. Except for a lucky few, the realization slowly and steadily comes to just about everyone that the top is out of reach.

But bullfighting works the other way around. A bullfighter rockets to the top. From first blush, he is a matador—that bold and arrogant swordsman who artfully entices the bull to its moment of truth. A matador monopolizes the spotlight long enough to convince the world of his incompetence. Then his own moment of truth arrives: the shock of failure and the dawning knowledge that he will never be on top again.

Barry Newman
"Banderillo"

Another option is to alternate points of the comparison or contrast, called the **alternating pattern,** which is illustrated in the following paragraph:

> Twenty-four-year-old Clark Wolfsberger, a native of St. Louis, and Kim Wright, twenty-five, who is from Chicago, live in Dallas. They've been going together since they met as students at Southern Methodist University three years ago. They are an attractive pair, trim and athletic, she dark and lissome, he broad-shouldered and square-jawed. They have jobs they took immediately after graduating—Clark works at Talent Sports International, a sports marketing and management company; Kim is an assistant account executive at Tracy-Locke, a large advertising agency—and they are in love.
>
> Bruce Weber
> "The Unromantic Generation"

A third option is to mix the two types of presentation: you present most of the comparison/contrast in the block pattern and then present the key points in the alternating pattern to highlight and emphasize significant similarities or differences.

Analogy

Develop your paragraph with **analogy** when you wish to stress comparisons between things that are unlike. In the following paragraph, the author presents an analogy of the crowd on the boardwalk in Atlantic City to a nest of social insects.

> Viewed from a suitable height, the aggregating clusters of medical scientists in the bright sunlight of the boardwalk at Atlantic City, swarmed there from everywhere for the annual meetings, have the assemblages of social insects. There is the same vibrating, ironic movement, interrupted by the darting back and forth of jerky individuals to touch antennae and exchange small bits of information; periodically, the mass casts out, like a trout-line, a long single file unerringly towards Childs's. If the boards were not fastened down, it would not be a surprise to see them put together as a nest of sorts.
>
> Lewis Thomas
> *On Societies as Organisms*

Example and illustration

Develop your paragraph by **example,** one or more short instances, or by **illustration,** a longer, sustained example that usually appears in the form of a story, when you want to make your ideas specific by supporting them with evidence. Examples work best when you use two or three that are truly representative. Because illustration consists of one sustained example of several sentences, its use is not as frequent but can be equally effective in relating to and supporting your topic sentence. In the following paragraph, the author uses illustrations as a lead-in to the topic (last) sentence.

> I have seen many students read a difficult book just as if they were reading the sports page. Sometimes I would ask at the beginning of a class if they had any questions about the text, if there was anything they did not understand. Their silence answered in the negative. At the end of two hours, during which they could not answer the simplest questions leading to an interpretation of the book, they would admit their deficiency in a puzzled way. They were puzzled because they were quite honest in their belief that they had read the text. They had, indeed, but not in the right way.
>
> Mortimer J. Adler
> *How to Read a Book,*
> *The Art of Getting a Liberal Education*

See also paragraphs 1 and 2 of the student's sample essay in Chapter 3 (pp. 49–50) for samples of short example.

Process

Develop your paragraph through explanation of a **process** when you wish to show how something is done or how something works. The following paragraph explains how we listen to music.

We all listen to music according to our separate capacities. But, for the sake of analysis, the whole listening process may become clearer if we break it up into its component parts, so to speak. In a certain sense we all listen to music on three separate planes. For lack of a better terminology, one might name these: (1) the sensuous plane, (2) the expressive plane, (3) the sheerly musical plane. The only advantage to be gained from mechanically splitting up the listening process into these hypothetical planes is the clearer view to be had of the way in which we listen.

Aaron Copland
"How We Listen to Music"

Cause and effect

Arrange your information through **cause and effect** when you want to discuss the causes behind certain effects or the reasons for certain results or consequences. Be certain that you have carefully thought out all the implications of your cause and effect statements. For example, one can write that candidate X lost the election because she did not get enough votes. Although this is true, a full treatment would include the reasons why enough people did not vote for candidate X. (See Section 7c on logical fallacies, pp. 120–130.) The following paragraph gives the result first—the transformation of the tartan into an instrument of Scottish nationalistic ideology. It then provides the reasons or causes that brought about this result.

A cluster of events transformed the tartan into an instrument of nationalist ideology. In the wake of the great defeat of Bonnie Prince Charlie in 1745, the British banned Highland wear, including tartans and the kilt, under penalty of six months in prison for a first offense and seven years' transportation for a second. The elder Pitt simultaneously formed the Highland regiments for service abroad. They alone were permitted to wear the plaid and the kilt, both for reasons of esprit de corps and, no doubt, to impede desertion: a man running about in a skirt south of the border or in France was a conspicuous object. This is, most likely, when tartans peculiar to certain regiments became established. Finally, Scottish nationalism, seeking to extirpate both Irish and Lowland roots of the culture, turned to the literal invention of an ancient Highland culture, kilt and all. The final triumph came when Lowland Scotland, offered this bogus tradition, eagerly accepted it.

Alexander Cockburn
"The Origin of the Kilt"

EXERCISE 5-1

Compose one paragraph on a suggested topic using any three of the following patterns of development.

1. Description: the face of an older person you know, a building you pass daily, a car you would like to own, a busy place—the cafeteria, library, student union

2. Definition: what you mean by "beauty," how the dictionary distinguishes between a "statesman" and a "politician," how the etymology of the word "umpire" is informative

3. Classification: varieties of students in your composition class, types of housing, current popular music

4. Comparison and contrast: two people you like very much, attitudes toward smoking, two classes you enjoy

5. Example and illustration: why some of your peers do not vote, attitudes toward birth control, underage drinking of alcohol

6. Process: tying a bow in your shoelace, starting a car, heating soup

7. Cause and effect: why a runner loses a race, something done carelessly, what caused an automobile accident

5d Transition

Even if all the sentences in a paragraph relate to a controlling idea and follow an organized method of development, it is still helpful to the reader's understanding to link sentences with **transitional devices** that provide smooth passage from one idea to the next. These devices include not only *transitional words and expressions* but also *pronouns, repetition of key words and phrases*, and *parallel grammatical structure*.

Transitional words and expressions

Transitional words and expressions show the relationship of one term to another term, one sentence to another sentence, one idea to another idea, and even one paragraph to another paragraph. They serve as signposts that direct the reader through the passage.

Below are some common transitional words and expressions and the relationships they may indicate:

ADDITION

again, also, and, besides, equally important, finally, first (second, third, and so on), furthermore, in addition, last, likewise, moreover, next, too

SIMILARITY

in a similar fashion, likewise, moreover, similarly, so

CONTRAST

although, but, even so, for all that, however, in contrast, nevertheless, on the contrary, on the other hand, still, yet

TIME

afterward, at the same time, before, earlier, finally, in the past, later, meanwhile, next, now, previously, simultaneously, soon, subsequently

PLACE OR DIRECTION
above, beyond, here, in the distance, nearby, opposite, overhead, there, to the side, underneath

PURPOSE
for this purpose, to this end, with this object in mind

RESULT
accordingly, as a result, consequently, hence, then, therefore, thus

EXAMPLES OR INTENSIFICATION
for example, for instance, indeed, in fact, in other words, that is

SUMMARY OR CONCLUSION
finally, in brief, in conclusion, in short, in summary, on the whole, to conclude, to sum up

In the following paragraph, the transitional words and expressions are printed in **boldface.**

There were other important applications of new technology that looked ahead to the future, **too**. Thaddeus Lowe was by no means the first to fly in lighter-than-air-balloons, **but** he was the first to use these craft for doing reconnaissance work on enemy positions. **Likewise,** the telegraph had been around for some years, **but** the Civil War was the first war in which it played a crucial role. **So, too,** railroads were already enjoying a robust adolescence, **but** it was during the Civil War that they found themselves making a major contribution. Barbed wire entanglements were **also** used for the first time in the Civil War, **as** were land and water mines.

Arthur M. Schlesinger, Jr.
The Almanac of American History

Pronouns

Pronouns link sentences by referring the reader to their antecedents (see pp. 282-288). In the following excerpt, notice how the pronouns in the second and third sentences link these clauses and sentences to the first sentence.

> There is always a teahouse wherever you go in the Orient. **Some** are big with red pillars and gleaming orange-yellow roofs; **many** have tables in a garden among scented flowers and lotus ponds; a **few** are huge houseboats carved to look like dragons floating on the water. But **most** of **them** are just plain, unornamented, regular restaurants.
>
> Maj Leung
> *The Chinese People's Cookbook*

Repetition and parallel structure

Repetition of key words and phrases and the use of **parallel grammatical structure** (see pp. 282-288) provide emphasis and clear transition from one thought to another. In the following paragraph, notice how the repetition of the word *know* drives home the author's point. Notice also that the last three sentences are in parallel form: each is made up of a clause beginning with *if* followed by a clause beginning with *you will*. This structure, along with the transitional words *then* and *Next* at the beginning of the second and third sentences, makes it easy for the reader to follow the progression of ideas from one sentence to the next.

> But I am wandering from what I was intending to do; that is, make plainer than perhaps appears in the previous chapters some of the peculiar requirements of the science of piloting. First of all, there is one faculty which a pilot must incessantly cultivate until he has brought it to absolute perfection. Nothing short of perfection will do. That faculty is **memory.** He cannot stop with merely thinking a thing is so and so; he must

know it; for this is eminently one of the "exact" sciences. With what scorn a pilot was looked upon in the old days, if he ever ventured to deal in that feeble phrase "I think," instead of the vigorous one "**I know!**" One cannot easily realize what a tremendous thing it is to **know** every trivial detail of twelve hundred miles of river and **know** it with absolute exactness. **If** you will take the longest street in New York, and travel up and down it, **conning** its features patiently until you **know** every house and window and lamp-post and big and little sign **by heart,** and **know** them so accurately that you can instantly name the one you are abreast of when you are set down at random in that street in the middle of an inky black night, you will then have a tolerable notion of the amount and the exactness of a pilot's **knowledge** who carries the Mississippi River in his head. And **then if** you will go on until you **know** every street crossing, the character, size, and position of the crossing-stones, and the varying depth of mud in each of these numberless places, you will have some idea of what the pilot must **know** in order to keep a Mississippi steamer out of trouble. **Next, if** you will take half of the signs in that long street, and *change their places* once a month, and still manage to **know** their new positions accurately on dark nights, and keep up with these repeated changes without making any mistakes, you will understand what is required of a pilot's peerless **memory** by the fickle Mississippi.

Mark Twain
Old Times on the Mississippi

5e Transitional Paragraphs

A **transitional paragraph** consists of one or two sentences whose purpose is to carry the reader from one paragraph to another. Usually a transitional paragraph sums up or emphasizes the thoughts in the preceding paragraph and announces the idea to be developed in the next paragraph. Notice how this is accomplished in the third (transitional) paragraph that follows:

I always find myself annoyed when "intellectual" men dismiss violence against women with a yawn, as if it were beneath their dignity to notice. I wonder if the reaction would be the same if the violence were directed against someone other than women. How many people would yawn and say, "Oh, kids will be kids," if a rock group did a nifty little number called "Lynchin," in which stringing up and stomping on black people were set to music? Who would chuckle and say, "Oh, just a little adolescent rebellion" if a group of rockers went on MTV dressed as Nazis, desecrating synagogues and beating up Jews to the beat of twanging guitars?

I'll tell you what would happen. Prestigious dailies would thunder on editorial pages; senators would fall over each other to get denunciations into the Congressional Record. The president would appoint a commission to clean up the music business.

But violence against women is greeted by silence. It shouldn't be.

But this does not mean censorship, or book (or record) burning. In a society that protects free expression, we understand a lot of stuff will float up out of the sewer. Usually, we recognize the ugly stuff that advocates violence against any group as the garbage it is, and we consider its purveyors as moral lepers. We hold our nose and tolerate it, but we speak out against the values it proffers.

Caryl Rivers
"Rock Lyrics and Violence Against Women"

EXERCISE 5-2

In the following excerpt, circle all the transitional words.

Propaganda. How do we feel about it? If an opinion poll were taken tomorrow, nearly everyone would be against it. For one thing it *sounds* so bad. "Oh, that's just propaganda" means, to most people, "That's a pack of lies." But propaganda doesn't have to be untrue—nor does it have to be the devil's tool. It can be used for good causes as well as for bad—to persuade people to give to charity, for example, or to love their neighbors, or to stop polluting the environment, or to treat the English language with more respect. The real problem with propaganda is not the end it's used for, but the means it uses to achieve the end. Propaganda works by tricking us, by momentarily distracting the eye while the rabbit pops out from beneath the cloth. This is why propaganda always works best with an uncritical audience, one that will not stop to challenge or question. Most of us are bamboozled, at one time or another, because we simply don't recognize propaganda when we see it.

Donna Woolfolk Cross
"Politics: The Art of Bamboozling"

EXERCISE 5-3

Identify the topic sentence (topic) in each of the following paragraphs.

1. It took infinite power to produce these little electrons, to raise them from the possible to the actual state, to throw them out of the realm of nothing into the simple, dimensional existence. No matter how insignificant they are in the order of creaturehood—they have neither intelligence, freedom, nor

reflection—they are tremendously more wonderful than nothing. And to prove their excitement at the fact of existence, they expand as water, evaporate as air, explode as fire, congeal as rock. In their congealed state (minerals) they are proletarian or aristocratic as the case may be: junk or jewels. I admire them very much massed in the magnificence of a mountain, diffused in the plume of a cloud, banked in the brilliance of a star.

Leonard Feeney
"You'd Better Come Quietly"

2. A suburban lady comes staggering out of the cocktail bar of a hotel which is making money, begins to yodel and perform the split in the lobby and is firmly but gently shoved outside by the house detective in the honest performance of his duty. Two weeks later it develops through the affidavits of friends who were lushing with her at the bar, that the plaintiff drank nothing but mild, nutritious stingers, prescribed by her physician as a remedy for anemia, and that she was not plastered but just suddenly faint, not yodeling but crying for help, not doing the split but swooning. Therefore she has been publicly humiliated to an extent which cannot be compensated for a nickel less than $50,000.

Westbrook Pegler
" 'T Aint Right"

3. In any science, the hardest question to answer is "why?" In many cases, the question is unanswerable. From one point of view, it is strange that human beings speak so many languages and that these languages undergo any changes at all. Other human activities are identical and unchanging everywhere—all human beings smile, cry, scream in terror, sleep, drink, and walk in essentially the same way. Why should they differ in speech, the one aspect of behavior that is uniquely human? The answer is that, whereas the capacity to learn language is innate, the particular language that anyone uses is learned. That is, the ability to learn languages is universal and

unchanging, but the languages themselves are diverse and constantly changing.

C. M. Millward
The Biography of the English Language

4. One of the ends of life, and therefore one of the ends of education, is to understand our place in the universe, our relation to our surroundings, human and physical; and so the relation of our civilization to the factors that have made it what it is. For everything about us has a history, and if we know something of the history, we understand the thing better. He is but ill-educated who cannot read with intelligence the literature of his country, understand broadly how it comes to be clothed in the shapes in which it is expressed, respond to the appeals it makes to ideas and emotions through words which store up literary energy and give it forth, as radium stores and gives out physical energy; who cannot apprehend the terms in which the sciences indispensable for the conduct of his everyday life name their elements and processes; who has no vision of the background of his religious worship, his standards of conduct and taste, and the social and political institutions of the nation to which he belongs.

H. R. James
Our Hellenic Heritage

5. When we read for information, we acquire facts. When we read to understand, we learn not only facts but their significance. Each kind of reading has its virtue, but it must be used in the right place. If a writer does not understand more than we do, or if in a particular passage he makes no effort to explain, we can only be informed by him, not enlightened. But if an author has insights we do not possess and if, in addition, he has tried to convey them in what he has written, we are neglecting his gift to us if we do not read him differently from the way in which we read newspapers or magazines.

Mortimer J. Adler
*How to Read a Book,
The Art of Getting a Liberal Education*

EXERCISE 5-4

In each of the paragraphs in Exercise 5-3 (pp. 95–97), identify the words that give the paragraph *unity (u);* then identify the words that serve the function of *transition (t).*

EXERCISE 5-5

Describe the method of development used for each of the following paragraphs. Some of the paragraphs may use more than one method. Underline the topic sentence in each paragraph. Does the topic sentence indicate the type of development in the paragraph?

1. A shoe is a form of clothing, a covering for the foot. Designed to fit about the foot in a snug but comfortable fashion, it often makes the foot feel as if it has incorporated the shoe as part of its being. Modern shoes usually have some strong agent such as rubber or leather on the bottom, called the sole, which proves helpful in protecting the foot from uncomfortable walking surfaces. The top half of the shoe that crosses over the foot, attached to the sole, is generally made of a more flexible material, in order to take on the shape of one's foot. Some shoes simply slip onto the foot, whereas others have tightening devices such as shoestrings, buckles, or velcro to prevent the shoe from falling off the foot.

   From a student's essay

2. They tumble down mountain sides; they meander through flat farm lands. Valleys trail them; cities ride them; farms cling to them; roads and railroad tracks run after them—and they remain, permanent, possessive. Next to them, man's gleaming cement roads which he has built with such care look fragile as paper streamers thrown over the hills, easily blown away. Even the railroads seem only scratched in with a penknife. But rivers have carved their way over the earth's face for centuries and they will stay.

   Anne Morrow Lindbergh
   North to the Orient

3. It might be well to take a brief look at the ends which are in fact being aimed at in this country. There are four of these; they are the same life objectives which inexperienced adolescents usually think supremely worth while. Two of them—the quest for money and the quest for pleasure—are the goals which increasingly, for a half century at least, have determined the cultural pattern of America. The other two—the quest for power and the quest for erudition—are equally inadequate, but to the pursuit of them more than a few are already turning as they find themselves increasingly bored by what has become the American way of life.

Bernard Iddings Bell
Crisis in Education

4. By literature, then, is meant the expression of thought in language; where, by "thought" I mean ideas, feelings, views, reasoning, and other operations of the human mind. And the art of letters is the method by which a speaker or writer brings out in words, worthy of his subject, and sufficient for his audience or readers, the thoughts which impress him. Literature, then, is of a personal character; it consists in the enunciations and teachings of those who have a right to speak as representatives of their kind, and in whose words their brethren find an interpretation of their sentiments, a record of their own experience, and a suggestion for their own judgments.

John Henry Newman
The Idea of a University

5. While many writers, and among them not a few men of science, are convinced that we live at a crisis in western civilization, opinions are divided about the nature of the crisis and the role which science has to play in helping to resolve it. According to some, science will be responsible for our ruin, because it has given mankind the power to destroy itself. According to others, science will work our salvation, because it is only another name for reason, and if we drop our outworn modes of thought we can use it to build a new metaphysic, a new ethic, and a new religion. According to others

again, science can put an end to want, and if we abolish want we shall abolish also hatred, envy and avarice; therefore we need science for both the physical and the moral health of society.

E. F. Caldin
The Wind and the Rain

6   Combining Sentences

A **sentence** is a group of words that contains a subject and predicate and functions as an independent clause. Writing correctly is a mechanical act of applying rules of grammar, but writing *effectively* involves more. It involves the choices you make in forming sentences by combining the various types of clauses and phrases with directness of assertion and devices of emphasis. To make a strong impression on the reader, you need to use your ear as much as your eye; that is, you need to listen to your sentences as well as write them. Writing **effective sentences** helps you to achieve a distinctive writing **style.**

6a Variety of Sentence Structure

As a writer, you have a responsibility to hold your reader's interest. Besides, if you don't get and hold interest, you have little chance of achieving your writing goal. One way to hold interest is to vary your sentence structure. Just as the speaker who talks in a monotone will quickly lose the listener's attention, the writer who uses only one sentence structure will soon lose the reader's attention.

The following passage has been rewritten in a monotonous style. Notice that most of the sentences are short and choppy and that all begin with the word *you*.

> You see things vacationing on a motorcycle in a way that is completely different from any other. You are always in a compartment in a car. You are used to it. You don't realize that through that car window everything you see is just more TV. You are a passive observer. You are bored by everything moving by you in a frame.
>
> You lose the frame on a cycle. You are completely in contact with it all. You are *in* the scene. You are not just watching it anymore. You are overwhelmed by the sense of presence. You know that the concrete whizzing by five inches below your foot is the real thing. You know it is the same stuff you walk on. You see it is right there. You can't focus on it because it is so blurred. You can, however, put your foot down and touch it anytime. You are always immediately conscious of the whole thing. You are conscious of the whole experience.

Consider how the passage is improved by varying the sentence structure.

> You see things vacationing on a motorcycle in a way that is completely different from any other. In a car you're always in a compartment, and because you're used to it you don't realize that everything you see is just more TV. You're a passive observer and it is all moving by you boringly in a frame.
>
> On a cycle the frame is gone. You're completely in contact with it all. **You're** *in* the scene, not just watching it anymore, and the sense of presence is overwhelming. That concrete whizzing by five inches below your foot is the real thing, the same stuff you walk on; it's right there, so blurred you can't focus on it, yet you can put your foot down and touch it anytime, and the whole thing, the whole experience, is never removed from immediate consciousness.

Robert M. Pirsig
Zen and the Art of Motorcycle Maintenance

Do not be afraid to make your sentences long enough and complex enough to express complex ideas. Using several short sentences to state what amounts to one complete thought causes a choppy and disjointed effect. Such writing gives the reader no idea what you consider important or relevant but less important. For example, read the following paragraph.

> Francis opened the trunk lid. An odor filled the attic air. It was the odor of lost time. The odor was a cloying reek of imprisoned flowers. It unsettled the dust. It fluttered the window shades.

Now read how the novelist William Kennedy combined the ideas in these short, choppy sentences into a single sentence.

> When Francis opened the trunk lid the odor of lost time filled the attic air, a cloying reek of imprisoned flowers that unsettled the dust and fluttered the window shades.

William Kennedy
Ironweed

Notice that the ideas in the second and third sentences of the paragraph form the main clause of Kennedy's sentence (*the odor of lost time filled the attic air*), whereas the ideas in the other sentences are expressed as subordinate clauses and appositives. Thus the idea of the odor filling the air is given the most importance, and the other ideas are given less emphasis.

Many professional writers use short, clipped sentences to create a sense of urgency or suspense in narrative writing. In most of the writing you will do for school or other purposes, however, you will often need to use a mixture of both shorter and longer, more complex sentences to express your ideas. As you write and as you revise your earlier drafts, consider whether two or more short sentences might be more effective if they were combined into one. Some of the more common ways to combine sentences are by the use of appositives; adjective and adverb clauses; and prepositional, verbal, and absolute phrases.

Appositives

An **appositive** is a word or group of words that defines or renames the noun that precedes it. Notice how the choppy sentences in the following examples can be combined through the use of appositives.

SEPARATE: The ailanthus was brought to America by a distinguished Philadelphia importer. His name was William Hamilton.

COMBINED: The ailanthus was brought to America by a distinguished Philadelphia importer, William Hamilton.

SEPARATE: The ailanthus grows in the most meager of environments. Its name means "the tree of heaven."

COMBINED: The ailanthus, "the tree of heaven," grows in the most meager of environments.

SEPARATE: Beside the river was a grove of tall, naked cottonwoods so large that they seemed to belong to a bygone age. These cottonwoods were trees of great antiquity and enormous size.

COMBINED: Beside the river was a grove of tall, naked cottonwoods—trees of great antiquity and enormous size—so large that they seemed to belong to a bygone age.

Willa Cather
Death Comes for the Archbishop

Adjective clauses

An **adjective clause** is a group of words with a subject and a predicate that modifies a noun or a pronoun. Usually, an adjective clause begins with a relative pronoun. Notice how the choppy sentences in the following examples can be combined through the use of adjective clauses.

SEPARATE: The birthplace of Jean Rhys is Dominica. Dominica is one of the Windward Islands.

COMBINED: The birthplace of Jean Rhys is Dominica, which is one of the Windward Islands.

SEPARATE: William W. Warner described blue crabs as "beautiful swimmers." He wrote a study of the Chesapeake Bay. The book won a Pulitzer prize.

COMBINED: William W. Warner, who wrote a study of the Chesapeake Bay that won a Pulitzer prize, described blue crabs as "beautiful swimmers."

SEPARATE: Holmes had been seated for some hours in silence with his long, thin back curved over a chemical vessel. In this vessel he was brewing a particularly malodorous product.

COMBINED: Holmes had been seated for some hours in silence with his long, thin back curved over a chemical vessel in which he was brewing a particularly malodorous product.

Sir Arthur Conan Doyle
"The Adventure of the Dancing Men"

Adverb clauses

An **adverb clause** is a group of words with a subject and a predicate that functions as an adverb in a sentence. Usually, an adverb clause begins with a subordinating conjunction (such as *because, after*, or *so that*) that shows the relation of the adverb clause to the word or words it modifies. Notice how the choppy sentences in the following examples can be combined through the use of adverb clauses.

SEPARATE: He was never in a battle. Nevertheless, he wrote movingly about war.

COMBINED: Although he was never in a battle, he wrote movingly about war.

SEPARATE: My wife and I both work at home. Quintana therefore has never had any confusion about how we make our living.

COMBINED: Because my wife and I both work at home, Quintana has never had any confusion about how we make our living.

> John Gregory Dunne
> "Quintana"

SEPARATE: The purple and red jukebox belted accommodating rhythms. A couple slow-dragged. Billy spun yarns about his adventures.

COMBINED: While the purple and red jukebox belted accommodating rhythms, and while a couple slow-dragged, Billy spun yarns about his adventures.

> James Alan McPherson
> "The Story of a Dead Man"

Prepositional phrases

A **prepositional phrase** consists of a preposition, a noun or pronoun called the object of the preposition, and all the words modifying this object. Notice how the choppy sentences in the following examples can be combined through the use of prepositional phrases.

SEPARATE: Jack London died at the age of forty. He had become an extremely popular writer.

COMBINED: Before his death at the age of forty, Jack London had become an extremely popular writer.

SEPARATE: She had a genius for painting. She also had a talent for writing.

COMBINED: In addition to her genius for painting, she had a talent for writing.

SEPARATE: His Royal Highness Prince Philippe gave me an audience. He was prince of Araucania and Patagonia. The audience was on a drizzling November afternoon. It was at his public relations firm. The firm was on the Faubourg Poissonière.

COMBINED: On a drizzling November afternoon, His Royal Highness Prince Philippe of Araucania and Patagonia gave me an audience at his public relations firm on the Faubourg Poissonière.

Bruce Chatwin
In Patagonia

Participial phrases

A **participial phrase** consists of a participle and all its modifiers and complements. Notice how the choppy sentences in the following examples can be combined through the use of participial phrases.

SEPARATE: Washington resigned as general. He then returned to his plantation.

COMBINED: Having resigned as general, Washington returned to his plantation.

SEPARATE: The producers planned a two-part miniseries. This miniseries would tell the story of the native American experience from the native American point of view.

COMBINED: The producers planned a two-part miniseries telling the story of the native American experience from the native American point of view.

OR: The two-part miniseries planned by the producers would tell the story of the native American experience from the native American point of view.

SEPARATE: We are given a thimbleful of facts. We rush to make generalizations as large as a tub.

COMBINED: Given a thimbleful of facts, we rush to make generalizations as large as a tub.

Gordon W. Allport

Absolute phrases

An **absolute phrase** is a group of words with a subject and a nonfinite verb (a verb form that cannot function as a sentence verb). When the verb is a form of *be*, it is sometimes omitted but understood. Notice how the choppy sentences in the following examples can be combined through the use of absolute phrases.

SEPARATE: The war was over. The nation turned its attention to reconstruction of the Union.

COMBINED: The war being over, the nation turned its attention to reconstruction of the Union.

OR: The war over, the nation turned its attention to reconstruction of the Union.

SEPARATE: The plane finally came to a stop. The passengers were breathing sighs of relief.

COMBINED: The plane finally came to a stop, the passengers breathing sighs of relief.

SEPARATE: Breakfast had been eaten. The slim camp outfit had been lashed to the sled. The men turned their backs on the cheery fire and launched out into the darkness.

COMBINED: Breakfast eaten and the slim camp outfit lashed to the sled, the men turned their backs on the cheery fire and launched out into the darkness.

Jack London
White Fang

EXERCISE 6-1

Use appositives, adjective clauses, or adverb clauses to form one sentence from each of the following groups of sentences.

1. The student senate will consider three issues this afternoon.

   The three are recycling paper, the alcohol policy on campus,

   and election campaigns.

2. The British medieval poet's name is Chaucer. He wrote *The Canterbury Tales*. It is a collection of stories and some poems.

3. Your feelings are not facts. Your feelings really count. Your feelings can count as a mirror of the way you are thinking.

4. Some drugs are used to treat hypertension. Hypertension means high blood pressure. The drugs lower amine chemical levels in the brain. These drugs cause side effects for some people.

5. All addictions can be considered neurotic. Addictions are departures from usual, healthy impulses. Healthy impulses can also be exaggerated.

6. Perfectionists are very hard to live with. Perfectionists cannot accept flaws. Most things they see are flawed. Everything, then, is unacceptable, even personal relationships.

7. Thick blue smoke from a car's exhaust pipe means the engine is burning oil. The engine probably needs an overhaul. An overhaul is expensive.

EXERCISE 6-2

Use prepositional phrases, participial phrases, or absolute phrases to form one sentence from each of the following groups of sentences.

1. Literary interpretation means explaining what has been read. What you read is fiction, drama, and poetry. Many believe that poetry is hard to explain. Not everyone agrees.

2. The surgeon rose to her feet. Her face was smiling. Her eyes sparkled. She shook hands with the nervous patient.

3. Not enough people study nursing these days. A shortage of nurses exists. There are both male and female nurses.

4. Tortilla chips have become popular in the Midwest. They are salted or unsalted. They are made from corn, soybean oil, and a trace of lime. They are stone ground.

5. The main building is located south of town. It is beside the highway. A stream flows on one side of it. Evergreen trees grow on the other side.

6. The local candidates for the senate appeared on television. Both are male. Both are wealthy. Both are young. Both failed to impress most of the viewers.

7. We walked through the field. It was waist-high with wheat. It felt like we were walking in water.

EXERCISE 6-3

Revise the following passages by combining short, choppy sentences to form strong, effective sentences.

How do trees affect our environment? First, trees help to control the greenhouse effect. Most scientists believe the greenhouse effect causes global warming. Global warming is a gradual trend. The trend is toward a warmer planet. It will have serious effects. It can cause floods, loss of forests and agricultural land. It can also cause extremes of hot and cold weather. This can lead to economic chaos. No one knows how fast this is happening. We now face rising temperatures every summer. We pump new gases into the atmosphere. The gases thicken the earth's blanket. The blanket traps too much heat. The main gas is carbon dioxide. It is released by burning fossil fuels. Trees slow down the greenhouse effect. They slow down global warming. They counteract the carbon dioxide in our atmosphere. Trees do not release carbon dioxide. It is absorbed by the trees. Every family should plant one tree. This would make a difference. Trees absorb carbon dioxide. They also provide shade. Shade reduces the demand for air conditioning. A cluster of trees can cool the air. The cool air reduces the amount of energy used. It is not expensive to plant a cluster of trees. It is more expensive to pay for air conditioning each year.

Trees also supply fresh oxygen. They filter out the toxins. The toxins come from the soil. Trees prevent soil erosion. Trees help retain rain water. Trees reduce noise if planted in clusters in cities. Some trees provide us with food. Trees grace our landscapes with beauty.

Adapted from a student's essay

EXERCISE 6-4

Revise the following passage by combining short, choppy sentences to form strong, effective ones.

Human language is flexible. It is also creative and complex. These things cause it to be variable. It changes over time. Language is very changeable. Speakers from one generation often are not able to understand speakers from a different generation. Today, speakers read Shakespeare. Shakespeare's language is barely intelligible to today's speakers. But language changes slowly. It does not happen over night. The change is spread over a period of time. And our own language today continues that change. Some day people will need footnotes to understand our English. The word "silly" meant "blessed." That was a hundred years ago. What will it mean in 2100?

Adapted from a student's essay

6b Directness of Assertion

In general, try to construct your sentences so that your ideas are expressed as forcefully and directly as possible. You can achieve force and directness by using action verbs and by writing in the active voice.

Action verbs

Action verbs give power and precision to your writing, whereas the overuse of the verb *be* weakens your writing. Note how the sentences in the following examples are strengthened when the verb *be* is replaced with an action verb.

WEAK: Her face **was** a wall of brown fire.
STRONG: Her faced **flashed** a wall of brown fire.

James Alan McPherson
"The Story of a Scar"

WEAK: Everywhere, in the bathroom too, there were prints of Roman ruins that **were** brown with age.
STRONG: Everywhere, in the bathroom too, there were prints of Roman ruins **freckled** brown with age.

Truman Capote
Breakfast at Tiffany's

WEAK: Their feet **were** no longer on firm sand but **were** on slippery slime and painful barnacled rock.

STRONG: Their feet **lost** the firm sand and **slipped** on slime, **trod** painfully on barnacled rock.

Michael Innes
The Man from the Sea

The active voice

As its name suggests, the **active voice** is usually more direct and forceful than the passive voice.

UNEMPHATIC: Kronos **was overthrown** by Zeus, his son.
EMPHATIC: Zeus **overthrew** Kronos, his father.

UNEMPHATIC: At the Rubicon a decision **was made** by Caesar.
EMPHATIC: At the Rubicon, Caesar **made** a decision.

UNEMPHATIC: Infinitely less **is demanded** by love than by friendship.
EMPHATIC: Love **demands** infinitely less than friendship.

George Jean Nathan

If you wish to emphasize the receiver of the action instead of the agent, use the **passive voice.**

The father **was granted** custody of the child by the court.

The schools **were consolidated** in 1953.

6c Emphasizing Important Elements of a Sentence

Construct your sentences to emphasize the important elements. You can achieve emphasis through careful choice of words, through proper subordination, and through any one of the following methods.

1. Achieve emphasis by placing important elements at the beginning or at the end of a sentence, particularly at the end.

   UNEMPHATIC: It is not known why more boys than girls are autistic.

   EMPHATIC: Why more boys than girls are autistic is unknown.

   UNEMPHATIC: The trip was not as bad as, but worse than, I feared it would be.

   EMPHATIC: The trip was not as bad as I feared it would be—it was worse.

2. Achieve emphasis by changing loose sentences into periodic sentences. In a loose sentence, the main clause comes first; modifying phrases, dependent clauses, and other amplification follow the main clause.

   Jane Eyre would not declare her love for Mr. Rochester, although the fortune-teller pressed her for the information when they were alone together on that dark and mysterious night.

   In a periodic sentence, the main clause comes last.

   Although the fortune-teller pressed her for the information when they were alone together on that dark and mysterious night, Jane Eyre would not declare her love for Mr. Rochester.

   Periodic sentences are less commonly used than loose sentences and therefore are more emphatic. They give emphasis to the idea in the main clause by saving this idea for last.

   LOOSE: The fortune-teller was really Mr. Rochester, although she claimed to be a gypsy from a nearby camp who had come simply to tell the ladies' futures.

PERIODIC: Although she claimed to be a gypsy from a nearby camp who had come simply to tell the ladies' futures, the fortune-teller was really Mr. Rochester.

LOOSE: It's easy to choose between love and duty if you are willing to forget that there is an element of duty in love and of love in duty.

PERIODIC: If you are willing to forget that there is an element of duty in love and of love in duty, then it's easy to choose between the two.

Jean Giraudoux

LOOSE: Emancipation will be a proclamation but not a fact until justice is blind to color, until education is unaware of race, until opportunity is unconcerned with the color of men's skins.

PERIODIC: Until justice is blind to color, until education is unaware of race, until opportunity is unconcerned with the color of men's skins, emancipation will be a proclamation but not a fact.

Lyndon B. Johnson

3. Achieve emphasis by writing balanced sentences. A balanced sentence presents ideas of equal weight in the same grammatical form, thus emphasizing the similarity or disparity between the ideas. (See parallelism, pp. 282–288.)

UNBALANCED: Generally the theories we believe we call facts, and the facts that we disbelieve are known as theories.

BALANCED: Generally, the theories we believe we call facts, and the facts we disbelieve we call theories.

Felix Cohen

UNBALANCED:	Money—in its absence we are coarse; when it is present we tend to be vulgar.
BALANCED:	Money—in its absence we are coarse; in its presence we are vulgar.

Mignon McLaughlin

4. Achieve emphasis by inverting normal word order. In most English sentences, the usual word order is subject-verb-complement. Changing this order makes a sentence stand out.

UNEMPHATIC:	He gave his property to the poor.
EMPHATIC:	His property he gave to the poor.
UNEMPHATIC:	Indiana Jones walked into the Temple of Doom.
EMPHATIC:	Into the Temple of Doom walked Indiana Jones.
UNEMPHATIC:	Long hours of hard work lie behind every successful endeavor.
EMPHATIC:	Behind every successful endeavor lie long hours of hard work.
UNEMPHATIC:	The lens, which helps to focus the image, is in the front of the eye.
EMPHATIC:	In the front of the eye is the lens, which helps to focus the image.

EXERCISE 6-5

Revise each of the following sentences to make it more forceful or to emphasize important elements. Where appropriate, change the verb *be* to an action verb, change the passive voice to the active voice, place important words at the beginning or the end of the sentence, turn a loose sentence into a periodic sentence, turn an unbalanced sentence into a balanced sentence, and invert word order.

1. Many politicians say that transporting garbage from the eastern states to the midwestern states is caused by greed and not a lack of space for landfills.

2. There are many reasons for opposing capital punishment.

3. A proposal to abolish grading in all freshman courses was made in the student senate just before the preannounced time for adjournment.

4. A New York court recently ruled that a gay lover had the right to remain in his deceased partner's rent-control apartment having qualified as a member of the deceased's family.

5. Slanting can be interpreted as presenting something with a special interest but propaganda is simply called disseminating one's beliefs.

6. All great cultures of the past were dependent on creativity and creativity depended on intelligent people.

7. As expected, the soprano was a vision of beauty and stepped up to the footlights.

8. The little boy's wagon was struck by the ice cream vendor's truck.

9. Some people believe that there is nothing positive about being in isolation, and that it is merely a remote place or a frame of mind that results in loneliness and depression.

10. Being in a state of solitude and daydreaming are not the same things because there exists a fine line between the two.

---

7 Thinking Critically and Writing Arguments

To write effectively, you need to think clearly and critically. The effectiveness of any writing depends on the validity of the reasoning behind it; hence, a well-written paper must be a well-reasoned one. The concept of critical thinking has already been discussed to some extent in the sections on drafting and revising. As you'll see here, thinking about your writing and evaluating it with a critical eye, important in all writing, is especially important when writing arguments.

7a Inductive and Deductive Reasoning

The two major kinds of reasoning are inductive and deductive reasoning. **Inductive reasoning** is reasoning from the specific to the general. The word *inductive* comes from a Latin word that means "to lead into." In the inductive method, you observe a number of particulars or specifics, and these particulars lead you to a general principle or conclusion. For example, imagine you are studying folk medicine. For a year you live in a society that practices folk medicine, and you carefully observe the practices of the healers. You observe that they use a preparation made from a particular plant to treat boils. In all cases, the boil disappears within two days of the application of the plant. On the basis of your observations of these particular cases, you reason that this plant helps cure boils.

Deductive reasoning is reasoning from the general to the specific. The word *deductive* comes from a Latin word that means "to lead from." In the deductive method, you start with a general principle and apply it to specific instances. For example, imagine you are a doctor. As a general principle, you accept that penicillin is effective against the bacteria causing strep throat. When a patient with strep throat comes to you, you apply the general principle to this specific case and prescribe penicillin.

The deductive method can be expressed as a three-step process, called a **syllogism.** The first step, the general principle, is called the **major premise;** the second step, the specific instance, is called the **minor premise;** and the third step, the application of the general principle to the specific instance, is called the **conclusion.**

MAJOR PREMISE:	Penicillin cures strep throat.
MINOR PREMISE:	This patient has strep throat.
CONCLUSION:	(Therefore) This patient will be cured by using penicillin.

Although inductive and deductive reasoning are powerful tools in writing, their misuse can lead to errors. To make effective use of the inductive method, make sure that you have made enough observations, that your observations are accurate and representational, that you have noted and accounted for any exceptions, and that your conclusion derives from these observations. For example, suppose the plant mentioned earlier did not cure three cases of boils. If your conclusion is to be valid, you must note these exceptions and explain them in terms of the conclusion. Perhaps this plant will not cure boils in people who have been treated with it previously, or whose boils are especially severe. The more observations and information you accumulate, the more likely that your conclusion will be accurate.

To make effective use of the deductive method, make sure that the general principle you start with is true and that the situation to which you apply it is relevant. Note and account for any exceptions. For example, imagine that the bacteria in the strep throat patient mentioned earlier have developed an immunity to penicillin. Then the principle would not be applicable to this patient's case. The more information you have about the specific situation, the more likely you will be to apply the relevant principle.

7b Truth in Reasoning

The relationship of truth to critical thinking is the same as the relationship of truth to anything else. We usually try to think in accord with the dictates of logic or accurate reasoning, and if we do, the result will be truth or, at the least, strong probability. Inductive reasoning, used properly, will result in probability. Consider the following example. Every week for two months you purchase a loaf of bread on Saturday at the supermarket. And each time the bread has been fresh. Therefore, when you purchase a loaf of bread this Saturday, the probability that it will be fresh is very strong, but it is not a certainty. On the other hand, deductive reasoning, done properly, will of necessity result in certitude, not probability. Consider this example: Only one newspaper is published in this city. All editors, despite their attempts to be objective, have biases; therefore, the one newspaper in town contains biased news. If the premises of this example are true, then the result is also true. In your writing, then, be careful to distinguish between certainty and probability.

7c Logical Fallacies

All thinking is subject to **logical fallacies,** or errors in reasoning. Test your own writing to make sure you have avoided false analogies, overgeneralizations and stereotyping, unstated assumptions, appeals to the emotions, confusion of cause and effect, improper either-or thinking, non sequiturs, and circular reasoning.

False analogies

Analogies, which are used often in inductive reasoning, are comparisons. For an analogy to be sound, or true, the comparison must make sense; that is, the things being compared must correspond in essential ways, and the ways in which they do not correspond must be unimportant in terms of the argument or conclusion. Consider the following analogies:

> These are not books, lumps of lifeless paper, but *minds* alive on the shelves. From each of them goes out its own voice . . . and just as the touch of a button on our set will fill the room with music, so by taking down one of these volumes and opening it, one can call into range the voice of a man far distant in time and space, and hear him speak to us, mind to mind, heart to heart.
>
> Gilbert Highet

First the writer compares books with minds. These two things are alike in essential ways. Both contain the thoughts of a person, and from both these thoughts are communicated. Then the writer compares pushing the button on a radio with taking down a book from a shelf and opening it. These acts are alike, since both call into range the voice of a person who is not present.

Here are some other sound analogies:

News is the first rough draft of history.

Ben Bradlee

The individual who pollutes the air with his factory and the ghetto kid who breaks store windows both represent the same thing. They don't care about each other—or what they do to each other.

Daniel Patrick Moynihan

If a State can prescribe, as a rule of civil conduct, that whites and blacks shall not travel as passengers in the same railroad coach, why may it not so regulate the use of the streets of its cities and towns as to compel white citizens to keep to one side of the street and black citizens to keep to the other?

Justice John Marshall Harlan

Although analogies help readers to understand a point, they are not proofs of a conclusion. In fact, many analogies that appear in writing are misleading, or false. A **false analogy** does not make sense. Although the things being compared may correspond in some ways, they are dissimilar in other ways that are crucial to the argument or conclusion, or their similarities are blown out of proportion. Consider the following false analogy.

Buying a car is like buying a steak. You can't be sure how good the product is until you've bought it and used it.

This analogy is false because you can test-drive the car, but you cannot test-eat the steak; moreover, the economic difference between the items is so great that a comparison between the purchase of one and the purchase of the other has little meaning.

EXERCISE 7-1

Explain why the following analogies are false.

1. Mr. Brown will be an excellent member for our school board because he was a colonel in the army.

2. A city council that can spend all the money it did to install electric traffic signals at the mall can afford four stop signs at the corner intersection in our neighborhood.

3. Think of writing your first essay in a course as an interview where you try to make a good first impression on someone.

Overgeneralizations and stereotyping

An **overgeneralization** is a conclusion based on too little evidence or on evidence that is unrepresentative or biased. For example, imagine you go to a major-league baseball game with your friends. You observe that attendance at this game is very low. On the basis of this observation, you conclude that attendance at major-league baseball games has fallen off drastically. This is an overgeneralization, since one observation—or even two or three—are not a sufficient number from which to draw a conclusion.

Now imagine that while you are visiting a large city for a week, you ride the subway every evening at nine. You find the ride quick and comfortable, since there are never any crowds and you always get a seat. On the basis of your observations, you conclude that the subway provides pleasant and reliable transportation. This is an overgeneralization since your evidence is not typical of a commuter's ride on the subway during rush hour.

Here are some other examples of overgeneralization:

Since neither of my parents smokes, the number of adults who smoke must be rapidly diminishing.

Melinda and her friend had dinner at a new local restaurant. Melinda's steak was undercooked and her friend's chicken was cold. They concluded that the restaurant was poor.

A candidate for mayor makes a door-to-door survey of all the houses in the neighborhood to find out whether voters are willing to pay higher taxes to improve the public schools. Most of them express enthusiasm for the idea, and the candidate decides to campaign on this platform.

Stereotyping is overgeneralization about groups of people. **Stereotypes** are the standardized mental images that are the result of such overgeneralization. Almost everyone believes stereotypes about one group or another, and we encounter them every day in advertising, television programs, and other media. For example, we are all familiar with these stereotypes:

STEREOTYPE

the absentminded professor	the passionate French lover
the dumb blonde	the stoical male
the genius with glasses	the man-hunting female

Because stereotypes of this kind are so widely recognized as such, you can easily avoid them in your writing. A greater danger is that you will develop your own stereotypes by treating an individual as representative of a group to which the individual belongs. Try to eliminate stereotyping not only from your writing but also from your thinking.

Unstated assumptions

An **assumption** is an idea that we accept as true without any proof. Sometimes **unstated assumptions** enter into our reasoning and confuse our thinking. Many of these assumptions are really stereotypes. For example, consider the following statement:

> His autobiography must be fascinating because he is such a famous actor.

This reasoning does not make sense. It is based on the unstated assumption that someone who has had a glamorous or exciting career will be able to write about it in an interesting way. That may be true in this particular case, but it cannot be assumed as a general principle.

EXERCISE 7-2

Identify the overgeneralization or the unstated assumption in each of the following statements:

1. He could not possibly be guilty of the crime since he is a devoted family man.

2. Attaining success in politics is the goal of every student who majors in political science.

3. She stands six feet tall and must be an excellent basketball player.

Appeals to the emotions

Avoid drawing a conclusion for yourself or tempting others into drawing conclusions on the basis of an appeal to the emotions instead of reason. Writers use various techniques to arouse an emotional rather than a rational response. Among these are name calling, using loaded words, creating a bandwagon effect, using flattery, and creating false associations.

Name calling

Name calling, which is sometimes referred to as the **ad hominem** ("to the man") **fallacy,** is an attempt to discredit an idea or conclusion by attacking not the idea or conclusion but the person presenting it.

> Griffin claims that the legal drinking age should be raised in order to reduce the incidence of drunk driving. Are you going to let someone who was once himself convicted of drunk driving tell you when you can take an innocent drink?
>
> Gardner claims that teaching is attracting mediocre people. Yet she herself is a hick from a backwater town. What can she know of quality?
>
> So what if Mr. Klein told you you shouldn't drop out of school? He's only an old man with old ideas. What does he know about youth and adventure?
>
> If the nature kooks had their way, America would still be a wilderness from coast to coast.
>
> Harley G. Waller

Loaded words

Loaded words are highly charged emotional words that appeal to readers' prejudices. Readers who do not already share these prejudices are as likely to be irritated as to be convinced by the use of loaded words.

> Because of this nation's **giveaway** policies, the **hardworking** man or woman lives in squalor while the **lazy bum** drives a Cadillac.
>
> Democracy is a system in which the **screeching** and **caterwauling** of the **vulgar masses** drown the pronouncements of the **enlightened** few.

Our library shelves are **infested** by the **filth** of **effete intellectuals** who crave the **corruption** of the **innocent youth** of this country.

Bandwagon technique

The **bandwagon technique** attempts to influence people by encouraging them to put aside their own powers of reasoning and simply join the crowd.

Don't be left out—see the film that all America has been waiting for.

Everyone in the neighborhood is signing the petition. You're going to sign it, aren't you?

ColaRite is the most popular soft drink in the country. Buy some and join the fun!

Flattery

Flattery is often used to try to persuade a reader or listener to do something or to accept the validity of a conclusion.

The voters of this city are too intelligent to be taken in by my opponent's promises.

You're young. You're on top of things. And you want to stay on top. That's why you need *Lifestyle*, the magazine that helps you be what you want to be.

A person of your sensitivity could not help being moved by the plight of these unfortunate victims.

False association

False association, sometimes called the **association fallacy**, attempts to convince people of the strength or weakness of a conclusion by suggesting that by agreeing or disagreeing with it, they will become associated with other people doing the same.

> Many people active in the movie and theater world belong to this health club. Since you are young and talented, you should join it, too.

> All of the best people in town support this proposal. Of course, you must support it, too.

> Only eggheads and clods belong to that fraternity. You're not planning to pledge it, are you?

EXERCISE 7-3

Each of the following statements contains a logical fallacy. For each statement, indicate whether this fallacy is a false analogy (FA), an overgeneralization (OG), an unstated assumption (UA), or an appeal to the emotions (AE).

1. Why would you want to live on a street where people have paved driveways but no garages?

2. He cannot possibly succeed in graduate school because he was a star athlete in college.

3. All the dentists in town endorse this toothpaste, so it must be effective.

4. A person with your good taste and integrity will not enjoy that movie.

5. That restaurant must serve good food because truckers stop there.

6. Purchasing a gun is no more dangerous than getting a driver's license.

7. You can't possibly understand grief unless you've had a loved one die recently.

8. It's really the place to be seen because many wealthy and famous people go there on Saturdays.

9. They must contribute a lot of money to the university because they always have season tickets for the football games.

10. All patriotic citizens will object to any burning of the flag.

Faulty cause-and-effect analysis

Often called the **post-hoc** ("after that") fallacy, this reasoning, which assumes that one event causes another event simply because it precedes the second event, is faulty. Many superstitions are based on this error in reasoning.

It didn't rain today because, for once, I brought my umbrella.

He won the game because he was wearing his lucky T-shirt.

I now have a cold because I forgot to take my vitamin pill this morning.

Either-or thinking

Either-or thinking is a type of oversimplification that assumes that there are only two alternatives in a situation when usually there are many possibilities in between.

You are either with us or against us.

We have to decide: do we want clean air and water or do we want a higher standard of living?

Every woman today must make a choice. She can have a family or she can have a career.

Non sequiturs

The Latin words *non sequitur* mean "it does not follow." A **non sequitur** is a logical fallacy in which the conclusion does not follow from the premise.

Many wild animals live longer in zoos than in the wild. Therefore, all wild animals should be placed in zoos.

Since Henderson does not beat his children, he is a good father.

It is important to honor our parents, and so we should actively participate in the celebration of Mother's Day and Father's Day.

Circular reasoning

Do not try to prove that something is true by merely re-stating it in other words or assuming that it has been proven. This error is called **circular reasoning** or **begging the question.**

Public transportation is necessary because everyone needs it.

The play is unsophisticated because it displays a naive simplicity.

The vest will protect an officer against a person with a gun because it is bulletproof.

EXERCISE 7-4

Each of the following sentences contains a logical fallacy. For each statement, indicate whether this fallacy is faulty cause and effect

(CE), either-or thinking (EO), a *non sequitur* (NS), or circular reasoning (CR). Explain the error.

1. She scored very high on the test because her grandmother prayed for her success on it.

2. Either James or Bill took the wallet; James was not here so Bill must have taken it.

3. Louella does not drink or smoke; she'll be a good parent.

4. If we vote for a state lottery, the poor people will have less money.

5. This house is cold today because you forgot to turn up the thermostat.

6. My car wouldn't start this morning; the battery must be dead.

7. He exercises everyday because thin people live longer.

8. Poetry is what poets do.

9. I enjoy Broadway musicals; therefore, I enjoy the musicals of Rogers and Hammerstein.

10. Our team lost the soccer match because it was so cold.

7d Writing Arguments

We write arguments to convince our readers of a fact, to persuade them to act or accept a certain point of view, or to resolve a disagreement. Arguments can be devised on whether a longer school year enhances learning, on the need to stop smoking, or on the need for laws against sexual harassment in the workplace. But it would be difficult to devise an argument on a verifiable fact (how many pints constitute a quart), on generalities (how bored some troops were during the Persian Gulf War), or on matters of mere taste (whether basketball is more exciting than tennis).

Propositions

Arguments on specific issues are framed into statements called **propositions:** for example, recycling household wastes will help preserve the environment. A proposition sentence serves as the thesis for an argumentative essay and can be a proposition of **fact** or **action.** A proposition of fact states or validates that something is, indeed, true (for example, that our representation in the United Nations is beneficial to the United States and other nations). A proposition of action states that something *should* be done (for example, that women in the military must be granted all the responsibilities in combat that men have). The point of an argumentative piece of writing is to argue and prove the proposition in accordance with the dictates of reasoning and logic, and critical thinking plays an especially important role in writing effective arguments. To build a strong argument we must consider premises and issues, evidence, reasoning, fallacies, and tone. We also need to apply the various stages in the process of writing—prewriting, drafting, and revising as presented in Chapters 1, 2, and 3.

Premises and issues

A proposition contains one main point, called a **premise.** The appearance of *two* ideas in one proposition does not mean that you have *one* premise.

idea 1   idea 2
Julio is **a good student** and will be **an effective student senator.**

An effective proposition contains a premise, or the main point, and a subordinate idea (or ideas) that serve as the **issue.**

issue   premise
Because Julio is **a good student,** he will be **an effective student senator.**

In this proposition the writer has opted to place the premise in the independent clause; but the subsidiary idea, the issue, in the dependent clause must also be argued. Additionally, the fact that *two* ideas relate to one and the same situation does not mean that you have *one* premise:

idea 1 (cause)   idea 2 (effect)
issue   premise
Ever since **Fatima injured her foot,** she has not **run to her potential.**

Despite the connection of cause and effect in this situation, the issue must first be argued before the premise can be argued and accepted. In some cases, a number of issues may have to be argued before the premise is argued:

issue 1
Despite **the bombing of Israel and Saudi Arabia,** the **pollution**

issue 2
of the Persian Gulf waters with oil, and the **inhumane treat-**

issue 3
ment of the Kuwaiti nationals, the **military leaders in Iraq**

premise
had the support of their citizenry.

Use the various prewriting techniques outlined in Chapter 2 to arrive at premises, issues, and then a proposition. Try positing a temporary proposition as you work on your argument, do research, and consider opposing perspectives. Expect that your proposition may change and evolve as you write your drafts. As in all writing, be prepared to revise and rethink your initial ideas, and talk with friends to help you evaluate the validity of your argument.

EXERCISE 7-5

1. Compose three propositions of fact that contain at least one issue. Label each issue and premise. Example:

           issue   premise
   Since **you worked as a lifeguard, you can instruct us on some lifesaving techniques.**

2. Compose a proposition of action that contains at least one issue on three of the following topics:

sexual harassment	cigarette smoking	energy conservation
civil rights	free college tuition	free medical care

Evidence

Once you have formulated a temporary proposition, you are ready to begin supporting your argument with **evidence.** Evidence consists of either fact or authoritative opinion. A fact must be verifiable either by appeal to natural law (water freezes at 32° Fahrenheit) or by authoritative testimony (the President indicated today that more money needs to be spent on public education). Opinion also serves as evidence, but only if it, too, is authoritative, attested to by oral or printed testimony. You will need to do research to find the evidence for your argument. Your personal experiences can serve as evidence if you identify them as personal testimony; however, be aware that personal experience, although relevant to you, is usually not as convincing as other types of evidence.

Be sure to cite evidence that your audience will understand and respect. You won't convince many voters that a raise in the tax rates will not be a burden by citing only the opinions of wealthy people. You will also want to cite the most recent evidence you can obtain. Surveys on the role of women in the armed forces taken during World War II, aside from their historical interest, will probably not be helpful in an argument designed to convince readers that women today are willing to serve in combat. When citing evidence, always anticipate the opposing arguments and try to refute them. An intelligent and successful argument considers all sides of a proposition.

Reasoning

Evidence alone does not prove a proposition or result in a convincing argument. You must organize the evidence into some meaningful sequence that will support the proposition. To do this, you need to think about the ways in which we reason, namely by induction (from the specific to the general) and deduction (from the general to the specific). See pp. 117–19 for a more detailed discussion of these types of reasoning. By carefully applying these methods of reasoning, your arguments will be stronger and more effective. Also be sure that your proposition, like the thesis, appears in your introduction and that your conclusion restates the idea of your proposition in different words and serves as a device of emphasis. Remember, arguments that are not well organized simply confuse the reader and are not convincing.

Fallacies

An argument that contains a **fallacy,** an error in reasoning, will not succeed. Most people do not intentionally build fallacies into their arguments; fallacies occur when we are careless

QUESTIONS FOR WRITING ARGUMENTS

1. Have I written a proposition of fact or of action?
2. Have I analyzed my proposition into a premise and issues? How many issues are there?
3. Have I gathered enough appropriate evidence for both the premise and the issue(s)?
4. Is my reasoning about the evidence sound? Have I checked for fallacies?
5. Is my tone appropriate?
6. Have I organized the argument properly and convincingly?

about our reasoning process and either arrive at invalid conclusions based on valid evidence or valid conclusions based on invalid evidence. For a full discussion of various types of fallacies, see pp. 120–129. Be sure to evaluate your argument carefully throughout your drafting to avoid any illogical phrasing or claims.

Tone

The **tone,** or attitude, you convey is important in all types of writing and especially in arguments. Written arguments should not resemble the arguments you might have with siblings or friends in which you raise your voice, call names, resort to biased language, or rely on falsehood. Remember, in written arguments reason, not emotion, must prevail. The words you select and their arrangement reveal your tone and will determine whether you can retain the interest of your audience members and then convince them or persuade them of your point of view. The wrong tone may alienate your readers or undermine your argument. Avoid chronic complaining, emotional appeals, rebellion for the sake of rebellion, enraged defenses, cynicism, and a know-it-all smugness. Instead, rely on responsible criticism, appeals to reason, informed analysis, forceful but fair explanations, optimistic skepticism, and intelligent observations.

EXERCISE 7-6

Identify the proposition in the following argumentative paragraph. Is it one of fact (PF) or of action (PA)? What is the premise (P)? What are the issues (I)?

> By now, there's nobody left in the world who needs convincing that America is a violent society. Handgun sales alone announce the obvious. Children patrol their neighborhoods armed with baseball bats. Young men with wild ideas stalk the rich and celebrated. Peddlers of door locks and guard dogs are a booming business, and the evening stroll has become a subject for nostalgia. "So, that's capitalism," say the Russians. "Cowboy mentality," sniff the Israelis. "A sick society," agree the media. But they're wrong, all wrong. America is not becoming more violent. It is, in fact, becoming less inclined to tolerate violence in all its forms than ever before.

Helen Fox
"Violence in America?"

EXERCISE 7-7

Identify the proposition (P) in each of the following argumentative paragraphs. Discuss the evidence used and how it is arranged.

A common myth about the nature of mathematical ability holds that one either has or does not have a mathematical mind. Mathematical imagination and an intuitive grasp of mathematical principles may well be needed to do advanced research, but why should people who can do college-level work in other subjects not be able to do college-level math as well? Rates of learning may vary. Competency under time pressure may differ. Certainly low self-esteem will get in the way. But where is the evidence that a student needs a "mathematical mind" in order to succeed at learning math?

Sheila Tobias
"Overcoming Math Anxiety"

Of all the changes that have altered the topography of childhood, the most dramatic has been the disappearance of childhood play. Whereas a decade or two ago children were easily distinguished from the adult world by the very nature of their play, today children's occupations do not differ greatly from adult diversions.

Infants and toddlers, to be sure, continue to follow certain timeless patterns of manipulation and exploration; adolescents, too, have not changed their free-time habits so very much, turning as they ever have towards adult pastimes and amusements in their drive for autonomy, self-mastery, and sexual discovery. It is among the ranks of school-age children, those six-to-twelve-year-olds who once avidly filled their free moments with childhood play, that the greatest change is evident. In the place of traditional, sometimes ancient childhood games that were still popular a generation ago, in the place of fantasy and make-believe play—"You be the mommy and I'll be the daddy"—doll play or toy-soldier play, jump-rope play, ball-bouncing play, today's children have substituted television viewing and, most recently, video games.

Marie Winn
"Children Without Childhood"

PART II

GRAMMAR

Grammar is the formal study of the features and constructions of language; in other words, it is a description of how a language works. The word *grammar* comes from the ancient Greek work *grammatiké*, which meant the study of written texts, in the broad sense of "the way written language is put together." The purpose of studying grammar is to gain an understanding of language so that you can use it effectively.

The basic pattern for writing in English is the **sentence.** A useful definition of a *sentence* is "a word or group of words that expresses a complete thought" and contains a subject and a verb. A sentence may be as short as one word or as long as fifty words or more.

8   The Parts of a Sentence

Regardless of its length, a sentence always contains at least one **clause,** consisting of a subject and its verb. (Sometimes the subject is implied rather than stated.) Study the parts of the sentences that follow.

<pre>
          subject predicate
             ↓   ↓
The scientist's research won.
</pre>

<pre>
implied
subject predicate
   ↓   ↓
(You) Consider the situation.
</pre>

<pre>
                    direct object
                         ↓
The scientist's research won recognition.
</pre>

indirect
object
↓

The scientist's research won her recognition.

objective
complement
↓

Research made the scientist famous.

                        predicate
subject   predicate   nominative
↓   ↓   ↓

The scientist is Barbara McClintock.

predicate
adjective
↓

Her research is remarkable.

These are the seven basic sentence patterns—all the patterns possible. Notice how the following sentences grow by the addition of modifiers to the basic *subject-verb patterns.*

The scientist investigated.

In her laboratory, the scientist investigated.

In her laboratory at Cold Spring Harbor, the scientist investigated.

In her laboratory at Cold Spring Harbor, the scientist investigated gene development.

In her laboratory at Cold Spring Harbor, the scientist investigated gene development in maize.

In her laboratory at Cold Spring Harbor, the scientist investigated gene development in maize, and her discovery won.

In her laboratory at Cold Spring Harbor, the scientist investigated gene development in maize, and her discovery of jumping genes won.

In her laboratory at Cold Spring Harbor, the scientist investigated gene development in maize, and her discovery of jumping genes won recognition.

8a Subjects

The **subject** of the sentence answers the question "who?" or "what?" about the predicate, or verb. The subject is the part of the sentence about which something is being said.

How can you identify the subject of a sentence? Form a question by putting "who" or "what" before the verb. In some sentences, the subject *performs* the action expressed by the verb.

Halfway through her performance, the **soprano** *hit* a flat note.

Captain Cook *searched* for a northwest passage to China.

Mass extinctions *mark* the boundaries between eras on the geological time scale.

Who hit a flat note? The *soprano*. Who searched for a northwest passage to China? *Captain Cook*. What marks the boundaries between eras? *Mass extinctions*.

In other sentences, the subject *receives* the action of the verb; that is, it is acted upon.

The deer *was wounded* by the hunters.

Former president **Lyndon Johnson** *was educated* at Southwest Texas State Teachers College.

The first modern bank in the United States *was established* by Robert Morris, a Philadelphia financier.

What was wounded by the hunters? *The deer.* Who was educated at Southwest Texas State Teachers College? *Lyndon Johnson.* What was established by Robert Morris? *The first modern bank in the United States.*

If the verb is a linking verb, such as *be* or *seem,* the subject is the person or thing identified or described.

> **James Boswell** was both the friend and the biographer of Samuel Johnson.
>
> **George Eliot** was the pseudonym of Mary Anne Evans.
>
> **Aaron Burr's reputation as a traitor** seems unjustified.

Who was both the friend and the biographer of Samuel Johnson? *James Boswell.* What was the pseudonym of Mary Anne Evans? *George Eliot.* What seems unjustified? *Aaron Burr's reputation as a traitor.*

The second way to identify the subject of a sentence is to pay attention to word order. In most English sentences, the subject appears before the predicate (the verb). However, there are exceptions. Sometimes word order is reversed for effect.

> On his head sits **a crown.**
>
> Through the ice-covered streets walked **the funeral cortege.**
>
> From these schools will come **tomorrow's leaders.**

Sometimes word order is altered to ask a question.

> Did **Miró's art** influence Pollock and Motherwell?
>
> Should **reporters** be required to disclose their sources?
>
> Does **classical music** have an audience among the young?

Sometimes one of the expletives *there* and *here* appears at the beginning of the sentence. These words are never the subject but simply serve to postpone the appearance of the subject, which is midsentence. The word *it* can also be used as an expletive. The result of using initial expletives and placing the subject in midsentence is an unemphatic sentence. Placing the subject at the beginning and end of a sentence will help you achieve sentence *emphasis*. In each of the following sentences, the subject is printed in **boldface.**

> There are **six books** in this series.
>
> Here are **four ways to increase productivity at this plant.**
>
> It is necessary **to read the instructions before starting.**

Sometimes the sentence is a command. In a command, the subject *you* is implied rather than stated.

> [You] Help me with this word-processing program.
>
> Please read this chapter before the next class.
>
> List five twentieth-century American composers.

Because a prepositional phrase ends with a noun or noun substitute, people sometimes look to it for the subject of the sentence. However, the simple subject is never found in a prepositional phrase. In each of the following sentences, the simple subject is printed in **boldface** and the prepositional phrase in *italics.*

> **Each** *of the states* chooses delegates to the convention.
>
> **Neither** *of the pandas* is female.
>
> **One** *of Charlemagne's achievements* was the development of an effective administrative system.

The simple subject

The **simple subject** is the main noun or noun substitute in the subject.

> A New Jersey **farmer** won a prize in London in 1986 for a 671-pound pumpkin.
>
> Growing **conditions** in 1987 made the pumpkins smaller.
>
> That year a **Canadian** took first place with a 408-pound entry.
>
> **It** won its grower a cash prize and a trip to San Francisco.
>
> There are **competitions** for other vegetables—giant carrots, radishes, onions.
>
> **Growing monstrous vegetables** can be a profitable hobby.

A simple subject may consist of two or more nouns or noun substitutes (pronouns) that take the same predicate.

> **Economics and health** are much in the news lately.
>
> In ancient Greece, **war and athletics** were believed to be influenced by Nike, the winged goddess of victory.
>
> **Desire, anger, and pain** must be annihilated in order to reach Nirvana.

The complete subject

The **complete subject** consists of the simple subject and all the words that modify it. In each of the following sentences, the simple subject is printed in **boldface** and the complete subject in *italics*.

> *Wide-visioned, close-fisted* **George Halas,** *originator of the Chicago Bears,* can be described as the George Washington of pro football.

A hot **bath and** *a vigorous* **massage** are good remedies for aching muscles.

Note: Throughout this book, we use the term *subject* to mean the simple subject.

EXERCISE 8-1

Circle the simple subject in each of the following sentences, then underline the complete subject.

1. Most members of our society learn early to recognize the language of advertising.

2. There are many examples of this kind of language on children's television programs.

3. Advertising attempts to alter our behaviors or to motivate us.

4. How often do we succumb to the pressure tactics of such language?

5. Through the efforts of advertising agencies, many of us purchase things we don't even want.

8b Predicates

The **predicate** of a sentence tells what the subject does or is. It is the part of the sentence that comprises what is said about the subject. The predicate consists of a verb (a word that expresses action or a state of being) and all the words that complete the meaning of the verb.

How can you identify the predicate of a sentence? Form a question by putting "does what?" or "is what?" after the subject.

The pianist **played a complicated piece.**

The amateur treasure hunters **found a few valuable pieces.**

The bald eagle **is the symbol of the United States.**

The pianist did what? *Played a complicated piece.* The amateur treasure hunters did what? *Found a few valuable pieces.* The bald eagle is what? *Is the symbol of the United States.*

The simple predicate

The **simple predicate** is the verb, which may consist of more than one word.

The town meeting **is** the epitome of a democratic society in action.

Early in her reign Elizabeth **had reestablished** the Church of England.

The Cultural Revolution in China **was headed** by Mao Zedong.

Many accidents **could have been prevented.**

A simple predicate may include two or more verbs that take the same subject.

The small group of colonists **boarded** the British ships and **threw** their cargoes of tea overboard.

Poe **fell** in love with his cousin Virginia and **married** the thirteen-year-old child.

Thoreau **opposed** the poll tax and **had been speaking** against it for years but **had** never before **broken** the law.

The complete predicate

The **complete predicate** consists of the simple predicate and all the words that modify it and complete its meaning. In each of the following sentences, the simple predicate is printed in **boldface,** and the complete predicate is in *italics.*

A jet flying overhead **broke** *the stillness of the night.*

The Connecticut River **divides** *the state into two almost equal regions.*

The goal of landing Americans on the moon and returning them to Earth **was accomplished** *by Apollo 11.*

EXERCISE 8-2

Circle the simple predicate in each of the following sentences, then underline the complete predicate.

1. What does it mean to be different?

2. Many students—minorities especially—have to confront this dilemma.

3. Differences are most often relative.

4. What is different in one environment does not necessarily transfer to a new environment.

5. Campuses have become much more aware and appreciative of multicultural differences in the past five years.

8c Complements

A **complement** completes the meaning of a verb. The five major types of complements are the *direct object*, the *indirect object,* the *objective complement*, the *predicate nominative*, and the *predicate adjective*.

Direct objects

A **direct object** is a noun or noun substitute that specifies the person or thing directly *receiving* the action of a transitive verb. A verb becomes transitive when it gives its action to that object (see pp. 156–158).

To identify the direct object, form a question by putting "whom?" or "what?" after the verb.

> Darwin accepted a **position** aboard H. M. S. *Beagle.*
>
> In addition to his other accomplishments, William James achieved a **reputation** as a literary figure.
>
> The congresswoman greets **us** warmly and then opens the **discussion.**

Darwin accepted what? A *position*. William James achieved what? A *reputation*. The congresswoman greets whom? *Us*. She opens what? *The discussion.*

Indirect objects

An **indirect object** is a noun or noun substitute that tells to whom or for whom or what the action of the verb is performed. A sentence can have an indirect object only if it has a direct object; the indirect object always comes just before the direct object. Further, indirect objects follow only those verbs that describe a "giving" action of some kind.

The director gave the **plans** her approval.

He wrote **her** a poem expressing his admiration.

In one of Aesop's fables, a mouse does a **lion** a favor.

Usually, sentences containing indirect objects can be rewritten by putting *to* or *for* before the indirect object.

The director gave her approval **to the plans.**

He wrote a poem **for her** expressing his admiration.

In one of Aesop's fables, a mouse does a favor **for a lion.**

Objective complements

An **objective complement** is a noun or an adjective that completes the action of the transitive verb in relation to its object. A sentence can have an objective complement only if it has an object. Further, the action of the verb must produce a "change" of some kind in that object.

The storm made the bridge **unsafe.**

The news report declared it a **hazard.**

You can recognize objective complements by inserting a form of the verb *be* before the objective complement.

The storm made the bridge *to be* **unsafe.**

The news report declared it *to be* a **hazard.**

The noun objective complement always follows the object. Occasionally, the adjective objective complement may precede the object.

The judge ruled **impossible** the impartiality of a trial held in the victims' community.

Predicate nominatives

A **predicate nominative** is a noun or noun substitute that follows an intransitive linking verb and renames the subject (see pp. 158–159).

> The culprit is **he.**
>
> Martha Graham became **one** of the principal innovators of modern dance.
>
> E. B. White's closest companion at the *New Yorker* was **James Thurber.**

The pronoun *he* renames *culprit.* The pronoun *one* renames *Martha Graham.* The noun *James Thurber* renames *companion.*

In a construction of this type, the linking verb serves as an equal sign. The noun on the left-hand side of the linking verb equals the noun on the right-hand side.

Predicate adjectives

A **predicate adjective** is an adjective that follows an intransitive linking verb and describes the subject (see pp. 158–159).

> Isadora Duncan's style of dancing seemed **revolutionary** to her contemporaries.
>
> The drama critic's review was especially **acrimonious.**
>
> Halfway through their journey over the mountains, the pioneers felt too **weary** to travel on.

EXERCISE 8-3

First circle the simple subject and the simple predicate in each of the following sentences. Then identify any complements. Underline each complement and classify it as a direct object (DO), an indirect object (IO), an objective complement (OC), a predicate nominative (PN), or a predicate adjective (PA).

1. Bilingual education is a popular program in many areas of our country.

2. Such programs have met with opposition by those who want English to be the official language of the United States.

3. Some European nations have successfully encouraged the official use of two and even three languages.

4. Should we not give our students every opportunity to master English, even if it means teaching it via another language?

5. Without such education some parts of our country will need signs in languages other than English.

9   The Parts of Speech

Words have traditionally been classified into eight categories, called **parts of speech**—noun, verb, adjective, adverb, pronoun, preposition, conjunction, and interjection. The function a word performs in a sentence determines which part of speech it is. A word may function as more than one part of speech, as shown in the following examples.

The committee is seeking ways to make a **ride** on the bus more comfortable. (*noun*)

Thousands of commuters **ride** the bus to work every day. (*verb*)

For many years **New England** dominated literary life in America. (*noun*)

Emily Dickinson's poems carry traces of other **New England** writers. (*adjective*)

Some scholars feel that the story of Jason and the Argonauts reflects trading expeditions that occurred **before** the Trojan War. (*preposition*)

Before Schliemann excavated the ruins of ancient Troy, most people believed that the story of the Trojan War was pure myth. (*conjunction*)

Any civilization is the product of those who came **before.** (*adverb*)

9a Nouns

A **noun** is a word that names. Nouns may name persons.

Shakespeare	actor	women
Margaret Mead	citizen	scholars

Nouns may name places.

Pittsburgh	prairie	suburbs
Pacific Ocean	camp	Great Lakes

Nouns may name animate or inanimate objects.

reindeer	Bunsen burner	cassettes
baboon	veranda	word processors

Nouns may name events, ideas, concepts, or activities.

meeting	freedom	frustration	fire
French Revolution	honor	philanthropy	smoke

In the following sentences, the nouns are printed in **boldface.**

> While in his **bath, Archimedes,** a Greek **mathematician** and **inventor,** worked out the **principle** of **buoyancy.**

> **Barbara Tuchman** argues that the **acceptance** of the **Wooden Horse** by the **Trojans** was the **epitome** of **folly.**

> The **discovery** of the **Rosetta stone** led to an **increase** in **knowledge** of the ancient **world.**

Proper, common, concrete, and abstract nouns

Nouns can be classified in other ways: as proper or common nouns, and as concrete or abstract nouns. **Proper nouns** name particular persons, places, objects, or ideas. Proper nouns are capitalized.

Milton	Honda	Martin Luther King, Jr.
San Francisco	Hinduism	New Mexico

Common nouns are less specific. They name people, places, objects, and ideas in general, not in particular. Common nouns are not capitalized.

poet-dramatist	motorcycle	preacher
port city	religion	democracy

Concrete nouns name things that can be seen, touched, heard, smelled, tasted, or felt.

horizon	marble	music
peanut butter	garbage	heat

Abstract nouns name concepts, ideas, beliefs, and qualities. Unlike concrete nouns, abstract nouns name things that cannot be perceived by the five senses.

love   justice   creativity
inspiration   kindness   monotheism

Compound nouns

As you read the preceding lists, you probably noticed that some nouns are made up of more than one word. Nouns that consist of more than one word are called **compound nouns.** Some compound nouns are written as one word, some are hyphenated, and some are written as two or more separate words. (When in doubt, check your dictionary.)

bedroom   tomato plant   cathode-ray tube
heartland   fire insurance   father-in-law

Nouns are characterized by several features.

1. Nouns show **number.** Most nouns can be either singular or plural. (For guidelines on forming the plural of nouns, see pp. 417–420.)

   SINGULAR: computer success   criterion woman sheep
   PLURAL: computers successes criteria   women sheep

2. Nouns have **gender.** They are either masculine, feminine, or neuter (sometimes called "indeterminate").

   MASCULINE: Abraham Lincoln   tenor   boy
   FEMININE: Harriet Tubman   soprano   girl
   NEUTER: human being   attendant child
                Eiffel Tower   chair   justice

3. Nouns have **case.** Case refers to the structural function of a noun in a sentence. English has three cases—subjective (nominative), objective, and possessive—obvious in pronouns (see pp. 172, 246–254). The form of

the noun changes only when it is used in the possessive case. (For more information on forming the possessive case, see pp. 384–387.)

The subjective case is used for subjects and predicate nominatives. The objective case is used for direct and indirect objects and for objects of prepositions. The possessive case is used to show possession.

SUBJECTIVE:	**Harrison** worked late.	**He** worked late.
OBJECTIVE:	The boss trained **Harrison.**	The boss trained **him.**
POSSESSIVE:	**Harrison's** proposal was accepted.	**His** proposal was accepted.

9b Verbs

A **verb** is a word that expresses action—physical or mental—or a state of being. In the following sentences, the verbs are printed in **boldface.**

Isaac Bashevis Singer **wrote** his stories and novels in Yiddish. (*physical action*)

Puritans **valued** industry and thrift. (*mental action*)

That young man **is** a famous singer. (*state of being*)

Action verbs

An **action verb** may be *transitive* or *intransitive*. An action verb that takes an object is **transitive.** An **object** is a word (a noun or noun substitute) that completes the idea expressed by the verb. (See pp. 149–151.)

Marie and Pierre Curie successfully **isolated** *radium*.

Professor Higgins **introduced** *Eliza Doolittle* to society.

In Shakespeare's play, Iago **hates** *goodness* and **loves** *evil.*

Othello never **suspects** *him.*

When the subject of a transitive verb performs the action received by the object, the verb is said to be in the **active voice.** The verbs in the preceding sentences are **transitive active.** A transitive verb is in the **passive voice** when the active voice object has become subject of that verb.

Radium **was** successfully **isolated** by Marie and Pierre Curie.

Eliza Doolittle **was introduced** to society.

In Shakespeare's play, *goodness* **is hated** by Iago and *evil* **is loved.**

He **is suspected** by Othello.

Only transitive verbs can be described as having voice. (For more about voice, see pp. 111–112 and 167–168.) An action verb that has no object is **intransitive.**

> Sometimes even good old Homer **nods.**
>
> Horace

> Consider the lilies of the field, how they **grow;** they **toil** not, neither **do** they **spin.**
>
> Matthew 6:28

> People **hate,** as they **love,** unreasonably.
>
> William Thackeray

An action verb may be transitive in one sentence and intransitive in another.

> The narrator **mourned** the *loss* of his beautiful Annabel Lee. (*transitive*)

> After the death of the President, the nation **mourned.** (*intransitive*)

> The audience **howled** its *derision* at the speaker. (*transitive*)

> Out on the tundra, the wolves **howled.** (*intransitive*)

> Queen Victoria **ruled** *Great Britain, Ireland, and India.* (*transitive*).

> In the midst of battle, death **ruled.** (*intransitive*)

Some action verbs are always **intransitive**—for example, *sit, lie, rise, die, reminisce.*

State-of-being verbs

State-of-being verbs may be *linking* or *nonlinking.* They are, however, always **intransitive** because they never take objects. Instead, they take complements: a predicate nominative or a predicate adjective.

Linking verbs

A **linking** verb expresses a state of being or condition and connects its subject to a word that describes or identifies that subject. The most common linking verb is *be* and its forms—*am, is, are, was, were, will be, have been,* and so on.

> Radiotherapy **is** the treatment of disease with radiation.

> Woody Guthrie **was** a popular folksinger.

> Americans **were** aghast at the sinking of the *Lusitania.*

Other common linking verbs are *appear, become, feel, grow, look, remain, seem, smell, sound,* and *taste.*

> Compared to other warm-blooded animals, hummingbirds **appear** extravagant in their use of energy.

> Houdini **became** world-famous for his daring escapes.

> The true fate of Amelia Earhart still **remains** a mystery.

A linking verb connects the subject to a predicate nominative or to a predicate adjective. A predicate nominative identifies the subject, whereas a predicate adjective describes the subject.

> *Napoleon* was a brilliant **general.** (*predicate nominative*)

> After his defeat at Waterloo, **Napoleon** was *disconsolate.* (*predicate adjective*)

> The *macadamia* is Australia's only edible **nut.** (*predicate nominative*)

> The macadamia's *shell* is nearly **impregnable.** (*predicate adjective*)

> The *bobcat* remains North America's most common native **cat.** (*predicate nominative*)

> Despite the trainer's efforts, the *bobcat* remains **wild.** (*predicate adjective*)

Nonlinking verbs

A **nonlinking,** state-of-being verb is not followed and completed by a predicate noun or adjective but may be followed by an adverb modifier.

> Yesterday we **were** *upstream* from their camp.

The plane **_was_** directly _overhead_ when it burst into flames.

Fortunately, they **_were_** _not near_ the skunk when it sprayed.

It **_seems_** _so._

Note: A verb earns its label only as it operates with its subject plus object or complement if it has either.

Gregor Mendel **grew** his _plants_ in the monastery garden. (_action verb, transitive_)

The plants **grew** vigorously. (_action verb, intransitive_)

During the campaign, the arguments **grew** _heated_. (_state-of-being verb, linking_)

EXERCISE 9-1

Underline the simple components of the following sentences using these abbreviated labels: _S_ equals subject; _TV_ equals transitive verb; _IV_ equals intransitive verb; _LV_ equals linking verb; _PV_ equals passive voice verb; _O_ equals object; _PN_ equals predicate noun; _PA_ equals predicate adjective. See the following examples.

$$\text{S} \quad \text{TV} \quad \text{O}$$
Vandals destroyed Rome during Nero's reign.

$$\text{S} \quad \text{PV}$$
Rome was destroyed.

$$\text{S} \quad \text{IV}$$
Rome burned furiously.

$$\text{S} \quad \text{IV}$$
Nero remained in his palace.

```
   S   LV            PN
Nero was an evil emperor.
```

```
   S    LV        PA
Nero remained indifferent to the fate of the city.
```

1. A wave of patriotism swept across the country during the Gulf War.

2. It was a stark contrast to the time of the Vietnam War.

3. Yellow ribbons were attached to doors and trees in honor of our military personnel.

4. Many people flew flags day and night.

5. Rallies in support of our troops were held in most large cities.

6. It seemed a genuine outpouring of national pride.

7. The percentage of women in the military reached its highest point in our history.

8. The popularity of a military career soared.

9. Many of the troops were honored with parades throughout America.

10. The yellow ribbons are still visible in places.

Auxiliary verbs and modals

A verb has four basic forms, called **principal parts;** the present infinitive, the past tense, the past participle, and the present participle.

PRESENT INFINITIVE	PAST TENSE	PAST PARTICIPLE	PRESENT PARTICIPLE
compute	computed	computed	computing
analyze	analyzed	analyzed	analyzing
fall	fell	fallen	falling
bring	brought	brought	bringing

The **present infinitive** is the dictionary form of the verb. For example, if you wanted to know the meaning of the first verb in the chart above, you would look up *compute*, the present infinitive form, in your dictionary. The **present participle** of all verbs is formed by adding *-ing* to the present infinitive. The **past tense** and **past participle** of most verbs, called **regular verbs,** are formed by adding *-d* or *-ed* to the present infinitive. Verbs like *fall* and *bring* are **irregular verbs;** their past tense and past participle are formed in some other way. (For more information on irregular verbs, see pp. 218–221.)

A **verb phrase** is made up of the present infinitive, the present participle, or the past participle preceded by one or more auxiliary verbs or modals. As discussed in the following pages, the **auxiliary** verb *have* is used to form the perfect tense; the auxiliary verb *be* is used to form progressive tenses and the passive voice. In the following sentences, the verb phrase is printed in *italics* and the auxiliary in **boldface.**

> Edna St. Vincent Millay's first book of poems **was** *published* in 1917. (*passive voice, past tense*)

> Jacobo Timerman **has** *called* attention to the violation of human rights in Argentina. (*present perfect tense*)

Modals are used to form questions, to help express a negative, to emphasize, to show future time, and to express such conditions as possibility, certainty, or obligation. The words *do, does, did; can, could; may, might, must; will, shall; would, should;* and *ought to* are modals. A verb phrase may include both auxiliaries and modals. In each of the following sentences, the verb phrase is printed in *italics* and the modal in **boldface.**

> For a democracy to work, its citizens **must** *participate.*
>
> You **should** *practice* at least an hour a day.
>
> The election **may** *be decided* on the basis of personality.

Sometimes an auxiliary or modal is separated from the main part of the verb.

> **Do** you *know* the full name of the Imagist poet H. D.?
>
> The price of gold **has** not *been falling.*
>
> The teacher **is** now *computing* students' grade-point averages.

Verbs display three characteristics: *tense, voice,* and *mood.*

Tense

Tense is the time expressed by the form of the verb. The six tenses are the *simple present, present perfect, simple past, past perfect, simple future,* and *future perfect.* Each of these tenses has a progressive form that indicates continuing action.

	BASIC FORM	PROGRESSIVE FORM
SIMPLE PRESENT:	compose(s)	is (are) composing
PRESENT PERFECT:	has (have) composed	has (have) been composing
SIMPLE PAST:	composed	was (were) composing
PAST PERFECT:	had composed	had been composing
SIMPLE FUTURE:	will (shall) compose	will (shall) be composing
FUTURE PERFECT:	will (shall) have composed	will (shall) have been composing

Usually, the simple present, the simple past, and the simple future are referred to as the present, the past, and the future tense, respectively.

The time of an action does not always correspond exactly with the name of the tense used to write about the action. For example, in special situations the present tense can be used to write about events that occurred in the past or will occur in the future as well as events that are occurring in the present.

Present tense

In general, the **present tense** is used to write about events or conditions that are happening or existing now.

> She **lives** in Austin, Texas.
>
> An accountant **is preparing** our tax returns.
>
> They **are** dissatisfied with their grades.

The present tense is also used to write about natural or scientific laws or timeless truths, events in literature, and habitual action.

> Some bacteria **are** beneficial, but others **cause** disease.
>
> No one **lives** forever.
>
> Sherlock Holmes and his archenemy, Dr. Moriarty, apparently **perish** together.
>
> He always **begins** his speeches with an anecdote.
>
> She **goes** to work every day at eight.

The past tense can also be used to write about events in literature. Whichever tense you choose, be consistent.

The present tense can be used with an adverbial word or phrase to indicate future time. In the following sentences, the adverbs that indicate time are *italicized*.

This flight **arrives** in Chicago *at 7:30 p.m.*

Next week the class **meets** in the conference room.

She **begins** her campaign *tomorrow*.

The verb *do* is used with the present infinitive to create an emphatic form of the present tense.

You **do know** your facts, but your presentation of them is not always clear.

He certainly **does cover** his topic thoroughly.

After six weeks of training, they **do look** fit.

Present perfect tense

The **present perfect tense** is used to write about events that occurred at some unspecified time in the past and about events and conditions that began in the past and may still be continuing in the present.

The novelist **has incorporated** theories of psycholinguistics into his mysteries.

Their new line of greeting cards **has been selling** well.

The two performers **have donated** the profits from their concert to charity.

Past tense

The **past tense** is used to write about events that occurred and conditions that existed at a definite time in the past and do not extend into the present.

The study **explored** the dolphin's ability to communicate.

The researchers **were studying** the effects of fluoridation on tooth decay.

The patient **was relieved** when the doctor **told** him the results of the tests.

The word *did* (the past tense of *do*) is used with the present infinitive to create an emphatic form of the past tense.

In the end he **did vote** against the bill.

Despite opposition, she **did make** her opinions heard.

They **did increase** voter registration, but they lost the election.

Past perfect tense

The **past perfect tense** is used to write about a past event or condition that ended before another past event or condition began.

She voted for passage of the bill because she **had seen** the effects of poverty on the young.

The researchers **had tried** several drugs on the microorganism before they found the right one.

He **had been painting** for ten years before he sold his first canvas.

Future tense

The **future tense** is used to write about events or conditions that have not yet begun. (See the Glossary of Usage for *shall, will.*)

Her next book **will continue** the saga of the Anderson family.

The voters **will be deciding** the role of religion in the schools.

We **shall stay** in London for two weeks.

Future perfect tense

The **future perfect tense** is used to write about a future event or condition that will end before another future event or condition begins or before a specified time in the future.

Before I see him again, the editor **will have read** my short story.

If he keeps to this regimen, by the end of the month the boxer **will have lost** the necessary ten pounds.

By October, she **will have been singing** with the City Opera five years.

For more information on the use of tenses, see pp. 273–277.

Voice

Voice indicates whether the subject of the clause or sentence performs or receives the action of the transitive verb.

Active and passive voice

If the subject performs the action completed by an object, the verb and the clause are in the **active voice.** (See also pp. 112 and 157.)

The President **announced** his decision.

The journal **offers** insights into contemporary poetry.

Anxiety **can cause** a rise in blood pressure.

If the subject receives the action of the verb, that is, if the subject is acted upon, the verb and the clause are in the **passive voice.** The passive voice of a verb consists of a form of *be* followed by the past participle of the verb.

The decision **was announced** by the President.

Insights into contemporary poetry **are offered** by the journal.

A rise in blood pressure **can be caused** by anxiety.

The money **has been stolen** from the safe.

Many sentences written in the passive voice, like the first three preceding examples, contain a phrase beginning with the word *by.* This phrase usually tells who or what actually performed the action.

Mood

Mood refers to whether a verb expresses a statement, a command, a wish, an assumption, a recommendation, or a condition contrary to fact. In English there are three moods: the *indicative,* the *imperative,* and the *subjunctive.*

Indicative mood

The **indicative mood** is used to make a factual statement or to ask a question.

William Carlos Williams **lived** in Paterson, New Jersey.
Did William Carlos Williams live in Paterson, New Jersey?

Kublai Khan **was** the grandson of Genghis Khan.
Was Kublai Khan the grandson of Genghis Khan?

Forced from their land, the Cherokees **embarked** on the Trail of Tears.

Imperative mood

The **imperative mood** is used to express a command or a request. In a command, the subject *you* is often not stated, but understood.

Bring me the newspaper.

Come here!

Would you please **close** that door.

Subjunctive mood

The **subjunctive mood** is used to indicate a wish, an assumption, a recommendation, or a condition contrary to fact.

He wished he **were** rich. (*wish*)

If this **be** true, the validity of the collection is in doubt. (*assumption*)

It is mandatory that he **dress** appropriately. (*recommendation*)

If I **were** mayor, I would solve the problems of this city. (*condition contrary to fact*)

As you can see from these examples, the form of a verb in the subjunctive is often different from the indicative form. With most verbs the only difference is in the third-person singular form in the present tense, where the subjunctive does not have the final *s* of the indicative form.

INDICATIVE	SUBJUNCTIVE
he speaks	he speak
she manages	she manage
it works	it work

The subjunctive of the verb *to be* differs from the indicative in both the present and the past tenses.

PRESENT TENSE

INDICATIVE		SUBJUNCTIVE	
I am	we are	(if) I be	(if) we be
you are	you are	(if) you be	(if) you be
he/she/it is	they are	(if) he/she/it be	(if) they be

PAST TENSE

INDICATIVE		SUBJUNCTIVE	
I was	we were	(if) I were	(if) we were
you were	you were	(if) you were	(if) you were
he/she/it was	they were	(if) he/she/it were	(if) they were

The subjunctive appears to be falling into disuse. However, it is still preferred in writing for expressing a condition contrary to fact, and it is required in *that* clauses of recommendation, wish, or command and in a few idiomatic phrases.

If she **were** in command, we would not be having this problem.

In Kipling's tale, Danny wished that he **were** king.

He resolved that if need **be,** he would study night and day.

EXERCISE 9–2

Underline the verbs in the following sentences, circle their subjects, and name their tenses.

1. Most of us know that writing an essay is a process.

2. Writing well requires planning and revising.

3. Many of us have tried to shorten the process.

4. Some skip the prewriting activities or devote too little time to them.

5. Others decide that a first draft just needs editing.

6. These shortcuts most often result in inferior writing.

7. Did you ever confuse revising with editing?

8. Do you write an outline after you have written the essay?

9. Finding a topic does not constitute a major problem.

10. Allotting enough time for the writing process can be problematic.

9c Pronouns

A **pronoun** is a word that stands for or takes the place of one or more nouns. When a pronoun refers to a specific noun, that noun is called the **antecedent** of the pronoun. In the following sentences, the arrows indicate the *italicized* antecedents of the pronouns in **boldface** type.

Because *vitamins* can have toxic side effects, **they** should be administered with care.

Megadoses of *niacin,* **which** is a B vitamin, can cause nausea and vomiting.

A pronoun may also have another pronoun as an antecedent.

Most of the old records are scratched. **They** cannot be replaced.

Each of the mothers thought **her** child should receive the award.

Certain pronouns may lack a specific antecedent.

Who can understand the demands made upon a child prodigy?

Everyone knew that **something** was wrong.

There are seven categories of pronouns: *personal, demonstrative, indefinite, interrogative, relative, intensive,* and *reflexive.*

Personal pronouns

Personal pronouns take the place of a noun that names a person or a thing. Like nouns, personal pronouns have number, gender, and case. This means that they can be singular or plural; that they can be masculine, feminine, or neuter; and that they can function in the subjunctive, the objective, or the possessive case. (For more information about pronoun case, see pp. 246–253.) In addition, personal pronouns are divided into three "persons": **first-person pronouns** refer to the person(s) speaking or writing, **second-person pronouns** refer to the person(s) being spoken or written *to*, and **third-person pronouns** refer to the person(s) or thing(s) being spoken or written *about*. The following is a list of all the personal pronouns.

	SINGULAR	PLURAL
FIRST PERSON:	I, me, my, mine	we, us, our, ours
SECOND PERSON:	you, your, yours	you, your, yours
THIRD PERSON:	he, him, his	they, them, their, theirs
	she, her, hers	
	it, its	

Demonstrative pronouns

Demonstrative pronouns point to someone or something. The demonstrative pronouns are *this* and *that* and their plural forms *these* and *those*.

Demonstrative pronouns are usually used in place of a specific noun or noun phrase.

The sandwiches I ate yesterday were stale, but **these** are fresh.

The goddess of retributive justice was called Nemesis, and **this** is the word we use today to refer to an avenger or an unbeatable rival.

James named the character Mrs. Headway, for **that** was her chief characteristic, her ability to make headway.

In addition, demonstrative pronouns are sometimes used to refer to a whole idea.

> Should we welcome the electronic age? **That** is a good question.

> This is the challenge new sergeants face: finding ways to make recruits respect you, not just fear you.

If you use a demonstrative pronoun in this way, be sure that the idea it refers to is clearly stated and not just vaguely suggested (see pp. 241–244).

Indefinite pronouns

Indefinite pronouns do not take the place of a particular noun, although sometimes they have an implied antecedent. Indefinite pronouns carry the idea of "all," "some," "any," or "none." Some common indefinite pronouns are listed below.

everyone	somebody	anyone	no one
everything	many	anything	nobody

Some indefinite pronouns are plural, some are singular, and some can be either singular or plural.

> **Everything** *is* going according to plan. (*singular*)

> **Many** *were* certain that the war which officially started on July 28, 1914, would be over before autumn. (*plural*)

> **Some** of the material *was* useful. (*singular*)

> **Some** of the legislators *were* afraid to oppose the bill publicly. (*plural*)

For more information on the number of indefinite pronouns, see pp. 231–232.

Interrogative pronouns

Interrogative pronouns are used to ask a question.

who   whom   whose   what   which

Who, whom, and *whose* refer to people. *What* and *which* refer to things.

> **What** were the effects of the Industrial Revolution on Europe during the first decade of the twentieth century?
>
> **Who** is Barbara McClintock, and for **what** is she best known?
>
> **Which** of the economic depressions have been most damaging?

Relative pronouns

Relative pronouns are used to form adjective clauses and noun clauses (see pp. 196–200).

| who | whom | that | whoever | whichever |
| whose | which | what | whomever | whichever |

Who, whom, whoever, and *whomever* refer to people. *Which, what, that, whichever,* and *whatever* refer to things. *Whose* usually refers to people but can also refer to things.

> The Black Emergency Cultural Coalition is an organization **whose** members have dedicated themselves to the elimination of racism in the arts.
>
> Betye Saar's *The Liberation of Aunt Jemima,* **which** was purchased by the University Art Museum at Berkeley, is a multidimensional work **that** uses a collage of labels from pancake-mix boxes.
>
> The food was given away to **whoever** wanted it.

For more information about the relative pronouns, see pp. 231–233, 239–240, 251–253.

Intensive pronouns

Intensive pronouns are used to emphasize their antecedents. They are formed by adding -*self* or -*selves* to the end of a personal pronoun.

The detectives **themselves** did not know the solution.

The producer wasn't sure **herself** why the show was a success.

Reflexive pronouns

Reflexive pronouns are used to refer back to the subject of the clause or verbal phrase in which they appear. They have the same form as intensive pronouns.

During her illness Marjorie did not seem like **herself.**

If you have young children in the house, take precautions to prevent them from electrocuting **themselves** accidentally.

This plant can fertilize **itself.**

EXERCISE 9–3

In each of the following sentences, underline the pronoun and identify it as personal (P), demonstrative (D), indefinite (I), interrogative (?), relative (REL), intensive (INT), or reflexive (REF). If it has an antecedent, circle it.

1. Whatever you select will be fine with us.

2. Many women themselves are not aware of sex bias in their writings.

3. Those look very attractive; however, I prefer to purchase these.

4. To whom do you wish to speak and what is the nature of your visit?

5. Although almost everyone might like candy, I myself have never had a taste for it.

9d Adjectives

An **adjective** is a word that modifies, or describes, a noun or pronoun. It limits or makes clearer the meaning of the noun or pronoun.

The **efficient** *secretary* organized the schedule. (*modifies a noun*)

He is **efficient.** (*modifies a pronoun*)

The songs of George Gershwin were antidotes to the **psycho-logical** and **financial** *depression* of the 1930s. (*modify a noun*)

They are still **popular** though **their** *composer* died in 1937. (the first *modifies a pronoun*; the second *modifies a noun*)

An adjective modifies by answering one of three questions about the noun or pronoun. These questions are (1) "what kind?" (2) "how many?" and (3) "which one?"

By describing a quality or a condition, an adjective answers the question "what kind?"

The England of the Anglo-Saxons was not a **unified** *country*, but a land divided into **separate** *kingdoms*.

Much of the poetry of the Anglo-Saxons was in the **heroic** *tradition*.

The *riddles* in **Anglo-Saxon** *poetry* were **clever** and **humorous.**

By telling quantity, an adjective answers the question "how many?" This quantity may be definite (*one, twenty*) or indefinite (*several, few*).

When writing about literature, keep in mind **six** *features*: plot, characterization, setting, theme, point of view, and style.

The report listed **several** *reasons* for the decline of literacy.

He has **many** *questions* but **no** *answers.*

An adjective answers the question "which one?" by showing possession or by pointing out people or objects. Possessive forms of both nouns and pronouns may be considered adjectives (*girl's, his*), as may the demonstratives *this, these, that,* and *those* and the articles *a, an,* and *the.*

Bauhaus sought to correct **the** *alienation* of factory workers from **their** *products.*

Asplund's *buildings* revealed **the** *possibilities* of steel and glass.

These *artists* were interested in everything from designing glassware to planning factories.

Adjectives are characterized by several features.

1. Most adjectives have a comparative form to compare two things and a superlative form to compare three or more.

	COMPARATIVE	SUPERLATIVE
rich	richer	richest
beautiful	more beautiful	most beautiful
bad	worse	worst

Chocolate mousse is a **rich** dessert.
Chocolate mousse is a **richer** dessert than apple pie.
Chocolate mousse is the **richest** of the three desserts.

The roses are **beautiful.**
The roses are **more beautiful** than the hyacinths.
The roses are the **most beautiful** flowers in the garden.

(For information about the comparative and superlative forms of adjectives, see pp. 259-262.)

2. Adjectives can usually be identified by their position in a sentence. For example, an adjective will fit sensibly into one of the following blanks.

The _____ person was very _____.

The _____ object was removed.

It seems _____.

The woman, _____ and _____, left early.

3. The adverb *very* can usually be placed before an adjective.

The **very large** object was removed.

It seems **very odd.**

The woman, **very tired** and **very cold,** left early.

Articles, which include the words *a, an,* and *the,* are a special subclass of adjectives that lack the ability to form the comparative and superlative forms. Also known as **noun markers** or **noun determiners,** the articles always precede the noun they modify and serve to identify (*the*) and quantify (*a, an,* meaning "one"). Use *a* before a noun beginning with a consonant and *an* before a word beginning with a vowel.

| **a** pen | **an** apple | **a** historian |
| **the** pen | **the** apple | **the** historian |

9e Adverbs

An **adverb** is a word that modifies, or limits the meaning of, a verb, an adjective, or another adverb.

During the Harbor Festival, the tall ships *sailed* **gracefully** into the bay. (*modifies a verb*)

The exhibition of art from Pompeii drew **extremely** *large* crowds. (*modifies an adjective*)

The accident at Chernobyl demonstrated **very** *powerfully* the hazards of nuclear energy. (*modifies an adverb*)

An adverb modifies by answering one of the following questions: (1) "when?" (2) "where?" (3) "to what extent?" (4) "how?"

Adverbs of time

Adverbs of time answer the question "when?"

We *will discuss* the matter **then.**

Environmentalists warn that we *must* **eventually** *reach* an equilibrium with nature.

Photography *is* **now** *accorded* equal status with painting and sculpture.

Adverbs of place

Adverbs of place answer the question "where?"

As the ambassador traveled through the Middle East and North Africa, he *encountered* an Islamic revival **everywhere.**

Faith healers *look* **upward** and **inward** for cures for disease.

The ceremony *was held* **outdoors** to accommodate the large crowd.

Note that nouns can function as adverbs of time and place.

The symposium *was held* **yesterday.**

Registration *began* last **week.**

Some students *go* **home** nearly every **weekend.**

Adverbs of degree

Adverbs of degree answer the question "to what extent?" In addition, they are used to heighten, or intensify, the meaning of a verb, adjective, or adverb.

The Empire State Building is **far more** *beautiful* than the World Trade Center.

After paying her medical bills, she was left **almost** *destitute.*

In his films the **very** *talented* Charlie Chaplin was able to make people laugh at the absurdities of life.

Adverbs of manner

Adverbs of manner answer the question "how?" They tell in what manner or by what means an action was done.

Disaster films *were* **enthusiastically** *embraced* by the movie-going public.

The Beatles proved that rock music *had to be taken* **seriously.**

People *are* **strenuously** *debating* whether the lives of comatose patients *should be maintained* **artificially.**

Characterizing adverbs

Adverbs are characterized by two features.

1. Adverbs can be formed from many adjectives by adding the suffix *-ly* to the adjective. An additional spelling change is sometimes required.

   The artist's style was **delicate.** (*adjective*)
   The artist painted **delicately.** (*adverb*)

   The general's actions seemed **heroic.** (*adjective*)
   The general acted **heroically.** (*adverb*)

2. Most adverbs have comparative and superlative forms.

	COMPARATIVE	SUPERLATIVE
profoundly	more profoundly	most profoundly
fast	faster	fastest
well	better	best

The soprano is singing **well** today.
The soprano is singing **better** than she sang yesterday.
The soprano is singing the **best** she has in days.

The plight of the homeless is **profoundly** moving.
The plight of the homeless is **more profoundly** moving than I had imagined.
The plight of the homeless is the **most profoundly** moving story in the paper today.

(For more information about the comparative and superlative forms of adverbs, see pp. 259–262.)

EXERCISE 9–4

Identify, underline, and label the adjectives (AJ) and adverbs (AV) in each of the following sentences.

1. Over 3,500 languages are spoken on this planet.

2. Many of the languages have important common features and are grouped together as a language family.

3. Phonological (sound) variations can vary greatly within a language family, but syntactical differences appear to be less numerous.

4. Contemporary English is a descendant of an older form of the Germanic language family usually called Low West Germanic.

5. Our language has borrowed immensely from the vocabulary of more than 200 languages over the years.

9f Prepositions

across	during	near	toward
below	from	on	with

The preceding words are **prepositions,** which are words used to show the relationship of a noun or a pronoun, called the *object of the preposition,* to another part of the sentence. The preposition and its object and any modifiers of the object *(the prepositional phrase)* then function in the sentence as adjective, adverb, or, occasionally, noun. Prepositions are among the most familiar and frequently used words in the language because they orient things in time and space. Some common ones are listed here.

COMMON PREPOSITIONS

about	concerning	past
above	despite	save (meaning
across	down	"except")
after	during	since
against	except	through
along	for	throughout
among	from	till
around	in	to
at	inside	toward(s)
before	into	under
behind	like	underneath
below	near	until
beneath	of	unto
beside	off	up
between	on	upon
beyond	onto	with
but (meaning	out	within
"except")	over	without

A **compound preposition** is made up of more than one word. The following are some commonly used compound prepositions.

ahead of	in addition to	on account of
as for	in back of	on top of
as well as	in case of	out of
because of	in front of	together with
by means of	instead of	with regard to

Prepositions appear only in and at the beginning of prepositional phrases. In the following sentences, the prepositions are printed in **boldface** and the prepositional phrases in *italics*.

> The term "metaphysical poets" was coined **by** *Samuel Johnson* **in** *the eighteenth century.*

> Metaphysical poets wrote **about** *human love* **in addition to** *religious love.*

> Often they used language normally associated **with** *human love* to describe their love **of** *God* and religious images to explain their love **for** *other human beings.*

Note: The *to* in the infinitive form of the verb (such as *to describe*) is not a preposition. (For more information on prepositional phrases, see pp. 105–106, 192–193, 342.)

EXERCISE 9–5

Identify the prepositions in each of the following sentences by underlining them.

1. Being in solitude often allows an individual an escape from the pressures in addition to the influences exerted by others.

2. In solitude an individual can forget about life in society for a while.

3. Instead of being in crowds all the time, we need time for ourselves.

4. Some find solitude by means of going to the lake shore on clear or even cloudy nights where the sounds of waves lapping at the beach repeat their cadence between steady rhythms.

5. For many people such experiences provide a relief from everyday pressures in many different ways despite the demands upon us.

9g Conjunctions

and   if   until   but   or   when

The preceding words are **conjunctions,** which are words used to join other words, phrases, clauses, or sentences. There are three types of conjunctions: *coordinating conjunctions, correlative conjunctions,* and *subordinating conjunctions.*

Coordinating conjunctions

A **coordinating conjunction** joins elements of equal grammatical rank. These elements may be single words, phrases, or clauses. The common coordinating conjunctions are:

and   or   for   yet   but   so   nor

In the following sentences, the coordinating conjunctions are printed in **boldface** and the elements being joined in *italics.*

> The children of *Queen Victoria* **and** *Prince Albert* married into many of the other ruling houses of Europe.

> *Some enjoy Matthew Arnold primarily for his poetry,* **but** *others respect him more for his criticism.*

> The flax is then soaked *in tanks, in streams,* **or** *in pools.*

Conjunctive adverbs

Words like the following, called **conjunctive adverbs,** may make clear the connection between *independent clauses* (clauses that can stand by themselves as sentences), but they cannot—as conjunctions can—join the clauses.

accordingly	hence	otherwise
also	however	still
besides	moreover	therefore
consequently	nevertheless	thus
furthermore		

In the following sentences, the conjunctive adverbs are in **boldface** and the independent clauses in *italics.* Notice that a semicolon precedes a conjunctive adverb that appears between independent clauses.

> *She wanted to photograph the building in the early morning light;* **therefore,** *she got up at dawn on Saturday.*

> *For years the elderly have moved from the North to Florida to retire;* **however,** *today many are returning to the North to be near their children.*

> *William Morris was a noted painter, weaver, and pattern maker;* **moreover,** *he was a respected poet, novelist, and critic.*

Correlative conjunctions

Correlative conjunctions are coordinating conjunctions that are used in pairs. The most common correlative conjunctions are these:

both . . . and	not only . . . but also
either . . . or	whether . . . or
neither . . . nor	

In the following sentences, the correlative conjunctions are in **boldface.**

Whether you go **or** stay makes no difference to us.

Both diet **and** exercise are necessary for losing weight.

Either the festival will be a success, **or** the city will have wasted taxpayers' money.

Subordinating conjunctions

Subordinating conjunctions join subordinate, or dependent, clauses to main, or independent, clauses. The following are some common subordinating conjunctions:

after	if	than
although, though	in order that	that
as	in that	unless
as if	inasmuch as	until
as long as	now that	when
as much as	once	where
because	provided that	whereas
before	since	wherever
even though	so long as	while
how	so that	whether

A clause that is structurally independent, that can stand by itself, is called an *independent clause*. A clause that is structurally dependent, that cannot stand by itself, is called a *dependent clause*. A subordinating conjunction is used at the beginning of a dependent clause to show the relation between this clause and the independent clause to which it is attached. In the following sentences, the subordinating conjunction is printed in **boldface** and the dependent clause in *italics*.

> The tepee was an improvement over the traditional tent, **because** *it had a smoke hole at the top.*

> **When** *a chief died,* his heir erected a totem pole to honor him.

> **Although** *the Japan Current makes winters in the Pacific Northwest mild,* it brings with it much rain.

(For more information on clauses, see pp. 103–105, 196–200, 338–340.)

EXERCISE 9–6

Underline the conjunctions in each of the following sentences, then label each as a coordinating (CO), a correlative (COR), or a subordinating conjunction (SUB).

1. Neither rain nor sleet nor hail nor snow is said to deter the delivery of mail in this country.

2. But it often seems that a missing stamp or illegible handwriting can.

3. The technology for sorting the mail has advanced; however, we still depend on people to deliver our mail although they may do so in vehicles.

4. Have you noticed that more and more women are employed as deliverers of mail but more men are administrators than women?

5. Working in the postal service appeals to many because of the benefits for employees.

9h Interjections

> Oh!   Wow!   Great!   Ouch!   Drat!   Whew!

The preceding words are **interjections,** words that express emotion. Grammatically, an interjection has no connection to the rest of the sentence or fragment in which it appears. In the following sentences, the interjections are in **boldface.**

> **Ouch!** I burned my finger.   The rescuers, **alas,** arrived too late.
> **Well,** there it is.   **What,** no kosher pizza?
> **Curses!** Foiled again!   **Ah,** what a life!

Interjections are used much more in speech than in writing, where they are used mostly in dialogue. An interjection may be followed by an exclamation mark or by a comma. An exclamation mark indicates a strong emotional response; a comma indicates a milder response.

9i Verbals

A **verbal** is not a "part of speech." Rather it is a grammatical form that is derived from a verb but does not function as a verb in a sentence. A verbal functions as a noun, an adjective, or an adverb. There are three types of verbals: *participles, gerunds,* and *infinitives.*

Participles

The **present participle** and the **past participle** of most verbs can be used as adjectives. (For information on how participles are formed, see p. 162.)

> A **dancing** bear is an image associated with Theodore Roethke.
>
> The peace between the two wars has been compared to a **held** breath.
>
> Countee Cullen used the image of **bursting** fruit as a symbol of abundance and fecundity.
>
> He prefers **iced** tea.

Gerunds

A **gerund** is a verb form that is spelled in the same way as the present participle, with an -*ing* ending, but a gerund is used as a noun, not an adjective, in a sentence.

> The problems of **parenting** were discussed at the symposium.
>
> The school taught **reading** and **writing** but little else.
>
> **Exercising** can help relieve stress.

Infinitives

The present infinitive and the present perfect infinitive of a verb can be used as a noun, an adjective, or an adverb. The **present infinitive** is the *to* form of the verb (e.g., *to go*); the **present perfect infinitive** is the *to have* form (e.g., *to have gone*).

> She wanted **to resign** at first but finally decided **to stay.** (*nouns*)
>
> *King Lear* is considered a difficult play **to stage.** (*adjective*)
>
> What he wanted most was someone **to love.** (*adjective*)

By the end of the day I was ready **to scream.** (*adjective*)

They were sorry **to have left** before you arrived. (*adjective*)

Sometimes the word *to* in the infinitive is understood rather than stated.

Therapists must help their patients cope with life's problems.

Therapists must help their patients **to** cope with life's problems.

Writers occasionally **split infinitives** by inserting words or phrases between the word *to* and the verb. In the following sentences, the infinitive is in **boldface** and the word that splits the infinitive is in *italics*.

To *exactly* **know.**

To *truly* **have known.**

Revise such awkward constructions to eliminate the split. Although recommendations on the use of split infinitives vary, it is best to avoid using them in formal writing.

EXERCISE 9–7

Circle the verbals in the following sentences and identify each verbal as a participle (P), a gerund (G), or an infinitive (I).

1. Should state governments be allowed to regulate the arts?

2. Do most people believe that listening, seeing, or hearing is the same thing as doing?

3. Labeling recordings with *parental advisory* warnings may actually help to boost the sales of such recordings.

4. Analyzing the effects of such warnings on purchases has not yet revealed an impact on sales.

5. Depending on where one lives, sales of certain recordings may be prohibited unless labeled.

10 Phrases

A **phrase** is a group of words that does not contain a subject and a predicate but which functions as a single part of speech. There are several types of phrases. This section discusses *prepositional phrases* and *verbal phrases*.

10a Prepositional Phrases

A **prepositional phrase** consists of a preposition, the object of the preposition, and all the words modifying this object. In the following sentences, the prepositional phrases are in **boldface** and the prepositions and their objects in ***boldface italics***.

> ***In* many *cultures*** whale meat has been an essential source ***of protein.***

> Some ***of* these cultural *groups*** resent efforts ***by conservationists*** to protect the whale, since these efforts would restrict the group's ability to obtain food and would conflict ***with* its *traditions.***

Conservationists, however, argue that the whale is an intelligent creature ***about which*** we know far too little and that if these creatures are not protected, they will disappear ***from the earth.***

Note: The word *to* with the infinitive (e.g., *to obtain*) is not a preposition and does not introduce a prepositional phrase.

Usually a prepositional phrase functions as an adjective or an adverb. Occasionally it may act as a noun.

> The *computer* **for the home** may become as common as the typewriter. (*adjective*)

> The phrase "fruit *fresh* **from the farm**" has become quite *popular* **in merchandising circles.** (*adverbs*)

> She wrote the book only **for the money.** (*noun*)

10b Verbal Phrases

A **verbal phrase** consists of a verbal and all its complements and modifiers. (To review verbals, see pp. 106 and 189–191.) There are three types of verbal phrases: *participial phrases, gerund phrases,* and *infinitive phrases.*

Participial phrases

A **participial phrase** consists of a present or past participle and all its modifiers and complements. It acts as an adjective in a sentence. In the following sentences, the participial phrases are in **boldface** with the participles in ***boldface italics.***

> Throughout his life, Whitman adhered to the beliefs ***summarized* in the preface of *Leaves of Grass.***

A man *curled* **in the fetal position** with his arm *covering* **his head** is the subject of one of Rodin's most moving sculptures.

Serenity is the chief quality *embodied* **in the pottery of Jade Snow Wong.**

Absolute phrases

A participle modifying its own subject instead of a noun or noun substitute in the sentence creates an **absolute phrase.** An absolute phrase must be set off from its sentence by a comma.

Their voices *raised* in song, the settlers rode out of sight.

The wind *having disappeared*, the boat drifted idly with the current, **sails *hanging* limp, the passengers *complaining* but *refusing* to touch the oars.**

Gerund phrases

A **gerund phrase** consists of a gerund and all its modifiers and complements. A gerund phrase acts as a noun in a sentence. In the following sentences, the gerund phrases are in **boldface** with the gerunds in ***boldface italics.***

For Freud, ***remaining* in Vienna** became impossible once the Nazi forces invaded Austria in 1938.

Today we use the term *sadist* loosely to mean any person who enjoys ***inflicting* pain.**

***Running* five miles a day** keeps a person in good condition.

Infinitive phrases

An **infinitive phrase** consists of the present infinitive or the present perfect infinitive form of the verb and all its modifiers and complements. It acts as a noun, an adjective, or an adverb. In the following sentences, the infinitive phrases are in **boldface** with the infinitives in ***boldface italics.***

>*To be* **a pilot on the Mississippi** was young Sam Clemens's dream. (*noun*)

>*To know* **him** is *to love* **him.** (*nouns*)

>Hard work is one way *to gain* **success in business.** (*adjective*)

>She is proud *to have dedicated* **her life to music.** (*adverb*)

EXERCISE 10–1

Underline all the prepositional phrases in the following sentences. Bracket each verbal phrase.

1. Constituting a formidable threat in this country, the AIDS virus, although preventable, continues to spread at an alarming rate.

2. Voluntary testing for the AIDS virus has become more widespread in many areas.

3. Practically without exception, public health officials, maintaining confidentiality on testing results, have succeeded in winning the confidence of frightened people.

4. Their voices raised in protest, many candidates for public office do not favor mandatory AIDS testing of people by insurance companies.

5. Testing people for AIDS and counseling those who are HIV-positive can be life-saving measures.

11   Clauses

A **clause** is a group of words with a subject and a predicate. A clause may be *independent* or *dependent*.

11a Independent Clauses and Coordination

An **independent clause** is a group of words with a subject and a predicate that expresses a complete thought. In other words, an independent clause is structurally independent and can stand by itself as a simple sentence.

> The Spanish conquistadors heard the legend of El Dorado, the Man of Gold.
>
> The bottom of the lake was encrusted with gold.
>
> Some soldiers of fortune traveled down the Amazon.

Coordination

Coordination occurs when two or more independent clauses are joined together with a coordinating conjunction. In the following sentence, the independent clauses appear in *italics* and the coordinating conjunction in **boldface.**

> *The football game ended at dusk,* **and** *all the local restaurants were crowded for three hours afterwards.*

11b Dependent Clauses and Subordination

A **dependent clause** is a group of words with a subject and a predicate. Dependent clauses cannot stand by themselves as sentences; they must be attached to or be part of an independent clause. They are often called *subordinate* clauses because they are structurally subordinate to the independent clause. Usually, a dependent clause begins with a subordinating word, which may be a subordinating conjunction or a relative pronoun. There are three types of dependent clauses—*adjective, adverb,* and *noun clauses.*

Subordination

Subordination occurs when a dependent clause, which cannot stand alone, is attached to an independent clause with a subordinating conjunction. In the following sentence, the independent clause appears in **boldface** and the subordinate clause in *italics.*

> *Because the football game ended at dusk,* **all the local restaurants were crowded for three hours.**

Adjective clauses

An **adjective clause,** or **relative clause,** functions as an adjective and modifies a noun or pronoun. Usually, an adjective clause begins with a relative pronoun: *who, whose, whom, that,* or *which.*

> Jazz is a musical *form* **that originated among black Americans.**

> *Charlie Parker,* **who was known as Bird,** played for a while with the Billy Eckstine band.

> Jazz critics have extolled *John Coltrane,* **whose penetrating, raspy sound has been imitated by many other players.**

> *Jazz,* **which began as an American art form,** is being internationalized by players such as the Argentinean Gato Barbieri.

In the first sentence in the preceding examples, the subject of the adjective clause is *that,* and the simple predicate is *originated.* In the second sentence, the subject of the adjective clause is *who,* and the simple predicate is *was known.* In the third sentence, the subject of the adjective clause is *sound,* and the simple predicate is *has been imitated.* In the fourth sentence, the subject of the adjective clause is *which,* and the simple predicate is *began.*

An adjective clause also can begin with a relative adverb—*when, where, why.*

The *shop* **where I bought the bracelet** is near here.

The old man told of a *time* **when the stars fell.**

The *reason* **why he acted** is unclear.

Sometimes an adjective clause modifies the entire idea expressed in the preceding clause.

On her birthday, John asked Susan to marry him, **which made her very happy.**

Adverb clauses

An **adverb clause** functions as an adverb in a sentence. It usually modifies the verb in another clause but sometimes modifies an adjective, an adverb, or an entire sentence. An adverb clause usually begins with a subordinating conjunction that shows the relation of the adverb clause to the word or words it modifies. (To review subordinating conjunctions, turn to p. 187.)

The grandfather clock *experienced* renewed popularity **after Henry Clay Works published his song "My Grandfather's Clock."** (*modifies the verb* experienced)

Because hash is an inexpensive meal, Americans *call* any cheap restaurant a hash house. (*modifies the verb* call)

Is the Golden Gate Bridge as *long* **as the Verrazano Bridge is?** (*modifies the adjective* long)

She speaks *more persuasively* **than I do.** (*modifies the comparative adverb* more persuasively)

Sometimes an adverb clause is elliptical, or incomplete, with the verb omitted but understood.

Is the Golden Gate Bridge **as long as the Verrazano Bridge** (is)?

She speaks more persuasively **than I** (speak).

(For information on using commas with adverb clauses, see pp. 344–345, 349, 353–354.)

Noun clauses

A **noun clause** acts as a noun in a sentence. In other words, it can function as a subject, an object, or a predicate nominative. Usually, a noun clause begins with one of the following subordinating words: *that, how, what, whatever, whenever, wherever, whichever, who, whoever, whose, why.*

That she would run for President seemed a certainty. (*subject*)

The book explains **why the United States refused to join the League of Nations.** (*direct object*)

His home is **wherever he stops his car for the night.** (*predicate nominative*)

EXERCISE 11-1

Bracket each dependent clause in the following sentences, and locate the subject (S) and verb (V) in each. Identify each dependent clause as an adjective clause (AJ), an adverb clause (AV), or a noun clause (NC).

1. Whenever one thinks of American classical music, the name of Leonard Bernstein comes to mind.

2. Because of his experience in conducting, composing, playing the piano, and teaching, Bernstein, who lived in New York, was considered a very significant musical celebrity.

3. Having attended the Boston Latin School, Bernstein graduated from Harvard, becoming, in 1943, assistant conductor of the New York Philharmonic Orchestra.

4. When Bernstein assumed the conductorship of the orchestra in 1958, he was the first native-born American to be named its music director, establishing another uniqueness in his career.

5. Although Bernstein enjoyed success as a pianist and composer, he also achieved acclaim when he narrated television programs featuring classical music.

12   Kinds of Sentences

Sentences can be classified into four basic groups according to the number and kinds of clauses they contain. These four basic types are *simple, compound, complex,* and *compound-complex sentences.*

12a Simple Sentences

A **simple sentence** contains only one independent clause and no dependent clause.

Hokusai and Kunisada are two important Japanese artists.

Sacajawea, a Shoshone Indian, worked as a guide and an interpreter on the Lewis and Clark expedition.

According to most authorities, Tutankhamen became pharaoh in 1361 BC and died in 1352 BC.

12b Compound Sentences

A **compound sentence** contains two or more independent clauses and no dependent clause.

The goddess Eos granted Tithonus his request for immortality, but he forgot to ask for eternal youth.

During the Crimean War, Florence Nightingale was appalled by the unsanitary conditions in British army hospitals; therefore, she introduced strict standards of cleanliness.

First dice the celery; then peel and chop the onion; next brown the meat in a frying pan.

12c Complex Sentences

A **complex sentence** contains one independent clause and one or more dependent clauses.

> Nihilists advocated the violent overthrow of all existing governments, but anarchists originally advocated freedom from governmental control through nonviolent evolution.

> After the museum bought one of his paintings, Cortez was interviewed on a local cable program.

> Because it is noted for its ability to weave intricate webs, the spider is a fitting symbol for the storyteller, or spinner of tales.

12d Compound-Complex Sentences

A **compound-complex sentence** contains two or more independent clauses and one or more dependent clauses.

> Unfortunately, the danger of crime in the cities is a bleak reality; therefore, some couples with small children choose to move to the suburbs, where they believe they can raise their children in safety.

> A group of painters called "neorealists" is turning back to representational styles, and the mass public, which never quite embraced abstract art, is responding enthusiastically to these artists' work.

> In the last twenty years, medicine has made major advances; doctors, for example, now perform bone-marrow transplants, procedures which, though risky, offer new hope to patients whose diseases were once considered terminal.

EXERCISE 12–1

Identify each of the following sentences as simple (SI), compound (CD), complex (CX), or compound-complex (CC). Underline the simple subject (S) and the simple predicate (P) of each.

1. Faced with both a shrinking student population and rising costs, many colleges and universities across the country are simultaneously attempting to raise more money and cut budgets.

2. Because colleges need to concentrate their funds, some deans are cutting budgets by eliminating entire academic departments.

3. Some colleges have hired strategic planners; others have contracted out their food service operations to cut back costs.

4. Because investments have stopped their rapid rise, schools no longer expect huge monetary returns on their endowments; however, some continue to expand their enrollments, although the majority do not.

5. The combination of deep budget cuts and five-figure tuition costs at some private colleges may force students to the less expensive public sector.

PART III

SENTENCE FORM

To write a good sentence, it is not enough to have a good idea. You have to express your idea in a form that your readers will understand. The form of a sentence has to follow certain conventions, traditional guidelines that are generally understood and accepted. The conventions of written English are much like rules of etiquette; they are essential for helping people to communicate clearly and effectively with one another. In fact, you know most of these conventions so well that you follow them without even thinking about them. Some, however, you may. need to review.

Sentence Fragments

Use sentence fragments judiciously. For formal writing avoid using them except in special situations.

A **sentence fragment** is an incomplete sentence punctuated as if it were a complete sentence. A sentence fragment lacks a subject, a predicate, or both or is a subordinate clause presented as if it were a sentence.

13a Fragments Lacking a Subject

Avoid punctuating as a sentence a group of words that lacks a subject.

To eliminate a sentence fragment lacking a subject, simply add a subject to this group of words or connect it to another sentence containing its subject.

NOT: Went dancing last night.

BUT: I went dancing last night.

NOT: Jean Rhys was born in the West Indies. And evoked the magic of these islands in *Wild Sargasso Sea.*

BUT: Jean Rhys was born in the West Indies and evoked the magic of these islands in *Wild Sargasso Sea.*

NOT: American public opinion became sharply divided. Most Americans had considered World War II a just war. Were willing to give their lives for their country. But many came to think Vietnam was an unjust war. And were repelled by the slaughter of their sons.

BUT: American public opinion became sharply divided. Most Americans had considered World War II a just war and were willing to give their lives for their country. But many came to think Vietnam was an unjust war and were repelled by the slaughter of their sons.

13b Fragments Lacking a Predicate

Avoid punctuating as a sentence a group of words that lacks a predicate.

A predicate must be a finite, or complete, verb. Some verb forms require an auxiliary verb or a modal in order to be finite. (To review auxiliary words and modals, see pp. 161–163.)

To eliminate a sentence fragment that lacks a predicate, add a finite verb or an auxiliary verb or modal to make the verb finite, or connect the fragment to another sentence that contains its verb.

NOT: People of many different nationalities together on the same block.

BUT: People of many different nationalities live together on the same block.

NOT: The sun rising over the rooftops.

BUT: The sun was rising over the rooftops.

NOT: The alumni already given millions of dollars for the new library.

BUT: The alumni have already given millions of dollars for the new library.

NOT: In the early twentieth century, Paris was the undisputed cultural capital of the Western world. At one point, for example, Aaron Copland, one of the foremost composers of our age, Tristan Tzara, a leading Dadaist, and James Joyce, the author of *Ulysses*, all living in Paris.

BUT: In the early twentieth century, Paris was the undisputed cultural capital of the Western world. At one point, for example, Aaron Copland, one of the foremost composers of our age, Tristan Tzara, a leading Dadaist, and James Joyce, the author of *Ulysses*, were all living in Paris.

NOT: In the back of the theater were standing-room-only ticket holders. And latecomers impatient for their seats.

BUT: In the back of the theater were standing-room-only ticket holders and latecomers impatient for their seats.

13c Phrase Fragments

Avoid punctuating a phrase as a sentence.

To eliminate a phrase fragment, simply make it part of an independent clause.

NOT: We swerved when we saw the deer. Running across the highway.

BUT: We swerved when we saw the deer running across the highway.

NOT: The professor rode with two officers in their squad car for six weeks. To learn about police work firsthand.

BUT:	To learn about police work firsthand, the professor rode with two officers in their squad car for six weeks.
NOT:	The highlight of the show was appearances by several guest stars. Cho Liu, for example, one of the country's finest ballerinas.
BUT:	The highlight of the show was appearances by several guest stars—Cho Liu, for example, one of the country's finest ballerinas.
NOT:	Because of public opposition. The city refused to grant permission. For a skyscraper to be built on the site of the church.
BUT:	Because of public opposition, the city refused to grant permission for a skyscraper to be built on the site of the church.
NOT:	Computer manufacturers use various gimmicks to attract users. In order to appeal to children. This writing program features a turtle. Instead of the ordinary cursor.
BUT:	Computer manufacturers use various gimmicks to attract users. In order to appeal to children, this writing program features a turtle instead of the ordinary cursor.

13d Dependent Clause Fragments

Avoid punctuating a dependent clause as a sentence.

A dependent clause usually begins with a subordinating word, which may be a subordinating conjunction or a relative pronoun. (To review dependent clauses, see pp. 196–200.)

One way to eliminate a dependent clause fragment is to remove the subordinating word. Another way is to connect the dependent clause to an independent clause.

NOT:	Because Charlene was fluent in French.
BUT:	Charlene was fluent in French.

NOT: Before Harrison wrote his term paper. He prepared an outline.

BUT: Before Harrison wrote his term paper, he prepared an outline.

NOT: Harold Macmillan felt it imperative for Britain to develop a firm relationship with de Gaulle. Even though the United States opposed official recognition of him.

BUT: Harold Macmillan felt it imperative for Britain to develop a firm relationship with de Gaulle, even though the United States opposed official recognition of him.

NOT: Although John Muir is often pictured as a genial and perhaps somewhat innocent nature guide. He was actually a shrewd, strong-willed, thoughtful man. Who was an effective political lobbyist for conservation.

BUT: Although John Muir is often pictured as a genial and perhaps somewhat innocent nature guide, he was actually a shrewd, strong-willed, thoughtful man who was an effective political lobbyist for conservation.

NOT: Since he was avidly interested in Holmesiana. He decided to apply for membership in the Baker Street Irregulars. Where he would be able to enjoy the company of other Sherlock Holmes enthusiasts.

BUT: Since he was avidly interested in Holmesiana, he decided to apply for membership in the Baker Street Irregulars, where he would be able to enjoy the company of other Sherlock Holmes enthusiasts.

EXERCISE 13-1

Revise the following items to eliminate any sentence fragments. One of the items contains no fragments.

1. I am no longer willing to go. Unless you also agree.

2. Where did you place the book? Over there?

3. Not long ago television in color was a rarity.

4. Through the cold and misty night. The race continued around the lake.

5. Placing the restaurant on top of the building. The view was magnificent.

13e Intentional Fragments

We use fragments often, especially in speech. We see them in advertising and in newspapers and magazines. In formal writing, they can be used appropriately, but only occasionally, to ask and answer questions and to emphasize a point, to record exclamations in dialogue, and to provide transition between ideas. Note the use of fragments in the following passages by professional writers. (The fragments are printed in *italics.*)

> There has been a flood of new studies of the Wild Child: historical, literary, psychological. The story is still evocative, "good to think with." But there is something new. There is a new focus for a forbidden experiment. A *new mind that is not yet a mind. A new object, betwixt and between, equally shrouded in superstition as well as science.* This is the computer.
>
> **Sherry Turkle**

> Hating to ask questions and never trusting the answers has defined the type of reporting I do. What I do is hang around. *Become part of the furniture. An end table in someone's life.* It is the art of the scavenger: set a scene, establish a mood, get the speech patterns right. What matters is that the subject bites his nails, what matters is that he wears brown shoes with a

> blue suit, what matters is the egg stain on his tie, the Reader's Digest Condensed Books on the shelves, the copy of *Playboy* with the centerfold torn out.
>
> John Gregory Dunne

As you can see from these passages, fragments can be used effectively in formal writing. However, unless you have a well-thought-out reason for using fragments, avoid them in formal writing and consult your instructor before using them.

14 Comma Splices and Fused Sentences

Separate sentences correctly from one another.

A **run-on sentence** occurs when two or more complete sentences are written as though they were one sentence. Two types of errors result in a run-on sentence: *comma splices* and *fused sentences.*

14a Comma Splices

Avoid separating two independent clauses with only a comma, unless the clauses are very short and closely related.

A comma is sometimes used between clauses of two or three words, especially if the clauses are in parallel grammatical form.

> One sings, the other dances.
>
> The grass withers, the flowers fade.

In general, however, using only a comma between two independent clauses is considered a serious grammatical error called a **comma splice.**

> **NOT:** Researchers are attempting to program robots to see, this procedure is much more complicated than you might expect.
>
> **BUT:** Researchers are attempting to program robots to see. This procedure is much more complicated than you might expect.
>
> **OR:** Researchers are attempting to program robots to see, but this procedure is much more complicated than you might expect.

> **NOT:** Some monasteries during the Middle Ages had fine libraries, in these libraries monks copied and illuminated manuscripts.
>
> **BUT:** Some monasteries during the Middle Ages had fine libraries; in these libraries monks copied and illuminated manuscripts.
>
> **OR:** Some monasteries during the Middle Ages had fine libraries, in which monks copied and illuminated manuscripts.

A comma splice also occurs when a comma (instead of a semicolon) is used between two independent clauses joined by a transitional phrase or conjunctive adverb (in **boldface**).

> **NOT:** The exhibit at the museum was well reviewed and well promoted, **consequently,** there were long lines for tickets.
>
> **BUT:** The exhibit at the museum was well reviewed and well promoted; **consequently,** there were long lines for tickets.

> **NOT:** When the smoke alarm sounded in the middle of the night, Melissa jumped out of bed and rushed to get her family out of the house, **in the meantime,** her neighbor called the fire department.

BUT: When the smoke alarm sounded in the middle of the night, Melissa jumped out of bed and rushed to get her family out of the house; **in the meantime,** her neighbor called the fire department.

14b Fused Sentences

Avoid writing two independent clauses without any punctuation between them.

This error is called a **fused sentence.**

NOT: The school was closed because of the snowstorm not knowing this, some students showed up for classes.

BUT: The school was closed because of the snowstorm. Not knowing this, some students showed up for classes.

OR: Not knowing that the school was closed because of the snowstorm, some students showed up for classes.

NOT: First boil the squash until it is tender then cut it open and scoop out its insides.

BUT: First boil the squash until it is tender; then cut it open and scoop out its insides.

OR: First boil the squash until it is tender, and then cut it open and scoop out its insides.

Although there are many ways of correcting run-on sentences, these are the four most common:

1. Make two sentences by adding a period at the end of the first clause and capitalizing the first word of the second clause.

   NOT: Doctors are again using leeches these creatures can prevent the problem of clotting that occurs after reattachment surgery.

BUT: Doctors are again using leeches. These creatures can prevent the problem of clotting that occurs after reattachment surgery.

2. Add a coordinating conjunction between the two clauses. Place a comma before the coordinating conjunction, unless the two clauses are very short.

NOT: Maria washed the car Carlos mowed the lawn.
BUT: Maria washed the car **and** Carlos mowed the lawn.

3. Rewrite one of the independent clauses as a dependent clause.

NOT: The cat wanted her breakfast she mewed loudly at the foot of the bed.
BUT: **When** the cat wanted her breakfast she mewed loudly at the foot of the bed.

4. If the two clauses are closely related, place a semicolon between them.

NOT: Cindy found the movie disappointing Lee thought it was wonderful.
BUT: Cindy found the movie disappointing; Lee thought it was wonderful.

EXERCISE 14-1

Eliminate the run-on sentence in each of the following items. Identify the error as a comma splice (CS) or a fused sentence (FS).

1. The billowing smoke burned my eyes, I realized the engine was overheated.

2. A crate of oranges fell to the street the children all ran toward it.

3. African bees originally imported to Brazil arrived in Mexico in 1986, they now are a threat to Texans.

4. Some cities recently banned cigarette vending machines it makes it harder for children to purchase cigarettes.

5. A Navajo reservation spreads for 17 million acres over Arizona, Utah, and New Mexico oil, gas, and coal reserves are found there as well as shopping centers.

EXERCISE 14-2

Eliminate the fragments and run-on sentences in each of the following items.

1. "Harassment" means "to trouble, worry, or torment someone" it comes from a French word that means "to set a dog on."

2. Harassment can be physical and verbal. Also sexual.

3. The results of physical harassment are easily seen the results of verbal harassment are harder to detect.

4. Because the verbal harassment can be sexual. Women are most often the victims.

5. Confronting the harasser is a way to stop it, people differ on the prevention strategies.

15   Verb Forms

15a Present Infinitive, Past Tense, Past Participle, and Present Participle

Use the appropriate form of the verb.

English verbs have four principal parts, or forms: present infinitive, past tense form, past participle, and present participle. The **present infinitive** is the base form of the verb, the form that appears in the dictionary. Regular verbs add *-ed* or *-d* to their present infinitive to form the **past tense** and **past participle.**

paint	painted	cook	cooked
dance	danced	slice	sliced

Irregular verbs form their past tense and past participle in a variety of other ways.

PRESENT INFINITIVE	PAST TENSE	PAST PARTICIPLE
begin	began	begun
catch	caught	caught
draw	drew	drawn
put	put	put
sing	sang	sung

You can use a dictionary to find the principal parts of a verb. In most dictionaries, after the abbreviation *v.* or at the end of

the definitions for the verb, the entry gives the principal parts
and the third-person singular present-tense form of the verb.
When the past tense and past participle are the same, the entry
lists only three forms of the verb. When the past tense and past
participle are different, the entry lists four forms.

The fourth form is called the **present participle,** always
formed by adding -*ing* to the infinitive (see p. 162).

> **dance** (dăns) *v.:* **danced, dancing, dances**
>
> **be•gin** (bĭ-gĭn′) *v.:* **began, begun, beginning, begins**
>
> **draw** (drô) *v.:* **drew, drawn, drawing, draws**

Most people have few problems using the proper forms of
regular verbs. Many, however, do have problems with the past
tense and past participle of irregular verbs. A list of common irregular verbs follows.

IRREGULAR VERBS

PRESENT INFINITIVE	PAST TENSE	PAST PARTICIPLE
arise	arose	arisen
awake	awoke	awaked
be	was, were	been
bear	bore	born (borne)
become	became	become
begin	began	begun
bind	bound	bound
bite	bit	bitten
blow	blew	blown
break	broke	broken
bring	brought	brought
build	built	built

PRESENT INFINITIVE	PAST TENSE	PAST PARTICIPLE
burst	burst	burst
cast	cast	cast
catch	caught	caught
choose	chose	chosen
cling	clung	clung
come	came	come
creep	crept	crept
deal	dealt	dealt
dig	dug	dug
dive	dived, dove	dived
do	did	done
drag	dragged	dragged
draw	drew	drawn
drink	drank	drunk
drive	drove	driven
eat	ate	eaten
fall	fell	fallen
feel	felt	felt
flee	fled	fled
fling	flung	flung
fly	flew	flown
forbid	forbade, forbad	forbidden
forget	forgot	forgotten, forgot
forgive	forgave	forgiven
freeze	froze	frozen
get	got	got, gotten
give	gave	given
go	went	gone
grow	grew	grown
hang (objects)	hung	hung
hang (people)	hanged	hanged
have	had	had
hit	hit	hit

PRESENT INFINITIVE	**PAST TENSE**	**PAST PARTICIPLE**
know	knew	known
lay	laid	laid
lead	led	led
lend	lent	lent
lie	lay	lain
lose	lost	lost
mean	meant	meant
pay	paid	paid
prove	proved	proved, proven
put	put	put
ride	rode	ridden
ring	rang	rung
rise	rose	risen
run	ran	run
say	said	said
see	saw	seen
seek	sought	sought
send	sent	sent
set	set	set
shake	shook	shaken
shine (give light)	shone	shone
shine (polish)	shined	shined
shrink	shrank	shrunk
sing	sang	sung
sink	sank, sunk	sunk, sunken
sit	sat	sat
slay	slew	slain
speak	spoke	spoken
spin	spun	spun
spit	spit, spat	spit, spat
spread	spread	spread
spring	sprang, sprung	sprung
steal	stole	stolen

PRESENT INFINITIVE	PAST TENSE	PAST PARTICIPLE
sting	stung	stung
stink	stank	stunk
swear	swore	sworn
swim	swam	swum
swing	swung	swung
take	took	taken
teach	taught	taught
tear	tore	torn
think	thought	thought
thrive	throve, thrived	thriven, thrived
throw	threw	thrown
wear	wore	worn
weep	wept	wept
win	won	won

Over the years some irregular forms have been eliminated from the language, and others are in the process of changing. As you can see from the preceding list, the preferred past tense form of *dive* is now *dived*, not *dove*. The preferred past participle form of *prove* is *proved*, not *proven*.

The following rules will help you select the appropriate verb form.

Use the past tense form to indicate simple past time.

NOT: We **seen** him in the library yesterday.
BUT: We **saw** him in the library yesterday.

NOT: Rhonda **swum** fifteen laps.
BUT: Rhonda **swam** fifteen laps.

NOT: His clothing **stunk** from the skunk's spray.
BUT: His clothing **stank** from the skunk's spray.

Use the past participle form with auxiliary verbs *have* and *be*.

NOT: **Have** you **chose** a major?
BUT: **Have** you **chosen** a major?

NOT: If you don't lock up your bike, it **will be took.**
BUT: If you don't lock up your bike, it **will be taken.**

NOT: Lenny **has wrote** home to his parents, asking for money.
BUT: Lenny **has written** home to his parents, asking for money.

Use the past participle form with a contraction containing an auxiliary verb.

NOT: **He's drove** all the way from Miami.
BUT: **He's driven** all the way from Miami.

NOT: **She'd** never **flew** in an airplane before.
BUT: **She'd** never **flown** in an airplane before.

NOT: **They've sang** in the choir for many years.
BUT: **They've sung** in the choir for many years.

15b Troublesome Verbs

Master troublesome pairs of words.

The following pairs of words often give people trouble: *lie* and *lay; sit* and *set; rise* and *raise; sneak* and *sneaked.*

Lie and lay

The verb *lie* means "recline." The verb *lay* means "put" or "place." Do not confuse the principal parts of these verbs.

PRESENT INFINITIVE	PAST TENSE	PAST PARTICIPLE	PRESENT PARTICIPLE
lie	lay	lain	lying
lay	laid	laid	laying

The problem most people have with these verbs is using a form of *lay* when they mean *lie*. *Lie* is intransitive; it does not take an object. *Lay* is transitive; it does take an object.

Lie on the floor. (*no object*)

Lay the *book* on the table. (*object*)

NOT: Why is Millie **laying** on the couch in the nurse's office?
BUT: Why is Millie **lying** on the couch in the nurse's office?

NOT: Peter **laid** in the sun too long yesterday.
BUT: Peter **lay** in the sun too long yesterday.

NOT: She had just **laid** down when the telephone rang.
BUT: She had just **lain** down when the telephone rang.

Sit and *set*

The verb *sit* means "be seated." The verb *set* usually means "place" or "put in a certain position." Do not confuse the principal parts of these verbs.

PRESENT INFINITIVE	PAST TENSE	PAST PARTICIPLE	PRESENT PARTICIPLE
sit	sat	sat	sitting
set	set	set	setting

The problem most people have with these verbs is using a form of *set* when they mean *sit*. *Sit* is intransitive; it does not take an object. *Set* is usually transitive; it does take an object.

Sit in the chair by the fireplace. (*no object*)

Please **set** the *table* for me. (*object*)

Note: Set is sometimes intransitive: *The sun sets.*

NOT:	Some people **set** in front of the television far too much.
BUT:	Some people **sit** in front of the television far too much.

NOT:	He **set** up until two in the morning, waiting for his daughter to come home from her date.
BUT:	He **sat** up until two in the morning, waiting for his daughter to come home from her date.

NOT:	After **setting** in the sun for five hours, Don was burned bright red.
BUT:	After **sitting** in the sun for five hours, Don was burned bright red.

Rise and *raise*

The verb *rise* means "go up" or "get into a standing position." The verb *raise* means "lift." Do not confuse the principal parts of these verbs.

PRESENT INFINITIVE	PAST TENSE	PAST PARTICIPLE	PRESENT PARTICIPLE
rise	rose	risen	rising
raise	raised	raised	raising

Rise is intransitive; it does not take an object. *Raise* is transitive; it does take an object.

Without yeast, the bread will not **rise.** (*no object*)

After they won the game, they **raised** the school *banner.* (*object*)

NOT:	They **rose** the curtain before the cast was fully assembled on stage.
BUT:	They **raised** the curtain before the cast was fully assembled on stage.

NOT:	Every morning they **rise** the blinds before leaving for work.
BUT:	Every morning they **raise** the blinds before leaving for work.

NOT: He **rose** his voice in order to be heard.
BUT: He **raised** his voice in order to be heard.

Sneak and sneaked

The verb *sneak* means "to move quietly and in a way to avoid detection." It is a regular verb and forms its past tense and past participle by adding *-ed* to the base form: *sneaked*. A tendency exists in the spoken language to treat *sneak* as if it were an irregular verb with a past tense and past participle of "snuck." This is considered inappropriate in writing.

NOT: I **snuck** around the house in my bare feet.
BUT: I **sneaked** around the house in my bare feet.

EXERCISE 15–1

Identify the inappropriate verb form in each of the following sentences. Replace it with the appropriate form.

1. We raise the curtain last night at 8:00 p.m.

2. The dish fall to the floor and breaked.

3. We were shook up by the car that past so close to us.

4. Sit the picture on top of the television set before it fell.

5. They snuck into the movie but drop the popcorn.

6. The cat stinked up the kitchen when the dog rose its howl.

7. I weared my new raincoat and it shined from the water.

8. The man ask for directions after he had go the wrong way.

9. I shone my shoes and polish them.

10. Lay on the couch while I sit this pillow beside you.

11. The man had rose the ladder before the carpenter said lifted it.

12. We could of went there if we was told early enough.

13. He was so happy that he past me some cake.

14. Someone's stole my notebook and trash it.

16   Subject-Verb Agreement

Make a verb agree with its subject in number and person.

For most verbs the only form change to indicate number occurs in the present tense and with a third-person singular subject. The change is the addition of *-s* or *-es* to the basic present-tense form.

The cushion **feels** soft.   The tomato **tastes** ripe.

The goose **flies** south.   He **brushes** his hair.

No change occurs with other singular subjects nor with all plural ones.

	SINGULAR	PLURAL
FIRST PERSON:	I **feel**	We **brush**
SECOND PERSON:	You **fly**	—
THIRD PERSON:	It **tastes**	They **taste**

Except for the verb *do*, modal auxiliaries (*may, can, will,* and so on) do not add *-s* or *-es* in third-person singular present tense. The auxiliary *have* changes form to *has*.

The verb *be* changes to indicate number in both the present tense and the past tense and in both the first person and the third person.

PRESENT TENSE		PAST TENSE	
I am	we are	I was	we were
you are	you are	you were	you were
he/she/it is	they are	he/she/it was	they were

Some kinds of subjects present special problems with subject-verb agreement. The following rules will help you choose the appropriate verb form.

16a Compound Subjects

Compound subject with *and*

In general, use a plural verb form with a compound subject joined by the word *and*.

A **compound subject** consists of two or more nouns that take the same predicate.

Shatonda and Sal **make** films for a living.

History and biology **were** his best subjects.

Ted and his friends **are supporting** Lopez for mayor.

Use a singular verb form with a compound subject joined by *and* if the compound is considered a single unit.

Pork and beans **is** a popular dish.

The *bow and arrow* **is** still regarded as a useful weapon.

Use a singular verb form with a compound subject joined by *and* if the parts of the compound refer to the same person or thing.

My *friend and guest* **is** the artist Katya Hyeska.

His *pride and joy* **was** his 1962 convertible.

Compound subject with *or* or *nor*

With a compound subject joined by *or* or *nor* or by *either . . . or* or *neither . . . nor,* make the verb agree with the subject closer to it.

The *cat or her kittens* **have pushed** the vase off the table.

Either the employees or their supervisor **is** responsible.

Neither the camera nor the lenses **were broken.**

16b Intervening Phrases or Clauses

Make the verb agree with its subject, not with a word in an intervening phrase or clause.

Intervening phrases

Several *people* in my club **subscribe** to that magazine.

The *books* by that writer **are** very popular.

The *picture* hanging between the windows at the top of the stairs **is** a portrait of the artist's mother.

Phrases introduced by *together with, as well as, in addition to, accompanied by,* and similar expressions do not affect the number of the verb.

The emerald *bracelet,* as well as her other jewels, **is** in the safe.

The *novel,* together with the plays that she wrote when she was much younger, **establishes** her reputation.

His *wit*, accompanied by his excellent grasp of the facts, **makes** him a sharp interviewer.

Intervening Clauses

The *books* that are in my briefcase **are** about Russian history.

The *people* who came to the concert that was canceled **are receiving** rain checks.

The *doctor* who is attending these patients **is** Ellen Okida.

16c Collective Nouns

A collective noun may take either a singular or a plural verb form.

Usually a collective noun refers to a group of people or things as a single unit. When this is the case, the collective noun is singular and the verb form should be singular.

The *army* **needs** the support of the civilian population.

The *flock* **is heading** toward the west end of the lake.

The *group* **is selling** tickets to raise money for charity.

Sometimes a collective noun refers to a group of things or people as individuals. When this is the case, the collective noun is plural and the verb form should be plural.

The *jury* **are arguing** among themselves; six believe the defendant is guilty, two think he is innocent, and four are undecided.

The *congregation* **disagree** about whether to keep the church open during the week.

Some people feel that using a plural verb form with a collective noun sounds awkward. You can avoid this problem by inserting "the members of" or a similar expression before the collective noun.

> The *members* of the jury **are arguing** among themselves; six believe the defendant is guilty, two think he is innocent, and four are undecided.

> The *members* of the congregation **disagree** about whether to keep the church open during the week.

16d Nouns Plural in Form but Singular in Meaning

Use a singular verb form with nouns plural in form but singular in meaning.

The following are some common words that are plural in form but singular in meaning.

checkers	ethics	molasses	pediatrics
civics	mathematics	mumps	physics
economics	measles	news	statistics

Checkers **is called** draughts in Great Britain.

Measles **is** a contagious childhood disease.

The *news* **is broadcast** around the clock on some radio stations.

The words *pants, trousers,* and *scissors* are considered plural and take a plural verb form. However, if they are preceded by the words *pair of,* the verb form is singular, since *pair* is the subject.

The *scissors* **need** to be sharpened.

The *pair* of scissors **needs** to be sharpened.

The *pants* **match** the jacket.

The *pair* of pants **matches** the jacket.

16e Indefinite and Relative Pronoun Subjects

Indefinite pronoun subjects

The following indefinite pronouns are considered singular.
Use a singular verb form with them.

anybody	either	neither	one
anyone	everybody	nobody	somebody
each	everyone	no one	someone

Neither **is** willing to go with me.

Everybody **is going to vote** on Tuesday.

Do not be confused by prepositional phrases that follow
the indefinite pronoun. The verb must agree with its subject,
not with the object of a preposition.

Each of the apartments in the north wing of the building **has** a
fireplace.

Either of those methods **is** feasible.

The following indefinite pronouns are considered plural. Use
a plural verb form with them.

both	few	many	several

Few **are** certain enough of their beliefs to take a stand.

Several **are** riding their bicycles to school.

Both of the paintings **were** sold at the auction.

The following indefinite pronouns may be singular or plural. If the noun to which the pronoun refers is singular, use a singular verb form. If the noun is plural, use a plural verb form.

all	any	enough	more	most	some

All of the *money* **was** recovered. (*singular*)

All **was** recovered. (*singular*)

All of these *records* **are** scratched. (*plural*)

All **are** scratched. (*plural*)

Most of the *cake* **was** eaten. (*singular*)

Most **was** eaten. (*singular*)

Most of the *guests* **were** hungry. (*plural*)

Most **were** hungry. (*singular*)

The indefinite pronoun *none* is considered singular because it means "no one." It takes a singular verb.

None of the books was missing.

Relative pronoun subjects

A verb whose subject is a relative pronoun should agree with the antecedent of the pronoun.

The man *who* **narrates** the film has a raspy voice. (*singular antecedent*)

The radios *that* **were made** in Japan are selling well. (*plural antecedent*)

The newspaper, *which* **was founded** in 1893, is closing. (*singular antecedent*)

The phrase *one of* is worth mentioning. Usually, the relative pronoun that follows this phrase is plural because its antecedent is a plural noun or pronoun. Therefore, the relative pronoun takes a plural verb form.

The man is one of the hostages *who* **are** in most danger.

Ralph is one of those *who* never **gain** weight.

However, when the words *the only* come before this phrase, the relative pronoun is singular because its antecedent is *one*. Therefore, it takes a singular verb form.

This is the only one of Mark's songs *that* **has been published.**

Mitch is the only one of those men *who* **is** athletic.

16f Titles

Use a singular verb form with a title, even if the title contains plural words.

Guys and Dolls **was** a popular Broadway musical.

Sixty Minutes **is** on television tonight.

Wuthering Heights **tells** the story of a doomed love.

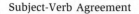
16g Units of Measurement, Time, and Money

Use a singular verb form with a plural noun phrase that names a unit of measurement, a period of time, or an amount of money.

> *Five miles* **is** too far to walk to school.
>
> *One hundred years* **is** the usual life span for the crocodile.
>
> *Twenty-five thousand dollars* **is** a good salary for this job.

16h Inverted Sentence Order

Use a verb that agrees with its subject, even when the subject follows the verb.

> Outside the building **were** *crowds of spectators.*
>
> From the chimneys **rises** thick black *smoke.*
>
> On the wall **are** *portraits* of her ancestors.

Do not be confused by sentences beginning with the expletives *there* and *here.* These words are never the subject.

> There **is** a *chicken* roasting in the oven.
>
> Here **are** the *groceries* you asked me to pick up.

16i Agreement with Subject, Not Predicate Nominative

Use a verb that agrees with the subject, not with the predicate nominative.

A firm *moral sense* and a *belief* in the goodness of human beings **were** his inheritance.

His *inheritance* **was** a firm moral sense and a belief in the goodness of human beings.

EXERCISE 16-1

Revise any of the following sentences in which a verb does not agree with its subject. Some of the sentences are correct as written.

1. Traveling to Rome and to Paris constitute his ultimate desire.

2. The person who took my book bag certainly realize how valuable those books are.

3. Does the chairperson or the registrar control class size limitations?

4. The approach to the airport and the train station are one and the same street.

5. Neither of us really want to go.

6. Getting dressed, sitting on a bus, and standing in a line is not my idea of a pleasant evening.

7. Your pair of pants are on the chair.

8. Either the clerk or the cashier made the error.

9. The team stand beside each other with the tallest members in the middle.

10. There is a shiny apple and two fuzzy peaches on the table.

11. She is the only one of our friends who have traveled to Europe.

12. Your instrument along with the music and a music stand seem appropriate to take.

13. My aunt and uncle along with a cousin are going with us.

14. *The Canterbury Tales* are considered Chaucer's best poetry.

15. Each of the notebooks and books in the pile were properly identified.

16. Are you sure that $72 are a fair price for that?

17. How many of you singing today has heard the famous cantata?

18. The tall buildings filled with lighted windows along the lake present an impressive sight.

19. The manager will welcome to the spa each of the prospective members who complete the application.

20. None from that group are here.

17 Pronouns: Agreement, Reference, and Usage

By themselves, most **pronouns,** or noun substitutes, have little meaning. For a pronoun's meaning to be clear, it usually must have a clear antecedent (the word or words to which the pronoun refers), and it must agree with its antecedent in number and gender.

> After the *pilot* checked **her** instruments, **she** prepared for takeoff.

> After the *pilots* checked **their** instruments, **they** prepared for takeoff.

17a Pronoun–Antecedent Agreement

Indefinite pronouns as antecedents

Use a pronoun that agrees in gender and number with an indefinite pronoun antecedent.

Use a masculine pronoun with an indefinite pronoun that refers to a masculine noun and a feminine pronoun with an indefinite pronoun that refers to a feminine noun. Use a neuter, or indeterminate, pronoun with an indefinite pronoun that refers to a neuter noun.

> Twenty men are in the training program. *Each* is a unique individual with **his** own goals and ideals.

> Twenty women are in the training program. *Each* is a unique individual with **her** own goals and ideals.

> Fifty businesses contributed to the charity. *Each* is unique with **its** own goals and aspirations.

Many times, however, a singular indefinite pronoun refers to a group consisting of both men and women, which implies plurality as in the following sentence:

> Everyone should cast _____ vote in the next election.

What should the pronoun in the blank be? Traditionally, a masculine pronoun (*his*) was used in such constructions to refer to an antecedent that included both men and women. Today, most people consider this usage sexist and prefer to use *his or her*. However, a paragraph or a paper can become tedious and calls attention to itself if it is filled with too many pairs of *his or her, he or she, him or her,* and so on. Here are three suggestions for rewriting sentences like this to avoid the problem of pronoun choice.

1. Make the pronouns plural.

   All should cast **their** votes in the next election.

2. Use an article (*a, an,* or *the*) in place of the possessive pronoun.

   Everyone should cast **a** vote in the next election.

3. Rewrite the sentence more extensively.

   Everyone should vote in the next election.

(See also Chapter 25, pp. 302–307.)

Although *everyone* and *everybody* are considered grammatically singular, they obviously refer to more than one person. Therefore, logic can lead to and legitimize the use of a plural pronoun with these antecedents, particularly when the pronoun is not in the same clause as the antecedent.

Although *everyone* made enthusiastic noises about the project, **they** fell silent when asked to contribute money.

The "correct" singular pronoun would, in fact, sound most illogical.

Although *everyone* made enthusiastic noises about the project, **each** fell silent. . . .

In such a case, *everyone* or *everybody* would be treated as a collective word. However, these two pronouns are different from other collectives in that usage still requires that they be considered singular in relation to their verbs. So with a present-tense verb and a pronoun in the same clause, logic of agreement still requires a singular pronoun or a recasting of the sentence using one of the three strategies suggested earlier.

Relative pronouns

Use the appropriate relative pronoun.

The pronouns *who, whom,* and *whose* refer to people. They also refer to animals thought of in human terms and called by name. The pronoun *that* usually refers to animals and things, but it is sometimes used to refer to people. The pronoun *which* refers to animals and things.

The *ballplayer* **who** broke Babe Ruth's career home run record is Hank Aaron.

The *movie* **that** Mikiko saw last night was *Terms of Endearment.*

Orwell's *1984,* **which** was published in 1949, is still in print.

Someone **whom** voters can trust will win the election.

Do not use *what* as a relative pronoun.

NOT: The stereo **what** I want costs $300.
BUT: The stereo **that** I want costs $300.

To avoid an awkward sentence, use the possessive pronoun *whose* to mean "of which."

> **NOT:** The car the windshield wipers **of which** are not working failed to pass inspection.
>
> **BUT:** The car **whose** windshield wipers are not working failed to pass inspection.

A relative pronoun takes its number from its antecedent. The number of the relative pronoun determines the number of any other pronouns used with it.

> *Students* **who** show **their** identification cards will get a discount.
>
> A *man* **who** cannot make up **his** mind is of no use to this company.

Compound antecedent

Use a plural pronoun to refer to a compound antecedent joined by *and*.

> *Evita and Juan* have finished **their** assignments.
>
> *The judge and the district attorney* have completed **their** terms of office.

When the antecedent is a compound joined by *or* or *nor* or by *either . . . or, neither . . . nor,* or *not only . . . but also,* make the pronoun agree with the part of the compound that is closer to it.

> Neither the district attorney nor the defense *lawyers* stated **their** cases clearly.
>
> Not only the jurors but also the *judge* found **his** attention wandering.

Collective nouns as antecedents

Use a singular pronoun with a collective noun antecedent if the members of the group are thought of as one unit. Use a plural pronoun if the members are thought of as individuals.

After winning the race, the *crew* placed **its** trophy on the mantelpiece.

The leader asked the *group* to lower **their** voices.

EXERCISE 17–1

Identify the pronoun in each of the following sentences. If the pronoun does not agree with its antecedent, rephrase the sentence. One of the sentences is correct as written.

1. The person which tossed that bottle was being careless.

2. Is it true that anything is better than nothing?

3. Not only the team but also the coach saw their chances of victory fade.

4. Somebody parked their car in front of the fire hydrant.

5. Each of those present displayed their badges at the conference.

17b Pronoun Reference

Vague reference

Provide a clear antecedent for each pronoun that needs one.

In general, do not use a pronoun to refer to the entire idea in a previous sentence or clause or to an antecedent that has not been clearly stated.

> **VAGUE:** Ahmed usually taps his feet, rolls his eyes, and fidgets when he is nervous, **which** annoys his girlfriend.

The pronoun *which* refers vaguely to the entire idea of Ahmed's behavior when he is nervous.

> **CLEAR:** Ahmed's habit of tapping his feet, rolling his eyes, and fidgeting when he is nervous annoys his girlfriend.

> **VAGUE:** Lou is an excellent mechanic, and she uses **this** to earn money for college.

The pronoun *this* refers vaguely to the idea of Lou's skill as a mechanic.

> **CLEAR:** Lou is an excellent mechanic, and she uses her skill to earn money for college.

> **VAGUE:** The tourists stared in awe as the great Christmas tree in Rockefeller Center was lit. They listened in rapt attention to the speeches and sang along with the carolers. **It** was something they would tell their friends about back home.

> **CLEAR:** The tourists stared in awe as the great Christmas tree in Rockefeller Center was lit. They listened in rapt attention to the speeches and sang along with the carolers. The spectacle was something they would tell their friends about back home.

> **VAGUE:** Now that her children were away at school, she felt free to pursue her own interests for the first time in years. Perhaps she would get a job. Perhaps she would go back to school. Suddenly she felt alive again. Until this moment, she hadn't realized how badly she had needed **this.**

CLEAR: Now that her children were away at school, she felt free to pursue her own interests for the first time in years. Perhaps she would get a job. Perhaps she would go back to school. Suddenly she felt alive again. Until this moment, she hadn't realized how badly she had needed a change in her life.

VAGUE: In the novel Christophine tries to discourage Antoinette from going to England. She says England is a cold place with bad weather and bad people, and she cautions Antoinette not to do **it.**

CLEAR: In the novel Christophine tries to discourage Antoinette from going to England. She says England is a cold place with bad weather and bad people, and she cautions Antoinette not to go there.

Ambiguous reference

Do not use a pronoun that could refer to either of two or more antecedents.

AMBIGUOUS: Malcolm told Henry that **he** had won a trip to France.

The pronoun *he* could refer to either Malcolm or Henry. If it refers to Malcolm, rewrite the sentence to make this reference clear.

CLEAR: Malcom told Henry, "I have won a trip to France."
OR: Malcolm, who had won a trip to France, told Henry the news.

If the pronoun refers to Henry, rewrite the sentence a different way.

CLEAR: Malcolm told Henry, "You have won a trip to France."

OR: Malcolm knew that Henry had won a trip to France and told him so.

AMBIGUOUS: Marika met Dr. McCluskey when **she** visited the lab last week.

The pronoun *she* could refer to either Marika or Dr. McCluskey.

CLEAR: When Marika visited the lab last week, she met Dr. McCluskey.

CLEAR: When Dr. McCluskey visited the lab last week, Marika met her.

AMBIGUOUS: In the saga, Luke Skywalker and Han Solo are at first rivals. Both want to win the affection of the princess. As the saga progresses, however, the two young men gain respect for each other, until finally the rivalry ends when **he** discovers he is Leia's brother.

The pronoun *he* could refer to either Luke or Han.

CLEAR: In the saga, Luke Skywalker and Han Solo are at first rivals. Both want to win the affection of the princess. As the saga progresses, however, the two young men gain respect for each other, until finally the rivalry ends when **Luke** discovers he is Leia's brother.

AMBIGUOUS: Fourteenth-century Europe was scarred by war and plague. It is hard to tell which was worse. The figures given by the chroniclers differ, but according to some accounts, **it** reduced the population by a third.

CLEAR: Fourteenth-century Europe was scarred by war and plague. It is hard to tell which was worse. The figures given by the chroniclers differ, but according to some accounts, **plague alone** reduced the population by a third.

17c Pronoun Usage

Do not use a personal pronoun immediately following its antecedent.

Pronouns are often used this way in conversation to emphasize the antecedent, but this construction is inappropriate in writing.

NOT: The dictator **he** would not give up any of his power.
BUT: The dictator would not give up any of his power.

NOT: Cuckoos **they** lay their eggs in other birds' nests.
BUT: Cuckoos lay their eggs in other birds' nests.

Use a pronoun ending in *-self* or *-selves* only when an antecedent for this pronoun appears in the sentence. (See reflexive pronouns, p. 175.)

I bought the tickets for Doris and **myself.**

NOT: Give the tickets to Doris and **myself.**
BUT: Give the tickets to Doris and **me.**

NOT: The invitation was addressed to his wife and **himself.**
BUT: The invitation was addressed to his wife and **him.**

EXERCISE 17–2

Rephrase any of the following sentences that contain pronoun agreement, reference, or usage problems.

1. Please accept this gift on behalf of my wife and myself.

2. Each of the people present lit their candles.

3. The people in the park, which traveled with us, were noisy.

4. After the drivers checked the tires, they were ready to go.

5. The people crowded around the car after the accident: it was a mess.

6. Some of the teachers, they were having a wonderful time.

7. Why hasn't anyone told Laura and myself about the trip?

8. John and Jim were no longer friends after he got a bid to join the fraternity.

9. The car, although very highly priced, it suited our needs in every way.

10. The police chief and the fire chief completed his plans this morning.

18   Pronoun Case

18a Subjective, Possessive, and Objective

Personal pronouns take the form of the *subjective*, the *possessive*, or the *objective case*, depending on their use in the sentence. The pronouns *who* and *whoever* also have different forms to indicate case.

SUBJECTIVE: I, you, he, she, it, we, they, who, whoever
POSSESSIVE: my, mine, your, yours, his, her, hers, its, our, ours, their, theirs, whose
OBJECTIVE: me, you, him, her, it, us, them, whom, whomever

He wrote *The Way to Rainy Mountain. (subjective)*

Scott Momaday has increased **our** awareness of the daily struggle of Native Americans. (*possessive*)

Many awards have been given to **him.** (*objective*)

The author is **he**. (*subjective*)

Most people have little trouble choosing the appropriate case when a personal pronoun is used by itself. Many do have trouble, though, when the pronoun is part of a compound structure. Almost everyone has trouble at times with *who* and *whom* and with *whoever* and *whomever.*

In compound subjects and objects

Place a pronoun that is part of a compound subject in the subjective case.

NOT: Fanny and **me** have tickets for the football game.
BUT: Fanny and **I** have tickets for the football game.

NOT: Neither Wally nor **him** is on the wrestling team.
BUT: Neither Wally nor **he** is on the wrestling team.

Place a pronoun that is part of a compound direct object or a compound indirect object in the objective case.

NOT: The fly ball bounced off the fence and then hit Christine and **I.**
BUT: The fly ball bounced off the fence and then hit Christine and **me.** (hit . . . me)

NOT: Give Mel and **she** the blueprints so that they can check the measurements.
BUT: Give Mel and **her** the blueprints so that they can check the measurements. (Give . . . her)

Place a pronoun that is part of a compound object of a preposition in the objective case.

NOT:	Although there are thirty people competing, everyone knows the race is really between you and **I.**
BUT:	Although there are thirty people competing, everyone knows the race is really between you and **me.**
NOT:	The symposium is being conducted by Dr. Fell and **she.**
BUT:	The symposium is being conducted by Dr. Fell and **her.** (by . . . her)
NOT:	Several of **we** amateurs were allowed to play in the pro tournament.
BUT:	Several of **us** amateurs were allowed to play in the pro tournament. (of us, *not* of we)

In predicate nominatives

Place a pronoun that is part of a predicate nominative in the subjective case. (See linking verbs, pp. 158–159.)

NOT:	The people to see for tickets are Juan and **him.**
BUT:	The people to see for tickets are Juan and **he.**
NOT:	The winners are Dara and **her.**
BUT:	The winners are Dara and **she.**

In speech, many people accept the informal use of the objective case of the pronoun following the verb *be.* In formal writing, however, the subjective case is still required in this construction.

INFORMAL:	It is **me.**
FORMAL:	It is **I.**
INFORMAL:	Was it **him** who asked you to the dance?
FORMAL:	Was it **he** who asked you to the dance?

After *than* or *as*

In an elliptical, or incomplete, clause, place the pronoun in the case it would be in if the clause were complete.

NOT: Demetrius is stronger than **him.**
BUT: Demetrius is stronger than **he.** (than he is)

NOT: No one could have worked more skillfully than **her.**
BUT: No one could have worked more skillfully than **she.** (than she did)

NOT: Luba knew she could love no one as much as **he.**
BUT: Luba knew she could love no one as much as **him.** (as she loved him)

In appositives

Place a pronoun that is part of a compound appositive in the same case as the noun to which the appositive refers.

An **appositive** is a noun or noun substitute that renames or identifies the noun or noun substitute preceding it.

NOT: The partners—Willie, Travis, and **me**—plan to open a bicycle repair shop in July.
BUT: The partners—Willie, Travis, and **I**—plan to open a bicycle repair shop in July.

NOT: Only two people, the manager and **him,** knew the combination of the safe.
BUT: Only two people, the manager and **he,** knew the combination of the safe.

Before verbals or verbal phrases

Place a pronoun that precedes a gerund or gerund phrase in the possessive case. A noun follows this rule also.

NOT: The audience applauded **them** dancing.
BUT: The audience applauded **their** dancing. (the performers')

NOT: I resented **him** criticizing me in front of my friends.
BUT: I resented **his** criticizing me in front of my friends. (my dad's)

NOT: Pauline liked everything about Ron but **him** singing first thing in the morning.
BUT: Pauline liked everything about Ron but **his** singing first thing in the morning. (Ron's)

Place a pronoun that precedes a participle or participle phrase in the objective case.

NOT: When Cedrica recalled her grandfather, she pictured **his** smiling.
BUT: When Cedrica recalled her grandfather, she pictured **him** smiling.

NOT: I heard **his** starting the car.
BUT: I heard **him** starting the car.

NOT: Phil had seen **their** racing to class.
BUT: Phil had seen **them** racing to class.

To decide which case of the pronoun to use, you have to decide whether the verbal following it is a gerund or a participle. Look at the next two sentences.

I can hear your singing.
I can hear you singing.

Both of these sentences are grammatically correct, but they have slightly different meanings. In the first sentence, *singing* is a gerund modified by the possessive pronoun *your*; in the second sentence, *singing* is a participle that modifies the objective pronoun *you*. The first sentence emphasizes an action, *singing*, while the second sentence emphasizes the performer of the action, *you.* Thus, in writing sentences like these, you can often convey different shades of meaning by using the possessive or the objective case of the pronoun.

Who and *whom; whoever* and *whomever*

In conversation, many people no longer use *whom* or *whomever* except directly after a preposition. In writing, however, you should always be careful to distinguish between *who* and *whom* and between *whoever* and *whomever.*

Use *who* and *whoever* as the subject of a sentence or clause.

Who founded the American Red Cross? (*subject of sentence*)
The book is about Clara Barton, **who** founded the American Red Cross. (*subject of clause*)
Whoever lost the book will have to pay for it. (*subject of clause*)

Use *whom* and *whomever* as the direct object or the object of a preposition.

Whom shall I call? (*direct object*)
Whomever the *Union Leader* endorsed enjoyed a substantial advantage. (*direct object*)
The person to **whom** I gave the packages was Pete. (*object of preposition*)

How can you tell whether the pronoun should be *who* or *whom?* For sentences, mentally rephrase the question as a declarative statement. Then substitute *who* for *he, she,* or *they,* or *whom* for *him, her,* or *them.*

(*Who/Whom*) founded the American Red Cross?
She founded the American Red Cross.
Who founded the American Red Cross?
(*Who/Whom*) shall I call?
I shall call **him.**
Whom shall I call?

For clauses, follow the same process. Rephrase the clause as a statement and substitute *who* for *he, she,* or *they,* or *whom* for *him, her,* or *them.*

> The person (*who/whom*) founded the American Red Cross was Clara Barton.
>
> **She** founded the American Red Cross.
>
> The person **who** founded the American Red Cross was Clara Barton.

> The writer (*who/whom*) she enjoyed most was Dickens.
>
> She enjoyed **him** most.
>
> The writer **whom** she enjoyed most was Dickens.

> (*Whoever/Whomever*) the *Union Leader* endorsed enjoyed a substantial advantage.
>
> The *Union Leader* endorsed **him.**
>
> **Whomever** the *Union Leader* endorsed enjoyed a substantial advantage.

If words intervene between the pronoun and the main verb of the sentence or clause, mentally delete them as you rephrase.

> (*Who/Whom*) <u>did he think</u> he had offended?
>
> He had offended **them.**
>
> **Whom** did he think he had offended?

> One person (*who/whom*) <u>the newspaper said</u> was killed was actually unhurt.
>
> **She** was killed.
>
> One person **who** the newspaper said was killed was actually unhurt.

> The stores gave away the food to (*whoever/whomever*) <u>they knew</u> could use it.
>
> **They** could use it.
>
> The stores gave away the food to **whoever** they knew could use it.

EXERCISE 18-1

Select the appropriate form of the pronoun in each of the following sentences.

1. Her family and (we/us) attended the special concert honoring Bach and Handel.

2. All the arrangements were made by Susan and (I/me).

3. Two of us—Kathleen and (I/me)—went to the recital early to get the tickets.

4. In the year 1882, both Bach and (he/him) died.

5. Perhaps Bach is a more prolific composer than (he/him), but Handel is more popular.

6. The two of them—Handel and (he/him)—were from Germany.

7. Some music lovers think that Handel is easier to listen to than (he/him).

8. Some organists object to (his/him) writing organ concertos because of his training.

9. Yet, (he/him) wrote great orchestral accompaniments for his oratorios.

10. (Who/Whom) are we to believe in these matters when others say that Bach is indeed more popular than (he/him)?

EXERCISE 18–2

Select the appropriate form of the pronoun in each of the following sentences.

1. If you scan the crowd carefully, you will locate the young woman (who/whom) you are looking for.

2. The woman in charge (who/whom) you must first see has gone to lunch.

3. Mary's brother, (who/whom) she admits is envious, will manage her mayoral campaign.

4. (Who/Whom) do you plan to see?

5. (Who/Whom) do you suspect has the higher grades?

6. (Whoever/Whomever) submits the least expensive bid will probably get the job.

7. The inspiration of the coach, (who/whom) never gives up, impressed the visitors.

8. The manager will employ (whoever/whomever) he can find (who/whom) is willing to work long hours.

9. (Whoever/Whomever) do you think that will be?

10. The musician, (who/whom) taught for many years, retired at the age of sixty.

19   Adjectives and Adverbs

An **adjective** is a word that modifies a noun or a pronoun. An **adverb** is a word that modifies a verb, an adjective, or another adverb.

Avoid confusing these two parts of speech.

ADJECTIVE	ADVERB
happy	happily
graceful	gracefully
most	almost

Although most adjectives and adverbs have different forms, a few words can function as both. Among them are the following:

deep	hard	late	loud	slow	very
far	high	little	low	straight	well
fast	kindly	long	parallel	tight	wild

19a Misused Adjective Forms

Avoid using an adjective to modify a verb, an adjective, or an adverb. Use an adverb instead.

NOT: The lawyer answered very **quick.**

BUT: The lawyer *answered* very **quickly.**

NOT: The director thought Marie's reading was **near** perfect.

BUT: The director thought Marie's reading was **nearly** *perfect*.

NOT: The group performing at the club plays **real** well.

BUT: The group performing at the club plays **really** *well*.

Do not be confused by words separating the adverb from the word it modifies. For example:

The lawyer *answered* each of her client's questions very **quickly.**

Avoid using an adjective ending in *-ly* in place of an adverb or an adverb phrase.

Although the suffix *-ly* usually signals an adverb, a few adjectives end in *-ly* too. For example:

earthly	ghostly	holy	lovely
friendly	heavenly	homely	manly

Do not mistake these adjectives for adverbs or try to use them as adverbs. Either use another word or express your idea as a phrase.

NOT: A figure was moving **ghostly** through the darkened room.

BUT: A figure was moving **like a ghost** through the darkened room.

OR: A figure was moving **ghostlike** through the darkened room.

NOT: They do not generally answer the questions of American tourists **very friendly.**

BUT: They do not generally answer the questions of American tourists **in a very friendly way.**

OR: They do not generally answer the questions of American tourists **very pleasantly.**

19b Misused Adverb Forms

Avoid using an adverb to modify a direct object. Use an adjective instead for this as objective complement. (See p. 150.)

Think about the difference in meaning between the following two sentences.

The instructor considered the student's paper careful.
The instructor considered the student's paper carefully.

In the first sentence, the adjective *careful* modifies the direct object *paper*. It tells what opinion the professor held of the paper. In the second sentence, the adverb *carefully* modifies the verb *considered*. It tells in what manner the professor considered the paper.

NOT: He keeps his work station **tidily.**

BUT: He keeps his *work station* **tidy.**

NOT: She considers her grades **excellently.**

BUT: She considers her *grades* **excellent.**

NOT: The jury found the defendant **guiltily.**

BUT: The jury found the *defendant* **guilty.**

Avoid using an adverb after a linking verb. Use the corresponding adjective instead for this as a predicate adjective. (See pp. 151, 158–159.)

NOT: After the operation, the patient felt **badly.**

BUT: After the operation, the *patient* felt **bad.**

NOT: This proposal sounds **sensibly** enough.

BUT: This *proposal* sounds **sensible** enough.

NOT: After he took that cooking course, his meals tasted **differently.**

BUT: After he took that cooking course, his *meals* tasted **different.**

Two words that are especially confusing are *good* and *well*. *Good* is always used as an adjective. *Well* is usually used as an adverb, but it can also be used as an adjective that means "healthy" or "satisfactory."

The preliminary *findings* look **good.** *(adjective)*

Janet *dances* **well.** *(adverb)*

The town crier shouted, "*All* is **well!**" *(adjective)*

Notice the difference between the following two sentences:

He feels good.
He feels well.

The adjective *good* describes the person's mood. The adjective *well* describes his health.

Some verbs can be used as both action verbs and linking verbs. (See pp. 156–161.) These verbs include the following:

die	grow	feel	turn
go	look	smell	taste

ACTION: The customs officer *looked* **carefully** through our luggage. *(adverb)*

LINKING: This *book* looks **interesting.** *(adjective)*

ACTION: The cute little puppy *grew* **quickly** into a 150-pound dog. *(adverb)*

LINKING: After drinking the potion, the old *man* grew **young** before our very eyes. *(adjective)*

ACTION: He *died* **peacefully** in his sleep. *(adverb)*

LINKING: The *poet* died **young.** *(adjective)*

19c Comparative and Superlative Forms of Adjectives and Adverbs

Form the comparative of most one-syllable adjectives and adverbs by adding the suffix *-er* (or *-r*) to the base, or positive, form of the word. Form the superlative of most one-syllable adjectives and adverbs by adding the suffix *-est* (or *-st*) to the base form.

POSITIVE	COMPARATIVE	SUPERLATIVE
slow	slower	slowest
late	later	latest
deep	deeper	deepest

Form the comparative of most longer adjectives and adverbs by placing the word *more* before the base word. Form the superlative of most longer adjectives and adverbs by placing the word *most* before the base word.

POSITIVE	COMPARATIVE	SUPERLATIVE
graceful	more graceful	most graceful
gracefully	more gracefully	most gracefully
sensible	more sensible	most sensible
sensibly	more sensibly	most sensibly

Some adjectives and adverbs have irregular comparative and superlative forms.

POSITIVE	COMPARATIVE	SUPERLATIVE
good } well }	better	best
bad } ill } badly }	worse	worst
many } much }	more	most
little (quantity)	less	least

A dictionary usually lists the *-er* and *-est* comparative and superlative forms for adjectives and adverbs that have these forms.

Use the comparative form to compare two things. Use the superlative form to compare three or more things.

> This dish is **spicier** than that one.
> This dish is the **spiciest** one on the menu.
>
> Harry is a **more skillful** carpenter than his partner.
> Harry is the **most skillful** carpenter in town.
>
> Lois works **harder** than Carol.
> Lois works the **hardest** of the three students.
>
> Sharon speaks **more distinctly** than her sister.
> Sharon speaks the **most distinctly** of anyone in her family.

Avoid using the superlative form when only two things are being compared.

> **NOT:** Of the two sexes, women live **the longest.**
> **BUT:** Of the two sexes, women live **longer.**

NOT: Both of the proposals were reasonable, but Johnson's was **the most complex.**

BUT: Both of the proposals were reasonable, but Johnson's was **more complex.**

NOT: Henry James and Edith Wharton both wrote of a certain type of society—the society of the very rich and the very secure—and of the effects of this society on the idealistic woman. It is hard to say whose vision was the **clearest.**

BUT: Henry James and Edith Wharton both wrote of a certain type of society—the society of the very rich and the very secure—and of the effects of this society on the idealistic woman. It is hard to say whose vision was the **clearer.**

Avoid making double comparisons (comparisons using both *-er* or *-est* and *more* or *most*).

NOT: He was **more wealthier** than John D. Rockefeller.
BUT: He was **wealthier** than John D. Rockefeller.

NOT: It is the **most sleekest** craft on the lake.
BUT: It is the **sleekest** craft on the lake.

Avoid comparing words like *complete, dead, perfect, round, square,* and *unique.*

These words, called *absolutes,* name conditions that cannot be compared. For example, people are either dead or not dead; one person cannot be *more dead* than another person. If something is perfect, something else cannot be *more perfect.* Except for *dead,* however, you can compare the steps in reaching these conditions. For example, something may be *more nearly perfect* than something else, or one thing may be *the most nearly complete* of three.

NOT: His solution was **more perfect** than John's.
BUT: His solution was **more nearly perfect** than John's.

19d Double Negatives

Use only one negative word to express a negative meaning.

A **double negative** occurs when two negative words are used to make a negative statement. Although this device was often used in earlier centuries to emphasize the idea of negation, it is not acceptable in standard modern English.

NOT:　Felicity **didn't** bring **nothing** to the party.
BUT:　Felicity **didn't** bring **anything** to the party.
OR:　Felicity brought **nothing** to the party.

NOT:　I **don't** know **no one** by that name.
BUT:　I **don't** know **anyone** by that name.
OR:　I know **no one** by that name.

NOT:　She **can't hardly** see in this light.
BUT:　She **can hardly** see in this light.

EXERCISE 19–1

Identify the incorrect adjective and adverb forms in each of the following sentences and explain why the usage is incorrect.

1. Visiting the showroom to view new cars makes many people feel happily.

2. Narrowing one's choices to two cars, it's always difficult to decide which one is the attractiver.

3. The colorfully instrument gauges look nicest in the day than at night.

4. The salesperson I met yesterday was not at work today because he felt badly and was sent home.

5. When I was asked to make a price offer, I didn't have nothing appropriate planned.

6. We couldn't hardly wait to go for a test drive.

7. After turning a corner, a truck came dangerous close to hitting us.

8. It happened so quick there wasn't hardly nothing to do but hit the brakes.

9. The salesperson with us sighed weary and shook his head.

10. When we got back, the salesperson anxious took the key from me and didn't speak to no one.

20 **Comparisons**

   In addition to using the appropriate comparative or superlative form of an adjective or adverb, a writer who is making a comparison has to keep a number of other points in mind. Be sure that your comparisons are sensible, complete, and unambiguous; do not leave out anything necessary to make your meaning clear.

20a False Comparisons

Be careful that your comparative statements compare what you intended to compare. Do not compare things that are essentially unlike.

> **FALSE:** Mark's smile was broader than Dora.

In the preceding sentence, the writer is trying to compare Mark's smile with Dora's smile. But the sentence as written compares Mark's smile with Dora herself.

> **VALID:** Mark's smile was broader than Dora's.
>
> **FALSE:** Her style of dressing is like the 1960s.

The preceding sentence compares a style of dressing with a period of time. Obviously, it should compare this style of dressing with the style of dressing popular in that period.

> **VALID:** Her style of dressing is like **that of** the 1960s.
>
> **FALSE:** Tuition at private colleges has become much more expensive than state colleges.
>
> **VALID:** Tuition has become much more expensive at private colleges than **at** state colleges.

20b Incomplete Comparisons

Avoid introducing the idea of a comparison without specifying one of the things being compared.

> **INCOMPLETE:** This cake tastes better.

Tastes better than what?

COMPLETE: This cake tastes better than any of the others.

INCOMPLETE: Growing up in a small town is different.

Different from what?

COMPLETE: Growing up in a small town is different from growing up in a large city or a suburb.

20c Ambiguous Comparisons

Avoid making a comparative statement that has two possible meanings.

AMBIGUOUS: I know Eliot better than Pound.

The preceding sentence is unclear. You can interpret it in two ways.

CLEAR: I know Eliot better than I know Pound.

CLEAR: I know Eliot better than Pound knows him.

AMBIGUOUS: I can recall the family vacation we took when I was five better than my sister.

CLEAR: I can recall the family vacation we took when I was five better than my sister can recall it.

CLEAR: I can recall the family vacation we took when I was five better than I can recall my sister.

20d Omitted Comparative Words

Avoid omitting the words *as* or *than* when they are necessary in a comparative construction.

NOT:	The candidate was better prepared although not as well spoken as her opponent.
BUT:	The candidate was better prepared **than,** although not as well spoken as, her opponent.

NOT:	His grades were as good, if not better than, his brother's.
BUT:	His grades were as good **as,** if not better than, his brother's.

NOT:	All of their friends were as poor or even poorer than they.
BUT:	All of their friends were as poor **as** they or even poorer. (*than they* is understood)

Use the word *other* or *else* when you compare one thing with other members of the group to which it belongs.

NOT:	The flutist plays more beautiful than any member of the orchestra.
BUT:	The flutist plays more beautifully than any **other** member of the orchestra.

NOT:	Hal can throw farther than anyone on his team.
BUT:	Hal can throw farther than anyone **else** on his team.

NOT:	The clipper cut through the water more gracefully than any of the ships.
BUT:	The clipper cut through the water more gracefully than any of the **other** ships.

EXERCISE 20–1

Rephrase the following sentences to eliminate any false, ambiguous, or incomplete comparisons. Where necessary, supply any comparative words that have been omitted.

1. Eating in Chicago is as enjoyable as many other big cities.

2. She has won more prizes than any student in her class.

3. This popcorn pops quicker.

4. He likes ice cream better than Mary.

5. The color of her hair is the same as the car.

6. Our quarterback throws as well if not even better than the other quarterbacks in our conference.

7. The Cadillac's chassis is longer than most other cars.

8. She wanted to go to the movies as much as he.

9. Some believe that the oboe is harder to play than almost any instrument.

10. He paid more for his stereo equipment than his father.

---

21 Shifts

Although variety is desirable in writing, some kinds of variety are not desirable. Shifting for no good reason from the active to the passive voice or from the past to the present tense is confusing and irritating to the reader. Be consistent in your use of number, person, tense, voice, and mood.

21a In Number

Avoid shifting awkwardly and inconsistently between the singular and the plural.

Many shifts of this kind are actually problems with pronoun-antecedent agreement (see pp. 236–241).

INCONSISTENT:	Just before **a person** speaks in public, **they** should do several relaxation exercises.
CONSISTENT:	Just before **a person** speaks in public, **he or she** should do several relaxation exercises.
OR:	Just before speaking in public, a person should do several relaxation exercises.
INCONSISTENT:	**A warthog** may appear ungainly, but **these animals** can run at a speed of 30 miles an hour.
CONSISTENT:	**A warthog** may appear ungainly, but **this animal** can run at a speed of 30 miles an hour.
OR:	**Warthogs** may appear ungainly, but **these animals** can run at a speed of 30 miles an hour.
INCONSISTENT:	**Anyone** who travels to Greece will see many sites about which **they** have read.
CONSISTENT:	**People** who travel to Greece will see many sites about which **they** have read.
OR:	**Travelers** to Greece will see many sites about which **they** have read.

21b In Person

Avoid shifting awkwardly between the second person and the third person.

All nouns and all indefinite pronouns are in the third person. However, personal pronouns may be in the first person, the second person, or the third person.

	SINGULAR	PLURAL
FIRST PERSON:	I, me, my, mine	we, us, our, ours
SECOND PERSON:	you, your, yours	you, your, yours
THIRD PERSON:	he, him, his she, her, hers it, its	they, them, their, theirs they, them, their, theirs

INCONSISTENT:	It has been said that unless **you** have a knowledge of history, **a person** is condemned to repeat the mistakes of history.
CONSISTENT:	It has been said that unless **you** have a knowledge of history, **you** are condemned to repeat the mistakes of history.
OR:	It has been said that without a knowledge of history, a person is condemned to repeat the mistakes of history.
INCONSISTENT:	When **a person** reads Jefferson's *Notes on Virginia*, **you** are amazed by his wide range of interests.
CONSISTENT:	When **people** read Jefferson's *Notes on Virginia*, **they** are amazed by his wide range of interests.
OR:	People who read Jefferson's *Notes on Virginia* are amazed by his wide range of interests.
INCONSISTENT:	As **we** read about the slaughtering of the rhinoceros for its horn and the elephant for its tusks, **one** becomes appalled by the selfishness of humankind.
CONSISTENT:	As **we** read about the slaughtering of the rhinoceros for its horn and the elephant for its tusks, **we** become appalled by the selfishness of humankind.
OR:	Reading about the slaughtering of the rhinoceros for its horn and the elephant for its tusks, one becomes appalled by the selfishness of humankind.

21c In Tense

Avoid shifting awkwardly between the present tense and the past tense.

When writing about literature or history, you can often use either the present tense or the past tense. However, if you start writing in the present tense, continue writing in this tense. If you start writing in the past tense, continue writing in this tense.

INCONSISTENT: At the end of the war, Ezra Pound **is accused** of treason. He **was confined** at St. Elizabeth's Hospital, where he **spends** the next twelve years.

CONSISTENT: At the end of the war, Ezra Pound **is accused** of treason. He **is confined** at St. Elizabeth's Hospital, where he **spends** the next twelve years.

INCONSISTENT: *The Day of the Scorpion* **is** the second book in Paul Scott's *The Raj Quartet*. It **tells** the story of an English family living in India in the last years of British rule. The book **opened** on August 9, 1942. On this day Gandhi and other prominent Indians who had voted for independence from Britain **were sent** to prison.

CONSISTENT: *The Day of the Scorpion* **is** the second book in Paul Scott's *The Raj Quartet*. It **tells** the story of an English family living in India in the last years of British rule. The book **opens** on August 9, 1942. On this day Gandhi and other prominent Indians who had voted for independence from Britain **are sent** to prison.

INCONSISTENT: Lincoln **came** to national attention as a result of a series of debates with Stephen A. Douglas. Although he **loses** the senatorial election to Douglas, two years later he **gains** the Republican nomination for president.

CONSISTENT: Lincoln **came** to national attention as a result of a series of debates with Stephen A. Douglas. Although he **lost** the senatorial election to Douglas, two years later he **gained** the Republican nomination for president.

21d In Voice

Avoid shifting awkwardly between the active voice and the passive voice.

INCONSISTENT:	John F. Kennedy **won** the presidency with only 49.7 percent of the popular vote because a majority of the electoral vote **was captured** by him.
CONSISTENT:	John F. Kennedy **won** the presidency with only 49.7 percent of the popular vote because he **captured** a majority of the electoral vote.
INCONSISTENT:	André-Jacques Garnerin **made** the first parachute jump, and the first aerial photographs **were taken** by Samuel Archer King and William Black.
CONSISTENT:	André-Jacques Garnerin **made** the first parachute jump, and Samual Archer King and William Black **took** the first aerial photographs.
INCONSISTENT:	A group of ants **is called** a colony, but you **refer** to a group of bees as a swarm.
CONSISTENT:	A group of ants **is called** a colony, but a group of bees **is referred** to as a swarm.

21e In Mood

Avoid shifting awkwardly between the indicative, imperative, and subjunctive moods.

INCONSISTENT:	First **brown** the onions in butter. Then you **should add** them to the beef stock.
CONSISTENT:	First **brown** the onions in butter. Then **add** them to the beef stock.
INCONSISTENT:	If I **were** president of this club and he **was** my second in command, things would be very different.

CONSISTENT: If I **were** president of this club and he **were** my second in command, things would be very different.

INCONSISTENT: First **proofread** your paper and **make** any necessary changes. Next you **ought to retype** it.

CONSISTENT: First **proofread** your paper and **make** any necessary changes. Next **retype** it.

(See also mood, p. 168.)

EXERCISE 21–1

Rephrase each of the following items to eliminate awkward shifts in number, person, voice, and mood.

1. In the novel the prisoners all gathered in the mess hall. Then they begin to shout and to throw dishes.

2. Because tuition is so expensive, a student should take their courses seriously.

3. Before you begin to criticize someone, one should consider what that person has been through.

4. In order to transplant a bush, dig deeply into the soil and loosen it. Then the plant should be placed carefully in the hole you made.

5. A person must bring a check, not cash, when you purchase license plates.

6. Anyone who reads these instructions will not understand what he or she have read.

7. A person cannot help but be impressed when you see the rock group perform.

8. The American company introduced a new model of automobile but it was made by workers in Europe.

9. The little dog runs into the street and was struck by the child on a skateboard.

10. In the drama the protagonist works hard at his job during the day but relaxed at night.

---

22 Sequence of Tenses

Maintain a logical sequence of tenses to indicate when events happen in relation to one another.

The English tense system may seem complicated, but most of the time, native speakers of the language have few problems using it correctly. One problem is shifting unnecessarily from one tense to another (see pp. 269–270). Some writers, on the other hand, have the opposite problem: they do not change tenses when they need to in order to show that one event happened before or after another. The following rules cover some of the most common problems with sequence of tenses.

22a With Clauses

If you begin a sentence in the present tense, shift to the past tense or the present perfect tense when you begin to write about past action.

> **NOT:** To a large extent, we **remember** Alice B. Toklas because she **is** Gertrude Stein's friend.
>
> **BUT:** To a large extent, we **remember** Alice B. Toklas because she **was** Gertrude Stein's friend.
>
> **NOT:** Today he **supports** moving the embassy, but just three weeks ago he **opposes** this action.
>
> **BUT:** Today he **supports** moving the embassy, but just three weeks ago he **opposed** this action.
>
> **NOT:** She always **goes** to the mountains on vacation because she **loved** them since childhood.
>
> **BUT:** She always **goes** to the mountains on vacation because she **has loved** them since childhood.

Use the past perfect tense to indicate that one past action occurred before another past action.

> **NOT:** Hitler **purged** the Nazi Party before he **gained** complete control of the state.
>
> **BUT:** Hitler **had purged** the Nazi Party before he **gained** complete control of the state.
>
> **NOT:** They **double-checked** the results of their experiment because they **made** an error.
>
> **BUT:** They **double-checked** the results of their experiment because they **had made** an error.
>
> **NOT:** Since spring **came** early, they **were hoping** for a long growing season.
>
> **BUT:** Since spring **had come** early, they **were hoping** for a long growing season.

Use the future perfect tense to indicate that an action in the future will occur before another future action.

> NOT: By next Tuesday we **will cover** half the course.
> BUT: By next Tuesday we **will have covered** half the course.
>
> NOT: When they **pay** off the loan, they **paid** twice the cost of the car.
> BUT: When they **pay** off the loan, they **will have paid** twice the cost of the car.

22b With Infinitives

Use the present infinitive to express action that occurs at the same time as or later than the action of the main verb. Use the present perfect infinitive to express action that occurs before the action of the main verb.

> NOT: They **need to purchase** their tickets by now.
> BUT: They **need to have purchased** their tickets by now. (*The need is in the present; the purchase, if it happened, was in the past.*)
>
> NOT: The artist **wanted to have captured** the variations in the light.
> BUT: The artist **wanted to capture** the variations in the light. (*The wanting occurred before the capturing.*)
>
> NOT: The designer **had hoped to have gotten** the job.
> BUT: The designer **had hoped to get** the job.

Compare the following three sentences.

> He **would like to review** the book favorably. (would like *in the present* to review *in the present*)
>
> He **would have liked to review** the book favorably. (would have liked *in the past* to review *in the past*)
>
> He **would like to have reviewed** the book favorably. (would like *in the present* to have reviewed *in the past*)

22c With Participles

Use the present participle to express action that occurs at the same time as the action of the main verb. Use the present perfect participle or the past participle to express action that occurs before the action of the main verb.

The present perfect participle of a verb consists of the word *having* followed by the past participle of the verb: *having done, having been, having seen,* and so forth.

NOT: **Winning** the battle, the general planned the next day's campaign.

BUT: **Having won** the battle, the general *planned* the next day's campaign. (*action of participle occurred before action of main verb*)

NOT: **Having hoped** for good news, he rushed for the telephone.

BUT: **Hoping** for good news, he *rushed* for the telephone. (*action of participle occurred at the same time as action of main verb*)

NOT: **Being encouraged** by her friends, she eagerly filled out the form for entrance in the marathon.

BUT: **Having been encouraged by her friends,** she *filled out* the form eagerly for entrance in the marathon. (*action of participle occurred before action of main verb*)

OR: **Encouraged** by her friends, she eagerly *filled out* the form for entrance in the marathon.

EXERCISE 22-1

Correct any error in the sequence of tenses in the following sentences. Identify any correct sentences.

1. After driving an hour to reach the mall, he discovered he lost all the money he got from the bank a day earlier.

2. Obtaining two evening jobs this week, the pianist decided to have given up his desire to continue taking music lessons.

3. We were all sorry to have missed your presentation.

4. He had been happy to travel to visit you having waited for the instructions for a week.

5. Most adolescents know about the mechanics of sex since they heard about them at an earlier age.

6. We were wishing for a long ski season even though winter had come late.

7. By the end of next week we will cover half of the course's syllabus.

8. Although our ticket sales fell a little this week, we still hope to have a good crowd at the dance.

9. He was late for the meeting, parking his car so far away.

10. After the performance, we told the actors we had a wonderful evening.

23   Sentence Structure

The parts of a sentence, like those of a building or a jig-saw puzzle, must be put together in a certain way in order to fit with one another. For example, verbs must agree with their subjects, and pronouns with their antecedents. In constructing sentences, you must also be sure to maintain a consistent structure throughout a sentence, to make subjects and predicates fit together logically, to express parallel grammatical elements in parallel form, and to place modifiers correctly.

23a Mixed Structure

Maintain a consistent sentence structure. Do not start a sentence with one type of structure and end it with another type.

> **INCONSISTENT:**   First rub olive oil over the outside of the chicken; then salt the chicken lightly, but no pepper.

The writer of the preceding sentence begins with an independent clause, continues with another independent clause, and then begins the third part of the sentence with the conjunction *but,* indicating that another independent clause will follow. However, the writer then ends the sentence with a phrase rather than a clause. The problem can be eliminated by turning the phrase into a clause.

CONSISTENT: First rub olive oil over the outside of the chicken; then salt the chicken lightly, but do not pepper it.

Another kind of mixed sentence structure is created by clauses that are not clearly related to one another.

INCONSISTENT: When your parents were poorly educated and you yourself have attended substandard schools, what kind of odds for success are those?

In this sentence, the writer begins with an adverb clause that should modify a word in an independent clause. However, the independent clause that follows does not contain any word for the adverb clause to modify. To correct the problem, simply provide such a word.

CONSISTENT: What kind of odds for success do you have when your parents were poorly educated and you yourself have attended substandard schools?

INCONSISTENT: Those black pilots who fought so valiantly during World War II, many people do not even know of their existence.

Here the writer begins with a noun modified by an adjective clause but does not provide a predicate for the noun. Instead, the sentence ends with an independent clause that is not grammatically related to what precedes it.

CONSISTENT: Many people do not even know of the existence of those black pilots who fought so valiantly during World War II.

The following sentence is from a television program about training business executives to answer (or evade) reporters' questions.

> **INCONSISTENT:**   How you could be a newsperson and work with people you might one day have to interview, I could not do it.
>
> **CONSISTENT:**   As a newsperson, I could not work with people I might one day have to interview.
>
> **OR:**   I do not understand how you could be a newsperson and work with people you might one day have to interview.

23b Faulty Predication

Make the subject and predicate of a sentence fit together both grammatically and logically.

A sentence with a poorly matched subject and predicate is said to have **faulty predication.**

> **NOT:**   More versatile and more manageable account for the popularity of the latest breed of home computers.

In the preceding sentence, the writer used two adjectives as the subject of the predicate *account for . . . computers*. A subject, however, must always be a noun or a noun equivalent.

> **BUT:**   Their greater **versatility** and the increased **manageability** account for the popularity of the latest breed of home computers.

Other sentences with faulty predication are grammatically acceptable but make no sense or do not say what the writer intended.

NOT: Flattery and snobbery are people who will not be effective as political advisers.

The nouns *flattery* and *snobbery* do not sensibly fit the predicate *are people.*

BUT: The flatterer and the snob will not be effective as political advisers.

NOT: My opinion of his latest movie is poorly directed and ineptly filmed.

According to the preceding sentence, it is the writer's opinion that is poorly directed and ineptly filmed. Obviously, the writer meant to say this of the movie, not of the opinion.

BUT: In my opinion, his latest movie is poorly directed and ineptly filmed.

OR: My opinion of his latest movie is that it is poorly directed and ineptly filmed.

NOT: Our criminal-justice system, which allows the victims of crime to suffer more than the perpetrators of crime, should be punished more severely.

The subject *our criminal-justice system* does not fit the predicate *should be punished more severely.*

BUT: Our criminal-justice system, which allows the victims of crime to suffer more than the perpetrators of crime, should be changed.

OR: Our criminal-justice system should be changed so that perpetrators of crime suffer more than their victims.

Avoid using an adverb clause as a subject or as a predicate nominative.

NOT: Because the British were occupying Philadelphia is the reason the Liberty Bell was moved to Allentown during the Revolutionary War.

The word *because* introduces what must be an adverb clause.

BUT: Because the British were occupying Philadelphia, the Liberty Bell was moved to Allentown during the Revolutionary War.

NOT: The reason the Liberty Bell was moved to Allentown during the Revolutionary War is because the British were occupying Philadelphia.

Change this *because* adverb clause to a noun clause, or omit it.

BUT: The reason the Liberty Bell was moved to Allentown during the Revolutionary War is **that** the British were occupying Philadelphia.

NOT: The year 1778 is when the Liberty Bell was returned to Independence Hall.

BUT: The Liberty Bell was returned to Independence Hall in 1778.

NOT: Ironically, England is where the Liberty Bell was cast.

BUT: Ironically, the Liberty Bell was cast in England.

23c Faulty Parallelism

Use the same grammatical form for elements that are part of a series or a compound construction.

The speech was **concise, witty,** and **effective.**

Today's "supermom" is both **a mother** and **an executive.**

He tried to be honest **with himself** as well as **with others.**

Sentence elements that have the same grammatical structure are said to be *parallel*. When elements that are part of a series or a compound construction do not have the same form, a sentence is said to have **faulty parallelism.**

Repeat articles, prepositions, and the word *to* before the infinitive to make the meaning of a sentence clear.

> The audience applauded the composer and lyricist.

The preceding sentence is clear if the composer and the lyricist are the same person. It is misleading if they are not the same person. Repeat the article *the* to indicate two people.

> The audience applauded **the** composer and **the** lyricist.

UNCLEAR:	She was a prominent critic and patron of young poets.
CLEAR:	She was **a** prominent critic and **a** patron of young poets.
UNCLEAR:	She quickly learned to supervise the maid and cook.
CLEAR:	She quickly learned to supervise **the** maid and **the** cook.
CLEAR:	She quickly learned **to** supervise the maid and **to** cook.
UNCLEAR:	His father had taught him to shoot and ride a horse.
CLEAR:	His father had taught him **to** shoot and **to** ride a horse.

Place elements joined by a coordinating conjunction in the same grammatical form. Balance a noun with a noun, an adjective with an adjective, a prepositional phrase with a prepositional phrase, and so on.

NOT PARALLEL: The scientific community in general regarded him

adjective   adjective   noun
↓   ↓   ↓

as **outspoken, eccentric,** and a **rebel.**

PARALLEL: The scientific community in general regarded him

adjective   adjective   adjective
↓   ↓   ↓

as **outspoken, eccentric,** and **rebellious.**

NOT PARALLEL: In *Searching for Caleb,* the protagonist is a

noun   noun   clause
↓   ↓   ↓

wife, a **mother,** and **she tells fortunes.**

PARALLEL: In *Searching for Caleb,* the protagonist is a

noun   noun   noun
↓   ↓   ↓

wife, a **mother,** and a **fortune-teller.**

adjective
↓

NOT PARALLEL: Reviewers praised the play for its **realistic**

noun
↓

portrayal of a sensitive young woman and

noun clause
↓

because it gave a penetrating depiction of a family.

adjective
↓

PARALLEL: Reviewers praised the play for its **realistic**

noun
↓

portrayal of a sensitive young woman and its

adjective   noun
↓   ↓

penetrating depiction of family life.

prepositional phrase
↓

NOT PARALLEL: A hobbit is a creature **with a hearty appetite**

adjective clause
↓

and **who loves home.**

verb
↓

PARALLEL: A hobbit is a creature who **has** a hearty appetite

verb
↓

and **loves** home.

Place elements joined by correlative conjunctions in parallel form.

NOT PARALLEL: He was not only **her husband** but also **she considered him her friend.**

PARALLEL: He was not only **her husband** but also **her friend.**

NOT PARALLEL:	Knute Rockne would be either **a science teacher** or **someone who coached football.**
PARALLEL:	Knute Rockne would be either **a science teacher** or **a football coach.**
NOT PARALLEL:	After his vision, Scrooge becomes not only **a generous man** but also **happy.**
PARALLEL:	After his vision, Scrooge becomes not only **a generous man** but also **a happy one.**

Take care with the placement of correlative conjunctions.

| NOT PARALLEL: | Solar energy is **both** used to heat houses **and** to run small appliances. |

In the preceding sentence, the first part of the correlative conjunction (*both*) is followed by a verb, but the second part (*and*) is followed by an infinitive. The problem can be corrected by moving the *both* to a later position in the sentence so that it, too, is followed by an infinitive.

PARALLEL:	Solar energy is used **both** to heat houses **and** to run small appliances.
NOT PARALLEL:	She would **either** run as the presidential candidate **or** the vice presidential candidate.
PARALLEL:	She would run as **either** the presidential candidate **or** the vice presidential candidate.
NOT PARALLEL:	He **not only** wanted money **but also** fame.
PARALLEL:	He wanted **not only** money **but also** fame.

23d Dangling Modifiers

An introductory phrase must clearly and sensibly modify the noun or pronoun that follows it.

A phrase that does not do this is called a **dangling modifier,** because it is not clearly attached to the rest of the sentence.

> UNCLEAR: **Frightened by the huge, gnarled tree outside his window,** his head dived under the covers.

In the sentence above, the introductory participial phrase seems to modify his head, but it was obviously not the boy's head, but the boy himself, who was frightened. A simple way to revise this sentence is to rewrite the independent clause so that it begins with the noun that the introductory phrase actually refers to.

> CLEAR: **Frightened by the huge, gnarled tree outside his window,** the boy hid his head under the covers.
>
> UNCLEAR: **Unable to make a living in Detroit,** relocating to Houston seemed a good idea.

The introductory phrase does not sensibly modify *relocating*, the gerund that follows it. This sentence can also be revised by rewriting the independent clause so that it begins with the noun or pronoun that the introductory phrase actually refers to.

> CLEAR: **Unable to make a living in Detroit,** she thought relocating to Houston was a good idea.
>
> OR: **Unable to make a living in Detroit,** she thought she might move to Houston.

Another way to revise the sentence is to turn the phrase into a clause.

> CLEAR: **Because she was unable to make a living in Detroit,** relocating to Houston seemed a good idea.

Here are some more examples of dangling modifiers.

UNCLEAR:	**While trying to control my temper,** the sergeant forced me to do a hundred push-ups.
CLEAR:	**While trying to control my temper,** I was forced to do a hundred push-ups by the sergeant.
OR:	**As I tried to control my temper,** the sergeant forced me to do a hundred push-ups.
UNCLEAR:	**As a young girl,** my grandfather told me stories of his life in Korea.
UNCLEAR:	**When I was a young girl,** my grandfather told me stories of his life in Korea.

A few introductory phrases are idiomatic. They modify the entire sentence, not a particular word.

To tell the truth, no one knows where he is.
Relatively speaking, my grades are not that bad.
As a matter of fact, the sea is not wine-red but blue.

23e Misplaced Modifiers

Place a modifying word or phrase as close as possible to the word it modifies. Carefully avoid placing it so that it seems to refer to a word other than the one you intended.

The placement of a modifier in a sentence is very important. Notice the difference in meaning between the following two sentences.

He **almost** spent two hundred dollars.
He spent **almost** two hundred dollars.

In the first sentence, *almost* modifies the verb *spent*. It tells us that he did not complete his action. In the second sentence, *almost* modifies *two hundred*. It tells us that the amount he spent came close to, but did not total, two hundred dollars.

Misplaced modifiers make a sentence confusing or even ridiculous, as shown in the following examples.

UNCLEAR:	He almost spoke for two hours.
CLEAR:	He spoke for **almost** two hours.
UNCLEAR:	She only quoted from three sources.
CLEAR:	She quoted from **only** three sources.
UNCLEAR:	He sang a ditty about filling a bottomless hole with his sister.
CLEAR:	**With his sister,** he sang a ditty about filling a bottomless hole.
OR:	He sang a ditty **with his sister** about filling a bottomless hole.
UNCLEAR:	He described his years spent alone on the island after the rescue.
CLEAR:	**After the rescue** he described his years spent alone on the island.

Avoid misplacing a modifier that will create a **split infinitive** (see Section 9i, p. 191).

23f Squinting Modifiers

Avoid placing a modifier in such a way that it could refer to either the preceding or the following element in the sentence.

Such a modifier is called a **squinting modifier.**

UNCLEAR:	The mayor announced **in March** he would run for reelection.

Was it the announcement or the election that was in March?

CLEAR:	The mayor announced he would run for reelection in March.

CLEAR:	In March, the mayor announced he would run for re-election.
UNCLEAR:	Carlson said **today** he is leaving for California.
CLEAR:	Carlson said he is leaving for California today.
CLEAR:	Today Carlson said he is leaving for California.
UNCLEAR:	Professor Quinn asked us **before we left** to turn in our papers.
CLEAR:	Before we left, Professor Quinn asked us to turn in our papers.
CLEAR:	Professor Quinn asked us to turn in our papers before we left.

EXERCISE 23–1

Revise each of the following sentences to eliminate the problem in sentence structure.

1. The boy scouts marched quickly turning their faces toward the flag.

2. Not only did we have to cut the grass but also rake the leaves.

3. Reaching into his pocket he found a coin and key.

4. For recreation she prefers to jog and play handball.

5. I could not believe it how people could act that way.

6. Searching for the coins she dropped on the sidewalk, the bus departed without her.

7. The reason I did not attend the game is because I lost my ticket.

8. Shipped directly from the farm every Saturday, shoppers are able to purchase fresh eggs.

9. Vacation is when we don't work or study.

10. The athlete nearly ate all his breakfast and then only rested an hour before the important game.

PART IV

DICTION AND STYLE

Diction is the choice and use of words in writing. Good diction helps you reach your audience, achieve your purpose, maintain an appropriate tone, and write with style.

24   Appropriate Word Choice

Whenever you write, the most basic decision you have to make about diction is whether to use formal or informal English. **Formal English,** as its name suggests, adheres strictly to the conventions of standard English. Most of the writing you do in college or in a profession—term papers, formal essays, theses, reports—should be in formal English. **Informal English** takes a more relaxed attitude to the conventions of standard English and may include contractions, colloquialisms, jargon, and sometimes even slang. It is appropriate for informal writing situations—journal and diary entries, informal essays, and creative writing in which you try to capture the sound of everyday speech.

INFORMAL: The delegates **were savvy of the fact** that the document they were signing **wasn't** perfect.

FORMAL: The delegates **understood** that the document they were signing **was not** perfect.

INFORMAL: The candidate **slammed** her opponent for often **changing his tune** on the issues.

FORMAL: The candidate **criticized** her opponent for often **changing his views** on the issues.

INFORMAL:	Stickley furniture may not be **real smooth,** but **it's pricey** and **fresh.**	
FORMAL:	Stickley furniture may not be **very comfortable,** but **it is expensive** and **fashionable.**	

A good dictionary will not only help you determine whether a word or expression is formal or informal but also provide other useful information. Following is a list of three good desk dictionaries and a sample listing from the first one.

1. *The American Heritage Dictionary.* 2nd coll. ed. Boston: Houghton Mifflin, 1982, 1985.

2. *Webster's New World Dictionary of the American Language.* 2nd coll. ed. New York: Simon & Schuster, 1982.

3. *Random House Webster's College Dictionary.* McGraw-Hill Edition, 1991.

Pronunciation

doubt (dout) *v.* doubt-ed, doubt-ing, doubts. — *tr.* **1.** To be undecided or skeptical about. **2.** To tend to disbelieve; distrust: *doubts the promises of all politicians.* **3.** *Archaic.* To suspect; fear. —*intr.* To be undecided. —*n.*

Forms and usage as a verb

Definition as a noun

1. A lack of conviction or certainty. **2.** A lack of trust. **3.** A point about which one is uncertain or skeptical. **4.** An uncertain state of affairs: *an outcome still in doubt.* —*idioms.* beyond (or without) doubt. Without question; certainly; definitely, no doubt. **1.** Certainly. **2.** Probably. [ME *douten* < OFr. *douter* < Lat. *dubitare,* to waver.] —doubt'er *n.*

Etymology

Explanation of usage

Usage: *Doubt* and *doubtful* are often followed by clauses introduced by *that, whether,* or *if.* A choice among the three is guided by the intended meaning of the sentence, but considerable leeway exists. Generally, *that* is used when the intention is to express more or less complete rejection of a statement: *I doubt that he will even try* (meaning, "I don't think he will even try"); or, in the negative, to express more or less complete acceptance: *I don't doubt that you are right.* On the other hand, when the intention is to express real uncertainty, the choice is usually *whether: We doubt whether they can succeed. It is doubtful whether he will come.* According to a majority of the Usage Panel, *whether* is the only acceptable choice in such examples; a minority would also accept *if* (which is more informal in tone) or *that.* In sum, *that* is especially appropriate to the denial of uncertainty or to implied disbelief but is sometimes used also when the intention is to express real uncertainty. *Doubt* is frequently used in informal speech, both as verb and as noun, together with *but: I don't doubt but* (or *but what*) *he will come. There is no doubt but it will be difficult.* These usages should be avoided in writing; substitute *that* or *whether* as the case requires.

Explanation of usage (label)

doubt•ful (dout′fəl) *adj.* **1.** Subject to or tending to cause doubt; uncertain: *It's doubtful if*

Syllabication (label)

Beginning of list of related words (label)

24a Slang

Slang is extremely informal language. It consists of colorful words, phrases, and expressions added to the language, usually by youthful or high-spirited people, to give it an exciting or ebullient flavor. Carl Sandburg described slang as "language that rolls up its sleeves, spits on its hands, and goes to work."

Slang is usually figurative and highly exaggerated. Each generation has its own slang; for example, in the 1960s someone who was approved of was *cool,* in the 1970s such a person was *with it,* and in the early 1980s, *awesome.* Although slang often begins as street language, some of it becomes so popular that with time it is accepted as part of formal language. Until a slang term becomes accepted, however, it is usually inappropriate in college writing.

> SLANG: Some parents **came apart** when they were **clued in to** how some children's programs on the **idiot tube** were really just extended commercials.

> FORMAL: Some parents **became upset** when they were **made aware of** how some children's **television** programs were really just extended commercials.

> SLANG: Elizabeth Blackwell was **spaced out** by the nineteenth century's view of the ideal woman, but she managed to find a doctor who was **wired with** her goal of studying medicine.

> FORMAL: Elizabeth Blackwell was **disheartened** by the nineteenth century's view of the ideal woman, but she managed to find a doctor who was **sympathetic to** her goal of studying medicine.

Slang can be used judiciously for effect in formal writing. When you use slang this way, do not enclose it in quotation marks or underline it.

> The educated were turning in their diplomas for guitars, the rich were trading in their furs for jeans and love beads, and the middle-aged were pretending they were fifteen, not fifty; in fact, during this topsy-turvy time, everyone seemed to be **going nuts.**

> She was thoughtful, politically aware, well spoken, and well educated, but the movie directors of the 1950s preferred **airheads.**

> As he grew older, he realized that his **old man** had been smarter than he thought.

24b Colloquialisms

Colloquial language is the conversational and everyday language of educated people. **Colloquialisms** are the words and expressions that characterize this language. Though not as informal as slang, colloquial langauge is generally still too casual to be considered appropriate for formal writing.

COLLOQUIAL: The meeting will begin at 7:00 p.m. **on the dot.**
FORMAL: The meeting will begin **promptly** at 7:00 p.m.

COLLOQUIAL: In *Bodily Harm*, Rennie realizes she is **in a jam** when she opens the box and finds illegal guns.
FORMAL: In *Bodily Harm*, Rennie realizes she is **in trouble** when she opens the box and finds illegal guns.

COLLOQUIAL: When Colonel Pickering expresses doubt as to Higgins's ability to make a lady of Eliza, Higgins **tells him to put up or shut up.**
FORMAL: When Colonel Pickering expresses doubt as to Higgins's ability to make a lady of Eliza, Higgins **invites him to make a bet.**

Notice how the following sentences are improved when the colloquial qualifiers are replaced by more formal adverbs.

COLLOQUIAL: Harriet Tubman was a **terribly** brave woman, for she made several trips back into slave territory to lead fugitives into freedom.

FORMAL: Harriet Tubman was a **truly** brave woman, for she made several trips back into slave territory to lead fugitives into freedom.

COLLOQUIAL: General Harrison considered Tecumseh's plan to force the United States to relinquish its claims to Indian lands **awfully** clever, but not workable.

FORMAL:	General Harrison considered Tecumseh's plan to force the United States to relinquish its claims to Indian lands **extremely** clever, but not workable.
COLLOQUIAL:	Television viewers were **pretty** moved by the program about nuclear war.
FORMAL:	Television viewers were **greatly** moved by the program about nuclear war.

24c Jargon

Jargon is the special language used by people in a particular field or group to communicate with others in the same field or group. The problem with jargon, or "shop talk," is that people outside the group have trouble understanding it. Language aimed at people with a specific technical or professional knowledge may be appropriate for some classes, but it is not appropriate for most general college writing. If you must use a technical term in general college writing, make sure you define it.

Consider the following excerpt which captures the strangeness of some computer jargon.

> A system for visual data interpretation should address format conversion, data storage and retrieval, the user interface, visualization methods, and capture of results on film or videotape. Frequently, data *format conversion* is required to convert floating-point numbers generated at irregular mesh points to integers in a rectilinear array. To ensure interactive speeds, it is important to consider *data storage and retrieval.*

> E. J. Farrell, et al.
> *Visual Interpretation of Multidimensional Computations and Transistor Design*

Someone who is familiar with computer programming will easily understand this paragraph. However, the general audience at which you aim most of your college writing will not; they will need to know the meaning of the terms *format, conversion, data storage and retrieval, user interface, visualization methods, floating-point numbers, irregular mesh points*, and *rectilinear array.*

24d Gobbledygook

Gobbledygook, or inflated diction, is stuffy, pretentious, inflated language that often contains an abundance of jargon. It is found in much government, legal, and academic writing, as well as in many other places, and it is sometimes called *governmentese* or *legalese*. Avoid gobbledygook, because it obscures meaning and lends both a timid and a pompous quality to your writing.

A major advocate of eliminating gobbledygook, especially from government writing, is Rudolf Flesch. In his book *How to Write Plain English*, he shows how Oregon's income tax instructions were rewritten to eliminate gobbledygook.

ORIGINAL

Deceased persons. A return must be made by the executor or administrator of the decedent's estate or by the surviving spouse or other person charged with the care of the property of the deceased. If the surviving spouse or next of kin desires to claim the refund, an affidavit should be submitted with the return. This affidavit (Form 243) is available at all Oregon Department of Revenue district offices, or it can be obtained by writing the Oregon Department of Revenue, State Office Building, Salem, Oregon 97310.

REVISED

My husband died last year. Can I file for him? Yes. The husband or wife of someone who dies, or the legal representative, must file the return. Use the form the person would have used if living. If you claim a refund, attach Form 243 to show you have the right to the deceased person's refund. Write for Form 243 to: Oregon Department of Revenue, Salem, Oregon 97310, or pick it up at any of our district offices.

EXERCISE 24-1

Rephrase each of the following sentences in formal English.

1. Grasp the circular receptacle by its protuberance and slowly rotate it until the minute particles deposited therein explode into almost weightless edibles.

2. Don't give me any jazz on the reasons why you miss the beat every time we're supposed to meet my parents.

3. He was caught red-handed with his hand in the cookie jar by the security guard.

4. Her shoes are rad but she still looks like a granola.

5. After an awesome scoring drive, the fullback hot dogged in the end zone and high-fived the other players.

6. I can't deal with all these problems anymore.

7. She kind of got mad when she got stood up for the dance.

8. His set of wheels cost a bundle.

9. I haven't a clue as to why people call her a "tie-dye."

10. His new specs have colored panes and he still visits a shrink.

25 Sexist and Other Biased Language

When writing, it is important to avoid language that may offend or alienate your audience and leave you open to charges of unfairness and prejudice.

25a Sexist Language

Sexist language is the use of words that inappropriately call attention to gender. Such language tends to stereotype individuals, usually women. It reflects outmoded usage, unfairly and incorrectly excludes an entire sex, and is often demeaning. Using the word *mankind* for instance, when you are referring to all people, discriminates against women by excluding them. Substituting the gender-neutral words *all people, humanity,* or *humankind* eliminates the sexist language; it is fair to both sexes.

As a writer, one of your most important jobs is to be as accurate as you can be. Avoiding sexist language will enable you to fulfill this goal. But sexist language, or any biased language, poses a bigger threat than simply affecting your accuracy. Words have incredible power; the images they create last a lifetime. Special care should be taken to choose the appropriate words that will enable you to communicate effectively and show consideration for another's point of view. The following

guidelines will help you recognize sexist language and eliminate it from your writing.

**Avoid using the word *man* or nouns ending in *-man* when
discussing both sexes.**

Replace any masculine-marked words in your writing with
gender-free alternatives such as these:

MASCULINE-MARKED WORDS	ALTERNATIVES
fellow man	other people, humans
forefathers	ancestors
kinsman	relative
layman	ordinary person, nonspecialist
man	human, person, individual
(to) man	to care for, to work
spokesman	speaker, representative
statesman	leader
workmanship	skilled work, quality job

Converting the suffix *-man* to *-person* often works, as in *chairperson* or *salesperson.* However, this practice can be awkward,
as in *cave person* or *committee person.* Using sex-free solutions
such as *cave dweller* or *committee member* is more effective.
Similarly, avoid using feminine-marked terms such a *schoolgirl*
or *mother tongue,* when *student* or *native language* would
work just as effectively.

Rewrite to avoid stereotyping jobs and social roles by gender.

Replace the words *salesman, chairman, mailman,* and
businessman with the gender-free terms *sales representative,
chair, mail carrier,* and *business executive.* Similarly, use such
terms as *housekeeper* instead of *cleaning woman, homemaker*

instead of *housewife,* and *flight attendant* instead of *stewardess* or *steward.* Recognize that the use of gender-specific terms for occupations is quickly disappearing as various groups and organizations substitute neutral job titles for those traditionally identified as male or female.

Watch for the use of language that expresses traditional and outdated assumptions about male and female occupations and roles.

Consider these sentences:

NOT: A doctor uses his skill and physical strength in the operating room while a nurse uses her compassion at the bedside.

BUT: Doctors and nurses use their skill, physical strength, and compassion in the operating room and at the bedside.

NOT: When cleaning their homes, women should be thorough.

BUT: It's important to be thorough when cleaning house.

Be consistent when naming individuals and identifying their occupations. Failing to do so implies a real or imagined value judgment about the person, the occupation, or both.

NOT: The corporate president, John Martinez, and his lovely wife Linda, a lawyer and mother of two, attended the gala.

BUT: The corporate president, John Martinez, and his lawyer wife, Linda Ostacco, attended the gala.

Also, it is appropriate to identify a married woman by her own name instead of her husband's name. When writing the names of male or female authors, artists, composers, and so on, write the full name the first time it appears. Subsequent references should be made by last name only, without a title: **not** Mr. Hemingway **but** Hemingway; **not** Miss Dickinson **but** Dickinson.

Check for demeaning language or for language that presents a stereotypical view of the way the sexes behave.

In your writing, avoid referring to women as *girls, ladies,* or *young ladies.* Sexist terms like *lady lawyer, coed,* and *gal Friday* should be avoided. Instead use the words *lawyer, student,* and *assistant.* Substitute terms such as *male dancer* and *male nurse* with *dancer* and *nurse.* Similarly, watch for phrases such as *cute girls* and *rowdy boys* that reinforce stereotypes about the way men and women act.

Rewrite your sentences to avoid using the generic pronoun *he* when referring to all human beings.

In the past *generic he* was acceptable when referring to men and women:

Nobody wants a failing grade to be on *his* record.

Everyone can be successful if *he* is given a chance.

In fact, for many years students were taught to use the male pronouns *he, him,* or *his* as antecedents or references for indefinite pronouns. In the first sentence, *his* refers to *nobody,* indirectly suggesting males only are in danger of failing. In the second, *he* refers to *everyone,* indirectly suggesting that males only are capable of success. Indefinite pronouns like *nobody* and *everyone* are gender neutral. Combining them with masculine pronouns like *he* and *his* results in sexist language. The following strategies may help you eliminate this inadvertent sexism.

1. Recast your sentences to make the pronouns plural.

   No *individuals* want failing grades on *their* record.

   People can be successes if *they* are given a chance.

2. Try eliminating the pronoun by using an article (*a, an,* or *the*) in its place.

    Nobody wants *a* failing grade recorded.

    Everyone can be successful if given *a* chance.

3. Rewrite the sentence using *he or she* (or *she or he*) whenever you refer back to a singular indefinite pronoun such as *everyone* or *nobody*.

    Nobody wants a failing grade to be on *his or her* record.

    Everyone can be successful if *she or he* is given a chance.

    Be aware that with repeated use this type of construction leads to stilted writing. Strings of *his or her* constructions quickly bore most readers. Note too that the use of *s/he* or *he/she* has not gained widespread acceptance.

Any of the methods shown here for revising sex-specific pronouns (see also Section 17a on pronouns) is correct, although you will probably find it easier to make words plural whenever appropriate. Plural is neither masculine nor feminine; it refers to both collectively.

25b Biased Language

Biased language, whether sexist language or any derogatory language directed at a group, race, religion, or nationality, should be avoided when writing. Identify all groups of people by their accepted proper names (see Section 7c on name calling, loaded words, and generalizations). Take care to avoid assigning stereotypical physical or behavioral characteristics to members of a particular group. Also, be aware that over time certain descriptive terms for groups of people acquire unfavorable connotations and that preferred terms for a group may change. As a matter of respect, be sensitive to these nuances and always use the terms that groups choose for themselves. Remember that language is powerful—it can wound by sending out a discriminatory message. Pay special attention to the language you choose. (See Section 2a, pp. 18–19 for additional information on audience.)

EXERCISE 25-1

Identify the biased language in the following sentences and supply an acceptable substitute. One sentence is acceptable as is.

1. The hard hats frequent that bar, but the chicks prefer the one downtown.

2. Our school has basketball teams for both men and girls.

3. Everyone was requested to move to her or his seat.

4. Mankind's inhumanity spreads throughout history.

5. Ask the kid at the desk what time the postman arrives.

6. Those guys play football like a bunch of old ladies.

7. The waitress tripped over the bus boy's foot.

8. In that coed dormitory, boys and girls live on alternate floors.

9. John is considered the black sheep of the family.

10. Firemen, policemen, scrubwomen, and hairdressers all joined in the singing.

26   Exact Word Choice

Choose words that express your thoughts precisely. Avoid settling for a near-synonym or an almost-right word, but pay attention to shades of meaning, nuances, and context.

26a Specific and General Words

Specific words are precise, focused, and restricted in scope. General words are not focused; they refer to a large group or a wide range of things. For example, compare the following general and specific words.

GENERAL:	painter	make	hungry	some
SPECIFIC:	Mary Cassatt	coerce	voracious	thirty-five

The word *painter* refers to a whole group of people. *Mary Cassatt* refers to just one. The word *make* refers to a wide range of actions; *coerce* limits this range, meaning "to make someone do something or to make something happen through the use of force or pressure." The word *hungry* indicates a desire for food or for something else, but *voracious* indicates that this desire is overwhelming and insatiable. The word *some* indicates a number larger than a few, but *thirty-five* indicates a specific number.

Consider how the following sentences are improved through the use of a specific word.

GENERAL:	The **official** was accused of **working** for a **foreign government.**
SPECIFIC:	**Alger Hiss** was accused of **spying** for the **Soviet Union.**

GENERAL: This **woman,** who is best known for **longer things,** also wrote **several good** ghost stories, which are collected in a **book.**

SPECIFIC: **Edith Wharton,** who is best known for her **novels,** also wrote **eleven riveting** ghost stories, which are collected in *The Ghost Stories of Edith Wharton.*

GENERAL: **Some writers** are **liked** for their **sense of humor.**

SPECIFIC: **Dorothy Parker and Robert Benchley** are **appreciated** for their **wry, and sometimes biting, wit.**

Of course, general words do have a place in your writing. They introduce topics that you can later elaborate on or narrow. When you use a general word, however, consider narrowing the scope of this word later in your writing, if not immediately. Always search for an alternative before using adjectives and adverbs such as *good, nice, bad, very, great, fine, awfully, well done,* or *interesting.* Words like these are so general, that is, have so many meanings, that paradoxically they convey almost no meaning at all.

26b Concrete and Abstract Words

Concrete words create vivid impressions. They name things that can be seen, touched, heard, smelled, or tasted—in other words, things that can be perceived by the senses. The words *skyscraper, microfilm, buzzer, gourmet, pizza,* and *porcupine* are concrete words. **Abstract words** name concepts, ideas, beliefs, and qualities—in other words, things that cannot be perceived by the senses. For example, the words *democracy, honesty, childhood,* and *infinity* are abstract words. Use abstract words with care, because, in general, they create less intense impressions and so are often ineffective.

ABSTRACT: He argued that this nation could no longer accept poverty.

CONCRETE: Hungry children crying themselves to sleep, families evicted from their homes and sleeping in the streets, old people in cold-water flats surviving by eating cat food—these are conditions, he argued, that we as Americans can no longer tolerate.

ABSTRACT: Immigrants came to America in search of a better life.

CONCRETE: Immigrants came to America to farm their own land, to earn a living wage, to put a roof over their heads and food in their stomachs, and to speak and believe as they wished without fear of being thrown in jail.

ABSTRACT: One reason supermarkets began to replace ma-and-pa grocery stores is that they offered more variety.

CONCRETE: One reason supermarkets began to replace ma-and-pa grocery stores is that they offered not one brand of peas, but seven brands; not one kind of coffee, but six kinds; not one type of paper towel, but ten in five different colors—all under one roof.

Abstract words do have a place in your writing. However, too many of them can create an impression of vagueness. When you use abstract words, try to provide concrete examples to make their meaning vivid. Compare the following pairs of sentences. The second sentence in each pair contains a concrete example that clarifies the meaning of the abstract word or words in the first sentence.

Hating people is self-destructive.
Hating people is like burning down your own house to get rid of a rat.

Harry Emerson Fosdick

Circumstance makes heroes of people.
A light supper, a good night's sleep, and a fine morning often made a hero of the same man who by indigestion, a restless night, and a rainy morning would have proved a coward.

Earl of Chesterfield

Americans are absorbed in the present but are unaware of the
past.

We Americans are the best informed people on earth as to the
events of the last twenty-four hours; we are not the best informed as to the events of the last sixty centuries.

Will and Ariel Durant

EXERCISE 26-1

Each of the following sentences is vague or unclear. Rewrite each
sentence, replacing general and abstract words with specific or
concrete ones.

1. Contemporary architects are designing new shapes for interior

   spaces.

2. People avoid unpleasantries.

3. Keeping a houseplant is not as time consuming as keeping a

   pet.

4. Some men's clothing was on sale sometime last week.

5. The media objected to the mayor's decision.

26c Denotation and Connotation

Besides their **denotation,** or basic dictionary definition,
many words also have **connotations**—associations that the
word brings to mind and emotions that it arouses. Words that
have the same dictionary meaning may have quite different connotations. For example, consider the following two sentences.

The clothes at this boutique are quite **cheap.**
The clothes at this boutique are quite **inexpensive.**

Both *cheap* and *inexpensive* have the dictionary meaning of "not expensive." However, *cheap* carries a negative connotation of low value, but *inexpensive* carries a positive connotation of fair value.

When you write, you must choose words with the appropriate connotations.

INAPPROPRIATE:	The quality of **childish** innocence shines through her poetry.
APPROPRIATE:	The quality of **childlike** innocence shines through her poetry.
INAPPROPRIATE:	The editorial praised the candidate for being **egocentric.**
APPROPRIATE:	The editorial praised the candidate for being an **individualist.**
INAPPROPRIATE:	In 1873, the Supreme Court prevented Myra Bradwell from becoming a lawyer, because it did not consider the law an **effeminate** profession.
APPROPRIATE:	In 1873, the Supreme Court prevented Myra Bradwell from becoming a lawyer, because it did not consider the law a **ladylike** profession.

Some words have such strong connotations that they are said to be *loaded.* When used, they go off with a deafening emotional bang. For example, the words *slumlord, witch-hunt,* and *imperialism* are all loaded. Their connotative effect drowns out their denotative meaning. Be careful of loaded words, because they can make your writing appear biased. (See pp. 20–22; 125–126.)

EXERCISE 26-2

In each of the following pairs, the words have the same or almost the same denotative meaning but different connotations. Write a sentence for each word that shows you understand its connotative value. You may use your dictionary to help you.

1. common/vulgar

2. donation/giveaway

3. hardy/bold

4. wrinkled/messy

5. effete/sterile

6. corrupt/dishonest

7. mutter/mumble

8. requests/demands

9. ignorant/moronic

10. customers/patrons

26d Wordiness and Repetition

Write as concisely as possible. Do not use five words where one will do. Avoid using empty words and unnecessary repetitions. Conciseness gives vigor to your style.

One way to achieve conciseness is to eliminate wordy expressions. Notice how each of the following phrases can be changed to a single-word equivalent.

WORDY	CONCISE
at all times when	whenever
at this point in time	now
at that point in time	then
because of the fact that	because
bring to a conclusion	conclude
by means of	by
due to the fact that	because
during the time that	while
in the event that	if

WORDY	CONCISE
in spite of the fact that	although
make reference	refer
be of the opinion that	think
on a great many occasions	often
prior to this time	before
until such time as	until
have a conference	confer

You can also make your writing more concise by deleting superfluous words, using exact words, and reducing larger elements to smaller elements. Notice how the following sentence is improved when the author uses these revision strategies:

WORDY: In the month of December in the year 1991, those who were flying in space on board the spaceship that was named *Challenger* made an attempt to catch hold of and perform a repair job on a satellite that had been disabled.

CONCISE: In December 1991, astronauts aboard the spaceship *Challenger* tried to grab and repair a disabled satellite.

The words *the month of* and *in the year* add nothing to the meaning of the sentence; they simply fill up space and can be deleted. The noun phrase *those who were flying in space* can be replaced by one exact noun—*astronauts*. The words *that was named* are also deadwood. The phrase *made an attempt* can be reduced to the more direct *attempted, catch hold of* to *grab*, and *perform a repair job on* to *repair*. The clause *that had been disabled* can be reduced to the single word *disabled*.

WORDY: A man named Allan Dwan, who was a pioneer in the field of filmmaking, began his career as a director in the year 1910.

CONCISE: Allan Dwan, a pioneer filmmaker, began directing in 1910.

WORDY:	The film that is called *The Birth of a Nation* and that was made by D. W. Griffith has caused a lot of controversy among people.
CONCISE:	D. W. Griffith's film *The Birth of a Nation* is highly controversial.

Avoid the wordiness that comes from overuse of prepositional phrases, the weak verb *be*, and relative pronouns.

WORDY:	The book examines the twentieth century **in terms of** its wars, depressions, and social changes.
CONCISE:	The book examines the twentieth century, its wars, depressions, and social changes.
WORDY:	1941 **was** the year **when, on** December 7, the Japanese bombed Pearl Harbor.
CONCISE:	On December 7, 1941, the Japanese bombed Pearl Harbor.
WORDY:	The car **that** was parked on the street, **close to** the curb is the **kind of** car **that** I have always wanted to own.
CONCISE:	I have always wanted a car like the one parked at the curb.

Using the active voice instead of the passive voice will usually make a sentence more concise (see voice, pp. 167–168). Sometimes, however, the passive voice is the simplest and most concise way to express an idea. For example, the sentences *Her husband was killed in Vietnam* or *The President is inaugurated on January 20* would be much wordier and more awkward if they were rewritten to make the verbs active. In general, however, the passive voice is wordier than the active voice. Notice how the following sentences are improved by changing the passive voice to the active voice and eliminating other kinds of wordiness. (See also jargon and gobbledygook, pp. 299–301.)

WORDY:	Studies **are being undertaken** by doctors who specialize in psychology to find out what effects the divorce of two parents has on the children of the two parents.
CONCISE:	Psychologists **are studying** the effects of divorce on children.

WORDY:	According to the author, whose name is Freeman Dyson, *Weapons and Hope* **was chosen** by him as the title for his book because a desire **was felt** by him "to discuss the gravest problem facing mankind, the problem of nuclear weapons."
CONCISE:	Freeman Dyson **titled** his book *Weapons and Hope* because he **wanted** "to discuss the gravest problem facing mankind, the problem of nuclear weapons."

WORDY:	Advice about gardening **is given** every day by Blair Michels, and this advice **is printed** on page thirteen of this newspaper.
CONCISE:	Blair Michels **gives** daily gardening advice on page thirteen of this newspaper.

Try to avoid the constructions *it is, it was, there is,* and *there was.* Like the passive voice, these constructions are sometimes useful and appropriate, but often they are an unnecessarily wordy way of introducing an idea. Notice how the following sentences are improved by eliminating the unnecessary constructions.

WORDY:	It is known that there is a need for security in children.
CONCISE:	Children need security.

WORDY:	It is a fact that the painting is a forgery.
CONCISE:	The painting is a forgery.

WORDY:	There is a need among modern people to gain an understanding of the risks of modern technology.
CONCISE:	We need to understand the risks of modern technology.

Another cause of wordiness is redundant elements, words or phrases that unnecessarily repeat the idea expressed by the word to which they are attached. For example, the phrase *to the ear* is redundant in the expression *audible to the ear* because *audible* itself means "able to be perceived by the ear." Here is a list of some other common expressions that contain redundant elements.

REDUNDANT	CONCISE
and etc.	etc.
bibliography of books	bibliography
mandatory requirements	requirements
refer back	refer
tall in height	tall
collaborate together	collaborate
visible to the eye	visible
repeat again	repeat
advance forward	advance
negative complaints	complaints
humorous comedy	comedy
close proximity	proximity
expensive in price	expensive
past history	history
continue to remain	remain
component parts	components
free gift	gift

NOT: The plot of Le Carré's **fictional novel** *The Little Drummer Girl* involves the **emotionally passionate** claims of the Israelis and the Palestinians.

BUT: The plot of Le Carré's novel *The Little Drummer Girl* involves the **passionate** claims of the Israelis and the Palestinians.

NOT: The **consensus of opinion** is that the **true facts** of the **fatal assassination** may never be known.

BUT: The **consensus** is that the facts of the **assassination** may never be known.

NOT:	Copies of the **biography of his life** quickly **disappeared from sight** on the shelves, although the book was **large in size** and **heavy in weight.**
BUT:	Copies of the **biography** quickly **disappeared** from the shelves, although the book was **large** and **heavy.**

Repetition has an important place in writing. It can be used effectively to emphasize a point or to complete a parallel structure. However, needless or excessive repetition weakens your writing. You can eliminate it by deleting the repeated words or by substituting synonyms or pronouns for them.

NOT:	Lady **Macbeth** urges **Macbeth** to murder the **king** so that **Macbeth** can become **king.**
BUT:	Lady **Macbeth** urges **her husband** to murder the **king** so that **he** can gain **the crown.**

NOT:	One admirer of the rock group Devo has found similarities between **the works of Devo** and the **works** of the Dadaists.
BUT:	One admirer of the rock group Devo has found similarities between **the band's works** and **those** of the Dadaists.

NOT:	After deciding to film the movie in a **shopping mall,** they examined thirty **shopping malls** until they found the right **shopping mall.**
BUT:	After deciding to film the movie in a **shopping mall,** they examined thirty **malls** until they found the right **one.**

26e Flowery Language

Wherever possible, use simple and direct words and phrases instead of showy and pretentious ones.

FLOWERY:	Travelers on the road of life cannot help looking back and considering the possibility of whether any companion on this lonely journey will remember them after they have passed from this vale of tears.
DIRECT:	People cannot help wondering whether anyone will remember them after they die.

FLOWERY: Even a person who passes his daily hours by contemplating the strange little tricks played on unsuspecting victims by cruel and relentless fate receives a jolt that shakes him to the depths of his being when, at the Huntington Library, he sets his eyes upon the pass that Lincoln inscribed in his own hand to allow his trusted bodyguard to be absent from his side on that fateful night of April 14, 1865.

DIRECT: Even people who appreciate the ironies of life receive a jolt when, at the Huntington Library, they see the pass that Lincoln wrote for his bodyguard to have the night off on April 14, 1865.

FLOWERY: The streets of this fair city were graced on this day of May 19, 1984, by the arrival of Hank Morris, an artist of more than well-deserved distinction.

DIRECT: The distinguished artist Hank Morris arrived in town on May 19, 1984.

EXERCISE 26-3

Review each of the following sentences to eliminate wordiness, needless repetition, or flowery language.

1. In this modern world of ours in which we find ourselves, no living and breathing human being can avoid the ravages of technological advances.

2. Studies that have been made by environmentalists decry the results of cutting the Amazon forests.

3. We will have our meetings on as many occasions as required.

4. We were beyond the announced starting time due to the fact that it snowed this evening.

5. The music was audible to the ear although the stage was barely visible to the eye.

26f Figurative Language

Franklin P. Jones once quipped, "You're an old-timer if you can remember when setting the world on fire was a figure of speech." In a **figure of speech,** or **figurative language,** words are used in an imaginative and often unusual way to create a vivid impression. For example, as a figure of speech, *setting the world on fire* means "doing something astounding that gains recognition." Literally, of course, setting the world on fire means burning it. Most figures of speech make a direct or indirect comparison between two things that are essentially unlike each other. Three common types of figures of speech are *simile, metaphor,* and *personification.*

Simile

A **simile** uses the word *like* or *as* to make a direct comparison between two unlike things: for example, "He was like a lion in the fight." Here are some other examples of simile.

> The land was perfectly flat and level but it shimmered like the wing of a lighted butterfly.
>
> Eudora Welty

> He wore faded denims through which his clumsy muscles bulged like animals in a sack.
>
> Ross MacDonald

> Art is like a border of flowers along the course of civilization.
>
> Lincoln Steffens

> The man's tie was as orange as a sunset.
>
> Dashiell Hammett

> He [Monet] paints as a bird sings.
>
> Paul Signac

Metaphor

A **metaphor** is an indirect comparison between two essentially unlike things that does not use the word *like* or *as*. In a metaphor the writer says or implies that one thing *is* another: for example, "He was a lion in the fight." Here are some other examples of metaphor.

> Advertising is the rattling of a stick inside a swill bucket.
>
> **George Orwell**

> His elegance was the thorn. And he was well aware that his aversion to coarseness, his delight in refinement, were futile; he was a plant without roots.
>
> **Mishima Yukio**

> Roads became black velvet ribbons with winking frost sequins. Pines became whispering flocks of huge, dark birds and the hilltop and pasture cedars were black candle flames.
>
> **Hal Borland**

> He gave her a look you could have poured on a waffle.
>
> **Ring Lardner**

> A California oak is a tough, comforting thing—half tree, half elephant—its gray, baggy elbows bending solicitously close to the ground, following the contours of the hill.
>
> **Phyllis Theroux**

Personification

Personification is the attributing of human qualities to inanimate objects or abstract ideas. You may have noticed the word *solicitously* in the preceding example of metaphor. This is an example of personification, since an oak cannot be solicitous; solicitousness is a human quality. Here are some other examples of personification.

> His clothes were dark and a white handkerchief peeped coyly from his pocket and he looked cool as well as under a tension of some sort.

> Raymond Chandler

> A painting in a museum hears more ridiculous opinions than anything else in the world.

> Edmond De Goncourt

> In all its career the Rio Grande knows several typical kinds of landscape, some of which are repeated along its great length.

> Paul Horgan

> I am for an art that is political—erotical—mystical, that does something other than sit on its ass in a museum.

> Claes Oldenburg

Mixed Metaphor

A **mixed metaphor** is one that is not logically consistent. Complete your figurative comparisons appropriately.

NOT: The river was a giant **snake** that **galloped** through the valley. (*Snakes cannot gallop.*)

BUT: The river was a giant **snake** that **slithered** through the valley.

NOT: The bill **rolled** the House with little opposition but it **ran aground** in the Senate. (*Something that is rolling cannot run aground, since one action occurs on a solid surface and the other on water.*)

BUT: The bill **rolled** through the House with little opposition, but it **hit a stone wall** in the Senate.

OR: The bill **sailed** through the House with little opposition, but it **ran aground** in the Senate.

NOT: Her **shallow** arguments were easily refuted by the more **solid** reasoning of her opponent. (*You cannot contrast something shallow with something solid;* shallow *refers to depth, whereas* solid *refers to firmness.*)

BUT: Her **shallow** arguments were easily refuted by the more **profound** reasoning of her opponent.

OR: Her **flimsy** arguments were easily refuted by the more **solid** reasoning of her opponent.

EXERCISE 26-4

Use figurative language to complete each of the following items in a vivid and consistent manner.

1. The pack of dogs (the lion's den/the crashing car) sounded

   like _____.

2. From the speeding car the houses (people/cornfields) looked

   like _____.

3. As the day for the final examination approached, she felt ___

   _____.

4. The darkness was like _____.

5. The dancing couple _____.

6. The addition of _____ was like _____.

7. The mattresses in the store were _____.

8. The child's face during the birthday party was as _____

    as _____.

9. Touching the chalkboard felt like _____.

10. Elephants and mice are as different as _____.

26g Clichés

A **cliché** is an overused phrase or figure of speech that has lost its freshness and its ability to express thoughts exactly. Clichés bore the reader and give the impression that the writer is lazy or unimaginative. Avoid staleness in your writing; strive for freshness and originality. Eliminate all clichés.

The following is a list of clichés. Avoid them and others like them.

shadow of a doubt	all walks of life
busy as a beaver	as luck would have it
bee in your bonnet	the crack of dawn
babbling brook	green with envy
depths of despair	take the bull by the horns
face the music	the acid test
bite the bullet	as happy as a lark
to the bitter end	in the nick of time
a thinking person	as sly as a fox
never a dull moment	as proud as a peacock
in the final analysis	callow youth
a crying shame	fly in the ointment
a bundle of joy	out of the woods
as quick as a wink	count on one hand
by the skin of our teeth	by hook or by crook
interesting to note	in the blink of an eye
slowly but surely	by the seat of my pants
in his heart of hearts	the depths of her soul

Clever writers or speakers often use clichés in an original way.

> Marriage is a great institution, but I'm not ready for an institution, yet.
>
> Mae West

> There nearly always is a method in madness. That's what drives men mad, being methodical.
>
> G. K. Chesterton

> Life is just a bowl of pits.
>
> Rodney Dangerfield

> Ecologists believe that a bird in the bush is worth two in the hand.
>
> Stanley C. Pearson

26h Euphemisms

Euphemisms are words that disguise seemingly harsh or offensive realities. Euphemisms are quite rightly used in many situations to be polite or to avoid giving offense. There is nothing really wrong with referring to old people as *senior citizens* or to dead people as having *passed on*. However, many euphemisms have become clichés; they also tend to be wordy and to give writing a timid quality. In addition, euphemism can be improperly used to cover up the truth. Euphemism is commonly used in this way in gobbledygook. (See pp. 300–301.)

> **NOT:** The employees who had been notified of an interruption in their employment were referred to their outplacement manager.

BUT:	The laid-off employees were told to speak to the person who would try to help them find new jobs.
NOT:	The official acknowledged that he had misspoken when he said the troops had not engaged in any protective-reaction missions.
BUT:	The official admitted that he had lied when he claimed the troops had not engaged in any offensive missions.
OR:	The official admitted he had been lying when he claimed the troops had not attacked any enemy positions.

NOT:	The prisoner's life will be terminated at dawn.
BUT:	The prisoner will be shot at dawn.

EXERCISE 26-5

Rewrite each of the following sentences to eliminate clichés and euphemisms.

1. Does anyone really believe that life is just a bowl of cherries?

2. In summation, the non-essential personnel in this division will be vacationed by next week.

3. To add insult to injury he then asked another girl to the party.

4. He looked as strong as an ox and acted as sober as a judge.

5. The remains will be taken to the cemetery.

6. Reaching the top of the ladder of success must be a moving experience.

7. After he was brought back to reality, he was cool, calm, and collected.

8. I was told that he did away with himself.

9. A sadder but wiser person, Mary appeared tired but happy.

10. He'll have to face the music despite his diabolical skill.

---

27 Correct Word Choice

27a Malapropism

A **malapropism** is a word or expression that sounds unintentionally humorous when it is used in place of the similar-sounding one that the writer intended. The term is derived from Mrs. Malaprop, a pretentious character in Richard Sheridan's eighteenth-century play *The Rivals*, who uses near-miss words with a hilarious effect. For example, she refers to an "allegory [*rather than* alligator] on the banks of the Nile" and to another character's "historical [*rather than* hysterical] fit."

Do not be a Mrs. Malaprop. If you are not sure of the meaning of a word, look it up. (Be sure to check the Glossary of Usage, pp. 601–620.)

NOT: Women charged with witchcraft were often accused of using spells and **incarnations** to cause their neighbors misfortune.

BUT: Women charged with witchcraft were often accused of using spells and **incantations** to cause their neighbors misfortune.

NOT: At the end of the book are several helpful **appendages.**

BUT: At the end of the book are several helpful **appendixes.**

NOT: The author argues that environmental damage is not necessarily a **coronary** of industrial development.

BUT: The author argues that environmental damage is not necessarily a **corollary** of industrial development.

27b Homonyms

A writer can get into difficulty with careless choice among **homonyms,** words that sound alike but have different meanings and spellings. Here are some examples of many that can give trouble.

altar/alter	presence/presents
cite/sight/site	there/their/they're
dual/duel	to/too/two
hole/whole	weather/whether
pair/pare	who's/whose
past/passed	your/you're

EXERCISE 27–1

Choose the word in parentheses that sensibly completes each of the following sentences. Use your dictionary when necessary or consult the glossary (see pp. 601–620).

1. In order (to/too/two) obtain (to/too/two) extra tickets for the game, they will need to contact (there/their/they're) parents.

2. The poem meant little to the (disinterested/uninterested) student.

3. (Who's/Whose) coat is that?

4. The handle on the door is (lose/loose).

5. The (percent/percentage) of people who smoke cigarettes is less than it was five years (ego/ago).

6. The (cite/sight/site) of the new building for the department of (pubic/public) works has not been selected.

7. The (ways/waves) hit the shore loudly during the stormy (weather/whether).

8. A loudly barking dog is an (affective/effective) burglar alarm.

9. Place the (hole/whole) bush in the (hole/whole) you dug for it.

10. In one (weak/week) many people (waste/waist) a (forth/fourth) of (their/there/they're) food servings.

PART V

PUNCTUATION AND MECHANICS

Punctuation marks are symbols designed to help people understand what they are reading. They tell readers when to pause, when to stop, and when to read something with emphasis or emotion.

Mechanics concerns the technical aspects of writing, such as when to underline for italics, how to form contractions, when to use abbreviations, and when to use numbers. Mechanics also includes manuscript form, which concerns the conventions followed when preparing your paper whether on a computer, with a typewriter, or by hand.

28 End Punctuation

End punctuation separates sentences and marks the end of other elements, such as abbreviations. The three end punctuation marks are the *period,* the *question mark,* and the *exclamation mark.*

28a The Period

Use a period to end a sentence that makes a statement.

> In 1979, the United States ceded control of the Panama Canal Zone to the Panamanian government.
>
> The Japanese painter Hokusai changed his style many times.
>
> Adlai E. Stevenson ran for the presidency against Dwight D. Eisenhower.

Use a period to end a sentence that makes a request, expresses a mild command, or gives directions.

> Please help the needy.
>
> Open your books to page 178.
>
> Turn left at the next corner.

If you wish the command or request to be given a great deal of emphasis or force, use an exclamation point instead of a period.

> Help!
>
> Sign up now!
>
> Quit smoking!

Use a period at the end of a sentence that asks an indirect question.

> The editorial questions whether NATO is effective.
>
> The reporter asked how the fire had started.
>
> The doctor wondered why the patient's temperature had risen.

Use a period at the end of a request politely expressed as a question.

> Will you please type this letter for me.
>
> Will you kindly keep your voices down.

(See pp. 367–370 for the use of the period with parentheses. See pp. 377–378 for the use of the period with quotation marks.)

Use a period after most abbreviations and initials.

If a sentence ends with an abbreviation requiring a period, use only one period.

> The first admiral in the U.S. Navy was David G. Farragut.
>
> The Marine Corps traces its beginnings to Nov. 10, 1775.
>
> Thomas Jefferson's home, Monticello, is near Charlottesville, Va.

The current trend in abbreviations is away from the use of periods. The following two rules are now considered standard. However, if you are in doubt about whether to use a period after an abbreviation, consult your dictionary.

Avoid using a period when abbreviating a unit of measure.

86 **m**	275 **kg**	2.4 **cm**	20 **ft**
10.5 **yd**	20 **lb**	20 **cc**	

Exceptions: For *mile* use *m.* or *mi.* to prevent confusion with *m* or *meter*. For *inch* use *in* only when there is no possibility of confusion with the word *in*; the abbreviation *in.* avoids all confusion.

Avoid using a period with acronyms or other abbreviations of businesses, organizations, and government and international agencies.

> The **NAACP** has not endorsed a presidential candidate.
>
> My mother served in the **WACs** for eight years.
>
> The impartiality of **UNESCO** is being questioned.

28b The Question Mark

Use a question mark at the end of a sentence that asks a direct question.

> Who invented the safety pin**?**
>
> Have you registered to vote**?**
>
> Why did Nixon go to China**?**

Use a question mark at the end of an interrogative element that is part of another sentence.

> How can I keep my job**?** was the question on every worker's mind.
>
> "Will he actively support women's rights**?**" she wondered.
>
> The telegram said that Malcolm is alive—can it be true**?**—and will be returned to the United States on Friday.

In general, when a question follows an introductory element, use a capital letter to begin the question and a question mark to end it.

> The question to be decided is "How can we improve our public transportation system**?**"
>
> Before buying on credit, ask yourself, Do I really need this**?**
>
> A good detective inquires, What was the motive for the crime**?**

Usage varies somewhat on capitalization of questions following introductory elements. The more formal the question, the greater the tendency to use a capital letter. The less formal, the greater the tendency to use a lowercase letter.

FORMAL: The book raises the question, What role should the
            United States play in the Middle East**?**
INFORMAL: I wondered, should I bring my umbrella**?**

**Use a question mark, usually in parentheses, to express doubt
or uncertainty about a date, a name, or a word.**

The *Vedas* (written around 1000 BC**?**) are the sacred books of
Hinduism.

A dialect of Germanic, called Angleish (**?**), is the basis of modern-
day English.

Sir Thomas Malory (**?**-1471) wrote *Morte d'Arthur*, an account of
the exploits of King Arthur and his knights.

28c The Exclamation Point

**Use an exclamation point at the end of a sentence, word, or
phrase that you wish to be read with emphasis, with surprise,
or with strong emotion.**

Don't give up**!**

We shall resist this onslaught**!**

Impossible**!**

What a terrible time**!**

Avoid using the exclamation point to express sarcasm, and try
not to overuse the exclamation point. Too many exclamation
points are distracting and ineffective. The more you use, the
less effective each one will be.

EXERCISE 28-1

Identify the end punctuation missing from the following sentences.

1. Have you ever been to a sculpture exhibition

2. Such an exhibition is opening here on Nov. 1

3. Suspense has been growing as people catch glimpses of unusual objects being installed in the gallery

4. One sculpture consists of a large wooden scaffold dripping
   with heavy chains

5. A lot of people would ask Is this a form of insanity

6. You might wonder

7. One sculptor is exhibiting a ceramic sink and toilet that look
   like they came from the land of Oz

8. Is it ironic that the night before the exhibit opens is Halloween

9. All Saints' Eve, or All Hallows' Eve, or Halloween, is on
   October 31

10. Will you please check the hours for the exhibit

29 The Comma

The **comma** groups elements within the sentence in four ways: a comma *separates coordinate elements*; it *sets off introductory elements*; it *sets off certain terminal elements*; and a pair of commas *sets off interrupting elements*.

29a Between Coordinate Elements

Independent clauses

Use a comma between two independent clauses (sentences) joined by a coordinating conjunction—*and, but, for, nor, or, so, yet.*

> Many Caribbean people emigrated to other countries, and 700,000 of these emigrants settled in the United States within a ten-year period.

> Halloween has its origins in the Celtic religious festival of the dead, but today Halloween is largely a children's holiday of tricks and treats.

> Travel to the countryside to buy fresh apples, for there at roadside stands you can find many varieties not available in supermarkets.

The comma may be omitted between two short independent clauses.

> *She handed him the note* and *he read it immediately.*
>
> *Take notes in class* and *study them.*

If in doubt, use the comma.

Items in a series

Use commas to separate three or more items—words, phrases, or clauses—in a series.

WORDS IN A SERIES

A zoo veterinarian is called on to treat such diverse animals as elephants, gorillas, and antelopes.

Murillo, Velázquez, and El Greco were three major seventeenth-century Spanish painters.

The sporting goods store carries equipment for skiing, track, hockey, and weight lifting.

PHRASES IN A SERIES

The subway carried children going to school, adults going to work, and derelicts going nowhere at all.

The children playing hide-and-seek hid behind boulders, under bushes, or in trees.

Running in the halls, smoking in the bathrooms, and shouting in the classrooms are not allowed.

CLAUSES IN A SERIES

Edward Steichen photographed the Brooklyn Bridge, Georgia O'Keefe painted it, and Hart Crane wrote about it.

Foster stole the ball, he passed it to Kennedy, and Kennedy made a basket.

The supermarket tabloid proclaimed boldly that the man's character was hateful, that he was guilty, and that he should be punished severely.

Note: The comma before the conjunction with items in a series is often omitted in newspapers and magazines. Follow your instructor's preference. Most handbooks recommend using the comma because it prevents misreading, as in the following cases.

Harry, Anita, and Jayne have left already.

Without a comma before the conjunction, it is possible to read such sentences as directly addressing the first person named.

Harry, Anita and Jayne have left already. (*Someone is addressing Harry and giving him information about Anita and Jayne.*)

The menu listed the following sandwiches: bologna, chicken salad, pastrami, ham, and cheese. (*five sandwiches*)

The menu listed the following sandwiches: bologna, chicken salad, pastrami, ham and cheese. (*four sandwiches*)

Coordinate adjectives

Use commas between coordinate adjectives that are not joined by *and*.

Coordinate adjectives each modify the noun independently.

The comic was censored for his *audacious, vulgar* routine.

The traveler paused before walking into the *deep, dark, mysterious* woods.

The advertisement requested a *cheerful, sensitive, intelligent* woman to serve as governess.

Avoid using a comma between cumulative adjectives.

Cumulative adjectives each modify the whole group of words that follow them.

He gave her a *crystal perfume* bottle.

On top of the stove was a set of *large shiny copper* pots.

She carried an *expensive black leather* briefcase.

How can you distinguish coordinate adjectives from cumulative adjectives? In general, coordinate adjectives would sound natural with the word *and* between them, since each modifies the noun independently.

The comic was censored for his audacious and vulgar routine.

The traveler paused before walking into the deep and dark and mysterious woods.

The advertisement requested a cheerful and sensitive and intelligent woman to serve as governess.

In addition, coordinate adjectives would sound natural with their order changed or reversed.

The comic was censored for his vulgar, audacious routine.

The traveler paused before walking into the mysterious, dark, deep woods.

The advertisement requested an intelligent, sensitive, cheerful woman to serve as governess.

The order of cumulative adjectives cannot be changed. For example, the following sentences make no sense:

He gave her a perfume crystal bottle.

On top of the stove was a set of copper shiny large pots.

She carried an expensive leather black briefcase.

EXERCISE 29-1

Place commas where they are needed in the following sentences. One sentence is correct.

1. Painters work with canvas and paints and sculptors use the same materials.

2. In that section of the store you will find snack crackers and gourmet coffee beans.

3. The heavy fortress-like table was made of oak.

4. A smaller oak table matched the large one.

5. Jim Abraham directed the movie Karen Hopkins wrote the script and Winona Ryder starred in it.

29b After Introductory Words, Phrases, and Clauses

Use a comma after an introductory word or expression that does not modify the subject of the sentence.

Why, we didn't realize the telegram was merely a hoax.

Yes, Washington did sleep here.

Well, that restaurant is certainly expensive.

On the other hand, its prices are justified.

By the way, what were you doing last night?

Use a comma after an introductory verbal or verbal phrase.

Smiling, she greeted us at the door.

While sleeping, Coleridge conceived the idea for "Kubla Khan."

To sketch a tree accurately, you must first study it closely.

Hoping to find happiness at last, Poe married his cousin.

Use a comma after an introductory series of prepositional phrases.

Under cover of night, the secret agent slipped across the border.

In this album of music from the 1960s, you will find several traditional songs.

In Jack London's famous story of a fight for survival in the Arctic, the man fails to light a fire.

Use a comma after an introductory phrase if there is a possibility that the sentence will be misread without it.

The day before, he had written her a letter.

After the tournament, winners received trophies and certificates.

Without hunting, the deer would soon become too numerous for the available food supply.

Use a comma after an introductory adverb clause.

Because John F. Kennedy was assassinated on the same day Aldous Huxley died, Huxley's death was given little attention by the press.

Although the alligator once faced extinction, its numbers are now increasing dramatically.

If the earth were to undergo another ice age, certain animals would flourish.

The comma after a very short introductory adverb clause is considered optional, unless its placement prevents misreading.

29c Before Certain Terminal Elements

Contrasted elements

Use a comma to set off an element that is being contrasted with what precedes it.

Robert Graves claims he writes novels for profit, not for pleasure.

Birds are warm-blooded animals, unlike reptiles.

Interrogative elements

Use a comma before a short interrogative element at the end of a sentence.

I don't know anyone who hasn't seen at least one of Hitchcock's films, do you?

Tom Stoppard's new play is wonderful, isn't it?

The Vietnam War was never officially a war, or was it?

Terminal adverb clauses

In general, do not use a comma before an adverb clause that follows the main clause.

Many people wept *when they saw the monument honoring the veterans of the war in Vietnam.*

A national holiday has been established *so that Americans can honor Martin Luther King, Jr.*

Who ruled England *before the Normans invaded it?*

However, there are several exceptions to the preceding rule.

Use a comma before a terminal adverb clause that begins with *although* or *even though*.

Columbus found a rich world for the Spanish, although it was not the world he set out to reach.

Use a comma before a terminal adverb clause that begins with *since* or *while* when these words express cause or condition. Do not use a comma when these words express time.

CAUSE:	He advocated prison reform, *since he knew first-hand the dehumanizing effects of prison life.*
TIME:	Mighty empires have come and gone *since the world began.*
CONDITION:	Many critics praised her new play, *while others felt it was the worst she had ever written.*
TIME:	She wrote her first play *while she was vacationing in Venice.*

Use a comma before a terminal adverb clause beginning with *because* if the clause does not modify the verb nearest it.

Notice the difference in meaning between the two sentences below.

I knew he *was absent* from work *because his supervisor was looking for him.*

I *knew* he was absent from work**,** *because his supervisor was looking for him.*

In the first sentence above, the adverb clause modifies *was (absent).* It tells why he was absent—because his supervisor was looking for him. In the second sentence, the comma tells us that the adverb clause does not modify the verb closest to it. Instead, it modifies the verb *knew.* It tells how I knew he was absent—because his supervisor was looking for him.

Use a comma before a terminal adverb clause that begins with *so that* when *so that* indicates result. Do not use a comma when *so that* indicates purpose.

RESULT: *Huckleberry Finn* combines strong plot and characterization with a profound insight into the human condition**,** *so that it can be read by children and adults alike.*

PURPOSE: Oliver Twist set out for London *so that he could escape punishment by the beadle.*

EXERCISE 29-2

Place commas where they are needed in the following sentences. One sentence is correct.

1. Wishing to make their friend happy they planned a surprise party.

2. It will be his twenty-first birthday won't it?

3. She took the test while she had a headache.

4. Nevertheless the cat still sheds fur.

5. If we hurry we will be in time for the movie.

29d Around Interrupting Elements

With nonessential appositives and adjective clauses

Use commas to set off a nonessential appositive. Do not use commas to set off an essential appositive.

A nonessential, or nonrestrictive, appositive gives additional information about the noun it refers to but is not essential for the identification of the noun it renames. In the following sentences, the nonessential appositives appear in *italics*.

Duke Ellington, *a famous composer and bandleader,* helped gain acceptance for jazz as a serious musical form.

St. Augustine, *the oldest city in the United States,* was founded by the Spanish.

An essential, or restrictive, appositive identifies the noun it refers to. As its name suggests, it is essential to the meaning of the sentence. In the following sentences, the essential appositives appear in *italics*.

My friend *George* works in a bookstore.

The word *nice* has undergone many changes in meaning.

Truman Capote's book *In Cold Blood* established a new literary form.

Use commas to set off a nonessential adjective clause. Do not use commas to set off an essential adjective clause.

A nonessential, or nonrestrictive, adjective clause provides extra information about the noun it modifies but is not essential to identify the noun it modifies. In the following sentences, the nonessential adjective clauses appear in *italics*.

Dinah Washington, *whom many consider the queen of the blues*, sang with Lionel Hampton's band.

Modern dance, *which was originated by Martha Graham*, has had a profound influence on the dance world.

An essential, or restrictive, adjective clause limits or identifies the noun it refers to. It is essential to the meaning of the sentence. In the following sentences, the essential adjective clauses appear in *italics*.

The person *who buys the first ticket* will win a trip to Mexico.

The scientist *whose research is judged the most important* will be given a grant.

The performance *that they gave last night* was not up to their usual standard.

Note: The pronoun *that* is used only with essential clauses. The pronoun *which* may be used with either essential or nonessential clauses.

Whether or not an adjective clause is set off with commas can make a major difference to the meaning of a sentence. For example, compare the following two sentences:

ESSENTIAL: The first president who was born in Virginia was George Washington.

NONESSENTIAL: The first president, who was born in Virginia, was George Washington.

The first sentence tells you that George Washington was the first Virginia-born president. The second sentence tells you that George Washington was the first president. As additional information, it mentions that he was born in Virginia.

Now compare the next two sentences.

ESSENTIAL:　The first president who was born in New York was Martin Van Buren.
NONESSENTIAL:　The first president, who was born in New York, was Martin Van Buren.

The first sentence tells you that Martin Van Buren was the first New York-born president. This statement is true. However, the second sentence says that Martin Van Buren was the first president. This statement is obviously not true.

Finally, compare these two sentences.

ESSENTIAL:　The tenants who did not pay their rent were evicted.
NONESSENTIAL:　The tenants, who did not pay their rent, were evicted.

The first sentence tells you that only the tenants who did not pay their rent were evicted. The second sentence tells you that all the tenants were evicted. As additional information, it tells the reason they were evicted: they did not pay their rent.

With adverb clauses and interrupting or parenthetical adverbs

In general, use commas to set off an internal adverb clause that is parenthetical or that separates the subject of the main clause from its predicate.

Harry Truman, although a newspaper headline prematurely declared otherwise, won the 1948 election over Thomas E. Dewey.

Columbus, as we have seen, died without his true accomplishments recognized or honored.

Use commas to set off adverbs (*however, accordingly, moreover, nevertheless,* and so on) and transitional phrases (*in addition, to sum up, on the other hand, for example*) used parenthetically.

Many acclaimed writers, however, have written mysteries.

A popular mystery set in a fourteenth-century monastery, moreover, was written by a professor of semiotics.

Edmund Wilson, on the other hand, considered mysteries simply a waste of time.

With parenthetical expressions

Use commas to set off a parenthetical expression within a sentence.

Expressions that comment on or give additional information about the main part of the sentence are considered parenthetical.

Jazz, many critics believe, is America's greatest contribution to the arts.

You, like most people, probably do not know that the person responsible for the completion of the Brooklyn Bridge was a woman.

George Washington, according to the old-style calendar used by the colonists, was born on February 11.

Use commas to set off words that identify the source of a quotation within a sentence.

"The advance for the book," said Calvin Trillin, "should be at least as much as the cost of the lunch at which it was discussed."

"You can be a little ungrammatical," Robert Frost claimed, "if you come from the right part of the country."

"Just get it down on paper," advised Maxwell Perkins, "and we'll see what to do with it."

Use commas after or around words in direct address.

Here, my fellow citizens, is an issue we can agree on.

Ladies and gentlemen, may I present our speaker.

Sam, you've won the prize!

With dates and addresses

With dates, use commas to separate the day of the week from the month, the day of the month from the year, and the year from the rest of the sentence.

Please reply by Tuesday, January 7.

The *Titanic* hit an iceberg and sank on April 15, 1912.

The Allies landed at Normandy on Tuesday, June 6, 1944, and began the offensive that would lead to the downfall of the Third Reich.

Note: Do not use a comma when only the month and the day (e.g., April 15) or only the month and the year (e.g., April 1912) are given or when the following form is used: 15 April 1912.

With addresses, use a comma to separate the name from the street address, the street address from the city, and the city from the state. Use a comma after the zip code (or after the state if no zip code is given) to separate the entire address from the rest of the sentence. Do not use a comma between the state and the zip code.

The book is available from the Macmillan Publishing Company, 866 Third Avenue, New York, New York 10022.

He lived at 579 Montenegro Avenue, Frisco, Colorado, until 1982.

EXERCISE 29-3

Place commas where they are needed in the following sentences. One sentence is correct as written.

1. Lyndon Johnson formerly a school teacher in Texas became president after John Kennedy was assassinated.

2. I did not know you lived there!

3. Her mail can be forwarded to 325 Allen Street Claypot Indiana after July 3 of this year.

4. "If we all pitch in and help" pleaded the group's chairperson "we can reach our monetary goal this week."

5. Despite what the officer claimed the traffic light had not turned green.

29e Unnecessary Commas

Avoid using a comma to separate a subject from its predicate.

NOT: The album that he cut last year, sold over a million copies.
BUT: The album that he cut last year sold over a million copies.
OR: The album, which he cut last year, sold over a million copies.

NOT: The painting hanging on the wall, was of the last duchess.
BUT: The painting hanging on the wall was of the last duchess.

NOT: How a bill becomes a law, was the subject discussed in class today.

BUT: How a bill becomes a law was the subject discussed in class today.

Avoid using a comma to separate a verb from its complement.

NOT: Did you know, that chimpanzees can communicate through sign language?

BUT: Did you know that chimpanzees can communicate through sign language?

NOT: After discussing the issue for several hours, we realized that our decision must be, to place safety concerns before cost considerations.

BUT: After discussing the issue for several hours, we realized that our decision must be to place safety concerns before cost considerations.

NOT: The speaker declared that the government must let us know, why we are involved in this conflict.

BUT: The speaker declared that the government must let us know why we are involved in this conflict.

Avoid using a comma between cumulative adjectives.

NOT: She declared him to be a handsome, young man.
BUT: She declared him to be a handsome young man.

NOT: He was sentenced to a nine-year, prison term.
BUT: He was sentenced to a nine-year prison term.

NOT: She wore a knee-length, red, suede shirt.
BUT: She wore a knee-length red suede shirt.

Avoid using a comma to separate the two parts of a compound subject, a compound verb, or a compound complement.

NOT: High ceilings, and cathedral windows are two features I look for in a house.

BUT: High ceilings and cathedral windows are two features I look for in a house.

NOT: The skier cleaned his boots, and then sprayed them with a water repellent.

BUT: The skier cleaned his boots and then sprayed them with a water repellent.

NOT: For breakfast she ordered a ham omelet, and a side dish of home fries.

BUT: For breakfast she ordered a ham omelet and a side dish of home fries.

Avoid using a comma to separate two dependent clauses joined by *and*.

NOT: They promised that they would obey the laws of their new country, and that they would uphold its principles.

BUT: They promised that they would obey the laws of their new country and that they would uphold its principles.

NOT: Anyone who attends this school, and who lives off-campus must sign this list.

BUT: Anyone who attends this school and who lives off-campus must sign this list.

NOT: He wrote that he would stop loving her when dogs could fly, and when fish could sing.

BUT: He wrote that he would stop loving her when dogs could fly and when fish could sing.

Avoid using a comma to separate the parts of a comparison.

NOT: During the five months she spent alone in the woods, she was more productive, than she had ever been before.

BUT: During the five months she spent alone in the woods, she was more productive than she had ever been before.

NOT: The situation is not as bad, as we had expected.
BUT: The situation is not as bad as we had expected.

NOT: It is difficult to imagine another museum containing such a magnificent collection of medieval art, as the Cloisters in New York City.
BUT: It is difficult to imagine another museum containing such a magnificent collection of medieval art as the Cloisters in New York City.

Avoid using a comma before an opening parenthesis. You may, however, use a comma after a closing parenthesis.

NOT: David McCullough, who wrote *The Path Between the Seas,* (winner of the National Book Award) visited the Panama Canal.
BUT: David McCullough, who wrote *The Path Between the Seas* (winner of a National Book Award), visited the Panama Canal.

EXERCISE 29-4

Circle any unnecessary commas that appear in the following sentences. One sentence is correct as written.

1. Things were not as bleak, on June 23, 1991, as they appeared to be later in the year.

2. Do you, by chance, know where to register for the marathon race to be held in Akron, Ohio?

3. They claimed that they did not see the intruder, and that they could not, therefore, identify him or her.

4. William Faulkner, an industrious and prolific writer, (who

won a Nobel Prize for Literature), lived in Oxford, Mississippi.

5. They decided to meet in Paris, France, on, July 25, 1995.

EXERCISE 29-5

Place commas where they are needed in the following sentences, and circle any unnecessary commas that appear. Some sentences are correct as written.

1. Computers are used in many writing classes although at one time (about fifteen years ago) the practice would have been considered odd.

2. Computers were first used as drill and practice machines to help students overcome problems with spelling punctuation grammar and even in some cases pronunciation.

3. Gradually, computers became accepted, in college writing classes, as students arrived with increasing computer literacy.

4. In many cases although teachers did not like to admit it their students knew more about using the machines than they did.

5. But software (computer programs) that operated on one manufacturer's machines, most often, did not operate on other machines.

6. The result, was a proliferation of software that, was very mixed in quality.

7. Nevertheless the computer market settled to a few major manufacturers and software improved, in both quality and quantity.

8. The next advance, in software for writing, around 1975-1980,
   occurred when programs appeared devoted to prewriting.

9. Students found these programs both helpful, and interesting
   because they could generate, much more writing much more
   quickly.

10. Some of these were based on freewriting and others on brain-
    storming clustering and the pentad.

11. At the same time many teachers (the enlightened ones!) rec-
    ommended that students use the computer's word-processing
    capabilities to write the final drafts of essays.

12. "A new age of anxiety" as one professor stated "began when
    students submitted essays with right-justified margins page
    numbers in the wrong places and paragraphs lacking indenta-
    tion."

13. Furthermore the students experienced anxiety because so
    many of them despite precautions "lost" their essays in the
    computer.

14. After overcoming this, particular problem students found that
    the advantages of editing essays, on the computer outweighed
    the disadvantages.

15. The finished product produced, on a laser printer looks so professional that it is worth the initial anxiety.

30 The Semicolon

The **semicolon** links independent clauses or separates items in a series. The semicolon indicates a pause longer than that taken for a comma but not so long as that taken for a period.

30a Between Independent Clauses

Use a semicolon between two closely related independent clauses not joined by a coordinating conjunction.

> Years ago caviar was an inexpensive food often given away free at taverns; today it is one of the most expensive foods in the world.

> Truffles are the food of the rich; turnips are the food of the poor.
> Truffles are the food of the rich; turnips, the poor.

The comma in the third sentence indicates that a part of the second clause has been left out.

Use a semicolon between two independent clauses joined by a conjunctive adverb or by a transitional phrase.

> Columbus sent cacao beans back to Spain; however, the Spanish were not particularly impressed.

Cortez brought back more cacao beans; moreover, he brought back the knowledge of how to prepare them.

In some cultures insects are considered delicacies; for example, the ancient Romans thought the cicada a delightful morsel.

Use a semicolon between two independent clauses joined with a coordinating conjunction if one or both of these clauses contain internal commas or if the clauses are particularly complex.

With fairly short clauses, either a comma or a semicolon is acceptable.

Persephone was the daughter of Demeter, the goddess of agriculture, and she was represented by the pomegranate, the symbol of fertility.

Persephone was the daughter of Demeter, the goddess of agriculture; and she was represented by the pomegranate, the symbol of fertility.

With longer and more complex clauses, the semicolon is preferred.

In Greek mythology Persephone was the daughter of Demeter, the goddess of agriculture; and she was represented by the pomegranate, the symbol of fertility, of which she ate the seeds after Hades carried her down into the underworld.

In Italy during the Renaissance, the inside of the opened pomegranate, which is divided into compartments containing colorful seeds, was used as the basis for a popular fabric design; and in the Middle East during ancient times, this beautiful fruit figured prominently in the decorative arts.

Because of its abundance of seeds, some Westerners find the pomegranate, which originated in the Middle East, unpalatable as a food, although pleasing as a decoration; but supporters of the pomegranate, of whom there are many, find the seeds no drawback, since they like to chew these crunchy tidbits.

30b Between Items in a Series

Use semicolons to separate items in a series if the individual items are long or contain commas.

> In the language of flowers, each flower represents a particular attribute: belladonna, which is a deadly poison, silence; citron, which produces a sour, inedible fruit, ill-natured beauty; blue periwinkle, which is small and delicate, early friendship.

> The guide grouped wildflowers into many families, four of which were the cattail family, Typhaceae; the arrowhead family, Alismataceae; the yellow-eyed grass family, Xyridaceae; and the lizard-tail family, Saururaceae.

30c Misused Semicolons

Avoid using a semicolon between noncoordinate elements.

> **NOT:** In Shakespeare's *Hamlet*, after Ophelia is rebuffed; she communicates her despair through the language of flowers.
> **BUT:** In Shakespeare's *Hamlet,* after Ophelia is rebuffed, she communicates her despair through the language of flowers.

> **NOT:** She became famous for her photographs of wildflowers; especially for those of mountain laurel.
> **BUT:** She became famous for her photographs of wildflowers, especially for those of mountain laurel.

EXERCISE 30-1

Circle sections where a punctuation mark should be replaced by a semicolon or where a semicolon should be placed in each of the following sentences. Insert a comma where needed after a conjunctive adverb. Two of the sentences are correct as written.

1. Several of the most beautiful bulbous flowers belong to the tulip family, others belong to the narcissus family.

2. Most tulips bloom in the early spring, others in late spring.

3. The colors of tulips range over the entire spectrum, however red appears to be the most favored color.

4. Wealthy people in eighteenth-century Europe, enchanted with tulips from the Middle East, paid vast sums of money for one bulb, in many cases, the cost exceeded thousands of dollars.

5. Today, tulip bulbs are sold for very reasonable prices nevertheless some varieties, especially hybrids, are very expensive.

6. The most popular varieties of tulips include the Darwin, which can be as large as a tennis ball and grow sixteen inches high, the lily-flowered, which have pointed petals resembling the day lily and also grow tall and the parrot whose petals resemble feathers and which grows about seven inches high.

7. Tulips are planted in the fall, bloom in the spring.

8. Tulips prefer a well-drained sandy soil; however, some varieties adapt to other soils easily.

9. Cutting some varieties of tulips for display in a vase can be risky; the cut flowers require a lot of water and, if the supply is not replenished often, the flowers quickly droop.

10. Most people associate the tulip with the country of Holland, nevertheless a major tulip festival occurs every spring in the city of Holland, Michigan.

31 The Colon

The **colon** introduces elements that explain, illustrate, or expand the preceding part of the sentence. It calls attention to the word, phrase, clause, or quotation that follows it.

31a Before Elements Introduced Formally

Use a colon when formally introducing a statement or a quotation.

Capitalize the first word of a formal statement or a quotation.

> One of the guiding principles of our government may be stated as follows: All people are created equal.

> Though Murphy's identity is not known, Murphy's Law seems to be a truth: "If anything can go wrong, it will."

Use a colon when formally introducing a series of items.

> The picture gallery at the Vatican contains magnificent treasures: Raphael's *Madonna of Foligno,* Titian's *Madonna of San Niccolô dei Frari,* Leonardo's *St. Jerome,* Caravaggio's *Deposition,* Rouault's *Autumn,* and Utrillo's *The Church of St. Auxonne.*

From 1933 through 1981, unsuccessful assassination attempts were made on the lives of the following presidents: Franklin Roosevelt, Harry Truman, Gerald Ford, and Ronald Reagan.

Nine planets circle the sun: Mercury, Venus, Earth, Mars, Jupiter, Saturn, Uranus, Neptune, and Pluto.

31b Before Formal Appositives

Use a colon before a formal appositive, including one beginning with a phrase such as *namely, that is, specifically,* or *in other words.*

In many cases a dash would also be appropriate in this situation.

The scholar wrote mysteries for one reason and one reason only: to make money.

Domenikos Theotocopoulos, whom many consider one of the greatest painters of all times, is better known by his pseudonym: El Greco.

In 1961, Kennedy made one of the toughest decisions of his presidency: namely, to back the invasion at the Bay of Pigs.

Notice that the colon in the third example appears *before* the word *namely.*

31c Between Two Independent Clauses

Use a colon between two independent clauses when the second clause explains or expands the first.

Cubism was more than a new movement: it was a revolution.

> After reading the letter, he did something that surprised me: he laughed.

The clause following the colon may begin with a capital or a lowercase letter. However, a lowercase letter is preferred.

31d In Salutations and Bibliographical Entries

Use a colon after a salutation in a formal letter or speech.

> Dear Dr. Jacoby:
>
> Ladies and Gentlemen:
>
> Members of the Board:

Use a colon between the city and the publisher in a bibliographical entry.

> New York: Macmillan
>
> London: John Murray
>
> Chicago: The University of Chicago Press

Use a colon between a title and its subtitle.

> *Tutankhamen: The Untold Story*
>
> *Nooks and Crannies: An Unusual Walking Tour Guide to New York City*
>
> *The Seeing Hand: A Treasury of Great Master Drawings*

31e Misused Colons

Avoid using a colon after a form of the verb *be,* after a preposition, or between a verb and its object.

NOT: Three devices the ancient Romans used to tell time were: sundials, water clocks, and sand-filled glasses.

BUT: Three devices the ancient Romans used to tell time were sundials, water clocks, and sand-filled glasses.

OR: The Romans used three devices to tell time: sundials, water clocks, and sand-filled glasses.

NOT: In 1966, France effectively withdrew from NATO, which thereafter consisted of: Belgium, Canada, Denmark, Great Britain, Greece, Iceland, Italy, Luxembourg, the Netherlands, Norway, Portugal, Turkey, the United States, and West Germany.

BUT: In 1966, France effectively withdrew from NATO, which thereafter consisted of Belgium, Canada, Denmark, Great Britain, Greece, Iceland, Italy, Luxembourg, the Netherlands, Norway, Portugal, Turkey, the United States, and West Germany.

NOT: The store manager ordered: six microwave ovens, four dishwashers, seven coffee makers, and eleven toasters.

BUT: The store manager ordered six microwave ovens, four dishwashers, seven coffee makers, and eleven toasters.

EXERCISE 31-1

Place a colon where it is necessary in each of the following sentences.

1. No one realized how exhausted the fullback was until the evidence became indisputable specifically, he collapsed.

2. She purchased the books for her courses English, math, science, French, and philosophy.

3. The teacher responded by quoting Michaelangelo "Trifles make perfection but perfection itself is no trifle."

4. She could not understand the speaker's logic in other words, his reasoning processes appeared to be faulty.

32 The Dash

The **dash** is less formal than the colon. It is used to give *emphasis* or clarity to extra information in a sentence. Dashes should be used sparingly in college writing. When typing, produce a dash by two hyphens without a space before, after, or between them (--).

32a With an Introductory Series

Use a dash to separate an introductory series from its summarizing clause.

> His own party, the opposition, and the public—all were astounded by his resignation.
>
> Chaucer, Shakespeare, Malory—these were her favorite writers.

32b With Parenthetical Elements

Use dashes to set off a parenthetical element you wish to emphasize.

> The castle was surrounded by a moat and contained—I found this astounding—an actual dungeon.
>
> On his first day as a volunteer, he fought a fire in—of all places—the firehouse.

Use dashes to clarify a parenthetical element that contains *commas*.

> Of our first five presidents, four—George Washington, Thomas Jefferson, James Madison, and James Monroe—came from Virginia.

> The first recorded Olympic Games—which, you will be surprised to know, this reporter did not see—were held in 776 BC.

32c With Terminal Elements

Use a dash to introduce informally a terminal element that explains or illustrates the information in the main part of the sentence.

> They pledged to prevent what seemed inevitable—war.

> He battled his worst enemy—himself.

> Willie little appreciated her greatest attribute—her sense of humor.

Use a dash to introduce informally a terminal element that is a break in thought or a shift in tone.

> Raquel confessed that she was desperately in love—with me.

> No one loves a gossip—except another gossip.

> "But she said she had—I can't believe it," Patrick exclaimed.

EXERCISE 32-1

Indicate where dashes may be placed in each of the following sentences.

1. Bach, Beethoven, Brahms, Bruckner all these composers were represented on one program.

2. Three of Beethoven's compositions the "Eroica Symphony," the "Leonore Overture," and the "Choral Fantasy" were performed before the intermission.

3. It was a long concert to put it mildly!

4. The Bach selection no one will believe this was an unknown, rarely played sinfonia.

5. When the concert ended, guess who the conductor had take a bow the cellist.

33 Parentheses

Parentheses enclose information or comments that break the continuity of the sentence or paragraph. Unlike the dash, which tends to emphasize, parentheses *minimize* the importance of the material they enclose and, therefore, should be used sparingly. The information within parentheses should be of such a nature that it may be omitted without changing the essential meaning of the sentence.

33a With Parenthetical Comments and Additional Information

Use parentheses to enclose comments or additional information that you do not wish to emphasize.

On August 11, 1960, Chad (see map) became independent.

Charles Darwin (1809–1882) was a contemporary of Abraham Lincoln.

Ibsen's *A Doll's House* (which was quite revolutionary for its time) ends with Nora's walking out on her husband.

Do not use a capital letter or a period for a parenthetical sentence within another sentence. Use a capital letter and a period for a parenthetical sentence that stands by itself.

SENTENCE WITHIN ANOTHER SENTENCE

After the Civil War, carpetbaggers (their name came from their habit of carrying their belongings in a bag made of carpet material) took advantage of Southern blacks who had just been given the vote.

Demosthenes warned the Athenians against King Philip of Macedon (he felt King Philip was a threat to their liberty).

The Democratic Party (this is the party founded by that lover of liberty, Thomas Jefferson) was divided on the question of slavery.

Notice that in the second example the period ending the main sentence goes *outside* the closing parenthesis.

SENTENCE STANDING BY ITSELF

In the fifteenth century, Christian I founded the Oldenburg dynasty. (In modern Denmark, the ruling family traces its roots to him.) Christian II, however, was removed from the throne in 1523.

Elizabeth Barrett Browning is remembered in part for her beautiful love poems. (She died in 1861.)

In the original *King Kong,* the huge creature climbed what was then the tallest building in the world, the Empire State Building. (In the second version of the movie, he climbed the World Trade Center.) There he was attacked by airplanes.

Notice that the period ending the parenthetical sentence goes *inside* the closing parenthesis.

33b With Items in a Series

Use parentheses to enclose numbers and letters designating items in a series.

> When accepting a credit card from a customer, you should (a) check the customer's signature against the card, (b) call the credit-card company for approval, and (c) write the approval code on the credit slip.

> In the nineteenth century, the United States was involved in four wars: (1) the War of 1812, (2) the Mexican War, (3) the Civil War, and (4) the Spanish-American War.

33c With Other Punctuation Marks

Place a comma, semicolon, or colon *outside* a closing parenthesis.

> Although most Americans have heard of the Battle of Lexington and Concord (which occurred on April 19, 1775), many do not know that it is commemorated as Patriots' Day in Massachusetts.

> Maine has successfully preserved its northern moose population (the moose is Maine's official state animal); however, the state's deer population is now endangered by the growing moose herd.

> The candidate carried only six states (plus the District of Columbia): Georgia, Hawaii, Maryland, Minnesota, Rhode Island, and West Virginia.

Place a question mark or exclamation point *inside* a closing parenthesis if the parenthetical expression itself is a question or an exclamation.

Sean was astonished when he opened the door to his room and found a letter (who could have put it there**?)** lying on the floor.

The Founding Fathers considered many different animals (Benjamin Franklin suggested the turkey**!)** before they decided to make the bald eagle the national symbol of the United States.

Place a question mark or exclamation point *outside* a closing parenthesis if the sentence is a question or exclamation but the parenthetical expression is not.

Did you know that Lewis Carroll wrote *Alice in Wonderland* for a real girl named Alice (Alice Liddell**)?**

Never was I more surprised than when I found wild berries growing in a New York City park (there were both raspberries and blackberries**)!**

34 Brackets

Brackets enclose information inserted into quotations, and they take the place of parentheses within parentheses. Brackets are used mainly in formal writing.

34a With Inserted Information

Use brackets to enclose information inserted into direct quotations for clarification.

"The fellow **[**Rubens**]** mixes blood with his colors," claimed Guido Reni.

The comedian quipped, "From the moment I picked your [S. J. Perelman's] book up until I laid it down, I was convulsed with laughter. Someday I intend reading it."

"Government [in a democracy] cannot be stronger or more tough-minded than its people," said Adlai Stevenson.

Use brackets to enclose editorial comments inserted into quoted material.

According to Clarence Darrow, "The first half of our lives is ruined by our parents [how many people under twenty agree with this!] and the second half by our children."

Notice that the exclamation point is placed inside the closing bracket because it is part of the editorial comment.

The word *sic* or *thus* enclosed in brackets is used to indicate that an incorrect or seemingly incorrect or inappropriate word is not a mistake on the part of the present writer but appears in the original quotation.

Jane Austen parodied the popular melodramatic fiction of her day in "Love and Freindship [*sic*]," which she completed at the age of fourteen.

Notice that the comma is placed *outside* the closing bracket and that *sic* is italicized.

34b With Parentheses

Use brackets to replace parentheses within parentheses.

Some humpback whales reach a length of over fifty feet. (See p. 89 [chart] for a comparison of the size of whales.)

> Several books are available on the life and times of "Boss"
> Tweed. (For a revisionist picture of Tweed, we suggest Leo
> Hershkowitz's *Tweed's New York* [Garden City: Anchor Press/
> Doubleday, 1977].)

Notice that the period is placed *inside* the closing parenthesis
because the entire sentence is enclosed by parentheses.

> The reading list contains several books dealing with the issue of
> freedom of the press (for example, Fred W. Friendly's
> *Minnesota Rag: The Dramatic Story of the Landmark Supreme
> Court Case that Gave New Meaning to Freedom of the Press*
> [New York: Random House, 1981]).

Notice that the period is placed *outside* the closing parenthesis
because only part of the sentence is enclosed by parentheses.

EXERCISE 34-1

Add parentheses and/or brackets where necessary to enclose information in each of the following sentences.

1. According to the famous British jurist, "The road to judgement

   sic is not a strait jacket."

2. During the Middle Ages, carols were also dances. They were

   not limited to the Christmas season either see examples 9 and

   10 in the text.

3. In the past thirty years the map of Africa see plate in text has

   changed drastically.

4. After agreeing on a budget compromise, the chair of the

   Senate budget committee Democrat-Indiana changed her mind.

5. We all helped to give him John a surprise birthday party.

35   Quotation Marks

Quotation marks enclose quoted material and certain kinds of titles. They are always used in pairs.

35a For Direct Quotations

Use quotation marks to enclose a direct quotation—the exact words of a speaker or writer.

> When one character says to Mae West, "My goodness, those diamonds are beautiful," West replies, "Goodness had nothing whatever to do with it."
>
> In *The Code of the Woosters,* Bertie vividly describes the aunt he fears: "Aunt Agatha, who eats broken bottles and wears barbed wire next to the skin."
>
> The opening lines set the tone of the poem: "I will be the gladdest thing / Under the sun!" (*The slash indicates the end of a line in a poem.*)

When writing dialogue, begin a new paragraph each time the speaker changes.

> "This coat costs $25.00," said the seller at the flea market.
>
> "That's too much," said the customer.
>
> "Did I say $25.00?" responded the seller. "I meant $15.00."

35b Block Quotations

When quoting a **prose** passage of considerable length, you omit quotation marks when you use the block quotation form. The Modern Language Association's (MLA) guidelines advise **block quotation** form for four or more lines of prose; the American Psychological Association (APA) specifies its use for passages of forty or more words. Type the material double-spaced. If you are using MLA form, indent ten spaces from the left-hand margin. Further indent three spaces for a paragraph, but only where a paragraph appears in the original. APA guidelines suggest that you indent only five spaces from the left-hand margin, indenting five additional spaces for a paragraph. Note that the right margin does not change and that double spacing separates the quote from the text. These instructions apply principally to material that is being prepared for publication. Your instructor may adjust these rules for class assignments and may suggest single-spacing in block form.

Here are two examples following MLA rules:

In "The American Scholar" Ralph Waldo Emerson gives a warning:

> Meek young men grow up in libraries, believing it their duty to accept the views which Cicero, which Locke, which Bacon have given; forgetful that Cicero, Locke, and Bacon were only young men in libraries when they wrote these books.
>
> Hence, instead of Man Thinking, we have the bookworm. Hence the book-learned class. . . . Hence the restorers of readings, the emendators, the bibliomaniacs of all degrees.

In a speech he made in New York in 1911, Woodrow Wilson underscored the importance of business:

> Business underlies everything in our national life, including our spiritual life. Witness the fact that in the Lord's Prayer the first petition is for daily bread. No one can worship God or love his neighbor on an empty stomach.

Following is an example of APA rules:

In Psychological Types, Jung stated the following:

> The dynamic principle of fantasy is play, which belongs also to the child, and as such it appears to be inconsistent with the principle of serious work. But without this playing with fantasy no creative work has ever yet come to birth. The debt we owe to the play of imagination is incalculable.

When quoting four or more lines of *poetry*, double-space lines and indent, according to MLA guidelines, ten spaces or five fewer if the poetic lines are long (APA style recommends spaces as with prose quotations). Type the poem line for line, following the spatial arrangement of the original. Do not use quotation marks.

Thoreau, as he explains in Walden, or Life in the Woods, lived less than two miles from the village of Concord and yet felt that he was living on a distant star, like the shepherd in the anonymous poem he quotes:

> There was a shepherd that did live,
> And held his thoughts as high
> As were the mounts whereon his flocks
> Did hourly feed him by.

35c For Quotations Within Quotations

Use single quotation marks to enclose quoted material contained within a quotation.

In "Silence," Marianne Moore wrote: "My father used to say, 'Superior people never make long visits.'"

The British humorist Robert Morley once joked, "Beware of the conversationalist who adds 'in other words.' He is merely starting afresh."

Jensen looked up from his research and declared, "I've found the answer. It was Henry Clay who said, 'I would rather be right than President.'"

35d For Titles of Short Works

Use quotation marks to enclose the quoted titles of short stories, short poems, one-act plays, essays, articles, subdivisions of books, episodes of a television series, songs, short musical compositions, and dissertations.

In his poem "Son of Frankenstein," Edward Field reveals the loneliness of the Frankenstein monster.

In the second half of *Brideshead Revisited*, which is entitled "A Twitch upon the Thread," Charles returns from South America, and Lord Marchmain returns to Brideshead to die.

Joan Didion details the pattern of shopping malls in "On the Mall."

Use underlining for the titles of longer works (see pp. 381–382).

35e With Other Punctuation Marks

Place a period or a comma *inside* a closing quotation mark.

In "Perseid," John Barth writes, "Stories last longer than men, stones than stories, stars than stones."

"I don't want to talk grammar," Eliza Doolittle says in *Pygmalion*. "I want to talk like a lady."

"After all," says Scarlett, "tomorrow is another day."

Place a semicolon or a colon *outside* a closing quotation mark.

The critic wrote that the play demonstrated the playwright's "dissatisfaction with satisfaction"; this comment, I felt, was more preposterous than the play itself.

In the American detective story, few women are private eyes. One of the best known of these women appears in Stuart Palmer's "The Riddle of the Twelve Amethysts": Hildegarde Withers.

Place a question mark or an exclamation point *inside* a closing quotation mark if the quotation itself is a question or exclamation.

The song I was trying to recall is "Will You Love Me in December?"

> Upon reaching the summit of Mount Everest, Sherpa Tensing declared, "We've done the bugger!"

Place a question mark or an exclamation point *outside* the closing quotation mark if the sentence is a question or exclamation but the quotation itself is not.

> Who first said, "Big Brother is watching you"?
>
> What a scene she caused by saying, "I don't want to"!

If both the sentence and the quotation are questions or exclamations, use only one question mark or exclamation point, and place it *inside* the closing quotation mark.

> Why did she cause a scene by asking, "Who is that woman?"

Of course, the rules for using other punctuation marks with quotation marks apply to single quotation marks as well.

> Harold asked, "Do you know who coined the term 'the brain trust'?" (*Question mark ends Harold's quotation.*)
>
> Gordon said, "I can hear the crowd shouting, 'Long live the king!'" (*Exclamation point ends quotation within quotation.*)

35f Misused Quotation Marks

Do not use quotation marks to enclose indirect quotations.

> **NOT:** The seer declared that "they would win the war against the Macedonians."
>
> **BUT:** The seer declared that they would win the war against the Macedonians.
>
> **NOT:** The editorial proclaimed that "the president would win the next election."

BUT: The editorial proclaimed that the president would win the next election.

Note: The word *that* is usually used to introduce an indirect quotation, *not* a direct quotation.

Do not use quotation marks to enclose a title used as the heading of a paper, theme, or essay.

Suicide and the Modern Poet

Science Fiction in the 1930s

Communication Among Chimpanzees

EXERCISE 35–1

Identify where quotation marks are needed in the following sentences. Three of the sentences do not need quotation marks.

1. Jonathan Swift ends his poem, A Description of a City Shower, with the line, Dead cats and turnip-tops come tumbling down the flood.

2. Michaelangelo claimed that trifles make perfection and perfection is no trifle.

3. The young lady asked, Did you see the latest episode of the program on Thursday?

4. Horace is credited with the now proverbial saying, Taste is not a matter to be disputed.

5. If you view Picasso's painting, *The Tragedy*, after reading Márquez's short story, Tuesday Siesta, the impact is astounding.

6. The best, said the announcer, is yet to come!

7. The professor advised, Remember to get a good night's sleep before writing the special examination.

8. The President advised that we would do all we could to maintain peace in the area.

9. James Whitcomb Riley, a native of Indiana, has become known as the Hoosier poet.

10. Although your intentions are praiseworthy, said the coach, nothing can substitute for practice.

---

36 Ellipsis Points

Ellipsis points are equally spaced dots, or periods. They indicate that part of a quotation has been omitted.

Use three ellipsis points within a quotation to indicate that part of the quotation has been left out, or omitted.

Partial quotations do not need ellipsis points at beginning and end.

> **NOT:** The politician declared that Indians have " a reverence for the life-giving earth● ● ● ●"
>
> **BUT:** The politician declared that Indians have "a reverence for the life-giving earth."

When typing, leave a space before the ellipsis point, a space between each of the points, and a space after the last point.

> In *The Other America: Poverty in the United States,* Michael Harrington writes: "They [the poor] are not simply neglected ● ● ● they are not seen."

> In *The Quiet Crisis,* Stewart Udall writes: "The most common trait ● ● ● is a reverence for the life-giving earth, and the native American shared this elemental ethic: the land was alive to his touch, and he, its son, was brother to all creatures."

> The Atlantic Charter states: "Eighth, they believe that all of the nations of the world ● ● ● must come to the abandonment of the use of force."

Use a period and three ellipsis points to indicate that the end of a sentence has been left out of a quotation.

> Huck said, "It most froze me to hear such talk● ● ● ● Thinks I, this is what comes of my not thinking."

> The review said, "The book promises a cornucopia of unusual characters● ● ● ● That promise is fully realized."

37   Underlining for Italics

Underlining in a typed or handwritten paper serves the same purpose as *italics* in a published or computer-generated work. It highlights, or sets apart, certain titles, words, or phrases.

Underline or, on the computer, use an italic font for the titles of books, full-length musical compositions, paintings, televi-

sion series, plays, and long poems and the names of newspapers, magazines, ships, boats, and aircraft.

> The Light in the Forest (*book*)
>
> Madame Butterfly (*opera*)
>
> The Rape of the Lock (*long poem*)
>
> the Mayflower (*ship*)

Be careful to underline only the exact title or name. Do not underline words added to complete the meaning of the title.

> The Atlantic magazine (*The word* magazine *is not part of the name.*)
>
> the London Times or The Times of London (London *is not part of the name.*)

Be careful to underline all the words that make up the title.

> The Decline and Fall of the Roman Empire (The *is part of the title.*)
>
> A Childhood (A *is part of the title.*)
>
> Standard & Poor's New Issue Investor (Standard & Poor's *is a part of the title.*)

(Do not underline the heading of your own paper.)

Underline foreign words or phrases that are not commonly used in English or use an italic font on the computer.

In general, a word or phrase need not be underlined if it is listed in a standard English dictionary. For example, the Spanish word *siesta*, the French phrase *coup de grace,* and the Latin phrase *ad infinitum* are now considered part of English and are not underlined.

German women were traditionally expected to confine themselves to <u>Kinder, Kirche, Küche</u>.

<u>Chacun à son goût</u> proved a difficult principle to apply in this case.

The great English public schools attempted to follow the ideal of <u>mens sana in corpore sano</u>.

Underline letters, words, or phrases being named or use an italic font on the computer.

How many <u>i</u>'s are in <u>Mississippi</u>?

His life demonstrates the meaning of the word <u>waste</u>.

What is the derivation of the phrase <u>on the ball</u>?

In most cases, it is also appropriate to use quotation marks instead of underlining for this purpose.

Underline words and phrases for emphasis or use an italic font on the computer.

I did <u>not</u> say I would do that.

You <u>must</u> stop overeating!

You plan to do <u>what</u>?

Do not overuse this device. Too much underlining weakens the effect. Emphasize only what deserves emphasis.

EXERCISE 37–1

Specifically identify which items require underlining in each of the following sentences, and explain why.

1. The novel Buffalo Girls was written after Larry McMurtry was awarded the Pulitzer Prize for his novel Lonesome Dove.

2. The word fallacy derives from a Latin word, fallacia, which means deceit.

3. Two popular magazines in the men's dormitory are Gentlemen's Quarterly and Popular Mechanics.

4. Beowulf was the first long epic poem in the English language.

5. His biography reveals that his grandparents sailed to this country on the Queen Elizabeth.

38 The Apostrophe

38a In Possessive Forms

The possessive case forms of all nouns and of many pronouns are spelled with an apostrophe. The following rules explain when to use an apostrophe for possessive forms and where to place the apostrophe.

Note: Do not be misled by the term *possessive.* Rather than trying to see "ownership," consider the possessive case form as an indication that one noun modifies another in some of the ways adjectives do. (See pp. 176–179.) Consider these examples:

a **week's** vacation   the **flower's** fragrance
Egypt's history   a **car's** mileage
the **river's** source   your **money's** worth

Singular nouns

To form the possessive of a singular noun, add an apostrophe and *s*.

> **Kirsoff's** review emphasized the **dramatist's** outstanding contribution to the arts.
>
> A **woman's** effort to free herself from the past is the concern of Alice **Walker's** novel *Meridian*.
>
> The Greeks tried to appease **Zeus's** anger, just as the Romans tried to avoid **Jupiter's** wrath.

Exception: Use only an apostrophe when a singular noun ending in *s* is followed by a word beginning with *s*.

> The **boss'** salary is three times that of her assistant.
>
> We discussed **Keats'** sonnets in class today.
>
> In Langston **Hughes'** story "Thank You, Ma'am," a young boy finds kindness where he expected punishment.

Plural nouns

To form the possessive of a plural noun not ending in *s*, add an apostrophe and *s*.

> The **women's** proposal called for a day-care center to be set up at their place of employment.
>
> Dr. Seuss is a well-known name in the field of **children's** literature.
>
> The store has introduced a new line of **men's** fragrances.

To form the possessive of a plural noun ending in *s*, add an apostrophe alone.

The **doctors'** commitment to their patients was questioned at the forum.

The course highlights two **composers'** works—Haydn and Mozart.

Compound nouns

To form the possessive of a compound noun, make the last word possessive.

Do most people welcome a **mother-in-law's** advice?

As a result of the **Vice President's** remarks, the student council members asked for his removal from the ticket.

The editorial defended the **police officers'** conduct in the case.

Noun pairs or nouns in a series

To show joint possession, add an apostrophe and *s* to the last noun in a pair or a series.

Sociologists were concerned that the **royal couple's** announcement would set off a new baby boom in Britain.

Lennon and McCartney's music had a dramatic effect on their contemporaries.

To show individual possession, add an apostrophe and *s* to each noun in a pair or series.

Anne Tyler's and **Sam Shepard's** styles have many similarities.

The **President's** and the **Vice President's** duties are clearly defined.

Nouns naming periods of time and sums of money

To form the possessive of a noun naming a period of time or a sum of money, add an apostrophe and *s* or an apostrophe if the noun is plural.

The value of **today's** dollar is less than the value of last **year's** dollar.

Taxes can easily swallow several **days'** pay.

Indefinite pronouns

To form the possessive of some indefinite pronouns, add an apostrophe and *s*. (Note that *each, both, all,* and some others can have no possessive form.)

> We can learn from **each other's** mistakes.

> How we can improve our care of the elderly is a subject on almost **everyone's** mind.

Personal pronouns

Do not use an apostrophe with the possessive forms of personal pronouns.

> Her analysis of the problem was more complete than **yours.**

> The Druids' methods of telling time were quite different from **ours.**

> Our troops are better prepared than **theirs.**

38b In Plural Forms

Add an apostrophe and *s* to form the plural of words being named, letters of the alphabet, abbreviations, numerals, and symbols. The apostrophe may be omitted with capitals without periods: TVs, UFOs, PhDs.

> One drawback of this typeface is the capital *i*'s and the lowercase *l*'s look exactly alike.

> Avoid weakening your argument by including too many *but*'s and *however*'s.

38c For Omissions

Use an apostrophe to indicate that part of a word or number has been omitted.

>In **'64** the Beatles invaded the United States with a new style of rock **'n'** roll.

>The manager told the singer to "go out and knock **'em** dead."

38d In Contractions

A **contraction** is a shortened form of a word or words. Contractions are widely used in speech and in informal writing.

Use an apostrophe to indicate a missing letter or letters in a contraction.

>Winning at cards **wasn't** Tony's only claim to success.

>Enrique claimed that enough attention **isn't** being paid to the threat of environmental pollution.

Note: It's is a contraction meaning "it is" or "it has." *Its* is a possessive pronoun meaning "belonging to it" and does not require an apostrophe.

>**It's** your turn to drive today.

>The dog covered **its** right eye with **its** paw.

Do not confuse the two.

In general, avoid contractions in formal writing.

INFORMAL: During his lifetime, Mark Twain **didn't** receive the serious critical attention he deserved.

FORMAL: During his lifetime, Mark Twain **did not** receive the serious critical attention he deserved.

EXERCISE 38–1

In each of the following groups, circle the items that show the incorrect use of an apostrophe or that omit a necessary apostrophe.

1. an hour's labor, a day's wages, a seasons toil

2. sheep's wool, mens' coats, women's scarves

3. one of your's, two of ours, brother-in-law's office

4. your home, it's house, its' there

5. do'nt do it, can't stop, didn't try

6. John's and Mary's apartment, Sue and Kathy's car, Tom and Ed's stereo (*joint ownership*)

7. Mary and Bill's book, Paula's and Sue's computer disk, Jim's and Louis' sonnets (*individual ownership*)

8. the silent '50s, TV's schedule, Elvis song

9. everyone's favorite, no ones friend, anyones' boss

10. her' bracelet, our chairs, it's fur

39   The Hyphen

39a In Compound Nouns

Use a dictionary to determine whether to spell a compound noun with a hyphen.

Relatively few compound nouns are hyphenated; most are written either solid (as one word) or open (as two or more separate words). The only kinds of compound nouns that are usually hyphenated are those made up of two equally important nouns and those made up of three or more words.

> philosopher-king   city-state   man-hour
> mother-in-law   free–for-all   jack-of-all-trades

39b In Compound Adjectives

Hyphenate two or more words that serve as a single adjective preceding a noun.

> **well-known** painter   **law-school** degree
> **soft-spoken** man   **sure-to-win** candidate
> **too-good-to-be-true** behavior

> Do you know the difference between **mass-market** paperbacks and trade paperbacks?

> Cheever's stories provide insight into **middle-class** suburban life.

> The company is investigating both the **short-term** and the **long-term** benefits of scattered work hours.

In general, do not hyphenate such words when they follow a noun.

painter who is **well known**   degree from a **law school**
man who is **soft spoken**   candidate who is **sure to win**
behavior that is **too good to
be true**

Do you know the difference between novels that are considered **mass market** and novels that are considered trade?

Cheever's stories provide insight into the lives of suburban people who are **middle class.**

The benefits of scattered work hours are both **short term** and **long term.**

Do not hyphenate two or more words that precede a noun when the first of these words is an adverb ending in *-ly.*

Critics attacked the President's **rapidly expanding** budget.

When the famous rock group first came to this city, the police were called in to restrain the crowd of **wildly screaming** teenagers.

The government's **widely criticized** policies are the subject of the debate on television today.

Use a hanging hyphen after the first part of a hyphenated compound adjective used in a series, where the second part of the compound adjective is implied but omitted.

both **paid-** and complimentary-ticket holders

both **short-** and long-term disability

all **first-, second-,** and third-year students

39c In Compound Numbers and Fractions

Hyphenate spelled-out numbers from *twenty-one* through *ninety-nine* and spelled-out fractions used as adjectives.

In spelled-out numbers larger than *ninety-nine,* do not use a hyphen before or after *hundred, thousand,* and so forth.

> **Two hundred fifty-seven** people were killed in the fire.
>
> The installation of computers has effected a **one-third** increase in productivity and an expected **three-quarter** growth in profits.
>
> The novel had **thirty-two** chapters in its first version, but the revised version has **forty-one.**

Do not hyphenate spelled-out fractions used as nouns.

> About **one half** of Yugoslavia is covered with mountains.
>
> Only **three eighths** of the adults in this community voted in the last election.

39d With Prefixes and Suffixes

In general, do not use a hyphen between a prefix and its root or a suffix and its root. However, there are several exceptions.

Use a hyphen between a prefix and its root to avoid ambiguity.

the **re-creation** of the world	*but*	tennis as **recreation**
to **re-count** money	*but*	to **recount** an event
a **co-op** apartment	*but*	a chicken **coop**

Use a hyphen between a prefix and its root when the last letter of the prefix and the first letter of the root are the same vowel or when the first letter of the root is capitalized.

sem**i-in**dustrial	ant**i-in**tellectual
supr**a-au**ditory	**re-e**cho
un-**A**merican	pro-**W**estern

Exceptions: Frequent usage may allow the elimination of the hyphen. (Consult the dictionary.)

cooperation	preempt	reexamine

Use a hyphen between the prefixes *all, ex* ("former"), and *self* and their roots and between the suffix *elect* and its root.

all-star	all-time
ex-senator	ex-husband
self-control	self-sufficient
mayor-elect	president-elect

39e For Word Division at the End of a Line

A hyphen is used to indicate that a word has been divided at the end of a line. However, some words may not be divided, and no word should be divided except between syllables. The following are some general rules for word division; consult a dictionary for words not covered by these rules.

Do not divide a one-syllable word.

truth	strayed	twelve
fifth	strength	gauche

Do not divide a word so that a one-letter syllable appears on a separate line.

NOT:	a-mount	e-rase	sand-y
BUT:	amount	erase	sandy

Do not divide proper names.

NOT:	Eliza-beth	Mal-ory	Mar-tin
BUT:	Elizabeth	Malory	Martin

In general, divide words between double consonants.

sad-dle	com-mit-ted	cor-ruption	refer-ral
daz-zle	as-sistant	im-mortal	dif-ferent

In general, divide words between the prefix and the root or between the suffix and the root.

non-violent	in-sincere	re-dedicate
appease-ment	fellow-ship	mother-hood

Note: Do not carry over a two-letter suffix—*loaded,* not *load-ed.*

Try to divide a hyphenated word at the hyphen.

NOT:	self-de-nial	quick-tem-pered	cold-blood-edness
BUT:	self-denial	quick-tempered	cold-bloodedness

EXERCISE 39–1

Circle the correct form of each word in parentheses in the following sentences.

1. (Twenty one/Twenty-one) lawyers worked on the case for the

   corporation and produced (well-researched/well researched)

opinions that proved to be (thought-provoking/thought pro-
voking).

2. The (all state/all-state) team included several (all-star/all·star)
players that became (all time/all-time) greats in football.

3. He said that (one fifth/one-fifth) of those people present were
fooled by (mass-media/mass media) efforts to sway opinion.

4. The (well-known/well known) speaker attended a university
that is (world-famous/world famous).

5. The (city-county/city county) building is located near the
(short-term/short term) parking lot.

EXERCISE 39–2

Circle any correctly hyphenated words in each of the following
groups.

1. self-discipline, semi-independent, un-intelligent

2. semi-dilapidated, mid-winter, all-ready

3. bishop-designate, chairperson-elect, old-senator

4. excitedly-screaming, true-to-life, a hundred-thirty-one

5. Kath-leen, occurr-ence, a-bout

EXERCISE 39–3

Imagine that the following words appear at the end of lines. Circle
any words in the groupings that are correctly divided.

1. th-irty, fif-ty, thir-teen

2. a-round, Chau-cer, oc-casion

3. New York, hymn-al, child-ren

4. trust-ed, regret-able, enlighten-ing

5. cof-fee, ei-ght, rein-deer

---

40   The Slash

Use a slash to indicate that a pair of options exist.

> She wants to go to the movies but he want us to go bowling; either/or will suit me fine.

> He prefers diet soda/low calorie yogurt.

Use a slash to indicate the end of a line of poetry when you are citing three lines or fewer and when you are not using the block form of citation. Note that a space precedes and follows the slash.

> Wordsworth's poem begins: "My heart leaps up when I behold / A rainbow in the sky."

Avoid using a slash to form the construction *s/he*, a nonstandard usage for *she and he;* instead, write the phrase as *she and he* or as *he and she.*

41   Abbreviations

In general, avoid abbreviations in formal writing. However, abbreviations are acceptable in certain situations.

Use an abbreviation for the following designations preceding names.

Mr.	Messrs.	St. (Saint)
Mrs.	Mmes.	Mt. (Mount)
Ms.	Dr.	Rev. (unless preceded by *the*)

Is **Mrs.** Dalloway a fully realized character?

For what musicals are **Messrs.** Rogers and Hart responsible?

Rev. James Spenser read the service.

Note: Spell out *Reverend* when it is preceded by *the*.

The **Reverend** James Spenser read the service.

Avoid using an abbreviation for any other designation preceding a name.

NOT: No one was surprised when **Pres.** Reagan said that he would run again.

BUT: No one was surprised when **President** Reagan said that he would run again.

NOT: Are you campaigning for **Sen.** Jones?

BUT: Are you campaigning for **Senator** Jones?

NOT: In his new book, **Prof.** Rosenthal discusses the use of imagery in the poetry of Ted Hughes.

BUT: In his new book, **Professor** Rosenthal discusses the use of imagery in the poetry of Ted Hughes.

Use an abbreviation preceded by a comma for a designation or an academic degree following a name.

Jr.

Sr.

B.A. or BA (Bachelor of Science)

M.A. or MA (Master of Arts)

M.S. or MS (Master of Science)

D.D.S. or DDS (Doctor of Dental Science)

D.D. or DD (Doctor of Divinity)

M.D. or MD (Doctor of Medicine)

Ph.D. or PhD (Doctor of Philosophy)

Ed.D. or EdD (Doctor of Education)

M.B.A. or MBA (Master of Business Administration)

J.D. or JD (Doctor of Jurisprudence)

D.V.M. or DVM (Doctor of Veterinary Medicine)

The speaker will be Thomas Dean, **Jr.**

The academy announced the appointment of Marion Unger, **Ph.D.,** as chair. (or **PhD** without periods)

Avoid using the abbreviation *Dr.* before a name that is followed by an abbreviation denoting a doctoral degree. Using both is redundant.

Use abbreviations without periods for many well-known agencies, organizations, and businesses, and also for other familiar abbreviations using capital letters.

The newspaper accused the **CIA** of covert activities in that country.

The **YMHA** is presenting a revival of Arthur Miller's *All My Sons.*

The candidate sought the support of the **AFL-CIO.**

An **acronym** is a pronounceable word made from initials or parts of words. Consult your dictionary about its capitalization, and be sure to explain, in parentheses, an acronym that might be unfamiliar to your readers.

> The next meeting of **OPEC** will be an important one.
>
> Bring your **scuba** (**S**elf **C**ontained **U**nderwater **B**reathing **A**pparatus) equipment with you.
>
> America's **ZIP** code (**Z**one **I**mprovement **S**ystem) has improved the postal service.
>
> The lecture explained **quasars** (quasi-stellar objects).

With numerals, use the abbreviations *B.C.* or *BC* (before Christ) and *A.D.* or *AD* (*anno Domini,* "in the year of the Lord") for dates. Use the abbreviations *A.M.* or *AM* or *a.m.* (before noon) and *P.M.* or *PM* or *p.m.* (after noon) for time.

> Confucius, China's most important teacher and philosopher, was born in 551 **BC.**
>
> In **AD** 37, Caligula was made emperor of Rome.
>
> The child was born at 6:37 **a.m.**

The abbreviation *B.C.* or *BC* should be put after the date, and the abbreviation *A.D.* or *AD* is usually put before the date. However, the practice of putting *AD* after the date is now also considered acceptable. *BC* and *AD* are sometimes replaced with the abbreviations *B.C.E.* (Before the Common Era) and *C.E.* (Common Era), respectively.

A.M. or *AM* and *P.M.* or *PM* may be written with either capital or lowercase letters, but be consistent within a single piece of writing. Lowercase letters require periods—*a.m.* or *p.m.*

Use the following abbreviations for common Latin words and expressions when appropriate.

c. or *ca.* (about)   *etc.* (and others)
cf. (compare)   *i.e.* (that is)
e.g. (for example)   *viz.* (namely)

Moses (**c.** 1350–1250 BC) led his people out of slavery.

Taoism is based on the teachings of Lao-zu (**cf.** Confucianism).

Monotheistic religions (**e.g.**, Christianity and Islam) worship only one god.

Do not overuse these Latin abbreviations. Where possible, try substituting the English equivalent.

Spell out the names of days and months.

NOT: The first game of the World Series will be played on **Oct.** 11
BUT: The first game of the World Series will be played on **October** 11.

NOT: It snowed heavily on the first **Sat.** in **Dec.**
BUT: It snowed heavily on the first **Saturday** in **December.**

Spell out the names of cities, states, and countries, except in addresses.

NOT: He came to **N.Y.C.** to study music.
BUT: He came to **New York City** to study music.

NOT: Emily Dickinson was born in Amherst, **Mass.**
BUT: Emily Dickinson was born in Amherst, **Massachusetts.**

Spell out first names.

NOT: The editor of the collection is **Thom.** Webster.
BUT: The editor of the collection is **Thomas** Webster.

In names of businesses, spell out the words *Brothers, Corporation,* and *Company,* except in addresses or in bibliographic information in research papers.

NOT: She was employed by the firm of Magnum **Bros.**
BUT: She was employed by the firm of Magnum **Brothers.**

NOT: The employees at Thomas Smythe and **Co.** are on strike.
BUT: The employees at Thomas Smythe and **Company** are on strike.

In formal, nontechnical writing, spell out units of measure.

NOT: The pamphlet claims that anyone who is more than ten **lbs.** overweight is a candidate for a heart attack.
BUT: The pamphlet claims that anyone who is more than ten **pounds** overweight is a candidate for a heart attack.

NOT: How many **qts.** of milk did you sell?
BUT: How many **quarts** of milk did you sell?

In technical writing, abbreviations are acceptable and often preferred.

42 Numbers

A **number** is a symbol that represents a specified quantity or location. In formal, nontechnical writing, we use numbers only in specific instances.

Use numbers for quantities that cannot be written as one or two words.

During its first year, the book sold only **678** copies.

Last Saturday this shop sold **1,059** doughnuts.

However, avoid beginning a sentence with a number.

> **Nine hundred seventy-six** people bought tickets for the concert, but only 341 attended.
>
> **Three hundred sixteen** photographs of San Francisco are on exhibit.

Spell out all numbers that can be written as one or two words and that modify a noun.

> She sang a medley of **sixteen** Sondheim songs.
>
> The gestation period for a rabbit is about **thirty-one** days.
>
> We need **one hundred** squares to make this quilt.

Use numbers for decimals or fractions.

> We had **2½** inches of rainfall last month.
>
> What do they mean when they claim that the average family has **2.3** children?

Use numbers for addresses.

> **702** West **74**th Street   **1616** South Street

However, it is acceptable to spell out the name of a numbered street in an address.

> 417 **Eleventh** Avenue   210 East **Seventh** Street

Use numbers to identify pages, percentages, degrees, and amounts of money with the symbol $ or ¢.

Turn to **page 82** for an analysis of the works of Van Gogh.

The survey found that **70.2 percent** of registered voters favor Brosnan.

An acute angle is an angle under **90°.**

The computer costs **$1,667.99.**

Use numbers for dates and for hours expressed with *a.m.* (AM) or *p.m.* (PM).

At **6:07 AM** the snow began to fall.

The First International Peace Conference, held at The Hague, began on May **18, 1899.**

Use numbers with units of measurement.

The course is **127** kilometers.

The room is **11'7" × 13'4".**

The tree is **6'5"** from the garage door.

However, simple numbers may be spelled out: ***six*** *feet.*

Use numbers with quantities in a series.

A grizzly bear can run at a speed of **30** miles per hour; an elephant, **25;** a chicken, **9;** but a tortoise, only **0.17.**

The commercial traveler logged his sales for his first five days on the job: **7, 18, 23, 4, 19.**

Use numbers recorded for identification purposes.

His social security number is **142-45-1983.**

For service call the following number: **(800) 415-3333.**

Flight **465** has been canceled.

When one number immediately follows another, spell out the first number and use a numeral for the second number.

He ran in **two 50**-meter races.

We have **three 6**-foot ladders in the garage.

EXERCISE 42–1

Underline the errors in the use of abbreviations and numbers in the following sentences. Two of the sentences contain no errors.

1. The Rev. Dr. Marianne Brown, Ph.D., will address us about Andrew Marvell's poetry.

2. The previous speaker in the lecture series was Dr. Louis Ambly, Jr.

3. She served on the board of directors for the Girl Scouts, the YMCA, and the Y.W.C.A.

4. The founder of the Hillready Bros. Corporation arrived in the U.S. by boat 100 years ago.

5. The NEH (National Endowment for the Humanities) supports many research projects.

6. The class begins at 11:10 am.

7. We will reconvene on Thurs., Nov. 21.

8. Wm. Brown has been appointed chair of the I.R.S. subcommittee on corporate taxation.

9. It is about four hundred and thirty-three miles from here to Chicago.

10. 199 delegates from around the nation assembled here at 9:30 a.m. today.

 Manuscript Form

The following specifications are standard guidelines for preparing all papers. Additional information on formatting computer-generated, typewritten, and handwritten papers follows. If your instructor specifies different or additional guidelines, be sure to follow them.

43a For All Papers

1. **Spacing**: Double space everything, including blocked quotations.

2. **Materials**: Use 8½" × 11" paper and use only one side of the paper.

3. **Title**: Center your title. Allow an extra line of space between the title and the first line of text. Do not underline or place quotation marks around your title. (Of course, if a part of your title is a quotation or the title of another work, use the appropriate punctuation for this part.) Do not use any symbols to decorate the title. Capitalize the first letter of all words in the title except

articles, short (less than five letters) conjunctions, and short prepositions. Do not place a period at the end of your title.

4. **Margins**: Allow an inch of space for the top and bottom margins and for both side margins.

5. **Hyphenation**: Use hyphens to divide words at the end of lines. (See Section 39e, pp. 393–394 for information on word division at line end.)

6. **Underlining**: When underlining, underline the complete item, including the space between words.

7. **Indentation**: At the start of each paragraph indent five spaces and begin the text on the sixth space. Indent block quotes ten spaces.

8. **Punctuation Format**: Leave two spaces after end punctuation marks and colons. Leave one space after all other punctuation marks. Avoid ending a line with an open bracket, parenthesis, or quotation mark. Beginning a line with any punctuation mark or separating ellipses over two lines simply confuses readers. Also, indicate a dash by using two hyphens without any space before or after the hyphen.

9. **Pagination**: Number each page with an arabic number in the upper right-hand corner. The number on the first page is normally omitted but may be centered at the bottom of the page.

10. **Identification**: Follow carefully your instructor's directions for writing your name and any other identifying information on your paper. Fold, staple, or clip your paper only if your instructor directs you to do so.

11. **Proofreading**: Always proofread your paper carefully before submitting it.

43b For Computer-Generated Papers

Using a computer or word processor can present unique problems in manuscript format. (See also Chapter 4, Sections 4e and 4f, pp. 66–68.)

1. Be certain that the print is dark enough to be clearly legible. If it is not, change the ribbon or use another printer.

2. Use unlined paper. Remove the perforated edges if any exist. Carefully tear the pages apart at the appropriate paper divisions if necessary.

3. Indent the first line of each paragraph five spaces from the left margin. Be aware that this spacing may vary in actual print due to the nature of the type font used. To avoid confusion use a tab for your margin indentations.

4. Use hyphens to divide words at the end of lines only if your computer does not have the "wrap" technique, which automatically eliminates hyphens.

5. Avoid underlining words to signal italics, since most computers can print in italic font.

6. If your computer has an automatic (justified) right-side margin feature that aligns type in the right-hand margin but causes extra spaces to appear between words, do not use it unless you have your instructor's approval.

7. Proofread at the computer terminal first. Then proofread your hard copy. Be certain to use the computer's spelling checker program if available, but remember that spelling checkers do not detect incorrectly used homonyms.

8. Use automatic style checker programs with caution. Many of these are designed specifically for business or

technical writing and may prompt suggestions that are inappropriate for college writing.

43c For Typewritten Papers

1. Use a black typewriter ribbon and be certain that the type bars are clean.

2. Use 8½" by 11" unruled white bond paper. Do not use onionskin.

3. If your keyboard lacks the numeral 1, use a lowercase letter *l* for the numeral.

4. Correct errors by erasing neatly and retyping the entry. Do not use white-out or correction fluid to cover errors unless your instructor approves.

43d For Handwritten Papers

Be sure to check with your instructor to see if a handwritten paper is acceptable.

1. Use blue or black ink. Writing with a pencil or felt-tipped pen is not appropriate.

2. Use 8½" by 11" ruled white paper. If you tear the paper from a spiral notebook, carefully trim the ragged edge. Paper with narrowly spaced lines is not appropriate.

3. Center your title on the top ruled line of the page.

4. The first rule on ruled paper is usually about an inch and a half of space from the top of the page. Use this as a guide for your top margin.

5. Some ruled paper has a vertical line on the left-hand side that can be used as a guide for your left margin.

6. Indent the first line of each paragraph about one inch from the left margin.

7. Correct an error by drawing one line through it and writing the correction above it. Use correction fluid only with your instructor's permission.

8. Write legibly. If your script handwriting is difficult to read, print.

SPELLING

Mastery of English spelling can be a frustrating task, though perhaps not as difficult as some students believe. Simply follow the guidelines outlined here, and always consult your dictionary when you are uncertain of a spelling. Keep a list of the words that you have misspelled in the past and refer to it when writing.

44 Spelling Accurately

Although spelling rules are not infallible, mastery of the few described here will help you. They include some of the most common spelling problems for both native and non-native English writers: adding suffixes to words, forming noun plurals, and choosing between *ei* and *ie*.

44a Doubling the Final Consonant

Words ending in a consonant-vowel-consonant (c-v-c) combination usually signal a short vowel sound.

bat	dot	shun
pen	begin	occur

When a suffix is added to such a word, sometimes the final consonant is doubled to maintain the short vowel sound.

With suffixes beginning with a consonant

Avoid doubling the final consonant of a c-v-c word when adding a suffix beginning with a consonant.

ship + ment = shipment   mob + ster = mobster
wet + ness = wetness   pen + man + ship = penmanship

With suffixes beginning with a vowel

Double the final consonant of a one-syllable c-v-c word when adding a suffix beginning with a vowel.

pen + ed = penned   brag +art = braggart
skip + er = skipper   grip + ing = gripping

Exception: bus + ing = busing

When adding a suffix beginning with a vowel to a c-v-c word of more than one syllable, double the final consonant if the word is accented on the last syllable. Avoid doubling the consonant, however, if the accent shifts to the first syllable when the suffix is added.

begín + er = begínner   regrét + ed = regretted
recúr + ence = recurrence defér + ence = déference
emít + ing = emitting   prefér + ence = préference

When adding a suffix beginning with a vowel to a c-v-c word of more than one syllable, avoid doubling the final consonant if the word is not accented on the last syllable.

pénal + ize = penalize   bánter + ing = bantering
lábor + er = laborer   abándon + ed = abandoned

Avoid doubling the final consonant when adding any suffix to any word that does not end in a consonant-vowel-consonant.

cheap + er = cheaper   ordain + ed = ordained
chant + ing = chanting   pretend + er = pretender

44b Dropping the Silent *e*

Many English words end with a silent *e*. At times the *e* indicates that the vowel before the consonant should have a long sound. For example, notice the difference in the vowel sound in each of the following word pairs.

hat—hate	rot—rote	pan—pane
din—dine	run—rune	spit—spite

At times the silent *e* indicates that the *c* or *g* preceding it should have a soft, rather than a hard, sound.

notice	trace	courage
peace	engage	outrage

Drop a final silent *e* when adding most suffixes beginning with a vowel.

fade + ing = fading	grimace + ed = grimaced
pleasure + able = pleasurable	cohere + ence = coherence
use + age = usage	escape + ist = escapist

EXCEPTIONS

acre + age = acreage	line + age = lineage
dye + ing = dyeing	mile + age = mileage
hoe + ing = hoeing	singe + ing = singeing

Retain a final silent *e* when adding the suffix *-able* or *-ous* to a word in which the silent *e* is preceded by a *c* or a *g*.

notice + able = noticeable	advantage + ous = advantageous
peace + able = peaceable	change + able = changeable
outrage + ous = outrageous	courage + ous = courageous

Retain a final silent *e* when adding a suffix beginning with a consonant.

delicate + ness = delicateness   move + ment = movement
loose + ly = loosely   decisive + ness = decisiveness

EXCEPTIONS

acknowledge + ment = acknowledgment
argue + ment = argument
judge + ment = judgment
nine + th = ninth
true + ly = truly
whole + ly = wholly

44c Changing *y* to *i*

When a final *y* is preceded by a consonant, change the *y* to *i* when you add most suffixes.

lovely + er = lovelier   happy + ly = happily
likely + hood = likelihood   lazy + ness = laziness
risky + est = riskiest   tally + ed = tallied

EXCEPTIONS

dry + er = dryer (machine)   sly + ly = slyly
dry + ly = dryly   sly + ness = slyness
dry + ness = dryness   wry + ly = wryly
shy + ly = shyly   wry + ness = wryness
shy + ness = shyness

However, avoid changing a final *y* to *i* when you add the suffix *-ing* or *-ist*.

spy + ing = spying   hurry + ing = hurrying
copy + ist = copyist   pacify + ing = pacifying

If a final *y* is preceded by a vowel, keep the *y* when you add a suffix.

employ + ee = employee   destroy + er = destroyer
essay + ist = essayist   convey + ance = conveyance
survey + ing = surveying   overstay + ed = overstayed

EXCEPTIONS

day + ly = daily   pay + ed = paid
gay + ly = gaily   say + ed = said
lay + ed = laid

44d Choosing Between *ei* and *ie*

In most cases, place *i* before *e* except after *c*. Place *e* before *i* when these letters are pronounced as *ā*.

i BEFORE e

pierce   niece   mien
believe   interview   shield

AFTER C

receive   deceit   deceive
conceive   perceive   ceiling

PRONOUNCED AS ā

neighbor   weight   feign
freight   vein   reign

EXCEPTIONS

either   height   neither   sufficient
feisty   heir   seize   efficient
heifer   leisure   weird

Note: The rule does not apply to words in which the *i* and the *e* or the *e* and the *i* are pronounced as parts of separate syllables: *piety, deity, hierarchy, science.*

44e Forming Noun Plurals

For most nouns, form the plural by adding *s* to the singular. (See also Section 9a on nouns, pp. 153–156.)

pot—pots	table—tables	magazine—magazines
lamp—lamps	picture—pictures	recorder—recorders

For nouns ending in *y* preceded by a vowel, form the plural by adding *s* to the singular.

monkey—monkeys	holiday—holidays
display—displays	jersey—jerseys
journey—journeys	odyssey—odysseys

For nouns (except proper nouns) ending in *y* preceded by a consonant, form the plural by changing the *y* to *i* and adding *es*.

jelly—jellies	theory—theories
quality—qualities	frequency—frequencies
heresy—heresies	fraternity—fraternities

For nouns ending in *s, ch, sh, x,* or *z,* form the plural by adding *es* to the singular.

genius—geniuses	miss—misses
ditch—ditches	brush—brushes
hoax—hoaxes	waltz—waltzes

For nouns ending in *o* preceded by a vowel, form the plural by adding *s* to the singular.

cameo—cameos	trio—trios
duo—duos	folio—folios
radio—radios	scenario—scenarios

For nouns ending in *o* preceded by a consonant, form the plural by adding either *s* or *es* to the singular.

ADD S

piano—pianos	memo—memos
burro—burros	dynamo—dynamos
alto—altos	magneto—magnetos

ADD es

hero—heroes	echo—echoes
mosquito—mosquitoes	tomato—tomatoes
potato—potatoes	mulatto—mulattoes

ADD S OR es

flamingo—flamingos *or* flamingoes
salvo—salvos *or* salvoes
banjo—banjos *or* banjoes
lasso—lassos *or* lassoes
domino—dominos *or* dominoes
cargo—cargos *or* cargoes

For most nouns ending in *f* or *fe* and for all nouns ending in *ff*, form the plural by adding *s* to the singular.

belief—beliefs	muff—muffs
waif—waifs	staff—staffs
safe—safes	rebuff—rebuffs

For some nouns ending in *f* or *fe*, form the plural by changing the *f* or *fe* to *ve* and adding *s*.

calf—calves	knife—knives
leaf—leaves	wife—wives
self—selves	life—lives

The following nouns ending in *arf* have alternative plural forms.

dwarf—dwarfs *or* dwarves
scarf—scarfs *or* scarves
wharf—wharfs *or* wharves

For compound nouns written as one word, form the plural by applying the preceding rules to the last part of the compound.

cupful—cupfuls	tablespoon—tablespoons
handful—handfuls	hemstitch—hemstitches
housewife—housewives	toolbox—toolboxes
takeoff—takeoffs	horsefly—horseflies

Exception: passerby—passer**s**by

For compound nouns in which the words are joined by a hyphen or written separately, make the chief world plural.

mother-in-law	mothers-in-law
sergeant at arms	sergeants at arms
runner-up	runners-up
attorney general	attorneys general
father-to-be	fathers-to-be

but

tape recorder	tape recorders
sound track	sound tracks
high school	high schools
hope chest	hope chests

EXCEPTIONS

drive-in	drive-ins
five-year-old	five-year-olds
jack-in-the-box	jack-in-the-boxes
frame-up	frame-ups
sit-in	sit-ins
stand-in	stand-ins

For numbers, letters, symbols, and words being named, form the plural by adding *'s* to the singular.

9's	*'s	*a*'s
and's	abc's	+'s

Learn the irregular plural forms.

Some nouns have an irregular plural or form the plural according to the rules of their language of origin.

woman—women	louse—lice	foot—feet
man—men	mouse—mice	tooth—teeth
ox—oxen	alumnus—alumni	analysis—analyses
child—children	radius—radii	crisis—crises

Learn the nouns that have the same form for both singular and plural.

deer	trout	species	moose
salmon	sheep	series	fish

Form the plural of proper nouns by adding *s* or *es*.

Tuesdays	the Joneses	the Kennedys

In the example on the right, note that no apostrophe is used and that the final *y* is not changed to *i*. (See also Section 38a on the apostrophe, pp. 384–387.)

EXERCISE 44–1

Have someone select words from the lists of troublesome words in Chapter 45 for you to spell aloud. Keep a list of the words you misspell, and use it for another oral spelling quiz.

45   Troublesome Words

A large number of spelling errors are caused by omitting one or two letters from a word or by adding letters where they do not belong. The most common errors of this kind are caused by failing to double a consonant or by doubling one incorrectly. The following is a list of words that are often misspelled. The part or parts of the word that commonly cause spelling problems are printed in **boldface.**

academic**ally**	arguing	conc**ei**va**b**le
a**cc**elerator	arg**um**ent	condem**n**
a**cc**ident**ally**	asp**i**rin	con**s**cience
a**cc**o**mm**odate	ath**ei**st	con**s**cient**ious**
a**cc**ompanied	ath**l**ete	contro**ll**ed
a**cc**umulate	a**th**l**e**tic	controv**er**si**a**l
achi**eve**ment	a**w**f**u**l	coo**ll**y
acknowle**d**ge	bankrup**t**cy	crow**d**ed
acknowled**gm**ent	bea**u**tiful	cruel**t**y
a**c**quaintance	begi**nn**ing	defe**rr**ed
admi**ss**ion	bound**ar**y	defi**n**itely
admi**tt**ance	busi**n**ess	defi**n**ition
adoles**c**ent	can**d**idate	de**s**cend
advantag**e**ous	chal**l**enge	desi**r**able
a**ll**otting	chang**e**able	desp**e**rate
a**l**most	choc**o**late	di**l**e**tt**ante
a**l**ready	colum**n**	di**n**ing
a**l**together	co**m**ing	disast**r**ous
amate**u**r	co**mm**i**tt**ee	dispe**l**
am**o**ng	compe**l**	di**ss**atisfied
a**n**aly**z**e	compe**ll**ed	di**ss**ervice
ar**c**tic	compe**ti**tion	drunke**nn**ess

ecstasy
efficiency
embarrass
empty
endeavor
enthusiastically
entrance
environment
equipped
especially
essential
exaggerate
excellent
excess
exercise
exhaustion
existence
familiar
fascinate
favorite
February
financially
foreign
forfeit
forty
fourth
frantically
fulfill
generally
government
grievous
guarantee
handicapped
handkerchief
harass
height
hindrance
hurriedly

hygiene
ideally
illogical
imitate
immediately
incidentally
indispensable
individually
ingenious
initially
initiative
intelligence
interfered
interrupt
irresistible
irritable
jewelry
judgment
knowledge
laboratory
lenient
liaison
lightning
literature
loneliness
manageable
maneuver
marriage
meanness
medieval
mileage
miniature
miscellaneous
mischievous
misspelled
mortgage
necessary
nineteen

ninety
ninth
occasion
occasionally
occurred
occurrence
omission
omitted
opponent
outrageous
pamphlet
parallel
pastime
peaceable
permissable
picknicked
playwright
pneumonia
possess
preference
preferred
prejudiced
privilege
probably
procedure
pronunciation
psalm
publicly
pumpkin
questionnaire
recession
reference
referring
remittance
restaurant
rhythm
satellite
sergeant

she**ph**erd	su**mm**ary	usua**ll**y
she**riff**	su**pp**osed	vac**uu**m
ski**i**ng	su**pp**re**ss**	valua**b**le
soph**o**more	sy**mm**etric	vi**o**lence
so**u**ve**n**ir	temp**e**rature	wa**rr**ing
specifica**ll**y	to**morr**ow	w**h**ere
stre**t**ch	transfe**rr**ed	w**h**ether
stu**bb**or**nn**ess	tr**u**ly	w**h**istle
su**b**tle	undou**b**tedly	who**ll**y
su**cc**ess	unmista**ka**bly	wri**t**ing
suffi**c**ient	u**nn**ece**ss**ary	wri**tt**en

Students trained in Canadian or British usage will note that U. S. spellings differ for some words:

UNITED STATES	BRITISH
behavior	behaviour
center	centre
color	colour
labor	labour

Avoid using British spellings.

EXERCISE 45–1

Underline any misspelled words in the following paragraph. Use a dictionary if you find it helpful. Circle those words which a computer's spelling checker would not detect.

The histery of education in hour country is one charac-
terised by slow but constant change. Especialy notible today
are the changes in the compesition of the student body which
now includes varyous multicultural representations. Some

think the changes have been to slow in comming. Others are anxous that change ocurs to fast. One thing apears clear: the campus of today is very diferent form that of yestreday.

46 Capitalization

Capitalize the first word of a sentence, the pronoun *I*, and the interjection *O*.

Many writers have created imaginary universes.

Do **I** think that life exists on other planets?

These creatures, **O** mighty Gork, come from the other side of the universe.

Capitalize the first word of a direct quotation that is a complete sentence.

At the climax of the movie, Rhett says, "**F**rankly, my dear, I don't give a damn."

The book begins with the present Mrs. de Winter recounting a dream: "**L**ast night I dreamt I went to Manderley again."

Capitalize the first word of every line of verse unless the poet has written the line with a lowercase letter.

Keats's poem ends with the lines, "**T**hough the sedge is withered from the lake / **A**nd no birds sing."

Note: In quotations, always capitalize whichever words the writer has capitalized.

Capitalize proper nouns.

Sharon	**K**eats
Andrew **J**ackson	**L**ake **M**ichigan
Portuguese	**H**awaii
Greta **G**arbo	the **E**mpire **S**tate **B**uilding
the **M**iddle **A**ges	the **R**evolutionary **W**ar

Avoid capitalizing compass points unless they are part of a proper noun: *northwest of Chicago* but *the Pacific Northwest.*

Capitalize an official title when it precedes a name.

The guest speaker will be **C**ongresswoman Katherine Murphy.

The nation mourned the death of **P**resident Lincoln.

The changes were supported by **G**overnor Celeste.

Capitalize the title of a high official when it is used in place of the person's name.

The guest speaker will be the **C**ongresswoman.

The nation mourned the death of the **P**resident.

The changes were supported by the **G**overnor.

Note: Do not capitalize a title that does not name a specific individual.

Capitalize abbreviations and designations that follow a name. Do not capitalize titles used as appositives.

Eugene Anderson, **J**r.

Anne Poletti, **P**h.**D.** (PhD)

Louise Tate, **A**ttorney at **L**aw

Seymour Rosen, a **c**hemistry **p**rofessor, submitted an article to the magazine.

Willie Mae Kean, a first-year **l**aw student, won the award.

Spike Kennedy, an **i**ntern at the hospital, was interviewed on television.

Capitalize the title of a relative when it precedes a name or is used in place of a name. Do not capitalize the title if it is used with a possessive pronoun.

Aunt Joan   **C**ousin Mary
Uncle Carlos   **G**randfather Tseng

Is **G**randmother coming to visit?

You look well, **G**randpa.

My **u**ncle Bill could not come to the performance.

Capitalize proper adjectives.

Shakespearean sonnet   **M**achiavellian goals
Parisian style   **G**recian urn
Islamic teacher   **C**hristian faith

Avoid capitalizing most proper adjectives that are part of a compound noun.

french fries   **d**anish pastry
roman numeral   **v**enetian blind

Note: Usage in this area varies. Consult your dictionary for capitalization of compound nouns formed from proper adjectives.

Capitalize the names of specific academic courses. Do not capitalize general subject areas unless the subject area is a proper noun, such as a language.

History 121	*but*	a world **h**istory course
The **M**odern **A**merican **N**ovel	*but*	an American **l**iterature course
Advanced **B**iology	*but*	a **b**iology course

Capitalize words naming the Deity, sacred books, and other religious documents and names of religions, religious denominations, and their adherents.

Jehovah	**A**llah	the **L**ord
the **B**ible	the **K**oran	the **U**panishads
Catholicism	**M**oslem	**L**utheran
Christ	**B**uddha	**G**od

Note: Pronouns referring to the Deity are usually capitalized.

Capitalize names of months, days of the week, and holidays.

April	**D**ecember	**J**anuary
Tuesday	**S**aturday	**W**ednesday
Halloween	**N**ew **Y**ear's **E**ve	the **F**ourth of **J**uly

Note: Do not capitalize the names of the seasons.

Capitalize the abbreviations *A.D. (AD)* **and** *B.C. (BC).*

A.D. 172	500 **B.C.**
AD 356	275 **BC**

For titles of literary works, capitalize the first and the last word and all other important words, including prepositions of five or more letters.

Avoid capitalizing articles, short prepositions, or coordinating conjunctions that do not begin or end a title. A short preposition is one that has fewer than five letters.

The Decline and Fall of the Roman Empire

"The Case of the Irate Witness"

Much Ado About Nothing

"On the Morning After the Sixties"

Capitalize both parts of a hyphenated word in a title.

"Home-Thoughts from Abroad"

"Good-Bye, My Fancy!"

EXERCISE 46–1

In each of the following items, change a lowercase letter to a capital letter wherever necessary.

1. The new gender studies program includes courses in women's literature from the middle ages and renaissance to the present time.

2. The puritans and separatists left England for holland and then came to america, abandoning forever the church of England.

3. At the camp david conference, the president, the prime minister, and the king all reached agreement.

4. Several cambodians opened a restaurant, the egg roll special, which instantly became popular.

5. Most tourists in paris visit the eiffel tower and the cathedral of notre dame.

6. The initial words of "the star spangled banner" are: "o say can you see by the dawn's early light / what so proudly we hailed at the twilight's last gleaming."

7. His short story, "Memories of the southwest," really portrays his aunt Iola and uncle Irving as a loving couple.

8. Was it F. D. Roosevelt who said, "we have nothing to fear but fear itself"?

9. In France, the fourteenth of July is a national holiday.

10. The course in comparative religions includes methodism, islam, confucianism, and the coptic Christians; however, it is offered only on Tuesdays and thursdays.

THE RESEARCH PAPER

The word *research* comes from an Old French word, *recercher*, meaning "to seek out" or "to search again." A research paper or essay is one in which you seek out information about a topic from a variety of sources. However, a research paper should not be merely a recapitulation of the findings of others. It should also reflect your own ideas, understanding, and analysis.

A research paper is both informative and objective. In it you provide information about a topic by examining a variety of sources objectively and by reaching a conclusion about these findings. The research paper will also contain a thesis or assertion supported by objective information.

A research paper is formal. It contains little, if any, colloquial language or slang and few, if any, contractions. A typical research paper contains between 2,000 and 3,000 words and runs five to fifteen pages long. A research essay contains all the characteristics of a research paper but is shorter.

47 Selecting and Limiting a Topic

Whether your instructor provides you with a list of topics on a specific subject matter or you have the freedom to select your own topic, begin with the question, "What really interests me?" Since you will be spending several weeks researching your topic, be certain you choose one that appeals to you. Are you interested in finding information about any particular person? Andrew Johnson? Diane Arbus? Spike Lee? Gwendolyn Brooks? Are you interested in studying any particular place? Fiji? Jupiter? Egypt? The Great Plains? Are you interested in exploring any particular time period? The turn of the century? The fifteenth century? The fifth century BC? The 1930s? Are you interested in examining any particular event? The Civil War? Columbus' landing in this hemisphere? The birth of religions in the Middle East? The first space flight to the moon? Are you interested in studying any particular object or activity? Clocks? Vitamins? MTV? Cooking? Are you interested in exploring any particular idea or doctrine? Colonialism? Multiculturalism? Transcendentalism? Marxism? Are you interested in investigating a controversial issue? Abortion? Steroid use by athletes? Nuclear power? Euthanasia?

When faced with the task of writing a research paper, many students go blank; they can think of nothing that interests them. Some solve this problem by thumbing through magazines, newspapers, and general encyclopedias. A letter in the *New York Times* book review interested one student, Gail Young, in Mercy Otis Warren, a minor author of Colonial New England. But what could Gail write about her?

Because your research paper will be between five and fifteen pages long, after deciding on a topic, you will need to limit it so that you can cover it effectively within these boundaries. What aspect of your topic do you wish to cover? Notice how the following topics are narrowed.

Spike Lee → his life → his life as an artist → his movies → *Jungle Fever* → the making of *Jungle Fever*

Egypt → the history of Egypt → the military history of Egypt → Egypt's role in Middle East peace negotiations

the fifth century BC → the fifth century BC in China → religion in China in the fifth century BC → the teachings of Confucius → modern Chinese reaction to the teachings of Confucius

the Civil War → important generals of the Civil War → General Sherman's role in the Civil War → General Sherman's Atlanta campaign

vitamins → types of vitamins → the use of vitamin supplements → vitamin therapy → the controversy over megadose vitamin therapy

transcendentalism → New England transcendentalists → the influence of transcendentalism on the works of Henry David Thoreau → the influence of transcendentalism in *Walden*

Of course, limiting your topic is not always a simple, straightforward process. It is more of a trial-and-error procedure. Your exploration of sources will lead to the discovery of a number of options or topics you can follow in your research. As you do further research you will find yourself revising and fine tuning that topic or finding better options to narrow down. Search for the option that not only interests you but also presents a new insight that will interest your audience. And be comfortable with the idea that limiting your topic involves experimentation and risk. This is normal.

47a Exploring Resources

A wide array of resources are available for you to explore: books, computerized data bases, periodicals, general encyclopedias, specialized encyclopedias, consultations with reference librarians, personal interviews. You most probably will not need to consult all of the resources available, but you will want to explore enough of them to help you select and limit your topic.

Gail Young first consulted a general encyclopedia in the reference area of the library. It seemed obvious to her from the brief entries therein that the life of Mercy Otis Warren would not be as interesting as that of Spike Lee. But the encyclopedias included with each of their entries a brief bibliography, a start for Gail's research. The encyclopedias also gave Gail several clues to possible areas for investigation. For example, Gail noted with surprise that the *Britannica* declares Warren's poems and plays to be of "no permanent value." What the *Americana* calls Warren's "chief work"—*History of the Rise, Progress, and Termination of the American Revolution*—was "bitterly resented" by John Adams, notes the *Britannica*. So Gail was on her way to choosing a topic: What did Warren's contemporaries think of her poems and plays? Why is her work apparently of so little worth today? What caused Adams' resentment? Was Warren an early feminist?

In Gail's case, encyclopedias provided sufficient impetus to limit the topic. But other sources of information should be consulted in order to validate points, to discover differing views, to help you determine the scope as well as the purpose of your research. The important principle to remember is to make your exploration of resources thorough. Avoid settling on a source or strategy that forces you to devise a specific topic or thesis too soon. On the other hand, you will not want to prolong unduly the exploration. If this searching activity does not help you limit your topic and direct you toward a purpose, perhaps you need to explore another topic.

47b Exploring Purpose

You write research papers and essays in academic and nonacademic settings for the same purpose: to gather together in one document materials from a variety of sources to provide knowledge and understanding for you and your audience. But a research paper is more than merely a collection of facts. It must also contain your reactions, analysis, and thought. To give your paper focus, it helps to explore various purposes and then settle on one that will act as your preliminary thesis, or as the main point of the paper. Finding a purpose carries the process of limiting the topic one step further toward the formulation of a preliminary thesis.

TOPIC LIMITATION

Spike Lee → his life → his life as an artist → his artistic output → his movies → *Jungle Fever* → the making of *Jungle Fever*

The purpose or preliminary thesis: Spike Lee, in producing the movie *Jungle Fever*, vividly portrayed racial tensions but unfairly exploited stereotypes in doing so.

Although your exact purpose in writing the research paper may change or remain unclear until you have actually explored sufficient resource materials, it is best to begin your project with at least a temporary purpose in mind. Try to arrive at a purpose that allows you to react to the topic and to get involved in the conversation of the topic as in the example on Spike Lee. In other words, apply the pentad or other prewriting devices to your topic to help generate more thoughts about it. (See also Chapter 2: Finding a Purpose, pp. 14–20.)

47c Exploring Scope

Scope concerns the size or range of your research topic. When selecting your topic, you will want to be sure that it indeed lends itself to research. If the scope of your topic is too broad, you will have difficulty finding a focus. If the scope of your topic is very narrow, very new, or subjective, you probably will not be able to locate sufficient objective information about it when exploring sources. For example, the topic *the rise in popularity of imported French cheese in the northeastern states during the last three months* will most likely not lend itself to adequate research. It is too recent. Additionally, the topic *why I like cheese* calls for subjective personal opinion, not research. The topic might be appropriate for a personal essay, but not for a research paper. You will have to consider a topic's scope even if your instructor gives you a list of research topics to choose from. Keep in mind the following questions.

DETERMINING SCOPE

Is my topic {
too broad?
too narrow?
too recent?
entirely subjective?

---

48 Doing Research

After you have chosen a potential topic, you will need to gather information. The best place to start is your library. Explore what your library has to offer and be sure to consult with the reference librarian, who can direct you to appropriate sources.

48a Finding Information

The library catalog

One way to begin your research is by consulting the **library catalog,** which lists alphabetically all the books, magazines, and journals in the library. The library catalog can be computerized or on-line, on cards, microfilm, or microfiche. Usually the catalog contains at least three listings for each book: a *subject* heading, a *title* heading, and an *author* heading. (Often a book is listed under more than one subject heading.) Start with the subject headings unless you have a particular title or author in mind.

Gail started her research by consulting the author/title headings in the computer on-line catalog, where she found entries listing Warren's works (see sample on-line catalog entry below) and some biographies, giving the location of the materials in the library, and providing other information such as publisher and date of publication, number of pages, number of illustrations, and presence of bibliography. Gail also discovered that although few of Warren's plays are available in book form, all are contained on microfilm in a collection of Colonial drama located in a special section of the library. Gail also found that Warren's history of the Revolution is in a special area for rare books because it is a facsimile of the original volume that

SAMPLE ON-LINE CATALOG ENTRY

Screen identification → Screen 1 of 2

NO HOLDINGS IN IND – FOR HOLDINGS ENTER dh DEPRESS DISPLAY RECD SEND
OCLC: 3355943   Rec stat: c Entrd: 771020   Used: 911114
Type: a Bib lvl: m Govt pub: Lang: eng Source: c Illus:
Repr: Enc lvl: I Conf pub: 0 Ctry: xx Det tp: r M/F/B: ˆo
Indx: 0 Mod rec: Festschr: 0 Cont:
Desc: Int lvl: Dates: 1953,1775
  1   010   a35-2531
  2   040   Wisconsin Univ. Libr.   ic OCP Id OCL Id m.c.
  3   050   0   PS858.W8 1b A
  4   092   B12 1b WE91
  5   049   INDU

Author → 6   100   1   Warren, Mercy (Otis) 1d 1728–1814. 1w dn
Title → 7   245   14   The Group. 1779.
  8   260   Ann Arbor, 1b William L. Clements Library, University of Michigan,
1c 1953.
  9   300   [9] p., facsims, 22 p. 1c 21 cm.
  10 500   A political satire in 2 acts, in verse,
  11 500   Reproduction of the William L. Clements Library copy of the 1st
Boston ed., with t.p. reading: The Group . . . Boston, Printed and sold by Edes
and Gill, 1775.

Screen identification → Screen 2 of 2
  12 651   0   United States 1x History 1y Revolution 1s Drama.

Technical data for librarians

City, publisher, date of publication

Number of pages and size

Introductory pages

Description

Warren autographed and sent to Thomas Jefferson. When Gail followed the call numbers of the books, she found, shelved with the Warren material, books by and about other authors of the period—suggestions for new topics if this research proved unproductive.

Gail also consulted the subject heading listing, where she found some duplicate listings. She was also able to find other

SAMPLE CATALOG CARDS

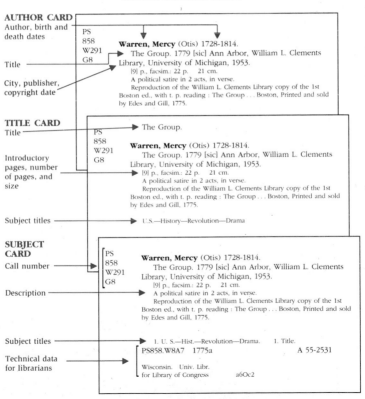

AUTHOR CARD
Author, birth and death dates

PS
858
W291
G8

Warren, Mercy (Otis) 1728-1814.
The Group. 1779 [sic] Ann Arbor, William L. Clements Library, University of Michigan, 1953.
[9] p., facsim.: 22 p.   21 cm.
A political satire in 2 acts, in verse.
Reproduction of the William L. Clements Library copy of the 1st Boston ed., with t. p. reading : The Group . . . Boston, Printed and sold by Edes and Gill, 1775.

Title

City, publisher, copyright date

TITLE CARD
Title

The Group.

PS
858
W291
G8

Warren, Mercy (Otis) 1728-1814.
The Group. 1779 [sic] Ann Arbor, William L. Clements Library, University of Michigan, 1953.
[9] p., facsim.: 22 p.   21 cm.
A political satire in 2 acts, in verse.
Reproduction of the William L. Clements Library copy of the 1st Boston ed., with t. p. reading : The Group . . . Boston, Printed and sold by Edes and Gill, 1775.

Introductory pages, number of pages, and size

Subject titles

U.S.—History—Revolution—Drama

SUBJECT CARD
Call number

PS
858
W291
G8

Warren, Mercy (Otis) 1728-1814.
The Group. 1779 [sic] Ann Arbor, William L. Clements Library, University of Michigan, 1953.
[9] p., facsim.: 22 p.   21 cm.
A political satire in 2 acts, in verse.
Reproduction of the William L. Clements Library copy of the 1st Boston ed., with t. p. reading : The Group . . . Boston, Printed and sold by Edes and Gill, 1775.

Description

Subject titles

1. U. S.—Hist.—Revolution—Drama.   1. Title.

PS858.W8A7   1775a   A 55-2531

Technical data for librarians

Wisconsin.   Univ. Libr.
for Library of Congress   a6Oc2

books listed here that were not under the author/title headings by looking on the shelves near the call numbers she had already gathered. Like Gail, you will want to note each source of possible relevance to your topic on a card (see sample cards on pp. 457 and 459) or in your computer file. Always remember to record the source's call number.

Some libraries have not computerized their catalogs, and you will find them on cards in drawers under the same three divisions; title, author, and subject. The subject catalog is often located away from the title/author catalog. In using a subject catalog in any form, you will find it helpful to consult, in the reference section of your library, the volumes called *Library of Congress Subject Headings* (LCSH). Gail checked several headings and found these for Warren: Colonial American Literature, American Historians, Dramatists, and Women, among others. Sample catalog cards are shown on p. 439.

Computer data bases

A **data base** is a computerized index of articles, books, and other materials *on a specific subject*. It should not be confused with a library's computerized (on-line) catalog, which lists all of the library's holdings. Information in the data base is indexed like the library catalog by author and title and, like the subject catalog, by key words called *descriptors*. A strong advantage of the computerized data base index is the fact that subjects, topics, and concepts can be combined, so the focusing and narrowing of your topic can be quickly accomplished. To access the materials in a data base, you will need to develop a set of *accurately spelled* descriptor terms; otherwise, your search will fail. Using many descriptors, both narrow and broad, will produce better results than using only one or two. These descriptors tend to be specific; for example, the descriptors *waste dump* will produce a limited number of entries, whereas the descriptors *nuclear waste repository* will produce many more entries. You will therefore need to break down your topic into its major subject concepts (consulting the LCSH is recommended) and to list terms to cover each concept. Some data bases have lists of standardized subject terms that are used within the data base. Such a list is called a **thesaurus** and is similar in function to the LCSH. Determine also how the subject terms you have chosen may be cross-referenced or combined, and use these descriptors as well. Next, you or the librarian should enter on the computer the terms you have chosen. The computer searches for all citations included in the data base indexed under your terms and provides you with a printout of the references that interest you. In some cases the data bases will provide you with a brief summary of each text. A library may permit you to search the data base yourself, but hundreds of data bases are available, and the process may be complicated. A sample subject search can also be made in some libraries via the newer CD-ROM (Compact Disc—Read Only Memory), which provides access to scholarly publications in specific fields. You should not hesitate to consult a reference librarian about the availability of a data base and fee, if any, for using it. A list of some of the data bases for different academic disciplines follows.

SPECIALIZED COMPUTER DATA BASES

ABI/INFORM (Business Administration)
Agricola (Agriculture)
America: History and Life
Art Literature International
Arts and Humanities Search
Biography Master Index
Biosis Previews (Biology)
CA Search (Chemistry)
*COMPEN DEX*PLUS* (Engineering)
Donnelly Demographics (Census Data)
ERIC, Educational Resources Information Center (Education)
Medline (Biomedics)
Mental Health Abstracts
Metadex (Metallurgy)

Philosopher's Index
PsychINFO (Psychology)
Religion Index
Social Scisearch (Social Sciences)
Sociological Abstracts
Software Directory (Microcomputer Software)
Ulrich's International Periodicals Directory
World Translations Index

Another student, Tim Gomez, chose the topic *sleep disorders* for a research paper. The data base Tim selected to search was *PsychINFO*, produced by the American Psychological Association and available on the Bibliographic Retrieval Services (BRS). The first descriptor Tim entered was the original broad topic, *sleep disorders,* and the query was the number of items on that topic. The computer's response—413 documents—confirmed Tim's earlier suspicion that his topic was too broad. He next entered a narrowed descriptor, *nightmares.* The number of documents now, though smaller, was still discouragingly high, so Tim continued the search by combining the descriptors. He requested the computer to search for material concerning first the *sleep disorders of young adults,* then of *students,* then of *young adult students,* and finally *college students' nightmares.* Within only a few minutes the computer narrowed the list of sources to a workable one of twenty-four items. After the computer had located the citations appropriate for Tim's topic, he requested that the computer provide him the titles of several articles and books with their subject headings to determine whether he was on target in his search. Then, after viewing this sample, Tim could obtain bibliographic information and an abstract (brief summary) of any or all of the citations.

Gail, also searching her topic in a data base, used the data base *America: History and Life,* produced by ABC Clio and available on the Dialog system. Before using it, Gail had spent hours searching only a few years of printed indexes and found listings for only four articles. With the data base, however, she searched 200,000 references dating back to 1964 and retrieved eleven articles in just a few minutes. Gail requested abstracts for all eleven of the articles on her topic; one of these abstracts is shown here.

SAMPLE DATA BASE ENTRY

380462 14A-00632

John Adams' Opinion of Benjamin Franklin

Evans, William B.

Pennsylvania Mag. of Hist. and Biog. 1968 92(2): 220–238.

Document Type: ARTICLE

Traces John Adams' animosity toward Benjamin Franklin in 10 1807 letters to Mercy Otis Warren questioning her favorable treatment of Franklin in History of the Rise, Progress, and Termination of the American Revolution. Differences between the two revolutionary giants began in 1776 when Franklin supported a unicameral legislature in Pennsylvania, and continued in Paris (1776–79) until their joint presence on the Peace commission in 1780 brought an open breach when Adams opposed Franklin's supposedly pro-French policy. Not only differences on policy but Adams' envy and pride may have colored his view of Franklin. Based primarily on the papers of John Adams; 67 notes. (R. B. Mitchell)

Descriptors: Adams, John (letters, opinion); Politics, 1774-1810; Franklin, Benjamin; Warren, Mercy Otis

Notice that because Warren's name is not in the title, Gail might have had difficulty in finding this article when she searched the printed indexes. The computer, however, could also search the abstract and find the descriptor.

Most often you will use the computer data base just as you use the computerized catalog, card catalog, and other sources like periodical indexes: to identify books and articles that may be useful in your research and that you will then locate in your library (or other libraries available to you through interlibrary loan with the help of your reference librarian). The abstracts available from computer data bases, like all abstracts, are merely brief summaries of the books and articles to which they refer. After reading the abstract, you will know whether the article or books are pertinent to your topic. You will then need to find and consult the article or book. Abstracts are often misused by researchers, who cite them in a paper instead of consulting and citing the actual source.

Occasionally, you may use a data base that provides the complete article or text from a select group of magazines, newspapers, and reference books. The data base systems used by Gail and Tim—Dialog and BRS—are among those that provide, in addition to references and abstracts, full texts of articles from a select list of magazines. A list of some of these data bases follows.

DATA BASES THAT PROVIDE COMPLETE TEXTS

AP News	*Magill's Survey of Cinema*
Bible	most major newspapers
Consumer Drug Information	*PsychINFO*
Consumer Reports	*Tax Notes Today*
Everyman's Encyclopedia	*UPI News*
Harvard Business Review	

Computer data base material requires documentation like any printed source. (Sample bibliographic entries for computerized sources appear on pp. 483 and 499.)

Periodical indexes

Periodical indexes are used to locate magazine and journal articles with more current information on a topic than you will find in most books. The more current your topic, the more likely you will benefit from using magazine, journal, and newspaper articles. Some researchers consult the periodical indexes before the library's catalog of books for this very reason. For topics in the humanities, the *Humanities Index* is useful, as is the *Essay and General Literature Index*, which will direct you to articles in books. Also helpful are the *Social Sciences* and the *General Science Index* in their specific areas. The *Readers' Guide to Periodical Literature* provides a monthly, quarterly, and annual index to almost 200 popular periodicals such as *Time, Newsweek,* and *Readers' Digest.* Although the *Readers' Guide* is one of the more widely used indexes, it is unlike scholarly indexes in that it will direct you to sources that do not contain bibliographies or documentation. This could lead you to a dead end in your further exploration of sources. The *Readers' Guide* is most valuable when used to find articles on contemporary topics. Another useful index is the *New York Times Index.* Following is a list of these and other indexes to periodicals. These indexes often appear in a data base version (noted in parentheses on this list).

GENERAL

Cumulative Index to Periodical Literature, 1959–
New York Times Index, 1851– (*National Newspaper Index,* 1979–)
Poole's Index to Periodical Literature, 1802–1906
Popular Periodicals Index, 1973–
Readers' Guide to Periodical Literature, 1900–; 1983–

SPECIALIZED

Abstracts of Popular Culture, 1976–
Agricultural Engineering Abstracts, 1975– (*Agris,* 1975–)
Agricultural Index, 1916–1964

The American Humanities Index, 1975–
Applied Science and Technology Index, 1958–; 1983–
Art Index, 1929–; 1984–
Bibliography and Index of Geology, 1961–
Biography Index, 1946–
Biological Abstracts, 1926— *(Biosis Previews, 1969—)*
Biological and Agricultural Index, 1964—
Book Review Digest, 1905–; 1983–
Business Periodicals Index, 1958–
Chemical Abstracts, 1907– *(CA Search* 1967–)
Computer Readable Databases, current
Cumulative Index to Nursing and Allied Health Literature, 1977–
Cumulative Index to Nursing Literature, 1961–1976
Current Index to Journals in Education, 1969–
Economics Abstracts, 1969–
Education Index, 1929–; 1983–
Engineering Index, 1906– *(Compendex Plus,* 1970–)
General Science Index, 1978–; 1984–
Humanities Index, 1974–; 1984–
Index to Legal Periodicals, 1908–; 1981–
Industrial Arts Index, 1913–1957
International Index to Periodicals, 1907–1965
International Political Science Abstracts, 1951–
International Who's Who, 1935–
MLA International Bibliography of Books and Articles on the
   Modern Languages and Literatures, 1921–; 1981–
Music Index 1949–
Physics Abstracts 1941– *(Inspec,* 1969–)
Psychological Abstracts, 1927– *(Psych Info,* 1967–)
Social Sciences and Humanities Index, 1965–; 1974–
Social Science Index, 1974–; 1972–
U.S. Government Publication (monthly catalog), 1895–

Tim Gomez, in researching his topic on sleep disorders, consulted periodical indexes in an attempt to restrict his topic to current information on sleep disorders. An excerpt from the

Readers' Guide entry for June 1991 under "Sleep" follows. Later in his research, Tim recalled the "See also" list of terms in this entry, which he found useful in narrowing his topic further.

READERS' GUIDE ENTRY

Subject heading	**SLEEP**
	See also
	Nightmares
Title of article	The promise of sleep research. il *The Futurist* 25:46–7 Mr/Ap '91
Related headings	**THE SLEEPING BEAUTY** [ballet] See Ballet Reviews— Single works
	SLEEPING PILLS *See* Hypnotics
	SLEEPING WITH THE ENEMY [film] See Motion picture reviews— Single works

Cross reference

Location of article

Should you become confused during your searches of the catalog, data bases, and periodical indexes, remember to consult the librarian or other personnel working in the library's reference section.

Nonlibrary sources

Depending on the nature of your topic, it might be appropriate for you to seek information outside of your library: mailings, experiments, questionnaires, and interviews. Most corporations, municipalities, colleges, and similar organizations will respond to your inquires for information by mailing you personal letters and/or brochures. You may opt to devise experiments modeled after the methodologies of the natural and social sciences (see pp. 569–570) to provide additional evidence for your research project. You might devise questionnaires that you distribute to others to obtain their opinions. Interviews are another good way to obtain information. If you decide to use an interview, you will want to carefully prepare for it in advance. Prepare a list of open-ended questions for the interview; avoid devising close-ended questions that can be answered with a simple "yes" or "no" because your goal is to gather information that will enhance your paper. Again, materials incorporated into your research from any source, whether correspondence, experiments, or interviews, require documentation in order to avoid plagiarism. (See pp. 482–484 on documenting nonprint sources and pp. 469–473 on plagiarism.)

48b Primary and Secondary Sources of Information

The sources of information for a research paper can be divided into primary and secondary sources. A **primary source** gives you firsthand information about a topic. For example, for a paper on the causes of and treatment of sleep disorders of college students, a primary source would be an article by a researcher or an interview with a person who had experienced nightmares. A book describing the experiments of others is a **secondary source.** For a paper on a literary subject, primary sources would include the literature itself and the writer's letters and diaries. For Gail's literary topic on writer Mercy Otis Warren or a historical study of Warren's quarrel with John Adams or the politics of the times, primary sources would include Warren's poems and plays, Adams' letters, and records of the proceedings of the Continental Congress. Secondary sources would include critical studies of the literature, histories of the period, and biographies of Warren and Adams.

In your research, try to use as many primary sources as possible. Although for many topics you will have to use secondary sources, remember that often the closer you are to the original source, the more accurate your information will be.

Keep in mind the reliability of your sources and ask yourself the following questions.

EVALUATING PRIMARY AND
SECONDARY SOURCES

If the source is primary:
1. Is the source objective?
2. Is the author of the source an expert in the field?
3. If the source reports the results of an experiment, did the experiment follow the established procedures?
4. How recent is the information? (Obviously, this question is not important for all situations.)

If the source is secondary:
1. What is the author's reputation in the field?
2. What sources did the author use?
3. How sound are the author's conclusions?
4. How recent is the book or article? (Again, in some situations, this will not be relevant.)
5. Does the book or article examine current literature on the topic or include a survey of current research and provide documentation?
6. Was the book published by a University Press or other respectable publisher or was the article published in a reputable magazine? (An article in a scholarly journal is more likely to contain reliable information than an article in a magazine that seeks to entertain its readers.)

Sources of information can also be divided into the three categories: you, others, and written and media materials. Your first source of information is yourself. What do you know about the subject? What experiences have you had that relate to the subject?

Your second source of information is other people. Interview people who have firsthand information about your topic. Interviews are always valuable, especially when your research topic is in the social sciences. Attend lectures and discussions about your subject. When suitable, take an opinion poll. Conduct a survey. When Tim Gomez began working on his research paper, he took an informal survey of students at his school to find out about their experiences with nightmares.

Your third source of information is books, magazine and journal articles, newspaper articles, films, and radio and television news programs and documentaries. Read as much about your topic as you can. View films and documentaries.

When you are beginning your research, you may find reference books helpful in getting an overview of your topic. Your library contains many general reference aids. Learn what they are and use them appropriately, but do not depend on encyclopedias or other general reference works for all your research. After getting an overview of your topic, you will need to consult more specialized books and articles for more detailed information.

The following is a sampling of general reference aids.

General encyclopedias

Collier's Encyclopedia, 24 vols.
Encyclopedia Americana, 30 vols.
The New Encyclopaedia Britannica, 32 vols.

Almanacs and yearbooks

American Annual, 1923–
Britannica Book of the Year, 1938–
Collier's Year Book (titled *National Year Book* before 1942), 1939–
Facts on File Yearbook, 1940–

United Nations Yearbook, 1947–
World Almanac and Book of Facts, 1868–

Agriculture

Bimonthly List of Publications and Visuals, U.S. Department of
Agriculture, July/Aug., 1973–
Guide to Sources for Agricultural and Biological Research, 1981–

Art and architecture

*Art Books 1876–1949: Including an International Index of
Current Serial Publications*, 1981
*Art Books 1950–1979: Including an International Directory of
Museum Permanent Collection Catalogs*, 1979
Art Books 1980–1985, 1985
Cyclopedia of Painters and Painting, 4 vols., 1978
Encyclopedia of World Architecture, 2 vols., 1979, repr. 1983
Encyclopedia of World Art, 16 vols., 1959–1968; and supplement,
1983
A History of Architecture, 19th ed., 1987

Atlases

Commercial Atlas and Marketing Guide, 1988
Hammond Gold Medallion World Atlas, 1990
National Geographic Atlas of the World, 6th ed., 1990
Oxford Economic Atlas of the World, 4th ed., 1972

Biological and life sciences

Biology Dictionary, 1989
Cambridge Encyclopedia of Life Sciences, 1985
Concise Encyclopedia of Biochemistry, 2nd ed., 1988
Dictionary of Life Sciences, 1984
Encyclopedia of the Biological Sciences, 2nd ed., 1970
Encyclopedia of Human Biology, 8 vols., 1991
Handbook of Genetics, 5 vols., 1976

Biography

Contemporary Authors: A Bio-Bibliographical Guide to Current Writers in Fiction, General Nonfiction, Poetry, Journalism, Drama, Motion Pictures, Television, and other Fields, rev. ed., 106 vols., 1962–
Current Biography, 1940–
Dictionary of American Biography, 20 vols., 1928–1937; and supplements, 1944–
Dictionary of National Biography (British), 22 vols., 1885–1901; and supplements, 1912–
Webster's New Biographical Dictionary, rev. ed., 1980
Who's Who in America, 1899–

Business and economics

American Business Dictionary, 1957–
Concise Dictionary of Business, 1990
Encyclopedia of Business Information Sources, 8th ed., 1991–92; with periodic supplements
Encyclopedic Dictionary of Accounting and Finance, 1989
International Dictionary of Management, 4th ed., 1990

Education

Cyclopedia of Education, 5 vols., 1968, reprint of 1911 ed.
Encyclopedia of Educational Research, 4 vols., 5th ed., 1982
International Encyclopedia of Higher Education, 10 vols., 1977

Engineering and technology

Concise International Encyclopedia of Robotics, 1990
Electronics Engineer's Reference Book, 1983
Encyclopedia of Computer Science and Engineering, 2nd ed., 1983
Encyclopedia of Computer Science and Technology, 16 vols., 1975–
Encyclopedia of Materials Science and Engineering, 1986

McGraw-Hill Dictionary of Mechanical and Design Engineering, 1984
Society of Automotive Engineers Handbook, 4 vols., 1991
Standard Handbook for Civil Engineers, 1983
Structural Engineering Handbook, 1990

Environment and ecology

Dictionary of the Environment, 3rd ed., 1989
Grzimek's Encyclopedia of Ecology, 1976
McGraw-Hill Encyclopedia of Environmental Science, 2nd ed., 1980

History and political science

Cambridge Ancient History Series, 12 vols., 3rd ed., 1984
Cambridge Medieval History, 9 vols., 2nd ed., 1967–69
Dictionary of American History, 8 vols., rev. ed., 1978
Encyclopedia of The Third World, 3 vols., rev. ed., 1981
Encyclopedia of World History, 4th ed., 1972
New Cambridge Modern History, 14 vols., 2nd ed., 1990

Literature, theater, film, and television

Bartlett's Familiar Quotations, 15th ed., 1980
Cambridge History of American Literature, 3 vols., 1943
Cambridge History of English Literature, 15 vols., 1907-1933
Cassell's Encyclopedia of World Literature, 3 vols., rvsd. and
    enlarged, 1973
Granger's Index to Poetry, 8th ed., rvsd. and enlarged, 1986
International Encyclopedia of Film, 1972
International Television Almanac, 1956–
Larousse World Mythology, 1965
McGraw-Hill Encyclopedia of World Drama, 5 vols., 2nd ed., 1984
Oxford Companion to American Literature, 5th ed., 1983
Oxford Companion to Classical Literature, 2nd ed., 1989
Oxford Companion to English Literature, 5th ed., 1985
Play Index, 1949–
Short Story Index, 1900–

Mathematics and physics

Encyclopedia of Physical Science and Technology, 15 vols., 1987
Encyclopedia of Physics, 2nd ed., 1991
Encyclopedia of Space, 1989
Encyclopedia of Statistical Sciences, 2 vols., 1988
Encyclopedia Dictionary of Mathematics, 4 vols., 2nd ed., 1986
Using the Mathematical Literature: A Practical Guide, 1979

Medicine/nursing

Encyclopedia and Dictionary of Medicine, Nursing, and Allied Health, 4th ed., 1987
Index Medicus (Bibliography of Medical Reviews), 1879–1927; New Series, 1960–; monthly supplements
International Dictionary of Medicine and Biology, 3 vols., 1986

Music

Encyclopedia of Pop, Rock, and Soul, 1977
Harvard Dictionary of Music, 2nd ed., 1969
International Cyclopedia of Music and Musicians, 11th ed., 1985
Musician's Guide, 6th ed., 1980
New Grove Dictionary of Music and Musicians, 20 vols., 1980

Philosophy and religion

Encyclopedia of Philosophy, 4 vols., 1973
Encyclopedia of Religion, 16 vols., 1987
The Interpreter's Dictionary of the Bible, 5 vols. and supplement, 1976

Science

Cambridge Encyclopedia of Astronomy, 1977
Cambridge Encyclopedia of Earth Sciences, 1982
Chemical Information Sources, 1991

Condensed Chemical Dictionary, 11th ed., 1987
McGraw-Hill Encyclopedia of Science and Technology, 15 vols.,
6th ed., 1987
Kirk-Othmer Encyclopedia of Chemical Technology, 1984

Social science

Dictionary of Psychology and Related Fields, 1974
Encyclopedia of Psychology, 2nd ed., 1984
Encyclopedia of Social Work, 2 vols., 18th ed., 1987; and supplement, 1987
International Encyclopedia of the Social Sciences, 18 vols., 1979

Special dictionaries

Dictionary of American Slang, 2nd ed., 1975
Dictionary of Modern English Usage, 2nd ed., 1965
Dictionary of Slang and Unconventional English, 8th ed., 1985
Harper Dictionary of Contemporary Usage, 2nd ed., 1985
Modern American Usage, 1966

Unabridged dictionaries

The Oxford English Dictionary, 13 vols., 1933
The Random House Dictionary of the English Language, 1987
Webster's Third New International Dictionary of the English Language, 1986

48c Compiling a Working Bibliography

A **working bibliography** is a record of sources you plan to consult for information about your topic. Since a working bibliography is open to change (you will add and delete books and articles as you do research), most instructors suggest that you record each source separately in your computer file or on 3" × 5" index cards. It is also a good idea to arrange your entries alphabetically, either by author or category. Organizing the data you collect makes it easier to add and delete sources and to compile your lists of **works cited,** which will appear at the end of your paper. To save time, you should also record the bibliographic information in the documentation format required by your instructor and appropriate to your discipline (see Chapters 50 and 51 on documenting research). Of course, the list of works cited will be shorter than the working bibliography because in it you will list only those works actually cited in your paper or essay.

For each entry that you record, be certain to include the following information.

1. The full name of the author, with the last name first (noting if the book has an editor or compiler rather than an author)

2. The complete title of the source (no abbreviations)

3. The city of publication, the publisher's name, and the date of publication

4. The library call number

5. Any other pertinent information, such as a volume or edition

When Gail Young was preparing a working bibliography, she first consulted the general encyclopedias (*Americana, Britannica, and Collier's*), checking the bibliography at the end of each article she read about Mercy Warren or John Adams. She then consulted the library catalog, a computer data base, and periodical indexes. As she worked, Gail kept adding titles to her working bibliography and eliminating titles that were irrelevant to her topic. Exploring resources and compiling a working bibliography also helped Gail settle on and limit her topic. One of Gail's informal bibliography entries follows. Notice that the book she listed has two editors rather than an author.

Berky, Andrew S., and James P. Shenton, eds.
The Historians' History of the United States
New York: Putnam's, 1966.
                        169.12
                        B39
                        1966

49 Writing the Research Paper

Once you have selected and limited a topic and started researching, you are ready to begin taking notes and writing.

49a Taking Notes

Note taking is a way of keeping track of information that
you think is important and that you may use later in your
paper. Many writers compile their research notes on a computer disk; others use 4" × 6" index cards. Using this size card
will prevent you from confusing your note cards with your bibliography cards. Either computer entries or note cards allow
you to organize your information and then rearrange it.

It is important to be judicious when taking notes. Do not record everything you read, but only what you think will be relevant. Being selective as you take notes will help you later on because when you write the paper, you will not use all the research entries you made but will cull them, using only the information that develops your thesis. It is also important to keep track of all your sources as you take notes to ensure accurate documentation and avoid plagiarism. (See pp. 469–473, in this chapter, on plagiarism.)

What information should you put in your research notes? Each note card or computer entry should have at the top of it a subject category heading, sometimes called a *slug,* which should correspond to the headings in your working outline (Section 49c). The slug will help you keep your research notes organized by topic. The entry itself should consist of a summary, paraphrase, or a quotation and should briefly indicate the source of the information. However, you need to include only the author and the page number, since you will already have more detailed source information in your working bibliography. It you are using more than one source by the same author, include the title or a shortened form of it.

Be sure to make a separate entry for each piece of information you record. This will help avoid any confusion and will make it easier for you to arrange your notes when it comes time to sit down and write the paper.

Summarizing

One method of taking notes is to write a summary of the information you wish to record. A **summary** presents the substance of the information in a *condensed* form. You do not use the words of the author but you convey the thoughts of the author *in your own words.* Following is a summary Gail Young wrote.

Adams - Quarrel
   Fritz 303
Adams' ten letters were an expression of
his own frustration at being retired, out of
favor, and "misunderstood," particularly
by his friend, Mercy Warren.

Compare the summary with the original source.

> Actually, these letters—ten in six weeks, some running to twenty pages—were his long pent-up cry of outrage at the world in general, at his age which had reduced him to the role of a spectator, at his enemies who had defeated him, at his friends who had misunderstood him, at himself for not being sufficiently dignified (like Washington) or sufficiently genial (like Franklin) to be forgiven his foibles, and at all historians, present and future, who would not write history as he would have it written, who would not let him play his part as he knew he had played it.
>
> Jean Fritz
> *Cast for a Revolution: Some American Friends and Enemies*

Paraphrasing

A second method of taking notes is to paraphrase the information. A **paraphrase** is a restatement of someone else's statement *in your own words*. A good paraphrase reflects your own style of writing and extracts important information but does not lose the original meaning of the statement. It is often equivalent in length to the original. Following is a paraphrase entry Gail Young wrote.

Governor Winthrop on Women
Brown 156
If the wife of the Governor of Hartford had not strained her weak wits by behaving like a man and neglecting her role and duties as a female, she would not have lost her mind.

Compare the paraphrase with the original.

> For if she had attended her household affairs, and such things as belong to women, and not gone out of her way and calling to meddle in such things as are proper for men, whose minds are stronger, &c., she had kept her wits, and might have improved them usefully and honourably in the place God had set her.

Alice Brown
Mercy Warren

Note that a paraphrase reproduces another's words without editorial comment (insertion of your own views about the text).

Recording quotations

A third method of recording information is to copy **quotations.** You may find that the information you wish to record has been so well expressed or contains such precise facts and details that you wish to use the exact words of the source rather than summarize or paraphrase the information. Following is a quotation Gail Young wrote.

> Women and reading
>   Warren, _The Group_ stage directions
>   n. p.
>
> "In one corner of the room is discovered a small cabinet of books .... Hobb's [sic] Leviathan, Winthrop's sermons, Hutchinson's History, Fable of the Bees ... Hoyle on Whist, Lives of the Stewarts ... and Acts of Parliament for 1774."

When quoting, you must be extremely careful to record _the exact words of the original_ if you use the quotation in your paper. (Review pp. 373–376 for the use of punctuation marks with quotations.) Be sure to analyze the content of your quotations. Remember that a research paper expresses your understanding of a subject based on the information gleaned from research. Avoid overusing quotations in your paper, because too many quotations leave the reader with the impression that you did not truly master the material. If you find that you are using too many direct quotations, you can always summarize or paraphrase the quotations when you write the paper. You must also integrate direct quotations into the text of your paper. Using lead-in phrases like the following samples helps with this integration.

As Carlos Artiz has reported,

Maury Joseph counters this argument as follows:

In support of these views, Laetitia Owen points out that . . .

A fourth method of recording your information is to combine quotation and paraphrase. This method allows you to record the information *in your own words* while retaining a few particularly well-chosen words from the original. The following is a combination quotation and paraphrase Gail Young wrote.

Political Situation, 1795
    Fritz 276
Neither side was pleased with John Jay's treaty. If the Federalists were "disappointed," the Republicans were "outraged." Mercy believed America "humiliated."

49b Prewriting

Once you have completed your preliminary research, you will want to formulate a plan for writing. It is always a good idea to start with some **prewriting.** The prewriting will be more goal oriented than the freewriting you do when writing personal essays, but like freewriting it will help you generate additional ideas and decide how to organize your paper. You can begin by sorting your research notes, whether on disk or on cards, by grouping together notes with similar subject headings.

Read each category and the entries. Record your reactions and use them as a basis for prewriting. You may brainstorm, cluster, freewrite, use the pentad, or use a variety of these methods. With these expanded reactions you will be able to sketch out an initial plan of how you will proceed. Try to group the entries according to point of view: those that support your view, those that oppose it, and those that are neutral. *Temporarily* set aside entries containing information that appears irrelevant at this time. (Never throw away your research entries because they may prove useful later on as your topic evolves.) Continue your research and note taking for any categories that are undeveloped, underdeveloped, or too controversial to lead, at this point, to a thesis. Do not be surprised or disappointed if you find yourself prewriting often. Prewriting is a recursive activity; you will probably have to do it more than once. (See Section 2a, pp. 7–23, for more information on prewriting.)

49c Formulating a Preliminary Thesis and Constructing a Working Outline

Having completed some prewriting based on your research, you will need to plan your paper by writing a preliminary thesis and constructing a working outline.

As in an essay, your **thesis** is a sentence that expresses the idea you wish to develop in your paper. The formulation of the preliminary thesis will help you focus your research. Word this thesis carefully, but at this point, do not worry about style, because you will most likely reword your thesis many times before you are satisfied with it. Gail Young's tentative thesis stated the following: *Colonial New England author Mercy Otis Warren is best known for insulting in print her friend John Adams*. Tim Gomez's was this: *Minor anxieties and the fear of* *death can cause college students' nightmares, which may be relieved sometimes by simple means, or, in serious cases, only with professional help.* (For more information on the preliminary thesis, see pp. 14–15.)

Your **working outline** is an organizational blueprint for all the main points in your paper. It is called a working outline because you will probably change it as you do more research and begin to write. You may discover that some of the research entries that you deemed irrelevant during prewriting become pertinent. Further research may also lead you to points overlooked earlier, which you should add to your working outline. Your working outline need not be in perfect form, but it should be complete enough to serve as a guide as you start organizing your ideas. Take some time with your working outline. Revise it as needed because it is easier to revise an outline than a garbled first draft. Gail Young developed the following outline based on her early research. The subject headings from her research notes appear in the outline and are underlined.

Title

Preliminary Thesis: Colonial New England author Mercy Otis Warren is best known for insulting in print her best friend John Adams.

1. <u>Attitudes</u> toward women writers at that time.
2. Successful <u>women writers</u> in colonial America.
3. <u>John Adams' reactions</u> to her writings.
4. <u>Contemporary reactions</u> to Warren's poems, plays, and history.

As she gathered more information about her topic, Gail added to the outline.

49d Constructing a Formal Outline

You will eventually want to revise your working outline and convert it into a formal outline. Many instructors require the submission of a formal outline with the paper. Your **formal outline,** in topic or sentence format, serves as a plan for your first and subsequent drafts and acts as a guide for your audience. (Review the procedures for outlining in Section 2c, pp. 29-32.) A formal outline includes a formal statement of your thesis, which has evolved from the preliminary thesis and working outline, and all of the supporting points that relate to your subject headings. Present these points in a logical sequence that you will use to develop your paper. As your paper develops, new ideas and insights on your topic may lead you to change the supporting points. Following is a portion of Gail Young's formal outline. Notice the addition of a possible title, the change in focus and point of view in her thesis, the appearance of supporting materials, and the new fourth point.

A New England Woman's War

Thesis: Mercy Otis Warren would probably be forgotten as an author and/or feminist but for her quarrel with John Adams.

I. Contemporary attitudes toward women
   A. Gov. Winthrop
   B. Lord Chesterfield
II. Women who succeeded as writers
   A. Anne Bradstreet
   B. Mercy Otis Warren
   C. Phillis Wheatley

III. Contemporary reception of Warren's writings

    A. Poems

    B. Plays

    C. History

IV. John Adams' reaction

    A. To poems and plays

    B. To history

       1. Political climate

       2. Adams' personal situation

       3. Politics of Warren's family

49e Writing and Revising the Paper

The process of actually writing your research paper is much like that of writing an essay, except that you are relying to a large extent on source material outside your own mind. But you need to read these sources carefully and think about them critically to develop your own ideas about them and the topic. Using your formal outline, write a first draft, let it sit for a while, and then go back to it and begin the process of criticism and revision. (See Section 3a on re-vision.) Also, be sure to consider your paper as a piece of research. Are you relying too heavily on one or two sources? Perhaps you need to do some more research. Do you seem to be using too many quotations? Perhaps it would be more effective to summarize or paraphrase some of them. Does any section of the paper need strengthening? Perhaps you could use some of the research entries you did not use in the previous draft. Does your paper seem like a collection of unrelated chunks of material? Perhaps you have overlooked key points in developing your topic or have failed to include logical transitions.

REVISING YOUR RESEARCH PAPER

Ask yourself the following questions to revise and complete your paper. Also, refer to Sections 3a, 3b, and 3c on revision (pp. 37–53) and to the sections noted in this checklist for more detailed information.

- **Purpose:** Is the purpose clear and the tone consistent and appropriate for that purpose? (See Section 2a, pp. 20–23 and Section 47b, pp. 435–436.) Have you avoided errors in reasoning? (See Section 7c, pp. 120–130.)
- **Title page:** If required, have you included a title page that lists all pertinent information? (See p. 508.)
- **Title:** Is your title brief? Does it suggest the topic, tone, and purpose of the essay, or does it effectively challenge interpretation? (See Section 3d, pp. 53–54.)
- **Outline:** If required, have you included an outline? (See Section 2c, pp. 29–32.)
- **Thesis:** Is the thesis clear? Does it give your reader adequate direction? (See Sections 2b, pp. 23–26 and 3a, pp. 38–39.)
- **Opening:** Does your opening state the topic effectively? (See Section 3d, pp. 55–56.)
- **Body:** Does every part of the body relate to the thesis and increase the reader's understanding of the problem being explored? Is the body coherent? (See Section 3d, pp. 56–58.)
- **Paragraphs:** Is the order of paragraphs logical, each relating to the thesis? (See Section 5a, pp.

78-82.) Are transitions between paragraphs clear and effective? (See Section 5d, pp. 90-93.) Is unity apparent in each paragraph as it develops its one idea? (See pp. 71-78.) Are supporting details specific, adequate, and logically arranged? (See Section 5c, pp. 75-78.)

- **Sentences:** Are sentences sufficiently varied in form to avoid monotony in style? Are your sentences constructed so that ideas are expressed forcefully and directly? Do you use action verbs and write in the active voice? Are important elements emphasized? (See Chapter 6, pp. 100-117.)
- **Words:** Does your choice of words express your thoughts precisely? (See Chapter 24, pp. 294-302.) Is the diction appropriate for purpose, tone, and audience? (See Chapter 26, pp. 308-327.) Have you edited out any wordiness, repetition, and vagueness? Have you avoided sexist language? (See Chapter 25, pp. 302-307.)
- **Conclusion:** Is the conclusion effective? Does it emphasize your points without undue repetition of the thesis? (See Section 3d, pp. 58-59.)
- **Documentation:** Are all sources acknowledged according to accepted guidelines in order to avoid plagiarism? (See Chapters 50 and 51, pp. 474-504.)
- **Manuscript form:** Have you followed standard guidelines or your instructor's requirements in formatting your paper? (See Chapter 43, pp. 405-409.)
- **Proofing:** Have you reread and edited your final version carefully, checking punctuation and mechanics? (See Section 3e, pp. 59-60.) Have you checked for errors in usage? (See the Glossary of Usage.) Have you read your sentences backwards, from the bottom of the page up, to check spelling? (See pp. 412-429.)

When Gail wrote her first draft, she gave a good bit of attention to Warren's plays and poems. As she worked, Gail realized her interest was in Warren's *History*, Adams' reaction, and Warren's response as part of the political controversy of the times. Gail had to revise her preliminary thesis and working outline as her first draft revealed a slightly different emphasis. Her formal outline, which we've just seen, reflects this change in emphasis. Such changes in both the outline and the paper are easier to make if you type your first draft on a computer. (See Chapter 4.)

The new emphasis that Gail arrived at in her first draft was refined further when she wrote second and subsequent drafts. Experienced researchers know that one draft is rarely sufficient. The topic and the paper itself develop during the process of researching and then during the writing and revising of various drafts. In her later drafts, Gail decided to give more emphasis to Adams' personal reactions to Warren's plays because it would enable her to present Warren as an early feminist unfairly treated by a famous person.

The following checklist for revising your research paper will help you work on your various drafts and then prepare a polished final draft.

49f Avoiding Plagiarism

In all the writing you do, it is essential that you acknowledge your sources of information and the ideas derived from those sources according to accepted guidelines. It is a matter of ethics and honesty. Although it is permissible to borrow words and ideas from sources, it is necessary to indicate clearly what is borrowed both in the body of the paper and in the works cited or bibliography (explained in Chapters 50 and 51). The failure to do so is called **plagiarism,** a term derived from the Latin words *plagiarius*, "plunderer," and *plagium*, "kidnapper,"

Some instructors will give students a failing grade on their papers or fail them for an entire course for committing an act of plagiarism.

Plagiarism falls into two categories: using someone else's *words* or using someone else's *ideas* as if they were your own. You must be scrupulous in avoiding both categories of plagiarism in your writing. Properly cite all quotations, paraphrases, and summaries of information from other sources. The only exception to this rule is **common knowledge,** or information commonly known and accessible to your audience. For example, it is common knowledge that the United States participated in the Persian Gulf War and that Mark Twain authored *Huckleberry Finn*, so you need not acknowledge sources for this information. However, information about the specific details of the air raids during the war or about Twain's use of specific dialects in the novel would not be common knowledge and would require research. You need to acknowledge your sources for such information. If you are unsure whether certain information constitutes common knowledge, document it.

Direct quotations

All direct quotations or material taken *word for word* from another source must be documented. (See pp. 460–462 on recording quotations.) Quotations should be enclosed in quotation marks or, if consisting of more than four lines of text, presented without quotations marks in block quotation form. (See pp. 373–376 on punctuation with quotations, pp. 374–375 on block quotations, and pp. 474–504 on proper methods of citing sources.)

Paraphrases and summaries

All paraphrases and summaries need to be properly documented. As we have seen, *paraphrasing* involves *stating* the words and ideas of another person in your own words using approximately the same number of words as the source. (See pp. 459–460.) *Summarizing* involves stating the ideas of another person in your own words in a greatly condensed form. (See pp. 458–459.) Acceptable paraphrases and summaries clearly present the idea, tone, and point of view of the author. Unacceptable paraphrases and summaries distort the idea, tone, and point of view of the author and often include words that are used in the original source but without quotation marks. Following are examples of unacceptable and acceptable paraphrases.

ORIGINAL TEXT OF SOURCE

Teachers have a choice. They can use word processing as a glorified typewriter, or they can use the new medium for scholarly community, creativity, and discovery. With CAI [computer-assisted instruction], software developers and teachers have the responsibility to work together to create and use software that respects the individuality of students and treats them honestly and humanely. Teachers can take good software and make it punitive, or they can soften the inflexibility of CAI programs by recommending it to certain students and, within a context, explaining its limitations.

Helen J. Schwartz
"Ethical Considerations of
Educational Computer Use"

UNACCEPTABLE PARAPHRASE

As Schwartz writes, teachers can make choices. They can use word processing just like a typewriter or use it creatively. With CAI, people can work together creating and using software designed individually for students that is honest and humane. Teachers can use the software for punishment or fun, especially for bright students.

The preceding paraphrase is unacceptable for several reasons. The author's full name does not appear in the lead-in phrase. Words that are directly quoted from the source lack quotation marks, and the paraphrase reflects an inaccurate reading of the source.

ACCEPTABLE PARAPHRASE

As Helen J. Schwartz reports, teachers can use word processing in uncreative and creative ways for "scholarly community, creativity, and discovery." Teachers and software developers "work together to create" and design software that either adapts to students' individual needs or is selectively assigned to students.

This paraphrase is acceptable. It correctly identifies the author and accurately restates the source author's idea, tone, and point of view. Most unintentional plagiarism results from paraphrases that are too close to the original source. After reading a source, put it away and write your paraphrase. Then go back to the source and check your work for accuracy. Use the checklist on avoiding plagiarism (p. 473) to help you evaluate your work.

Collusion

Collusion, a form of plagiarism, occurs when two or more people agree to devise a piece of writing that will be attributed to only one of them. Because all of your writing is considered to be your own work, it should not be wholly or partially written by another person. Additionally, the idea and the organization of ideas in your paper must be your own. (Ideas of others may appear in your writing, but in each instance the source must be properly cited.) You can incorporate into your writing ideas that have arisen from class discussion, lectures, and collaborative writing sessions, but you should not restate the ideas of the class or writing sessions simply to meet the needs of the assignment. You may revise and edit your writing with the help of others, and it is fine to discuss individual details with other people (see pp. 39–40 on collaboration and peer critiques). But you should not have others do your writing or revising for you. Ultimately, if someone helps you significantly with your writing, you must acknowledge that help.

AVOIDING PLAGIARISM

1. Are all direct quotations accurately reproduced in my paper? Are they cited properly?
2. Do all of my paraphrases and summaries reflect the author's idea, tone, and point of view? Have I cited the author properly? Are quoted words enclosed in quotation marks?
3. Am I clear on the distinction between what information is considered common knowledge (which would *not* require documentation) and what information has been quoted, paraphrased, or summarized and needs to be documented? If in doubt, have I documented anyway?
4. Have I acknowledged each source where it occurs in my paper as well as in the works cited list or bibliography?
5. Have I avoided collusion?

50 Documenting Sources— MLA Style

To credit your sources adequately you will need to convert your working bibliography into a formal bibliography or list of **works cited,** a list of all sources cited in your paper. It will appear on a separate page at the end of your paper and will enable your readers to verify your sources. (See p. 523 for an actual works cited listing.) Since the various disciplines have different bibliographic guidelines, before compiling your working bibliography, check with your instructor to determine which guidelines your paper should follow (whether MLA— Modern Language Association—form, APA—American Psychological Association—form, or some other form). The MLA style of documentation is used largely in the humanities and is set forth in the *MLA Handbook for Writers of Research Papers, 3rd ed.* (1988). The *MLA Handbook* explains how to format the list of works cited and recommends the use of in-text parenthetical citations. These MLA guidelines are explained and illustrated in this chapter. For a sample paper in MLA style, see Section 52a, pp. 505–523, and the literary analysis paper in Chapter 53, pp. 558–566. Consult the *MLA Handbook* for situations not covered in this chapter's examples. See also Chapter 51 on APA and other documentation styles.

50a Preparing the List of Works Cited

According to the *MLA Handbook*, your works cited page should be formatted as follows.

1. Start the list on a new page following the text of the paper. Number each page of the list in the upper right

corner, continuing the page numbers of the text. (For instance, if the text ended on page 7, the first page of the list would be page 8.)

2. Center the title "Works Cited" one inch from the top of the page. Do not underline it. (See pp. 523 and 566 for examples.)

3. Double space between the title and the first entry, and then double space the entire list, within entries and between entries.

4. List the sources alphabetically by author or by the title for works by unknown authors. (Disregard *a*, *an*, and *the* in alphabetizing titles.)

5. If you follow the guidelines for your working bibliography given on pp. 455–457, your sources will already be listed in the proper form; simply copy the information for each source that you actually used in your paper.

6. Begin each entry at the left margin; if an entry is longer than one line, indent the subsequent lines five spaces.

7. Remember the different formats of documentation: in-paper (parenthetical documentation, see pp. 484–489) and end-of-paper (works cited). Be sure to include both.

8. Look into the possibility of using a computer program to format your works cited list. This could help you save time.

Here are some guidelines for formatting works cited entries. A series of models of work cited entries follows.

1. Always include the author's full name (when given and as listed on the title page), the complete title, and the complete publication information. (See an actual list of works cited on p. 523.)

2. Separate these three items (and any additional information) with periods followed by two spaces.

3. Give the author's last name first. Names of second or third authors, or the name of an editor after the author, should not be inverted. (See p. 477.) For more than three authors, list only the first author and add "et al.," which is a Latin abbreviation for "and others." (See p. 477.)

4. Indicate an editor or compiler by the abbreviation "ed." or "comp." or "eds./comps." if there is more than one. (See p. 478.)

5. In the publication information for books, you may use the shortened form of publishers' names as listed in the *MLA Handbook* or other standard sources. Give the name of the city. Add the state or country *only* if the city alone would not be familiar or would be confusing to the reader: for example, Cambridge, MA, or Cambridge, England. Use the standard postal abbreviations for states. (See p. 477 for a sample entry.)

6. In publication dates for periodicals, abbreviate the names of months except May, June, and July. Place the dates in parentheses for periodicals with continuous pagination. (See p. 480.)

7. Include page numbers for a periodical article, for a work that is part of an anthology or collection, or for an introduction, preface, foreword, or afterword. Do not use *p.* or *pp.* in works cited entries. (See p. 480.)

8. Double space all entries and indent the second and subsequent lines of an entry five spaces. (See p. 480.)

50b Sample MLA Works Cited Entries

Books
ONE AUTHOR

Boorstin, Daniel J. The Image: A Guide to Pseudo-Events in
America. New York: Atheneum, 1961.

TWO AUTHORS

Commager, Henry Steele, and Elmo Giordanetti. Was America a
Mistake? An Eighteenth-Century Commentary. New York:
Harper, 1967.

THREE AUTHORS/EDITION AFTER THE FIRST EDITION

Millet, Fred B., Arthor W. Hoffman, and David R. Clark. Reading
Poetry. 2nd ed. New York: Harper, 1968.

MORE THAN THREE AUTHORS

Adams, Russell, et al. Great Negroes Past and Present. Chicago:
Afro-American, 1964.

MORE THAN ONE BOOK BY THE SAME AUTHOR

Skinner, Cornelia Otis. Madame Sarah. Boston: Houghton, 1967.
---. Nuts in May. New York: Dodd, 1950.

Note: three hyphens, a period, and two spaces. (List the works
alphabetically.)

A CORPORATE AUTHOR

Group for the Advancement of Psychiatry. Symposium No. 8:
    Medical Uses of Hypnosis. New York: Mental Health
    Material Center, 1962.

MULTIVOLUME WORK

Tolkien, J. R. R. The Lord of the Rings. 2nd ed. 3 vols.
    London: Allen, 1954–55.

ONE AUTHOR, PREPARED FOR PRINTING BY AN EDITOR

Franklin, Benjamin. Autobiography: An Authoritative Text. Ed.
    J. A. Leo. New York: Norton, 1984.

**ESSAY OR SELECTION FROM AN ANTHOLOGY, COLLECTION,
OR CRITICAL EDITION**

Bowen, Francis. "Life of James Otis." Library of American
    Biography. Ed. Jared Sparks, Boston: Little, 1847. 175–92.

(Note: you may omit the name of a publisher before 1900. The
previous entry might have listed Boston, 1847.)

**WITH TWO PUBLISHERS/REPRINTED/WITHOUT PUBLICATION DATE
(N.D. = NOT DATED)**

Boswell, James. Boswell in Search of a Wife, 1776–1779. Ed.
    Frank Brady and Frederick A. Pottle. 1956. New Haven:
    Yale UP; New York: McGraw, n.d.

WITHOUT PLACE OR PUBLISHER/REPRINTED (RPT.)

Warren, Mercy Otis. The Adulateur, a Tragedy. The
Massachusetts Spy. N.p.:n.p., 1722. Rpt. in The Magazine of
History 63. Tarrytown, NY, 1918.

AN INTRODUCTION, PREFACE, FOREWORD, OR AFTERWORD

Regan, M. Joanna, RSM, and Isabelle Keiss, RSM. Foreword.
Tender Courage, A Reflection on the Life and Spirit of
Catherine McAuley, First Sister of Mercy. Chicago:
Franciscan Herald, 1988.

A TRANSLATION

Aristotle. Poetics. Trans. John Warrington. New York: Dutton,
1963.

AUTHOR UNKNOWN

The Twelve Steps for Everyone. Minneapolis: Comp Care, 1990.

(Note: do not use "anonymous" or "anon.")

AN ENCYCLOPEDIA

Academic American Encyclopedia. 21 vols. Danbury: Grolier, 1987.

A DICTIONARY

The Agriculture Dictionary. Albany: Delmar, 1991.

Articles in periodicals

IN A MONTHLY JOURNAL OR MAGAZINE, PAGINATION BY ISSUE

Morrison, Samuel Eliot. "Three Great Ladies Helped Establish the
United States." Smithsonian Aug. 1975: 96–103.

IN A JOURNAL WITH CONTINUOUS PAGINATION

Breedan, Stanley. "The First Australians." National Geographic
173 (1991): 267–90.

IN A WEEKLY OR BIWEEKLY JOURNAL OR MAGAZINE

Seliger, S. "In the Dead of the Night." Interview with E.
Hartmann. People Weekly 11 Mar. 1985: 128–30.

IN A DAILY NEWSPAPER

Bohlen, Celestine. "Fragile Truce in Yugoslavia." New York Times
8 Aug. 1991, natl. ed.: A1.

AN UNSIGNED ARTICLE

"Executive Changes." New York Times 8 Aug. 1991, natl. ed.: C3.

AN EDITORIAL

"Breakthrough for Peace." Editorial. Miami Herald 2 Aug. 1991,
final ed.: 20A.

A BOOK REVIEW

"Do Surveys Give the Full Picture?" Rev. of <u>What They Know</u>
<u>About You</u>, by Bernard Asbell and Karen Wynn. <u>South Bend</u>
<u>Tribune</u> 4 Aug. 1991, metro ed.: C7.

A LETTER TO AN EDITOR

Haifley, Dan. Letter. <u>San Francisco Chronicle</u> 30 July 1991, A16.

Other printed sources

A GOVERNMENT DOCUMENT

United States. Dept. of Commerce. Bureau of the Census.
"Population Profile of the United States, 1977." <u>Current</u>
<u>Population Reports</u>. Series P-20, no. 808. Washington: GPO,
1979.

A BIBLICAL CITATION

<u>The New English Bible with the Apocrypha.</u> Oxford Study ed.
New York: Oxford, 1970.

AN UNPUBLISHED DISSERTATION

Glenn, Jonathan A. "A New Edition of Sir Gilbert Haye's <u>Buke of</u>
<u>the Ordre of Knychthede</u>." Diss. U of Notre Dame, 1987.

A PERSONAL LETTER

Hamel, Mohammed. Letter to the author. 12 Dec. 1992.

AN ABSTRACT

Herzberger, David K. "Narrating the Past: History and the Novel of
    Memory in Postwar Spain." Abstract. <u>PMLA</u> 106.1 (1991): 190.

A CARTOON

Gross, S. Cartoon. <u>New Yorker</u> 31 Dec. 1990: 33.

Wright, Don. Cartoon. <u>St. Louis Post-Dispatch</u> 3 Aug. 1991, 3-star
    ed.: 2B.

A MAP/CHART

<u>Wyoming</u>. Map. Boston: Rand, 1991.

<u>Phonetics Wheel</u>. Chart. New York: Holt, 1988.

A PAMPHLET

Hall, Steven. <u>The Alphabetical City</u>. New York, 1980.

Nonprint sources

PERSONAL OR TELEPHONE INTERVIEW

Wilfong, James. Personal interview. 23 Sept. 1989

Bethke, Teresa. Telephone interview. 1 Oct. 1990

MATERIAL FROM A COMPUTER SERVICE

Evans, William B. "John Adams' Opinion of Benjamin Franklin."
    <u>Pennsylvania Magazine of History and Biography</u> 92
    (1968):220–238. Dialog file 38, item 380462.

COMPUTER SOFTWARE PROGRAM

Davisson, W. I. <u>Macroeconomics.</u> Computer software. Emerald
   Distributing, 1987. 256KB, disk.

AUDIOTAPE AND VIDEOTAPE

Beethoven, Ludwig von. Piano Concerto no. 3 in C Minor, op. 37
   and Fantasy for Piano, Chorus and Orchestra, op. 80. Cond.
   Leonard Bernstein. Philharmonic Orch. New York, MYT
   38526, 1983.

<u>Alzheimer's Disease.</u> Videocassette. Prod. Hospital Satellite
   Network. American Journal of Nursing, 1985. 28 min.

FILM

<u>It's a Wonderful Life.</u> Dir. Frank Capra. With James Stewart,
   Donna Reed, Lionel Barrymore, and Thomas Mitchell. RKO,
   1946.

TELEVISION PROGRAM

<u>Beyond Our Control.</u> Narr. Joe Haas. Writ. and prod. Maureen
   Kline. Public Service Special. WNDU, South Bend, IN. 7
   Feb. 1993.

LIVE PLAY

<u>Hamlet.</u> By William Shakespeare. Dir. Mark Pilker. With Jeremy
   Wilde. Washington Hall, Notre Dame, IN. 7 Mar. 1991.

RECORDING

Goodman, Benny. With Teddy Wilson, Zoot Sims, Ruby Braff,
Roland Hanna, Urbie Green, Milt Hinton, and Paul Quinchette.
Never-Before-Released Recordings. Musical Heritage Society,
MHS 922277L, 1988.

LECTURE

Klein, Edward. "Computer-Assisted Instruction in English
Grammar and Spelling." MLA Convention. Chicago, 28 Dec.
1990.

RADIO BROADCAST

Amahl and the Night Visitors. By Gian Carlo Menotti. With
Robert Dure and Paula Harris. Indiana Opera North Inc.
WSJV, Elkhart-South Bend. 9 Dec. 1990.

WORK OF ART

Seurat, Georges. Sunday Afternoon at the Grand Jatte. Art
Institute, Chicago.

50c Sample In-Text Parenthetical Citations—MLA Style

The *MLA Handbook* recommends the use of in-text **parenthetical citations** to provide concise documentation directly
where a source is quoted, paraphrased, or summarized. In-text

parenthetical citations replace an outdated system of documentation requiring footnotes at the bottom of the page or at the end of the paper. A parenthetical citation must appear in the paper each time you use material from a source. You will credit your source by citing the author's last name and identifying the location of the borrowed information with its page number, line, act, scene, or chapter, as appropriate. These parenthetical acknowledgments refer the reader to the full source information contained in the list of works cited at the end of the paper.

At times, however, you may wish to refer to the entire work within the text. In this case, give the author's name and the title of the work in the text of the paper.

> In Cast for a Revolution: Some American Friends and
> Enemies, Jean Fritz tracks the political dissention
> surrounding the war.

Or your text may give both author and location of your reference.

> Alice Brown, on page 156 of her biography, Mary Warren,
> quotes Governor Winthrop's comments.

As you work through your paper, you will find yourself using parentheses for much of this information, as shown in the following examples illustrating the standard formats for MLA parenthetical citations. Consult the *MLA Handbook* for situations not covered here.

DIRECTLY QUOTED MATERIAL, AUTHOR'S NAME IN TEXT

> Brown says that John Adams' language was "warmer than
> that of the Courtier to Aspasia" (157).

DIRECTLY QUOTED MATERIAL, AUTHOR'S NAME IN PARENTHESES

"Governor Winthrop . . . consigned them to the limbo they
had earned" (Brown 156).

Note that the author's name and the page number are separated by one space without punctuation and that the punctuation closing the sentence belongs outside the end parenthesis.
    At other times, your textual citations will refer to para-
phrases and/or summaries.

REFERENCE TO MATERIAL, AUTHOR'S NAME IN TEXT

Fritz (259) lists the recipients of Warren's autographed copies.

REFERENCE TO MATERIAL, AUTHOR'S NAME IN PARENTHESES

Warren mailed complimentary copies to a list of distinguished
friends (Fritz 259).

WORKS LISTED BY TITLE, NOT AUTHOR

In this case you may include the title in the text or in
parentheses:

The Encyclopaedia Britannica finds Warren's poems "of no
value."

Judgment in our time contradicts the high praise Warren's
friends gave to her poems (Encyclopaedia Britannica).

Note that you need not provide page numbers for material
arranged alphabetically, as in an encyclopedia or a dictionary.

TWO AUTHORS WITH THE SAME SURNAME

(Kennedy, E. 137)

(Kennedy, J. F. 142)

TWO OR THREE AUTHORS

(Commanger and Giordaette 191-192)

(Jones, Millett, and Hoffman 21)

THREE OR MORE AUTHORS

(Adams et al. 42)

BOOK BY A CORPORATE AUTHOR

(Group for the Advancement of Nursing 75) or a shortened
version: (Group for Nursing 75)

BOOK, PAMPHLET, OR ARTICLE WITH NO AUTHOR

(The Architect's Guide to New York 47) or a shortened
version: (Architect's Guide 47)

VOLUME AND PAGE NUMBERS OF A MULTIVOLUME WORK

(Jones 4: 9-12)

The number to the left of the colon identifies the volume; the
number(s) to the right, the pages.

QUOTATION FROM AN INDIRECT SOURCE

Thomas Mann was only partly right (about the Romans, at least) when he wrote in The Magic Mountain: "the ancients knew how to pay homage to death" (qtd. in Crowin 139).

Always place your citation as close as possible to the material it acknowledges, even in midsentence if it is brief.

Brown quotes Governor Winthrop (156) in his harsh consideration of the sick wife of a fellow governor.

LITERARY PROSE WORKS

(121; ch. 4)
(231; bk. 2, ch. 3)

POEMS AND DRAMAS IN VERSE FORM

Act, scene, line(s):

(Hamlet 2.1 10-19)

Use Arabic numerals unless your instructor specifies otherwise. Book and line:

(Paradise Lost 4. 21). or (PL 4.21)

Consult the *MLA Handbook* for a listing of approved abbreviations for literary titles.

QUOTATIONS OVER FOUR LINES IN LENGTH

See p. 374 for the rules on quotations over four lines in length. Begin such quotations on a new line, indent ten spaces from the left margin, and double space the material. Do not use quotation marks. After the final punctuation mark of the quotation, skip two spaces and add the reference in parentheses. The introductory phrases for such quotations usually end with a colon.

> As Norman Corwin reports, escapism dominates our television viewing:

>> On New Year's day, the parade of bowl games begins early and ends late, stretching, like the old British Empire, across all time zones. And as though live football coverage was not enough, whole taped games are played back later, throughout the season, for those who may have missed them the first time around. (40)

50d Explanatory Notes

In MLA style, you can use **explanatory notes** to present supplemental reference information such as relevant references that do not appear in your list of works cited or additional text or commentary that might disrupt the flow of the paper. These notes appear at either the bottom of the page as footnotes or at the end of the paper as endnotes. Check with your instructor to determine which approach to use. Identify your explanatory notes with consecutive numbers typed as raised arabic numbers in the text of your paper. These raised numbers will then correspond to the numbered footnote or endnote. Set footnotes four lines from the last line of text. Indent five spaces to begin, and allow one space after the raised number at the bottom of the page. Note that footnotes are double spaced.

TEXT: In her novels Maria Edgeworth makes her model women daughters, wives, and mothers rather than wage earners.[1]

NOTE: [1] When she writes about tradespeople and farmers, as in *Popular Tales,* she stresses the need for women as well as men to learn a trade in order to be morally independent.

Format endnotes as you would footnotes, but place them on a separate page at the end of the paper. Place the title "Notes" one inch from the top of the page. Indent the first line of the entry five spaces from the left margin and signal the endnote with a raised arabic number. Examples of explanatory notes can be found at the end of the sample research paper on p. 521.

51 Documenting Sources— APA and Other Styles

Whereas MLA documentation style is used in the humanities, the guidelines of the American Psychological Association (APA) are usually required for documentation in the social sciences. In this chapter, we look at the APA style and the styles used in some of the other disciplines. If you use the APA style of documentation to cite sources, use the examples in this chapter as a guide in preparing your working bibliography. You will convert your working bibliography into a list of **references** (the APA equivalent of the MLA list of works cited), which will appear on a separate page at the end of your paper. (See p. 541 for an actual reference listing.) This chapter also contains examples for in-text parenthetical documentation in APA style. Consult the *Publication Manual of the American Psychological Association,* 3rd edition (1983) for situations not covered by these examples. See Section 52b, pp. 524–545, for a sample paper that uses APA style. If you have a computer program that offers APA style formatting, using it will allow you to save time when formatting your list of references.

51a Preparing the List of References

According to APA style, your references page should be formatted as follows:

1. Start the list on a new page following the text of the paper. Number each page on the list in the upper right corner two spaces beneath the running head. (See p. 541 for an example.)

2. Center the title "References" two spaces beneath the page number. Do not underline the title.

3. Double space between the title and the first entry, and then double space the entire list within entries and between entries.

4. List the works alphabetically by author, or by title for works by unknown authors. (Disregard *a, an,* and *the* in alphabetizing titles.) Works by the same author should be listed chronologically from the earliest to the most recent publication.

5. If you follow the guidelines for your working bibliography on pp. 455–456, all the information you need will be found in each entry.

6. Begin each entry at the left margin; if an entry is longer than one line, indent the second and subsequent lines three spaces.

7. Be sure to include both formats of documentation: in-paper (parenthetical documentation) and end-of-paper (references).

Here are some general APA guidelines for preparing your reference list entries. Model entries in APA style follow.

1. Include only those sources you have used in the paper.

2. Always include the names of all authors (when given and listed on the title page), the complete title, and the complete publication data for each entry in your list.

3. Separate these three items (or any additional information) with periods followed by two spaces.

4. Give the author's last name first, followed by his or her initials. Follow this format for each author of the work if there is more than one author. (See an actual list of references on p. 541.)

5. Use capital letters for proper nouns and for the first word of titles and subtitles of books and articles. Lowercase the other parts of the title. For the titles of periodicals use customary capitalization. (See p. 493.)

6. For more than one work by an author, repeat the author's name for each entry and arrange the works by publication date, the earliest first. (See p. 543.)

7. List all names of multiple authors (*et al.* is not used in the list of references). See p. 493 for an example of a listing with multiple authors.

8. Place all publication dates in parentheses directly after the final author's name, with a period after the end parenthesis. In dates for periodical articles, give the year first, then by the month and day. Do not abbreviate the months.

9. Do not enclose the titles of articles from periodicals in quotation marks. (See p. 495.)

10. Precede page numbers by "p." or "pp." in referring to articles or chapters in an edited book or to articles in popular magazines or newspapers, but *not* in reference to journal articles. (See pp. 494 and 495.)

51b Sample APA References

Books

ONE AUTHOR

Kennedy, E. (1977). On becoming a counselor: A basic guide of non-professional counselors. New York: Continuum.

TWO AUTHORS

Barron, J. M., & Lynch, G. P. (1986). Economics. St. Louis: Times Mirror/Mosby.

THREE OR MORE AUTHORS

Kagan, D., Ozment, S., & Turner, F. (1987). The western heritage (3rd ed.). New York: Macmillan.

A CORPORATE AUTHOR

Intermed Communication, Inc. (1983). Nurse's reference library: diagnostics. Spring House, PA: Intermed.

MULTIVOLUME WORK

Sandburg, C. (1939). Abraham Lincoln: The war years (Vol. 2). Orlando, FL: Harcourt.

IN A SERIES

Henle, M. (1986). <u>1879 and all that: Essays in the theory and history of psychology</u> (Critical assessments of contemporary psychology. D. Robinson, Gen. Ed.). New York: Columbia University Press.

EDITION AFTER THE FIRST/REVISED EDITION, AUTHOR AS PUBLISHER

American Psychiatric Association. (1987). <u>Diagnostic and statistical manual of mental disorders</u> (3rd rev. ed.). Washington, DC: Author.

ARTICLE OR SELECTION FROM AN ANTHOLOGY, COLLECTION, OR CRITICAL EDITION

Reed, I. (1991). America: The multinational society. In M. S. Layton (Ed.), <u>Intercultural journeys through reading and writing</u> (pp. 301–305). New York: HarperCollins.

AN INTRODUCTION, PREFACE, FOREWORD, OR AFTERWORD

Ogilvie, L. J. Forword. In L. and F. Bock. <u>Creating four-part harmony</u> (pp. 7-10). Carol Stream, IL: Hope.

A TRANSLATION

DeLa Varende, J. (1956). <u>Cherish the sea: A history of sail</u> (M. Savill, Trans.). New York: Viking.

AUTHOR UNKNOWN

Living sober. (1975). New York: Alcoholics Anonymous World
  Services, Inc.

AN ENCYCLOPEDIA

Disaster Aid. (1977). In Encyclopedia of social work (Vol. 1, pp.
  277-288). Washington, DC: National Association of Social Workers.

A DICTIONARY

Bourdon, R., & Bourricaud, F. (1989). Religion. In Critical
  dictionary of sociology (pp. 292-303). Chicago: University of
  Chicago Press.

Articles in periodicals

IN A JOURNAL, PAGINATION BY ISSUE

Lottmann, H. R. (1936). A bustling bologna. Publisher's Weekly,
  229(20), 26-30.

IN A JOURNAL WITH CONTINUOUS PAGINATION

Moize, E. A. (1991). Sidney's changing face. National Geographic,
  173, 247-265.

IN A POPULAR MAGAZINE, WEEKLY

Donahue, D., & Red, S. (1986, May 12). A hyannis hitching. People,
  pp. 53-56, 59.

IN A POPULAR MAGAZINE, MONTHLY

Morine, D. J. (1982, August). To trust, perchance to buy. Psychology Today, pp. 51-52.

NO AUTHOR, IN A POPULAR MAGAZINE

Tax cheats' hall of shame. (1991, August 5). Time, p. 43.

IN A NEWSPAPER

Bohlen, C. (1991, August 8). Fragile truce in Yougoslavia. New York Times, p. 1.

AN EDITORIAL

Help students—not the tax revolt. (1991, July 31). Los Angeles Times, p. B6.

A BOOK REVIEW

Morris, A. (1990). The body politic: Body, language, and power [Review of Sowing the body: Psychoanalysis and ancient representations of women]. College English, 52, 570-578.

A LETTER TO AN EDITOR

Silva, J. T. (1991, August 5). [Letter to the editor]. Houston-Post, p. A14.

Other printed sources
GOVERNMENT DOCUMENT

United States Department of Commerce. (1977). <u>Population profile</u>
<u>of the United States</u>. (Publication No. P-20, No. 808).
Washington, DC: U. S. Government Printing Office.

DISSERTATION

Anglin, M. K. (1990). A lost and dying world: Women's labor in
the mica industry of southern Appalachia. <u>Dissertation</u>
<u>Abstracts International</u>, <u>51</u>, 37981A.

Note: If the microfilm of the dissertation is used as a source,
add the university microfilms number in parentheses:
(University microfilms NO. DA 9110081).

ABSTRACT

Nicholson, A. N., Pascoe, P. A., & Stone, B. M. (1989). The sleep-
wakefulness continuum: Interactions with drugs which
increase wakefulness and enhance alertness. <u>Alcohol, Drugs</u>
<u>& Driving</u>, <u>5</u>, 287-301. (From <u>Psychological Abstracts</u>, 1990,
<u>77</u>, Abstract No. 27815).

Note: If only the abstract is cited and not the entire article, include the collection of abstracts in parentheses as above.

CARTOON

Benson. (1991, August). [Cartoon]. Chicago Sun-Times, p. 8.

MAP/CHART

Wyoming. (1991). [Map]. Boston: Rand McNally.

Phonetics wheel. (1988). [Chart]. New York: Holt.

Nonprint sources
PERSONAL COMMUNICATIONS (LETTERS, MEMOS, TELEPHONE CONVERSATIONS, INTERVIEWS)

These are cited in the text only and not in the reference list because they consist of nonrecoverable data.

E. A. Wonderly (personal communication, April 22, 1992)

AUDIOCASSETTE

Ringer, A. B. (Speaker). (1991). Problems of codependency (Cassette Recording No. 8512). Chicago: Alcoholics Anonymous.

VIDEOTAPE

Poe, K. L. (Producer). (1991). Alzheimer's disease. [Videotape]. New York: American Journal of Nursing.

FILM

Benjamin, R. D. (Producer), & Jeffries, M. K. (Director). (1990). AIDS in our schools [Film]. New York, Educational Products.

**PROCEEDINGS OF MEETINGS AND SYMPOSIA:
ABSTRACTS OR SUMMARIES**

Hansen, W. L., Saunders, P., & Welsh, A. L. (1980). Teacher
training programs in college economics: Their development,
current status, and future prospects [Abstract]. Proceedings of
the Sixth International Conference on Improving University
Teaching, 1, 149.

MATERIAL FROM A COMPUTER SERVICE

Bower, Bruce. (1987, January 17) The fragile, creative side of
nightmares. Science News, p. 37. (DIALOG file 647:
MAGAZINE ASAP, item 04645291).

COMPUTER SOFTWARE PROGRAM

Burns, R. E. (1981). History of western civilization [Computer
program]. South Bend, IN: Clover Distributors. (No. HIS42).

51c Sample In-Text Parenthetical Citations— APA Style

APA documentation style recommends the use of in-text
parenthetical citations, as does MLA, to provide concise documentation when and where a source is used. Each source included in your parenthetical citations should appear in the list
of references at the end of your paper.

The following guidelines for in-text parenthetical citations
are based on the *Publication Manual of the American Psychological Association*, 3rd edition, 1983.

1. Use a title in a parenthetical citation only if the author is unknown.

2. Give the year of publication in addition to the author's last name and page or line numbers for quotations.

3. Separate items in parentheses—the author's name, publication date, and page numbers—with commas. Signal page numbers with "p." or "pp." This notation is *required* for direct quotations.

4. For works with more than one and fewer than six authors, list the names of *all* the authors in the *first* textual reference. For subsequent references, if the work has two authors, cite both names; if the work has more than two authors, give only the surname of the first author followed by "et al."

Sample APA style parenthetical citations follow. Consult the APA Publication Manual for situations not covered here.

DIRECTLY QUOTED MATERIAL, AUTHOR'S NAME IN TEXT

According to Gringel (1991), drug habits . . .

DIRECTLY QUOTED MATERIAL, AUTHOR'S NAME IN PARENTHESES

Social behavior may be defined as the interaction of individual organisms (Judy, 1985).

SPECIFIC PART OF A SOURCE

Humans do not use these higher thought processes while speaking (Wittgenstein, 1965, p. 9).

SOURCE WITH TWO AUTHORS

Inconsistencies exist in the theories (Morris & Fox, 1978, pp. 16-17).

REFERENCE TO SEVERAL SOURCES IN THE SAME PARENTHETICAL CITATION

Some cruel experiments produce no knowledge (Oglive, 1954, p. 1195; Ryder, 1976, p. 3).

Note that multiple citations within the same parentheses are grouped alphabetically and separated by semicolons.

WORKS WITH AN UNKNOWN AUTHOR

Cite in the text the title and the year. Use double quotation marks around article or chapter titles; underline periodical and book titles.

. . . for beating the drug habit ("Saying No to Drugs," 1992).

. . . in the book Nurses as Enablers (1991).

The word "anonymous" is used with a title only if the work's author is designated as such.

PERSONAL COMMUNICATIONS (LETTERS, MEMOS, TELEPHONE CONVERSATIONS)

Give the initials as well as the surname of the source with as exact a date as possible.

R. H. Clymer (personal communication, December 8, 1992)

51d Other Documentation Styles

The MLA documentation style is generally accepted in the humanities and the APA style is preferred in the social sciences, but other areas of study, such as mathematics and the natural sciences, prefer their own documentation styles. If you are not certain which style to use for a particular course, consult your instructor. You will find that other styles of documentation may use different terminology. Other styles may, for example, refer to "bibliography" instead of "works cited" (MLA) or "references" (APA) and may prefer "footnotes" to "parenthetical citations." Regardless of the style you use, be consistent in its application. And remember when compiling your working bibliography that all documentation styles will require the same basic data: author, title, place of publication, publisher, date, and page numbers. Only the mechanics, or format, varies.

Following is a listing of some of the style manuals for other disciplines that should be available in your college library. These will give you the information you need to format citations for your courses outside of the humanities and social sciences. Also, see Sections 54b and 54c on writing in the natural and applied sciences (pp. 572-578).

Biology

Council of Biology Editors. Style Manual Committee. *CBE Style Manual: A Guide for Authors, Editors, and Publishers in the Biological Sciences.* 5th ed. Bethesda: Council of Biology Editors, 1983.

Business and finance

Harrison, David. *The Spreadsheet Style Manual.* Homewood, IL: Dow Jones-Irwin, 1990.

Chemistry

American Chemical Society. *Handbook for Authors of Papers in American Chemical Society Publications.* Washington: American Chemical Society, 1978.

Dodd, J. S., ed. *The ACS Style Guide: A Manual for Authors and Editors.* Washington: American Chemical Society, 1986.

Engineering and technology

Michaelson, Herbert B. *How to Write and Publish Engineering Papers and Reports.* 3rd ed. Phoenix: Oryx, 1990.

Weiss, Edmond H. *The Writing System for Engineers and Scientists.* Englewood Cliffs: Prentice, 1982.

Geology

United States. Geological Survey. *Suggestions to Authors of the Reports of the United States Geological Survey.* 7th ed. Washington: GPO, 1989.

Government and political science

United Nations Editorial Manual: A Compendium of Rules and Directions on United Nations Editorial Style, Publication Policies , and Practice. New York: United Nations, 1983.

Law

Neumann, Richard K. *Legal Reasoning and Legal Writing: Structure, Strategy, and Style.* Boston: Little, Brown, 1990.

United States Department of Justice. *Citation and Style Manual.* Chevy Chase, MD: U.S. Department of Justice, 1988.

Linguistics

Linguistic Society of America. *LSA Bulletin.* Dec. issue, annually.

Mathematics

American Mathematical Society. *A Manual for Authors of Mathematical Papers.* 7th ed. Providence: American Mathematical Society, 1980.

Medicine

International Committee of Medical Journal Editors. "Uniform Requirements for Manuscripts Submitted to Biomedical Journals." *Annals of Internal Medicine* 96 (1982): 766-770.

Huth, E. J. *How to Write and Publish Papers in the Medical Sciences.* 2nd ed. Philadelphia: ISIP, 1987.

Physics

American Institute of Physics. Publication Board. *Style Manual for Guidance in the Preparation of Papers.* 3rd ed. New York: American Institute of Physics, 1978.

General

The Chicago Manual of Style for Authors, Editors, and Copywriters. 13th ed. Chicago: U of Chicago P, 1982.

Turabian, Kate L. *A Manual for Writers of Term Papers, Theses, and Dissertations.* 5th ed. Chicago: U of Chicago P, 1987.

52   Sample Research Papers

Following are two model research papers. John Jansen wrote the first research paper for an English class and used the MLA documentation style, which is standard in the humanities. The paper argues the issue of equal pay for men and women for work judged to be of equal value. Eileen Biagi wrote the second sample research paper for a psychology class and documented it in the APA style, which is preferred in the social sciences. It reports on and analyzes career achievement motivation in women. Explanatory comments on the content and form of both papers appear on facing pages to highlight important elements. Remember that the MLA and APA styles of documentation differ on many points. Consult the appropriate sections of this handbook for specifics on each style. (See Chapter 50, pp. 474–490, for detailed guidelines on MLA documentation and Chapter 51, pp. 490–501, for APA guidelines.)

52a Sample MLA Paper

The sample paper that follows uses the documentation style recommended in the third edition of the *MLA Handbook for Writers of Research Papers.*

1   **Outline.** An outline, if required, precedes the first page of the paper on a separate, unnumbered page. The outline below is an informal, preliminary working outline that the author used to organize his ideas prior to and while writing the paper. The formal topic outline on the facing page could be submitted with the paper if required. Note that the formal outline uses only short phrases, omits an introduction, and uses standard outline form with Roman numbers for major categories, indented capital letters for the next series of ideas, and indented Arabic numbers for the third level. (See Section 2c, pp. 29–32, on outlining.) If your outline is longer than one page, number all the pages with lowercase Roman numerals.

Working Outline: Comparable Worth

Tentative Thesis: Sexual discrimination underlies the concept of not paying equal salaries to men and women who perform jobs of equal value to an organization.

1. Introduction: Proponents and opponents of the comparable worth positions have valid viewpoints.
2. Women earn less money than men for three reasons.
3. Can comparable worth theories be used to set wage standards?
4. What is the role of job evaluation in setting wages?
5. Can compensable factors be considered without sex bias?
6. Current job evaluation procedures that appear to be objective are really subjective.
7. In reality, jobs rank differently according to various job evaluation scales.
8. Can job evaluations serve as a basis for unequal pay, which is the result of sexual discrimination?

Note: In place of an outline, an *abstract* (a summary of the essay's content and organization in two hundred words or less) may be required. Place it on a separate page entitled "Abstract" before the essay. Double space and center the block form on the unnumbered page.

1   Outline: Comparable Worth in Salaries

Thesis: All jobs in organizations should be compared to one
another using an evaluative system that is blind to gender.

    I. Unfair wages for women

        A. Women's choices

           1. Hours

           2. Job types

           3. Temporary employment

        B. Custom and tradition

   II. Comparable worth determinants

        A. Job evaluation factors

        B. Sex bias

  III. Objectivity and subjectivity in evaluations

        A. The McArthur scale

        B. The Treimin scale

  IV. The solution

        A. The threat

        B. The promise

2   **Identification and title page format.**   A separate title page is not required by MLA guidelines; should your teacher require one, follow the specific instructions given. If you must submit an outline, place the identification on the same page as the outline.

Jansen properly omitted a separate title page. Following MLA guidelines, he placed his name and course information in a block beginning at the left margin about one inch from the top of the first page of the paper. He double spaced and centered the title. The title includes no punctuation, underlining, or quotation marks. Jansen doubled spaced to begin the text.

3   **Paper format.**   All pages of the paper, excluding the outline and any title page, are numbered with Arabic numerals in the upper right corner, typed one-half inch from the top of the page. MLA guidelines recommend typing your last name before the page number. Avoid using the abbreviation "p." before the page number.

Double space the text of your paper with a margin of one inch at the top and bottom and on both sides of the page. Indent the first word of a paragraph five spaces from the left margin. If using a computer, set the first tab at five and do not right-justify your margin without your instructor's approval.

4   **Introduction and thesis.**   Jansen's thesis statement appears in the first sentence in the form of an argumentative proposition that identifies a problem within industry. Although the thesis usually appears somewhere near the beginning of the paper, it need not be the opening sentence. By placing the thesis first, Jansen quickly informs his audience of his view on this issue. He realizes that many readers will not agree with him, so he includes opponents' views in this paragraph and offers a solution for the problem identified in the thesis. This is a good way to establish a reputation for fairness and to keep the attention of any opponents or undecided readers.

2   John Michael Jansen

Professor M. Hall

English 102

6 November 1992

Comparable Worth in Salaries

4   Industry needs to adopt an evaluative system that is blind to
gender in comparing all jobs in order to achieve comparable
worth in salaries. When jobs are worth the same to an
organization, those who staff the jobs should be paid the same
salary. However, opponents counter that the market system
properly determines wages and salaries, and that businesses and
professions must base wage and salary decisions on the free
market. How do we solve the dilemma, especially to provide
equity to women and minorities who have suffered the most
discrimination in comparable worth jobs? The solution appears to
lie in adopting fair job evaluation systems that award equal pay
to women and men who perform the same jobs. This would
reconcile the concerns of minority workers, including women, and
those of employers and taxpayers as well as labor economists, so
long as all share the economic and cultural costs of such
programs. As a start, this can be accomplished when all parties
concerned involve themselves in implementing and funding such
procedures within their own companies.

Women in the 1980s earned on the average about 30 to 35

5 **In-text documentation.**   Because the names of the authors are not incorporated into the text discussion, they appear in a parenthetical reference along with the page number on which the information is found. The abbreviation "p." for page is not used, and the parentheses are included within the sentence; a period follows them.

6 **Audience.**   Jansen gives his paper wide appeal by citing varied yet familiar occupations: janitors, secretaries, highway repair flagmen, truck drivers, teachers, female and male physicians.

7 **Common knowledge.**   Jansen does not provide documentation for the views expressed about janitors and flagmen because they do not come from any particular source; they represent common knowledge that most people have about this subject matter. (See p. 470 on common knowledge.)

8 **Use of evidence.**   Jansen cites published evidence and examples to support his thesis. In this case, he is using supporting evidence taken from a recent newspaper article. Note that the page number of the newspaper in parentheses also includes the section of the newspaper, A4.

9 **Developing the argument.**   After presenting some examples, Jansen shows how society places restrictions on the occupational choices that most women make. Note his use of the transitional phrase "on the other hand" in midparagraph to introduce two additional considerations: *custom* and *tradition.*

10 **Transition.**   Jansen accomplishes a smooth transition *between* paragraphs by writing the conjunctive adverb "however" to introduce the topic sentence of the paragraph.

5 percent less than men earned (Aaron and Loughy 4). It appears to
be common knowledge that within a corporation male janitors can
6 earn more money than female secretaries and that highway repair
7 flagmen earn more than the company's female nurse. The
inequities extend beyond one corporation. Truck drivers, usually
male, earn more than teachers, usually female. Problems exist
even within the professions. Paul Recer points out that "women
physicians in 1988 earned only 62.8 percent of the pay received
8 by male doctors . . . a decline from 1982, when female physicians
earned 63.2 percent of the pay of male doctors" (A4).

Although men and women freely make career decisions in the
same way, our culture places restrictions on women's choices.
Some of the differences between men's and women's earnings are
due to decisions women make about how many hours to work
each week, what occupations to choose, and when to enter or to
9 leave the work force. On the other hand, custom and tradition also
influence wages in different jobs and occupations, a view that
acknowledges that women improve their relative earnings by
entering jobs traditionally held by men. Women, who enter these
same jobs and work just as many hours, earn, in many cases, less
salary than their male counterparts. Recer also cites a study of the
American Medical Women's Association which reveals that female
physicians "are classed in the four lowest-paid specialities: general
practice, pediatrics, psychiatry, and internal medicine" (A4).

However, the narrower the definition of industries and
10 occupations, the greater the apparent segregation of women and
men who hold particular jobs becomes. According to the U. S.

11 **Use of evidence.** To exemplify and make specific his views in the previous paragraph, Jansen now cites a printed source and common knowledge.

12 **Direct quotation.** Jansen incorporates a direct quotation from Meeker, who is identified within the sentence, into his own sentence in order to define the concept of job evaluation. Note that a capital letter does not follow the opening quotation mark. The parenthetical reference includes only the page number because Jansen identified Meeker in the text, and a period follows the parentheses.

13 **Ellipsis within a quotation.** The three ellipsis points, each preceded and followed by one space, indicate that Jansen did not present Meeker's full sentence. If ellipsis points appear at the end of a sentence, they are followed by a space and the appropriate end punctuation mark.

14 **Explanatory note.** The superscript number "1" signals the presence of an explanatory endnote placed at the end of the paper on a separate page entitled "Notes." Jansen does not place the contents of the note within the paper itself because not all readers will need an example to understand the text.

15 **Developing the argument.** Jansen writes this expository paragraph to describe some of the complexities involved in devising systems of job evaluation.

16 **Quotation marks question validity.** Jansen has placed the phrase "compensable factors" within quotation marks because of its elusive use by job evaluators; in short, he questions the validity of the concept as described in the paper.

17 **Explanatory note.** The superscript number "2" signals another explanatory endnote, which Jansen places after the text of the paper.

11 Department of Labor classifications, 37 percent of all women work in industries in which at least 65 percent of the employees are women (Norwood 4). Furthermore, it seems to be common knowledge that the larger the proportion of female workers in an industry, the lower the average hourly wage they receive.

Can comparable worth be used to set wage standards? To do so requires some form of job evaluation, a method of ranking jobs according to their value to the employer. Its purpose, Meeker

12 says, is to provide a system of comparing "dissimilar work . . . to

13 determine appropriate wage levels" (674). The result of the evaluation process becomes a hierarchy of job values, a model reflecting the relative worth of jobs in a governmental unit, a plant, or a firm. It seems like a good system; however, it is not

14 always consistent.[1]

15 While a variety of job evaluation systems exist, they range from the simplest ranking procedures to more complicated

16 methods based on points or scores awarded to "compensable factors," which consist of a job's skill and training requirements, its working conditions, its demands on physical and mental efforts, and the amount of responsibility for people and materials that the job requires. In the more sophisticated evaluative systems, each job receives a rank based on compensable factors followed by an attempt to relate the resulting job rankings into a wage structure. Job evaluation in this model relates to jobs, not to the worker who performs the job, even though it is the worker who is

17 evaluated and rated.[2] Hutner writes that job content determines pay grades for each job, whereas a worker's characteristics—

18   **Indirect quotation.** Because Jansen introduces the quotation from Hutner with the conjunction "that," the quotation which follows is considered *indirect* rather than *direct*: therefore, he did not enclose it in quotation marks. The indirect quotation ends at the close of the next sentence, where he places the parenthetical page citation.

19   **Developing the argument.** Jansen closes this paragraph with a reference to *sex bias*, which he examines in the next paragraph.

20   **Block quotation.** Although it stands apart from the text as shown, a block quotation must have a logical connection with the sentence that precedes it. Jansen uses a colon, an appropriate punctuation mark to indicate that a block quotation will follow; however, other marks may be used or none, as required by the grammar of the sentence preceding the quotation. The block quotation is indented ten spaces on each line and double spaced. Notice that the right-hand margin of the blocked quotation is the *same* as that for the body of the paper. Because Jansen identifies the author and the title of the book from which he took the quotation in his text, the parenthetical reference includes only the page number. If he had not included this information in the text, the parenthetical reference would appear as follows: .(Hutner 16) Note also that the period ends the block quotation; the parentheses are not part of the direct quotation.

21   **Developing the argument.** Jansen selected the block quotation to close this paragraph because it emphasizes and summarizes the role of sex discrimination. In the next paragraph he turns to the inequities that result from subjective judgments in establishing job evaluation models.

Jansen 4

18 seniority, merit, productivity—determine the individual worker's
pay within each job grade (16). At first glance this appears to be
19 a fair system; however, it too has inconsistencies rooted in sex
bias.

A critical part of the job evaluation process, from the point of
view of pay equity, lies in eliminating sex bias when assessing
the compensable factors. For example, when examining working
conditions, most evaluators weight the rigors of traditionally male
jobs, such as dirt and noise, heavier than that of traditionally
female jobs, such as the stress of dealing with bosses or clients
or the eye and back strain of working at sewing machines and
word processors. More evaluative points may be assigned to so-
called typically male jobs that involve large salaries, such as
corporate sales managers, than to female jobs that involve contact
with consumers, like customer service. Furthermore, in Equal Pay
For Comparable Worth, Hutner reports the following:

20
> If, when dollar values are assigned to the compensable
> factors, market values for typically female jobs are
> used as benchmarks for female jobs in the
> establishment, then discrimination in the market place
21 > is carried over to the firm. (16)

Despite what appears to be the formality and objectivity of
job evaluation models, the procedures appear to be judgmental
throughout. In no sense do they represent an objective
determination of the value of the product of each job. Subjective
evaluations enter at every step of the way: in determining what

22 **Parenthetical citation of an author from an anthology.** Jansen identifies his paraphrase of material written by McArthur, which he discovered in an anthology (collection of essays) edited by Hartmann, and he includes the page numbers. Note that the abbreviation "pp." for pages is absent and that a hyphen mark with no spaces before or after it separates the numbers.

23 **Numbers.** Jansen properly uses Arabic numbers with percentages rather than spelling them out.

24 **Word choice.** Jansen opts to place the phrase "physical demand" in quotation marks to emphasize the elusiveness of the concept as well as the apparent use of the phrase by many people to apply only to occupations where physical labor is more obvious. Avoid the excessive use of quotation marks for this purpose because it may confuse your audience.

25 **Developing the argument.** Jansen, having explained some examples of job evaluation systems, now discusses the problems that ensue from the lack of a uniform evaluation system in order to stress the resulting inequities.

attributes to include in the job evaluation, in setting the point
weights for each attribute, in deciding how many points each job
should get for each attribute, and in calibrating the resulting point
scores with pay (McArthur 53–70). An example is the range of
weights attached to the degree of supervision required in an
office job: one job evaluation scale assigns a maximum of 7
percent of total points to this attribute, while another assigns 14.5
percent. "Physical demand" provides a maximum of 10 percent of
the points for shop jobs but none at all for office jobs. Some job
evaluation scales are meant to apply only to shop jobs, others
only to office jobs, and still others to both (Treiman 66–179).

The importance of a particular attribute in determining a
job's rank depends not on the maximum proportion of total points
it could account for, but on the proportion of the variation in total
points of the various jobs for which it actually accounts. Whatever
variations occur depend purely on the judgment of evaluators. In
other words, jobs rank differently according to various job
evaluation scales. The weights assigned to job attributes actually
determine the ranks of the jobs. In fact, different relative rankings
of jobs may arise for any of a variety of reasons: use of different
attributes or weights or variation in the application of a given
system by evaluators. The results of simple correlations between
the rankings of various evaluators applying the same job
evaluation are sometimes disturbingly low (Schwab 37–52).

26   **The essay's conclusion.**   In the last paragraph, Jansen concludes his essay by referring back to the introduction and summarizing his argument. The final sentence of the essay restates the thesis to remind the reader of the point of his essay: that companies will need to adopt evaluative systems that are blind to gender when comparing jobs to achieve comparable worth in salaries.

26   For comparable worth advocates, then, job evaluation
constitutes both a threat and a promise. Because it typically
rationalizes and solidifies sex discrimination in pay systems, job
evaluation, as presently used, becomes a threat. Because it offers
a way of measuring the relative value of jobs that are not
identical, it becomes a promise. Moreover, job evaluation may
provide the only evidence acceptable to the courts as proof of sex
discrimination based on salary. Wages resulting from
discriminatory pay will become an increasingly important issue,
not only to the large numbers of female, ethnic, and racial
members of the work force, but also to their employers, to the
consumers of their services, and to their male fellow workers
(Hutner 18). While advocates will continue to cite cases of
discrimination in salary, and opponents will argue that the labor
market dictates the lower salaries, it behooves all involved
(workers, employers, consumers, labor economists) to study and
share the benefits and sacrifices that will follow with the
elimination of salary discrimination. Companies will need (or be
required by federal dictate) to create and fund procedures that all
businesses must follow with job evaluations determined by a
panel composed of ethnically diverse members of both sexes.

27   **Explanatory notes.**   The endnotes begin on a separate numbered page entitled "Notes" with the word centered on the
page one inch from the top. Notes are double spaced and indented five spaces from the left margin. The note number,
which is raised slightly from the line of type without punctuation, precedes one space and the content of the note. Notes
that extend beyond the length of one line, as these do, begin
subsequent lines at the left margin, double spaced. Both of
these notes elaborate on points that Jansen makes within the
text of the paper but which he decided would impede the
paper's flow if contained in its body. Endnotes can also contain
bibliographic information related to the topic and of possible
interest to the reader but not contained in the list of works
cited. Endnotes are optional.

Notes

27   [1] Aaron and Lougy give an example. Ranking jobs entirely on the basis of two factors, "brain" and "brawn," and assigning from 0 to 100 points for "brain" and 0 to 30 points for "brawn," brain appears to be the more important factor because it can account for 100 out of 130 maximum points. But if one assigns to most jobs similar "brain" scores (say, clustering most jobs in a 10-point range from 40 to 50 points), and if the scores are widely disputed over the 30-point range for "brawn," brawn will be more important than brains in determining the rankings. The Comparable Worth Controversy, 28.

[2] Aaron and Lougy state another example. Suppose one ranks jobs according to two factors, A and B, and gives scores for each factor ranging from 1 to 10. Job I gets a score of 3 for factor A and 8 for factor B. Job II receives a score of 5 for factor A and 7 for factor B. Weighting each factor equally, job II ranks ahead of job I (12 points to 11). According factor B, for example, three times the weight of factor A, however, results in job I ranking ahead of job II (27 points to 26). The Comparable Worth Controversy, 29.

28 **Works cited.** "Works Cited" lists only the works that the writer directly cites in the text.

If your instructor requires you to list all works *consulted*, place the title "Works Consulted" on a separate page and present, in alphabetical order, all works consulted or cited. The format is the same as for works cited.

29 **Format of the list.** The list of works cited begins on a separate, numbered page; the heading is centered one inch from the top. All lines should be double spaced. Alphabetized entries begin with a capital letter. The first line of each entry begins flush with the left margin. Subsequent lines for an entry are indented five spaces from the left margin. Each entry begins with the author's surname. For works with multiple authors, invert the first author's name only. For works with more than three authors, list only the name of the first author followed by the abbreviation "et al."

30 **Page information.** If the book as a whole is the reference, page numbers are not included.

31 **Article within an anthology or collection of essays.** List the name of the author first, then the title of the essay in quotation marks. Note the end punctuation goes inside the closing quotation mark. The underlined title of the anthology or collection comes next, followed by a period. "Editor" is abbreviated as "Ed." The editor's name appears in noninverted order with a period, then the place of publication and a colon, the publisher and a comma, and the year of publication and a period. The page numbers for the *entire* article appear, not merely those that identify the location of citations or paraphrases.

32 **Periodicals using continuous pagination.** The date is identified by a volume number; the year appears in parentheses.

33 **Government documents.** Specific authors of government documents often are not known. If such were the case here, the entry would begin at "U.S. Department of Labor" relocated to appear in alphabetical order. But this government report contains signed essays; the entry begins with the author's name and the title of the essay.

28   Works Cited

29 Aaron, Henry J., and Cameron M. Lougy. The Comparable Worth
30   Controversy. Washington: The Brookings Institute, 1986.

    Hutner, Frances C. Equal Pay for Comparable Worth. New York:
          Praeger, 1986.

31 McArthur, Leslie Zebrowitz. "Social Judgment Biases in
          Comparable Worth Analysis." Comparable Worth: New
          Directions for Research. Ed. Heidi I. Hartmann. Washington:
          National Academy Press, 1985. 53–70.

32 Meeker, Suzanne E. "Equal Pay, Comparable Work, and Job
          Evaluation." Yale Law Journal 90 (1981): 674–92.

33 Norwood, Janet L. The Female-Male Earnings Gap: A Review of
          Employment Earnings Issues. U.S. Department of Labor.
          Bureau of Labor Statistics, Report 673. Washington: GPO,
          September 1982.

    Recer, Paul. "Study: Health Field Still Sex-Segregated." South
          Bend Tribune 8 Sept. 1991, metro ed.: A4.

    Schwab, Donald P. "Job Evaluation Research and Research
          Needs." Comparable Worth: New Directions for Research.
          Ed. Heidi I. Hartmann. Washington: National Academy
          Press, 1985. 37–52.

    Treiman, Donald J. Job Evaluation Research: An Analytic Review.
          Washington: National Academy of Sciences, 1979.

The sample research paper that follows uses the method of documentation recommended in the third edition of the *Publication Manual of the American Psychological Association.*

1 **Title page format.** APA guidelines do not explicitly prescribe a form for the title page, although the sample paper in the *APA Publication Manual* provides Biagi with a model to follow: the title, her name, and the name of the university she attends centered on the page and double spaced. Since Biagi's paper is a class assignment, she adds the course title, the instructor's name, and the date of submission about four inches beneath her university affiliation.

2 **Running head.** The running head is a brief encapsulation of the essay title that appears twice on the title page: at the top right corner above the page number and under the course information and date, where it is labeled "Running Head." Numbering and identifying pages will ease the reordering of pages in case of page misplacement and eliminates the need to include one's name alongside each page number (as is done in MLA style). Note that running heads most often appear on papers submitted for publication, so follow your instructor's directions on this point.

1

Career Achievement Motivation in Women

Eileen B. Biagi

University of Notre Dame

Psychology

Dr. W. Bartlett

May, 1993

2 Running Head: CAREER ACHIEVEMENT

3   **Abstract.** Papers written in the APA format usually include an abstract, a brief comprehensive summary of the contents of the paper. The abstract must be exact in its content and contain no abbreviations or acronyms. The abstract may contain paraphrasing but no direct quotations. The content should be as brief as possible, yet each sentence must be informative. The content reports; it does not evaluate. An abstract for a *review* or a *theoretical paper* may not exceed 100 words and should describe the topic in one sentence; the purpose, thesis, or organizing basis and scope of the paper; the sources used (such as published literature, personal observation); and the conclusions and implications or applications. An abstract of a *report* of an empirical study may not exceed 150 words and includes the problem under investigation, and, as appropriate, the subjects of the study (number, age, sex, species, etc.), the experimental method (apparatus, data-gathering method, drugs or medications used), the findings including statistical information, and the conclusions and implications or applications.

    If your instructor requires a formal outline, it will take the same form as the outline that accompanies the MLA style paper in this chapter (see p. 507). It begins on a separate unnumbered page, and only short phrases are used. Roman numbers indicate major categories; indented capitals and then Arabic numbers, indented further, indicate subsidiary categories.

3

Abstract

Historically, women and men have differed in their career orientations. Farmer (1987) attempts to explain these differences with her model of career and achievement motivation. She proposes that interaction among personal, environmental, and background factors determines an individual's level of achievement motivation. Specific results of her study are presented and compared with other research. Support exists for her assertion that gender differences in this area are evident and that achievement motivation will vary with age and social changes. Other studies suggest that this motivation construct differs between females and males. However, these studies conflict with Farmer's in that they detect other types of gender differences. As yet, a comprehensive model that explains achievement motivation for women and men does not exist. But the models we do have for women's career achievement motivation suggest that they can serve as bases for changing women's positions in the job market and their attitudes about achievement in the career world.

4   **Page numbering.** APA style requires that pages be numbered with Arabic numbers starting with 1 on the title page and continuing throughout the paper. The page number appears in the upper right corner, two lines under the running head.

5   **Format.** APA recommends double spacing between all lines in a paper. Margins should be one and one-half inches at the top, bottom, right, and left of each page. Lines are not justified on the right side, nor are hyphenated words permitted at the end of a line. No more than twenty-five lines of text should appear on a page, excluding the running title and page number. Paragraphs are indented five spaces.

6   **Introduction and thesis.** Biagi opens the paper by presenting her thesis and the particular problem under study. Although the thesis should appear near the beginning of the paper, it need not be the first sentence. By placing the thesis here, Biagi immediately establishes the nature of her analysis and what she intends to accomplish in the paper.

7   **In-text documentation.** Biagi follows APA documentation style. When the author's name is not given within the text itself, a parenthetical reference includes the name and page number. Commas separate the elements in the reference. The publication date is *always* cited, and "p." or "pp." accompanies the page number or numbers. No title appears in the text reference unless the author is unknown.

8   **Date reference.** Because Biagi cites more than one publication of Farmer's in the paper, each time she cites Farmer's name she includes the publication date of the material cited in parentheses.

9   **Developing the analysis.** As is appropriate in a study in the social sciences, Biagi begins a review of previously published research on the topic.

4

5   Career Achievement Motivation in Women

6   By identifying the factors that influence career achievement
motivation in women, we can recognize, understand, and perhaps
change the current position of women in the job market and
women's attitudes about achievement in the career world. Do men
and women differ in their career orientations? And, if they do,
why do these differences occur and what factors contribute to the
disparities? "Psychologists have generally viewed the need for
achievement [achievement motivation] as a learned motive, with
parents playing a major role in shaping their children's later
7   strivings" (Benner, 1985, p. 12). However, this single motive
cannot easily explain the historical differences between and
changes within women's and men's career orientations.

8   Farmer (1987) proposes one such model for explaining gender
differences in achievement motivation, basing the model on social
learning theory (Bandura, 1987) and on a sociocultural perspective
(Maehr, 1974, 1984). The model incorporates the idea of reciprocal
9   determinism, i.e., through interaction, the behavioral, cognitive,
and environmental factors influence one another. Farmer (1987)
further presents three constructs that interact both among
themselves and influence achievement motivation: personal,
environmental, and background. Academic self-esteem,
expressiveness, independence, ability attributes, and intrinsic
values comprise the personal factors. Environmental elements
include support from parents and teachers and support for
working women, while the components of the background

10   **Paragraph and essay development.** Biagi, following Farmer, enumerates the dimensions that have a significant influence on career motivations. These not only develop this paragraph but provide the organizational framework for the next several paragraphs.

11   **Citing a work by two or more authors.** When citing a source with two or more authors outside of parenthetical citation, use the word "and" as Biagi does; however, if citing the source *within parentheses*, use an ampersand (&) in place of the word "and."

12   **Paraphrasing.** Biagi paraphrases relevant research to present information economically (Farmer, Kaufman and Richardson, Ireson, and Lueptow), but she documents her sources just as she would if she had quoted them directly. (See paraphrasing in Chapter 49, pp. 459–460.)

construct are sex, special status, school location, race, age, verbal ability, and math ability. Yet each of these dimensions has a significant influence on the career motivation of both women and men.

10   Additionally, according to Farmer (1987), "Motivation is represented by three different but related dimensions: Aspiration, Mastery, and Career" (p. 5). Aspiration motivation refers to the level of education and occupation a person hopes to attain, while mastery motivation concerns the desire to achieve a challenging task until one masters the task. Finally, career motivation becomes the commitment to the long-range prospects of a career. Farmer provides us a model, then, which we can compare to current studies of the vocational development of women.

Examining the achievement motivations individually reveals that the aspiration motivation in adolescence is not a reliable predictor of achievement in adulthood (Farmer, 1985). In particular, highly achievement-motivated female adolescents did not attain (as adults) careers comparable to their previously

11   desired goals. Likewise, Kaufman and Richardson (1982) noted a study that found that occupational aspirations of girls change over time from equal to boys at the beginning of high school to lower than boys by the end of senior year (Ireson, 1978). If the female adolescent's aspirations to achieve diminish over time, she will undoubtedly lack the motivation necessary to develop a career corresponding to her initial aspiration level. Nevertheless,

12   Lueptow (1984) concluded that adolescent girls have higher levels

13   **Block quotation.**   APA guidelines require the indentation of a block quotation five spaces from the left margin. Place the period at the end of the last sentence of the quotation but before the citation. The right margin of the quotation is the same as that of the rest of the paper. In APA style, quotations of forty or more words should appear in block format with quotation marks omitted. Note that Biagi uses a lead-in sentence to prepare her audience for the quotation.

14   **Transition.**   Here, and at other places in the paper, Biagi uses transitional words and phrases such as *furthermore, additionally, finally*, and *on the other hand* in order to achieve coherence.

15   **Developing the analysis.**   As is often the case in reviewing research materials, Biagi notes a conflict between two sources and reports it. She then presents a practical application that originates from the second source cited in the paragraph, which reveals her stance in the conflict.

of achievement value orientation and academic achievement than
males. He offered two suggestions for these surprising results.

13   First, on the basis of these results it is likely that
achievement orientation is actually a component of the
female sex role, and not the male. Second, the author urges
that a distinction be made between achievement based on
excellence and accomplishment, which is the focus of the
female achievement orientation, and achievement through
assertion and aggressive competition, which are the
achievement themes favored by males. (Lapsley & Quintana,
1985, p. 255)

Unifying the study's results is the common discovery that
adolescent girls differ from adolescent boys on the achievement
issue. Whether one sex achieves and the other does not or
whether the sexes achieve in different realms remains unclear.

14   Furthermore, turning to mastery motivation, Farmer (1985) found
that men score higher than women on this construct and that
environmental factors have a stronger influence on women's mastery

15   motivation than on men's. These findings conflict with Lueptow's
(1984), whose results suggest that a part of the female ideal of
achievement consists of "excellence and accomplishment," mastering
the work. The results show that women do have some desire to
achieve mastery; however, the magnitude of this motivation is
debatable. Because environmental factors such as ethnic identification,
regional location, religion, and the educational and occupational
history of family members have a relatively strong impact on women's

16   **Paraphrase and personal opinion.** Note here how Biagi obtains a balanced blend of paraphrase and opinion. She paraphrases five different sources in this paragraph and adds her personal reflection and opinion.

mastery motivation, a vocational counselor may use this knowledge by offering support and encouragement to female clients on the high school and collegiate levels as well as in public and private agencies.

16   Finally, on the career motivation construct, adolescent girls score higher than adolescent boys (Farmer, 1985). But earlier research by Rooney (1983) shows that in adulthood women score lower than men in career motivation reflected, in part, by the positions these women hold in the job market. At the present time, young women expect to work outside the home, and data show that women are a major part of the occupational economy (Kaufman & Richardson, 1982). However, they work mainly in service and support jobs (Lueptow, 1984). Kaufman and Richardson point out that women experience difficulty gaining executive and managerial positions because of their limited access to the power centers of the professions and because of socialization that has encouraged them to be deferential to men. In addition to the socialization factor, Farmer (1987) finds that for those who have responsibilities at home, homemaking had a negative influence on career commitment for women. She suggests that conflicting role priorities may reduce women's career commitment. Several self-imposed and societal factors might hinder women from achieving as men do. Many women have refused promotions that require them to relocate away from their families or work longer hours. Others have welcomed the opportunity. The self-imposed factors may be then, partially, a product of socialization. The complex interaction between personal development and socialization makes measuring an individual's career motivation a delicate task.

17 **Audience.** Thinking of her audience, Biagi incorporates several examples into this paragraph, which benefits the reader by making specific the theoretical concerns she presents in the paper.

18 **Reference to a table.** At the close of this paragraph, Biagi refers to a study that she did in an earlier course. She places the table summarizing the study at the end of the paper. According to APA guidelines, she presents only the table's *highlights* in the text, not all of its details. Biagi properly identifies the author of the table by including a surname and the date in parentheses.

17   On the other hand, the role of women in society is not static. Women, except in some third-world countries, have become increasingly more independent and well-educated. Compared to women in the Victorian era, who were socialized to remain unemployed outside the home, women today are much more career-oriented. In particular, within the past twenty years, economic necessity, the recognition of what women can accomplish, and the feminist movement, coupled with the readiness of the culture to accept them, have resulted in drastic changes in the social mores and patterns of thought concerning women. Young children read stories about policewomen and male nurses. Adolescent girls, reversing a long-standing trend, enroll in classes in advanced math and the pure sciences. Adult women are entering the professions of law, medicine, accounting, and the professorate in greater numbers and are slowly attaining high-ranking positions. Recently, Congress approved the right of women pilots to fly into combat situations after exemplary performances observed during the Persian Gulf war. Additionally,

18 a preliminary study of career-oriented women showed that college-aged students rated a situation in which the woman works at home as more common than that in which the woman works in the business world. However, these same students asserted that when the woman remains at home it causes more strain on a marriage and is less fair than when the woman works outside of the home (Biagi, 1990).

19 **Table signal.** Biagi, following APA guidelines, signals the placement of the table in the text. The table, however, actually appears at the end of her paper. If the paper were to be published, an editor would insert the table in the text in place of the signal.

20 **Conclusion.** Biagi presents a conclusion in accordance with APA guidelines. She indicates how her analysis and research contribute to resolving the original problem posed in the thesis. Her conclusion is clear, direct, and unambiguous.

19

Insert Table 1 about here

As social and cultural values change, women push for the opening of more career opportunities. If it were possible to measure women's career motivation over the past one hundred years, it would most likely reflect this increase in women's interest in the career world. As personal and societal values change over time, women's career motivation will most likely vary with them.

20
Farmer's (1987) model for explaining career achievement motivation in women is at odds with other research on the topic. Although achievement motivation in high schools does not constitute a valuable predictor of adult career achievement, women's ideal of achievement may differ from men's and these differences must be incorporated into measurements of achievement motivation and models for prediction of career achievement. Environmental factors do influence women's mastery and career motivations. As social and cultural values change and we acknowledge economic necessity, women's desire to have careers increases along with an influx of women into the work force. These studies show that career achievement motivation in women fluctuates. Women have the power to develop it in themselves, and vocational counselors have the ability to nurture its growth through support and encouragement of female clients from the very earliest stages onward.

21 **Format of references.** The alphabetized bibliography at the end of a paper following APA style is titled "References." Center the word "References" on a separate, consecutively numbered page, and include all the works cited in your paper. Although APA style does not call for it, if Biagi's instructor suggested that she list her background reading as well, she would have titled her list "Bibliography."

22 **Edited book.** Use the abbreviation "*Eds.*" for "*editors*" or "*Ed.*" for "*editor*" within parentheses when referring to an edited book, as shown in Biagi's reference list. However, if the reference is to a chapter or article within an edited book, the author of the chapter or article appears first with the reference formatted as follows:

Author, A., Author, B., & Author, C. (1976). Can the chimpanzee

think? In T. Regan & P. Singer (eds.), <u>Animal rights and</u>

<u>human obligations</u> (pp. 15–20). Englewood Cliffs, NJ: Prentice-

Hall.

23 **Review of a book.** Because the review lacks a title, the information that describes it takes the place of the title, and Biagi places it in brackets to show that it is not the title. If the review had a title, this material would follow it, in brackets. Note also that by APA style, all publication dates appear in parentheses followed by a period.

24 **Publisher's name.** The name of a university press is spelled out in full form, but the name of a commercial publisher may be abbreviated: Macmillan Publishing Company, for example, becomes simply Macmillan.

21   References

Bandura, A. (1978). The self system in reciprocal determinism.
    American Psychologist, 33, 344–358.

22   Benner, D. G. (1985). Need for achievement. In D. G. Benner (Ed.),
    Baker encyclopedia of psychology. Grand Rapids: Baker Book
    House.

Farmer, H. (1985). Model of career and achievement motivation for
    women and men. Journal of Counseling Psychology, 32 (3),
    663–676.

Farmer, H. (1987). A multivariate model for explaining gender
    differences in career and achievement motivation. Educational
    Researcher, 16, 5–9.

Ireson, C. (1978). Girls' socialization for work. In A. Stromberg and
    S. Harkess (Eds.), Women working (pp. 128–139). Palo Alto:
    Mayfield.

Kaufman, D. R., & Richardson, B. L. (1982). Achievement and
    women. New York: Free Press.

23   Lapsley, D. K., & Quintana, S. M. (1985). [Review of Adolescent
    sex roles and social change]. Sex Roles, 12, 252–255.

24   Lueptow, L. B. (1984). Adolescent sex roles and social change.
    New York: Columbia University Press.

25 **Journal article.** The volume number, underlined, follows the name of a journal and a comma. A comma also follows the volume number. Pages are indicated here without the abbreviations "p." or "pp." but the abbreviations are used in referring to articles or chapters in an edited book and to articles in popular magazines and newspapers.

25   Maehr, M. (1974). Culture and achievement motivation. <u>American
        Psychologist,</u> <u>29</u>, 887–896.

Maehr, M. (1984). On doing well in science: Why Johnny no
        longer excels: Why Sarah never did. In S. Paris, G. Olson, &
        H. Stephenson (Eds.), <u>Learning and motivation in the
        classroom</u> (pp. 179–210). Hillsdale, NJ: Lawrence Erlbaum.

Rooney, G. (1983). Distinguishing characteristics of the life roles of
        worker, student, and homemaker for young adults. <u>Journal of
        Vocational Behavior,</u> <u>22</u>, 324–342.

26   **Table location.**   Tables should be placed on a separate numbered page after your references. Explain all abbreviations in
the table *except* those that are standard statistical abbreviations,
as is the case here.

27   **Note.**   Follow each table with a note, as Biagi does, and place
it beneath the table, double spaced. Cite the author and the
copyright holder. In this case, the table comes from a paper
that Biagi wrote a few semesters earlier. Even though it is her
own work, it must be cited when used in another paper.

26 Table 1

Means, Standard Deviations, and Univariate Analyses Results
for the Gender Role Main Effect

| Variable | Women Work at Home | | Women Work Outside of Home | | | |
	M	SD	M	SD	F	p
Common	4.29	.65	2.92	1.05	45.73	.000*
Strain	3.75	.67	3.27	.96	7.35	.009*
Fair	3.17	.79	3.62	.99	5.40	.024*

27 Note. From "How Typical and Atypical Gender Roles Are
Valued: A Pilot Study" by E. B. Biagi, 1990. Unpublished
manuscript, University of Notre Dame, Department of
Psychology, Notre Dame. Copyright 1990 by E. B. Biagi.
Adapted by permission.

*p<.05

PART VIII

ACADEMIC AND BUSINESS WRITING

Good writing is not confined to your English composition class. The processes that you undertake to produce an essay in a composition course are the same for all courses in any discipline in your college career and beyond. This section introduces you to the variety of writing assignments you may encounter: essays in the humanities and about literature; field research reports in the social sciences; lab reports in the natural sciences; technical reports in the applied sciences; essay examinations; and business memos, letters, and the resume. Academic writing and business writing should be clear, concise, and correct. Attention must also be given to purpose or focus, audience, and certain conventions of form.

53 Writing in the Humanities and About Literature

Disciplines in the humanities include communication arts, history, language and literature, philosophy, religion and theology, women's (gender) studies, and, in many instances, the fine and performing arts: painting and sculpture, music, dance, and theater. When you write in the humanities you concern yourself with human values as you focus on an individual work or collection of works within one of these disciplines (for example, on a poem, a novel, a drama, a painting, or a symphony). Your writing will most likely address *what* the author, artist, or composer communicates, *how* it is communicated, *where* it fits into or adjusts the tradition of which it is a part, and how you—the reader, viewer, or listener—*react* to it. Writing in the humanities, then, incorporates subjective information because you are reacting to or interpreting a work. Much of it relies on objective data as well, however, because you will use the work itself and perhaps outside sources to support your interpretation.

In the humanities you will encounter different types of writing that either *explain* (exposition) or *persuade* (argument). (See Section 5c on the expository patterns of development and Section 7d on writing an argument.) The types of papers you will be asked to write can take several forms. A **reaction paper** is one in which you record your thoughts, feelings, and ideas about a work, as in your reactions of pity and sorrow to Blake's poem, "The Chimney Sweeper." An **interpretive paper** is one in which you discuss what the author or artist is communicating, as in writing about the feelings of loneliness and isolation in Picasso's painting *The Tragedy* from his blue period. An interpretive paper can also reflect what a work means to you. Or, you might write a review of a book, film, art work, ballet, or concert. An **analysis paper** or a **review paper** is one in which you discuss the relationship of the parts of a work to the whole (see pp. 87–89 on analysis); for example, how each individual composition performed during a concert contributes to or detracts from the success of the concert itself. In your college career, the type of analysis paper you will most likely encounter is literary analysis, which is discussed in the following section.

53a Writing About Literature

Writing about literature is a specialized type of writing within the humanities. It involves careful reading of texts, critical thinking (see Chapter 7, pp. 117–130), and your response to the literature, whether a reaction, an interpretation, or a review.

Reading critically

Writing about literature begins with careful reading and *rereading* of the literature, whether works of fiction, poetry, or drama. As you read, be certain that you know the meaning of each word you encounter; if you don't, look it up. Constantly ask questions as you read: who? what? where? when? why? how? Who is the main character? What options are open to all of the characters? Where is the action occurring? When does the action take place? Why do the characters behave as they do? How do the characters solve their problems? You may not find all the answers, but keep asking the questions. Underline striking words or phrases like this line from a sonnet by Hopkins:

> It gathers to a greatness, like the *ooze of oil.*

Take notes and record your reactions to what you read in the margins or in a notebook. Use your imagination. Put yourself in the character's place: How would you react to particular situations? Then record your insights. The truths that we encounter in literature are universal truths that engage us by appealing to our imagination and intellect. However, these truths are not always obvious or transparent. We need to look for clues to find the truths the characters and their actions reveal. For example, what does Hester Prynne's confession of guilt in Hawthorne's novel *The Scarlet Letter* reveal? As a result, when you are reading, you will need to look for patterns, such as recurrences in the character's behavior, responses to adversity, or the use of dialect. You will want to be alert to symbols and the meanings that lie beneath them, as in the phrase *two roads* in Frost's "The Road Not Taken." Look for images, the pictures created by the use of figurative language (similes, metaphors, personification), such as the simile *like a thunderbolt* in Tennyson's poem "The Eagle." Be certain to think critically about and analyze the characters, the plot, the form of the text, the climax and crisis, and the resolution of the action. The topics listed in the "Literary Topics" checklist (p. 552) can help guide you on what to be attuned to when reading. And, of course, remember that writing about literature is possible only with *careful* and *close* reading and rereading of literary texts.

Finding a topic

If your instructor has not given you a general topic to write about, you will need to find your own. In either case, avoid topics that are too broad, such as Captain Ahab's preoccupation with vengeance in Melville's *Moby Dick*, because you cannot write about every implication related to the topic in a literary selection. Instead, you will need to devise a limited topic such as Ahab's lapses from sanity as revealed in some of his interactions with other characters in the novel. Use the notations you wrote in the margins and the underlined words and phrases in your text as starting points for prewriting (see pp. 7–23). Be certain that your prewriting, (whether freewriting, devising a scratch outline, using the pentad) centers on the literary work. Most readers have personal reactions to literature, but few instructors desire that you use the literary work solely as a springboard for your personal feelings. When prewriting and then writing about a literary text, examine the aspects of it as listed on page 552. Any one of these possibilities can serve as a topic for a paper.

Also, think carefully about your prewriting, the literary text, class notes, and any study aids distributed in class. Use them to posit a preliminary thesis and a working outline, which will eventually lead you to a more focused thesis. (See Sections 2a and 2b.)

Developing the topic

Once you have decided on a topic or thesis, you need to develop it. Like most papers written in the humanities, papers

LITERARY TOPICS

Subject	What the poem, story, novel, or drama is about
Theme	The main idea or message about the subject
Characterization	How you come to know the characters; how they are presented
Plot	The chain of cause and effect that takes the narrative from its beginning to its end
Setting	The actual or imagined place where the action occurs
Point of View	The viewpoint from which the story is told: first or third person, author's voice
Tone	The attitude toward the subject matter, the reader, or both
Devices of Sound	End rhyme, internal rhyme, slant rhyme, alliteration, consonance, assonance
Images	Pictures evoked by figurative language
Figurative Language	Personification, simile, metaphor, oxymoron, symbols
Symbolism	Use of a word to represent more than one idea or thing
Meter	Patterns of rhythm: iamb, anapest, and so forth

about literature involve reaction to and interpretation of the work. To develop your topic, you will analyze the text and argue your response or reaction to the literary work using it and perhaps other sources as support.

When writing about literature, the literary work is considered the **primary source,** and many writers of essays about literature confine themselves to working with the primary source. Other writers, by choice or necessity, investigate **secondary sources**—books, reviews, and journal articles written about the primary source—and write their papers citing these secondary sources, as the author of the student paper on pp. 558–566 does. You can, of course, consult secondary sources in order to discover a topic; you can also consult these sources to find support for your interpretations. You would then cite the sources to provide evidence for your analysis or argument and to avoid plagiarism.

You can develop your thesis by using the following options for structuring a literary analysis.

1. **Textual analysis.** Consider the literary work in and for itself independent of any biographical, environmental, temporal, or other influence.

2. **Canon analysis.** Consider the literary work in relation to other works by the same or another author.

3. **Biographical analysis.** Consider the literary work in relation to one or more aspects of its author's biography.

4. **Theoretical analysis.** Consider the literary work in relation to a particular theory of literature.

5. **Artifact analysis.** Consider the literary work in relation to the historical era in which it was written.

6. **Literary tradition analysis.** Consider the literary work in relation to the tradition of which it is a part.

7. **Literary process analysis.** Consider the literary work as a whole in relation to the parts of which it is composed, and analyze how the parts relate to one another.

8. **Character analysis.** Consider the literary work in relation to the development and interaction of characters. Ask yourself why they behave as they do.

9. **Combinations of the above.**

Regardless of the option you select, you can develop it by using one or more of several methods: definition, comparison, contrast, classification, analysis, and so on. (See Section 5c, pp. 82–89.) Always arrange the ideas that support your topic and thesis in a meaningful sequence. Develop the body of your paper using only your own thoughts, or incorporate appropriate secondary sources into your discussion with proper documentation. Organize your presentation to reflect an analysis (see pp. 87–89) or an argument (see pp. 117–136) in order to show how your thesis contributes to understanding, interpreting, or reacting to a literary work. In your conclusion, restate the main points of your thesis. And always reread your writing to ensure that you do not lose sight of your purpose: to present an exposition or argument that abides by your thesis.

Avoiding plot summary

Bear in mind that you are writing for an audience. Assume that your readers have read the literary work, and avoid using excessive, nonrelevant plot summaries of fiction or paraphrases of poetry in place of genuine analysis or interpretation. Instead of summarizing plot, look for patterns in the behavior, speeches, and actions of the characters or sequences of events that relate to your topic. Note how these and the choices that characters make support your interpretation, and back your ideas up with relevant passages from the primary source. Remember to document such passages accurately.

Presenting the topic

As best you can, incorporate the vocabulary of literary criticism into your paper to be exact. Avoid writing *story* when you mean *narrative, short story, novel,* or *plot.* Avoid referring to a character as "that guy" or "that woman"; instead, name the character. Use the present tense when referring to the author and the literary work.

> **Not** "As Chaucer wrote" **but** "as Chaucer writes"
> **Not** "when Huck addressed Jim" **but** "when Huck addresses Jim"

When writing your first references to an author, use her or his full name: Katherine Ann Porter. In subsequent references use only the author's surname: Porter, without any titles such as Ms., Mr., or Dr.

Enclose the titles of short stories, essays, and shorter poems in quotation marks (for example, "Noon Wine," "A Modest Proposal," "Stopping by Woods"). See Section 35d. Underline the titles of novels, dramas, nonfiction books, and longer poems to indicate italics (for example, Tom Jones, Death of a Salesman, The Idea of a University, and Beowulf). See Chapter 37.

Accurately refer to subdivisions in literary works by using specific references instead of phrases like "the place where." Specifically refer to "Chapter 7" or "the third stanza." Refer to subdivisions in drama in this order: act number, scene number, and line number (if the latter two exist) separated by periods; for example, "The last sound heard in *The Cherry Orchard* is that of an ax against a tree" (4) and "In despair, King Lear tore off his clothes" (3.4.115).

When quoting from literary texts, always check your accuracy. See Sections 35a and 35b, pp. 373–376, on formatting direct and block quotations.

Select a title for your essay that relates to the content of the paper. In your introduction include the name of the literary work, its date, the author, your thesis, the necessary background material relating to your thesis, and your approach to the topic. (See the sample literary paper on p. 558.)

Follow the MLA documentation style (see Chapter 50, pp. 474–490) when writing and documenting your essay unless your instructor expects another format. As in all writing, carefully document all quotations, paraphrases, and summaries (see pp. 457–462) to properly acknowledge all primary and secondary sources and to avoid plagiarism (see Section 49f, pp. 469–473).

53b Sample Literary Analysis

Following is an essay about a work of literature that Jennifer Neidenbach wrote for a composition course. Jennifer arrived at her topic after a class discussion of the novel *Emma* by Jane Austen. From her careful reading of the novel, Jennifer knew that marriage played an important part in the novel. When Jennifer learned that Austen herself had never married, and that in her time an unmarried woman was both socially and economically disadvantaged, Jennifer wondered if Austen's own experience might have affected the portrayal of unmarried women in the novel. After doing some prewriting, Jennifer concluded that Austen did indeed portray unmarried women with deliberate sympathy, describing them as unfortunate victims of the existing social order. To develop her essay she used character analysis and devoted a paragraph to each of the main unmarried female characters to show how Austen used each woman's individual misfortunes to create a composite portrait of the unmarried woman's plight. Jennifer's analysis includes her own reactions and interpretations as well as evidence from secondary sources to support her thesis:

> Jane Austen sympathetically illustrates both the social role and the individual persona of the spinster through the characters of Emma Woodhouse, Harriet Smith, Jane Fairfax, and Miss Bates.

Note that Jennifer uses the MLA style format in her paper and that the essay has been annotated to show how her analysis develops and how she uses primary and secondary sources as support for her interpretation of the novel.

Neidenbach 1

Student
identification

Jennifer M. Neidenbach

English 103

Professor F. Augustus

14 March 1992

Title

Thesis: An
interpretation

Secondary
source

Emma and the Plight of the Spinster

In her 1815 novel Emma, Jane Austen
sympathetically illustrates both the social role
and the individual persona of the spinster through
the characters of Emma Woodhouse, Harriet
Smith, Jane Fairfax, and Miss Bates. Austen first
examines the social role as dictated by essays,
sermons, and other popular conduct literature of
the eighteenth century written by male authors,
which demanded that women serve only as wife
and mother and labeled women who deviated
from that role as meddling "spinsters." Yet
Austen also demonstrates that these social roles
created an individual persona within each
character, resulting in empowerment in the
private world of women and the relinquishment of
that power in the public world of men. "The
Austenian heroine, like Austen herself, must
exercise extra-ordinary ingenuity to keep her
autonomous selfhood intact" (Litvak 763).

Neidenbach 2

Background
information

Essays and sermons designed to teach the reader proper social behavior grew in popularity in England during the eighteenth century. According to this popular conduct literature, the woman's province is the home, where she dedicates herself to the duties of wife and mother. Most people agreed with moralist

Secondary
source

Wetenhall Wilkes that spinsterhood "is an affliction too severe for any of the fair sex, because in these kingdoms it is a kind of imputed scandal" (Jones 33-34): not only was the unmarried woman unable to fulfill the roles of wife and mother, she imposed an economic burden upon the male members of her family. The spinster also endured criticism from conduct book writers and felt the barbs of the satirists, but some writers such as Jane Austen treated the unmarried woman with compassion.

Analysis of
Emma

Emma Woodhouse, whom we know to be "handsome, clever, and rich, with a comfortable home and a happy disposition" (Austen 3), could easily find a husband. But instead she declares without any hesitation: "I am not only not going to be married at present, but I have no intention

Primary
source

of ever marrying at all" (Austen 75). But, when Harriet Smith expresses concern that her friend

Neidenbach 3

"will be an old maid—and that is so dreadful!"
Emma reassures her.

Lengthy quote
from primary
source

> Never mind, Harriet, I shall not be a poor
> old maid; and it is poverty only which
> makes celibacy contemptible to a
> generous public! A single woman
> with a very narrow income must be a
> ridiculous, disagreeable old maid!
> [sic] the proper sport of boys and
> girls; but a single woman of good
> fortune is always respectable, and
> may be as sensible and pleasant as
> anybody else! (Austen 76)

Emma believes that her wealth will enable her to
live independently and that her status as the
daughter of the wealthiest man in the village of
Highbury will protect her from the scorn usually
accorded to spinsters. Emma also does not
impudently plan to reject or avoid the domestic
sphere, for she intends to remain unmarried in
order to care for her agoraphobic, hypochondriac

Primary
source

father. And as she tells Harriet, "I believe few
married women are half as much mistress of
their husband's household as I am of Hartfield;
and never, never could I expect to be so truly
beloved and important; so always first and

Neidenbach 4

always right in any man's eyes as I am in my
father's" (Austen 76). By being economically
independent but still within the woman's
traditional domestic province, an unmarried
Emma Woodhouse will avoid the contempt of
society, the typical plight of the spinster, thereby
redefining the concept of womanhood in her day.

Secondary source

This point is underscored by James Edward
Austen-Leigh's comment in his Memoir of Jane
Austen that the novelist "created in Emma a
heroine whom she suspected no one but herself
would like" (qtd. in Gilbert and Gubar 158).

Character analysis of Harriet

Emma's fortunate situation far surpasses that
of the other spinsters in the village, for they lack
the education or wealth necessary for achieving
some sort of security for themselves. Her friend
Harriet Smith lacks both, and, although Emma
schemes to find Harriet a good husband among
the gentry, Harriet's sweet temperament, beauty,

Primary source

and "proper and becoming deference" (Austen 19)
cannot make up for her ignorance, poverty, and
illegitimacy. Perhaps most readers cannot help
but sympathize with the unfortunate girl,
especially when Harriet foolishly, albeit
reluctantly, rejects the worthy suitor she truly
loves in order to pursue Emma's ambitious

Writing in the Humanities and About Literature

Neidenbach 5

advice and retain her friendship. With Emma's
encouragement Harriet unwisely ventures beyond
her class, because the wealthy gentlemen of
Emma's acquaintance will surely dismiss Harriet as
unmarriageable, just as Mr. Elton does. What this
action suggests is that both women believed it is
indeed proper to enter into a marriage that crosses
socio-economic lines, so proper that Harriet would
not risk losing Emma's friendship. But social mores
prevented Harriet from taking a commanding role.
Emma, on the other hand, feels no such
constraints in selecting a husband for Harriet.

Character
analysis of
Jane

Primary
source

Socio-economic considerations also affect Jane
Fairfax, as talented as Harriet is awkward, but
sharing Harriet's impoverished condition. Even
though Jane is intelligent, beautiful, educated,
elegant—in short, as Mr. Knightley suggests, "the
really accomplished young woman which she
[Emma] wanted to be thought herself" (Austen
144-45)—she will also share Harriet's spinster fate,
for the orphaned Jane has no money to provide a
dowry. Accordingly, her foster parents provide
her with the best education available to a
woman, well aware that one day Jane will have
to support herself by taking a position as a
governess. With no other alternative, Jane

Neidenbach 6

anguishes over her future, certain that she will
soon be banished from the elegant, comfortable
world of her childhood and be forever separated
from her gentry-class lover, thus being punished
for her audacity in rejecting socially defined
behavior.

Character
analysis of
Miss Bates

Harriet, Jane, and even Emma thereby
subscribe to the unattractive stereotype that they
might become like Miss Bates, who "is neither
young, handsome, rich, nor married," has "no
intellectual superiority to make atonement to
herself, or frighten those who hate her into

Primary
source

outward respect" (Austen 17). Emma treats the
unlucky woman with disturbing harshness, but
this behavior misleads both the readers who
accept her attacks on unmarried women at face
value as well as those who object to her
apparent cruelty. As Alison Sulloway explains,

> Austen loved to exploit the literary
> device of the court fool or the villain
> who tells a variety of unpleasant truths
> that conventional people would rather

Secondary
source

> not hear. Emma is ungenerously
> indulging herself in the national sport of
> spinster-baiting, partly to distance
> herself from economically and socially

Neidenbach 7

> deprived spinsters such as Jane Fairfax,
> Harriet Smith, and Miss Bates, and the
> little crowd of lonely female hangers-on
> who keep Mr. Woodhouse amused. But
> Emma is a ruthless truth-teller: she has
> identified poverty and social humiliation
> as a feminist issue, as it was for her
> creator, but not for her. (Sulloway 21)

Though caricature distorts much of Emma's
portrait, Miss Bates' difficulties indicate just how
anxious and lonely an unmarried woman's life
could become. Austen's sympathetic treatment of
unmarried women as victims of the existing
social order is set against that ironic view of
them as suitable targets of derisive laughter.

Conclusion

     The rich and undisciplined Emma finally
marries Mr. Knightley, the benevolent authoritarian,
but, as Austen suggests with apprehensive irony,
he plans to direct her along the course of a
proper conduct book wife. Austen ultimately
demonstrates that women can deviate from social
roles only in their relationships with other
women. In the patriarchal world women must
return their newly acquired power to men.
Emma, Jane, and Harriet are "rescued" in time

for a happy ending—not by resolutely asserting
their independence and denouncing society's
treatment of the spinster, unfortunately, but by
making dignified marriages that would please
even the most solemn conduct book writer and
re-enforcing the stereotype by being driven by it.
Harriet happily weds the young farmer who
adores her, and the intelligent Jane, as if in
recognition of her abilities and in recompense for
her suffering, wins the most wealthy man in the
novel. These women escape the spinster's fate
and enter new lives largely determined by their
educational and economic resources. However,
Susan Kneedler points out, "Austen's books teach
that traditional ends like marriage will not solve
the problems women face (928A). Austen did not
see marriage as the solution to every problem in
a woman's life, for as a wife she must be subject
to her husband's rule. Miss Bates, like the
creator of these women, remains unmarried and
in uncertain financial straits. Austen, then,
portrays both the social role and the individuality
of the four women in the novel with sympathy
and understanding.

Reference to
thesis

Neidenbach 9

Works Cited

Primary source

Austen, Jane. Emma. New York: Heritage Press, 1964.

Secondary sources

Gilbert, Sandra M., and Susan Gubar. The Madwoman in the Attic: The Woman Writer and the Nineteenth-Century Literary Imagination. New Haven: Yale UP, 1984.

Jones, Vivien, ed. Women in the Eighteenth Century. London: Routledge, Chapman, and Hall, 1990.

Kneedler, Susan. "Feminist Hope in the Novels of Jane Austen." DAI 40 (1987):928A. U of Southern California.

Litvak, Joseph. "Reading Characters: Self, Society, and Text in Emma." PMLA 100 (1985):763-73.

Sulloway, Alison G. Jane Austen and the Province of Womanhood. Philadelphia: U of Pennsylvania P, 1989.

54 Writing in the Social, Natural, and Applied Sciences

54a Writing in the Social Sciences

Disciplines in the social sciences include anthropology, economics, government, political science, psychology, sociology, and social services, and their focus is often group behavior. Writing in the social sciences can cover, for example, the causes and effects of diverse social phenomena, the values and traditions shared by different social groups, and hypotheses and theories that explain particular types of behaviors in population groups. Research in the social sciences is ongoing. Social scientists react to new theories by carefully examining the **data bases** (the raw material on which a theory is based, such as a tally of city dwellers' preferences for waste disposal) and the **methodologies** used to obtain the data (for example, interviews or mail-in questionnaires) in order to judge the validity of the results. Other social scientists study how these new theories alter or advance previous research. Social scientists rely on either quantitative or qualitative data. **Quantitative data** are statistical or numerical measures—the results of surveys, tests, or experiments. **Qualitative data** are descriptive rather than numerical and include interviews, oral histories, and descriptions of people, their cultures, and their experiences. Writing in the social sciences tends to be objective, based on fact and observation, rather than subjective, based on personal impressions, emotions, and reactions, and it takes the form of field research reports, summaries, reviews of research, case analysis, or research papers.

The field research report

One of the most commonly used types of writing in the social sciences is the **field research report.** This type of report involves observing human behavior or obtaining information on attitudes or opinions, which then serve as data bases. You may find it helpful to consider your field research report as an exercise in problem solving. You may seek a solution, for example, to the problem of New Jersey's waste disposal now that the Midwestern states are refusing to accept its garbage because of a landfill shortage. The information you gather through various methods, such as questionnaires or interviews (see pp. 447–448), leads you to some sort of solution. Writing a field research report often involves the use of statistical data in table or chart form or as figures. As in most scientific writing, writing field research reports requires objectivity. Before you begin your field research, you will find it helpful to plan specifically how you will obtain the data you need (a *methodology*) and the order in which you will seek it (*random* or in a *planned sequence*).

Each part of your report, other than the title, consists of complete sentences; is subject to the processes of prewriting, revision, and proofing; and has a thesis, topic sentences, and a recognizable developmental pattern. The field research report contains the following parts.

- **Title.** The title consists of a descriptive phrase, preferably short, that summarizes the purpose or results of the report. Humorous titles are considered inappropriate.
- **Running head.** The running head is an abbreviated title that is typed in the upper right corner of each page of the paper or report, including the title page. (See the model APA paper, p. 525.) The student authors of the report "Would You Choose this College Again?" (p. 570) might use "College Choice" as their running head.

- **Abstract.** The abstract is a brief summary of 100 to 150 words that provides an overview of the problem investigated, the method used, and the results.

- **Introduction.** In the introduction you report why you did this particular research (the problem), explain why you consider it important, and offer any background information necessary for understanding the problem. What results did you *expect* to obtain? Many introductions contain references to source materials used to define a problem and provide a rationale for conducting the research.

- **Methodology.** In the methodology section you report how you gathered the data. Examples of your methodology, such as a questionnaire or a copy of your interview questions, should appear in an appendix. Identify the number of participants and note their age, sex, race, religion, socio-economics, and other appropriate identifying characteristics. Also list any other sources consulted such as computer data banks, census bureau figures, and printed sources. If you use a computer in tallying your results, identify the software and hardware.

- **Results.** The expression of your results (the solution to the problem) will usually be a mixture of prose and statistical information accompanied by tables and figures. But do not allow the statistical information to become an end in itself. What is its significance? What exactly did you discover? The answers separate the results from raw data.

- **Conclusions.** In the conclusion, provide *your* own interpretation of the results. If you incorporate or compare and contrast other studies with your results, be certain to provide accurate citations.

- **Appendices.** The appendices are the support and documentation for your methodology. Begin each appendix on a new page and head it "Appendix." Use identifying capital letters, as in "Appendix A," "B," or "C," if you include more than one appendix. Double space the text.

■ **References.** See the section on documentation that follows.

Documenting your field research report

Most writers in the social sciences use the APA documentation style covered in Chapter 51 or the *Chicago Manual of Style* (see p. 504). Document all methodology used, including computer software programs and any printed or nonprint sources that you quote, summarize, or paraphrase. Do this both in-text (see pp. 493–499) and in your list of references (see pp. 499–501). Finally, be careful to avoid plagiarism (Section 49f); check the accuracy and format of each of your citations.

See Chapter 52, pp. 524–545, for a sample research paper in APA style for a social science course. Following is the introduction to a field research report that two students, working as a team, wrote for an introductory sociology course.

Would You Choose This College Again?

Introduction

In April, 1992, 512 students participated in a survey designed and administered by the authors and mailed to all graduating seniors. Our purpose was to ascertain how many of these graduating students would or would not select this college again in light of the experience and knowledge they now possess. Our survey covered three main areas in the undergraduate experience: (1) relationship to one's major department of study (availability of desired courses, quality of teaching, accessibility of faculty, responsiveness of departmental administration, quality of the writing courses in this department); (2) support services (library holdings, hours, and quality of service; availability of computer services, bookstore, placement office, housing office, and financial aid office); and (3) extracurricular activities (cultural and recreational).

Of our respondents, 51.8% received the Bachelor of Arts degree and 44.6% the Bachelor of Science degree. Sixty-five percent of the respondents were men, 33% women. Only 3% of the total were married. In terms of ethnic diversity, 3% were Asian-American, 7% Hispanic, 14% African-American, and 76% other. Eighty-eight percent of responding students received financial aid from sources as follows: 45% partial tuition scholarships, 21% student-work assistantships, and 50% guaranteed loans. A number of students received financial support from more than one source.

We anticipated that a very high percentage of students, 90% or more, would select this college again. Our expectations were too optimistic.

54b Writing in the Natural Sciences

Disciplines in the natural sciences include biology, the health professions, chemistry, earth sciences, mathematics, and physics. Writing in these areas will be concerned with the natural world, particularly the causes and effects of natural phenomena, and related laboratory experiments. Researchers in the natural sciences follow the **scientific method:** (1) formulating a **hypothesis,** which is an initial attempt to explain phenomena; (2) presenting information, including previously published research, to support the hypothesis; (3) planning the investigation or experiment; (4) performing the experiment, carefully observing and recording the procedures and results; and (5) analyzing the results and providing conclusions that may or may not support the hypothesis. Scientists use only **empirical evidence,** or objective data, to support the hypothesis, and this evidence, gathered from observing natural events, is quantitative (based on numbers and statistics) rather than qualitative (based on subjective data such as ideas and emotions). Successful scientific writing is also based on empirical validation (another scientist, using the same materials and methodologies, should be able to achieve your results).

Lab reports

The **lab report** is the most common type of writing students do in the natural sciences. Lab reports are written after you complete an experiment or project and document not only your results but also the procedure leading to your results. You will, then, need to keep careful notes in a lab notebook. This notebook is very important. If you overlook something while taking the notes, you may have to redo the experiment. The notes will serve as the raw material from which you fashion the lab report. When preparing the lab report, write preliminary and final drafts for each part of the report. Be sure that the report is well written and that you proofread all parts. As much as possible, try to avoid using the passive voice (see p. 167).

When formatting the lab report, label all parts and use complete sentences except for the title. Each part of the report should have a recognizable organization and include a topic sentence and a developmental pattern. Process analysis and cause and effect analysis are most common (see Section 5c). The standard parts of a lab report are as follows.

- **Abstract.** The abstract should not exceed 250 words in length and should be composed of complete sentences. It summarizes the purpose of the report, the nature of the experiment, and the results.
- **Title.** The title usually consists of one or a few words that are related to the experiment. Humor in the title is inappropriate.
- **Introduction.** The introduction provides the background information (a summary of previous research on the problem), introduces the hypothesis or problem that the experiment addresses, and states what is relevant about the problem as well the objectives of the experiment. The introduction should also explain the experiment's organization.
- **Methods and materials.** The methods and materials section provides the theory which underlies the solution to the problem and then enumerates all the steps followed in the experiment. It includes a list of the apparatus and materials used, employing graphics and details of assembly, as appropriate. If you used computer programs, present detailed information on the software and hardware. You must present the steps of the experiment in the proper order; a flowchart may be required by your instructor.

- **Results.** In the results section you will record and discuss the results of your experiment. Since the results serve as the solution to the problem, be certain to discuss their significance. If any discrepancies occurred during the experiment, you must report and, if possible, account for them.
- **References cited.** See the documentation section that follows.

Documenting your lab report

Some scientists use the style and documentation formats specifically designed for their disciplines (see pp. 502–504 for a listing of style manuals for use in the sciences). Others use the APA format, which is explained in Chapter 51. Ask your instructor which is preferred. The format will determine what to name the final part of your lab report: "References," "Works Cited," or "Bibliography." Here you will list the lab manual and your course textbook, as appropriate, and all journal articles, books, and reference materials you may have consulted. Successful lab reports not only conform to the methodologies of the scientific disciplines but also present accurate, precise documentation. Plagiarism (pp. 469–473) should be avoided through careful documentation. Following are an abstract and portions of the methods and materials section of a lab report.

S. Reike
Chemistry 329
28 April 1993

Gas-Liquid Chromatography

Abstract

In this experiment, the author used gas-liquid chromatography to
evaluate the individual components of a two-component system, a technique
based on the speed with which the individual components move through
the column in the chromatography. A detector evaluates the retention time
and the relative concentrations of each component. Four individual components
were used and the retention times noted. Six two-component systems were
then run and the components determined by matching the retention times
of the individual components with the retention times for the four single
systems; hence, the individual components in the two-component system
could be determined. The components of the six systems studied are

System A:	2 and 3	System D:	did not separate
System B:	did not separate	System E:	2 or 4 and 3
System C:	3 and 2 or 4	System F:	3 and 4

Methods and Materials

In gas-liquid chromatography, one injects a sample into the apparatus
with a microsyringe. I used two microliter samples. The sample was
introduced into an inert mobile phase of helium. The mobile phase carries
the sample to the column which contains the stationary phase. Once the
sample encounters the stationary, it may be retained. Since the sample can
move only in the mobile phase, the amount of time it spends in the two
different phases determines the rate at which the sample moves through
the column. The more time it spends in the mobile phase, the faster it
moves throughout the detector. Mixtures separate based on the different
times they spend in each phase. Once the sample reaches the detector, it
responds according to the concentration of the component. A higher
concentration creates a large area under the corresponding curve.

54c Writing in the Applied Sciences

The applied sciences include all branches of engineering, including aerospace, architectural, biotechnical, chemical, civil, computer science, electrical, marine, petroleum and mining, and pollution control. The type of writing used is called **technical writing.** It includes program reports, proposals, investigative reports, and technical reports.

The technical report

The **technical report** is comprised of data collected, analyzed, and presented in an organized form that responds to the needs of a specific audience. Write the report objectively (using quantitative data such as statistics and numbers) and include visuals such as graphs, charts, maps, and tables that offer support for the conclusions or recommendations presented. Divide your technical report into sections, each beginning on a new page, with the following headings.

- **Title page.** Include a title page that briefly and clearly presents the title of the report, your name, and the date, centered on the page. Humor in a title is inappropriate.
- **Table of contents.** The table of contents functions as the outline for the report and consists of the report's headings and the related page numbers. If you devise any subheadings for your report, indent them.
- **List of tables, charts, figures.** If applicable, present the list of tables (or charts, maps, figures) on a separate page and include in it the captions of the tables and their page numbers. Number the tables consecutively with Arabic numbers: for example "Table 1."
- **Abstract.** The abstract, which should not exceed 250 words, summarizes the nature of the report, the procedures followed, and the results, conclusions, and/or recommendations.

- **Introduction.** The introduction provides an overview of the report and whatever background information the audience may need (a summary of research related to the subject and description of the topic). Explain the purpose, scope, and function of the report, including who commissioned it, if appropriate. Present the plan and organization of the report, define appropriate terminology, and include the materials and methodology used.
- **Body.** In the body include a detailed account of the methodology used, a description of equipment as appropriate, a statement of the results, and your analysis of the results.
- **Conclusion and recommendations.** Your conclusions will describe the results of your project, include recommendations that derive from the evidence, and suggest possible future applications of the project. If you have more than one conclusion, recommendation, or both, list them numerically in order of·importance.
- **References.** See the following documentation section.

Documenting your technical report

All sources and references used in a technical report must be accurately documented with in-text and end-of-text citations. The varying branches in the applied sciences use different documentation styles. The manuals for some of these appear on p. 502; ask your instructor if you are uncertain which style to use. Your report may include appropriately numbered footnotes or endnotes (see Section 51c) and may close with either a bibliography or list of works cited. Check your citations and carefully document your sources to avoid plagiarism (pp. 469–473).

Following is the introduction from a technical report entitled "Computer Implemented 'Concentration'" that a team of four students collaborated on for an electrical engineering course.

Introduction

"Concentration" is a game which tests a person's ability to retain information. Playing the game requires cards similar to a regular deck of playing cards except that symbols or pictures are used instead of numbers. Exactly one pair of cards exists for every different symbol in the deck. At the beginning of a game all the cards are laid out face down. A player's turn consists of trying to match two cards face up. If a player makes a match, he or she claims the two cards and plays again. If no match is made, the next player receives a turn. At the end of the game, the player with the most cards is the winner.

Our team built a computer implementation of the concentration game for two reasons. First, building this particular digital system would provide us with valuable experience in hardware design, system software development, and assembler design. Second, the end result of our efforts would be a game which is both challenging and enjoyable. Specifically, our team's objective was to implement the concentration game on a system memory card inserted into an IBM personal computer (PC). Since the size of the memory card is finite, our goal was to keep the hardware simple. We used the IBM PC monitor to simulate output comparable to the actual card game.

We developed a flowchart for our system code, defined an instruction set, and created a new flowchart that generated the AHPL code, implemented and successfully simulated the AHPL code, and completed the hardware design, which includes four different XILINX chips, the application source code, and the two pass assembler. We then designed the printed circuit board layout for the game.

55 Writing Essay Examinations

An **essay examination** gives you the opportunity to show what you have learned in a course and gives your instructor an effective way to examine your grasp of the material studied. Essay examinations tend to be more demanding than multiple-choice tests because you are called upon to recall information, analyze and evaluate it, and draw up a well-reasoned and well-written essay under time restrictions. Essay tests can be administered in any course of study but are more common in the humanities. Whatever the course, this chapter will help you prepare for and then take essay examinations.

55a Preparing for the Examination

To write a successful essay examination begin by studying. Reread your course notes, textbooks, and any assigned readings. Mark the important points in the texts by underlining or highlighting them. Review all of this material several times until you believe you know it. Try outlining to familiarize yourself with key points. Then try testing yourself by anticipating possible test questions—compare and contrast, analyze, define and exemplify, cause and effect, classify—and then actually write responses. Time yourself and try to simulate realistic examination conditions as best you can. If your instructor is able to provide old examinations, take them. The more practice you get at thinking through the subject matter and writing about it, the better prepared you will be for the actual examination. And, most important: give yourself enough time to prepare. If you can, begin a week before the test; at the very least, three or four days before. Cramming, especially for essay examinations, is rarely effective.

55b Evaluating the Question and Timing Yourself

When writing an essay examination, you must respond to the question asked. The first thing to do, then, is to read the question all the way through to get a general sense of what is being asked. Then read the question again and evaluate it. Underline the key words. Pay particular attention to the verbs, especially such words as *analyze, argue, classify, compare, contrast, defend, describe, develop, evaluate, enumerate, exemplify, explain, identify, judge, justify, list, persuade, refute,* and *trace.* These words will give you clues for organizing your response. For example, on a literature examination you might be asked to "*classify, define,* and *exemplify*" the character types in Katherine Porter's short story "Noon Wine." Will you need to write an argumentative essay or construct a response with some crucial facts? Pay particular attention to the nouns in the question to determine what you are expected to write about (*reason* or *reasons, cause* or *causes*) as well as the adjectives (*main, intermediate, principal, contributing, relevant, succinct*). Keeping these key words in mind will help you write relevant responses. If you're ever unsure about a question, be sure to ask your instructor for clarification.

When evaluating examination questions, think about how much you will need to write. After you have determined what you are expected to write in the examination, plan how much time to devote to the process of writing the response. Many college examinations require you to respond to more than one essay question. Timing yourself, then, becomes very important to ensure enough time to answer all questions fully. How much total time is to be devoted to the question: a full class period or twenty-five minutes? An incomplete essay response due to your running out of time is rarely given full credit no matter how accurate or well written it is. Remember to bring a watch to the examination, and use it to pace yourself. Try to allow some time for prewriting and drafting to help you generate and organize ideas. Also allot time for revision and editing.

For example, if you have twenty minutes, you might allow five minutes for prewriting, twelve for producing a draft, and three for editing and proofing.

55c Deciding on a Response Strategy

Essay examination responses can be classified as objective, subjective, or a blend of the two, depending on the question asked. When you write an objective response you present factual data that can be verified. When you write a subjective response you interpret or react to something. But subjective responses do not give you total liberty to write whatever comes into your mind; you respond to the question asked. Careful evaluation of the question will indicate whether an objective, subjective, or combined response strategy is best. For example, a question that reads "list the main causes for X" will require an objective strategy; "explain the effects of the causes of X on Y" will call for a subjective strategy; and "list, classify, and explain the effects of X on Y" will call for a combination objective/subjective strategy.

55d Planning and Prewriting

To write a final draft that is clear and logical, do some planning and prewriting before you actually begin writing your response. Make notations or draw up a scratch outline on the inside cover of the examination booklet, on a separate sheet of paper, or in the margins. As you jot down ideas, ask yourself these questions: What is my thesis? What will my main points be? How will I organize them? What type of supporting examples or information will I use? How will I begin? Which patterns of paragraph development will best suit the response I have planned? How will I conclude the essay? Sketching out a blueprint of your response is a useful tactic.

55e Drafting Your Response

Having done some prewriting, look for logical relationships in the material, and draw arrows or make other notations to impose order. Write a first draft if time permits; otherwise, proceed with the final draft. Be sure to state your thesis at the outset and to support it with examples and other information. Essay examination responses are often analytical and subjective in nature, but you should incorporate appropriate objective data into your response as relevant: dates, accurate citation of lines of poetry, or excerpts from well-known writings or speeches. After all, your examination response should show your instructor that you know your topic. But your essay response should not be a hodgepodge of facts. Strive to achieve an appropriate blend of analysis and fact. Also, be sure to check the logic of your response. Does the essay support your thesis? Did you avoid digressions? Are transitions used effectively? Refer back to your outline or prewriting to keep yourself on track. Also, read your response as you go along. Check each paragraph. Is there a topic sentence? Does everything within the paragraph flow logically? Are you answering the question effectively? Try to evaluate your response as you write it.

55f Revising

Although it is a good idea to read and evaluate your response as you write, you will certainly want to allow yourself some time to proofread the final copy of your response before you turn it in. Is your prose clear and precise? Is it grammatically and mechanically correct? Have you responded to the question asked? Essay responses filled with fragments, spelling errors, punctuation errors, illogical sequencing, faulty evidence, and digressions to do not impress readers. Admittedly, instructors are aware that writing under time constraints produces anxieties and that your prose may not be as polished as it is in papers that are written more leisurely. However, do take time to revise. To make this process easier, skip lines between sentences, so that you have room to make changes. If your instructor will allow it, write your essay in pencil so that you can erase. This way your revisions will be neater.

55g Sample Essay Examination Response

Following are an essay examination question for an abnormal psychology course and the student's effective response.

Question
Discuss the behaviors which indicate that a person is an alcoholic (30 minutes).

Response
See student response on p. 584.

STUDENT RESPONSE

Thesis responds to the question

A person who is alcohol-dependent will be subject to varying behaviors which act alone and in combinations to signal departures from the norm. These include difficulties with personal relationships (complaints from spouse and children or friends about drinking), with employment (frequent absenteeism due to hangovers), with the law (more than one DUI offense), with social situations (isolating oneself in order to drink), and with spirituality (turning further away from God and more to drinking for strength).

Types and examples of behavior

Other types of behavior and examples act as supporting evidence

These specified behaviors accompany other types of behavior which become routine to the alcohol-addicted person. The addict is often preoccupied with the thought of drinking and has regularized the time of day at which drinking begins, a time which is approached with anticipation and oftentimes anxiety. Once drinking, many addicts undergo personality changes: the mild-mannered suddenly become loud and boisterous. Blackouts, not to be confused with fainting spells or deep sleep, occur more frequently. These are periods of memory lapse when the drinker does not remember where or when or other circumstances surrounding the drinking and constitute a middle stage of the affliction.

Conclusion—note reference back to thesis

Denial is the behavioral defense mechanism the addict uses when confronted with any of the behavioral patterns of his or her drinking. Any of these behaviors, singly or in combination, are indications that a person is or might become alcohol-dependent.

STRATEGIES FOR TAKING ESSAY EXAMINATIONS

1. Begin preparing for the examination in advance.
2. Study by rereading your texts and class notes.
3. Anticipate possible exam questions and practice writing responses.
4. At the test, read the question carefully and evaluate it. Underline the key words to determine what you are being asked to do.
5. Note your time limitations. Allot time for prewriting, drafting, proofing, and editing. Bring a watch to the test so that you can pace yourself.
6. Decide upon your response strategy. Do some planning and prewriting, and begin drafting your response once you have an idea of what you want to say.
7. Proofread the essay before turning it in. Check your thesis, supporting evidence, grammar, and punctuation.
8. Good luck!

EXERCISE 55-1

Evaluate the preceding essay response. React to the thesis. How is it supported? What patterns of development are used? Circle all transition words. Would you organize your response differently?

56   **Writing for Business**

Like all good writing, business writing should be clear, concise, and correct. In addition, writers in a business setting must meet certain conventions of form, record information accurately for later referral (sometimes with legal implications), and pay special attention to the needs of their readers.

56a The Memo

The most common form of communication in business is the memo. A **memo** addresses one or many readers within an organization or company. It is generally short (no more than a page or two), focuses on a single topic, is clearly directed to its audience, and, to a noticeable degree, follows conventions or formulas in form and content. A memo can be sent on paper or electronically through mail systems that link company offices.

The parts of a memo

The memo has two parts: heading and message. The memo **heading** is often printed on company memo sheets and looks something like this:

Date:

To:

From:

Subject:

The writer fills in these elements to record vital information for the file and to inform the reader directly about the message to come.

In writing the **message,** the memo writer focuses on a single topic. Short paragraphs and company abbreviations that are clear to readers are used. For example, the abbreviations for Emergency Services (ES) and Intensive Care Unit (ICU) are used in the following sample memo. Important information is highlighted in headings and lists, and these items are kept parallel. Further, drawings and diagrams often accompany the memo to support its purpose and message and to avoid lengthy discussion. The sample in the following section is a good example of a typical business memo.

Sample memo

Date: 23 March 1993

To: All Employees, Emergency Services

From: Demetrius Jones

             Director, Patient Services

Subject: New Procedure for Patient Admission to ICU

Effective April 15, new procedures will be implemented in the Patient Records Office to ensure that patient admissions from ES to ICU will be handled quickly.

After that date, ES personnel must complete the new Form ES-27 for any patient transferred to ICU. A copy of this form should be sent to ICU and to Patient Records.

All ES employees are asked to cooperate with this new procedure. Address any questions to me at ext. 8887.

cc: Patient Records Office

56b The Business Letter

A **business letter** is appropriate when you write to an organization or when you write on behalf of an organization to customers or clients. The letter is more formal than the memo and thus also may be used for recording important matters of policy or confidential personnel decisions within an organization.

Business letter formats

Business letters generally follow one of three formats: the block format, a modified block format (sometimes with indented paragraphs), and a simplified format. Check with your company to see which format is preferred. Each format is shown in a model business letter on pp. 593–596.

If you use a typewriter or computer, type or print the business letter on 8 1/2" x 11" white or off-white bond paper (erasable paper is not popular because it tends to smudge). Center the text vertically on the paper and use wide margins. The text of the letter must be neat: messy erasures, cross-outs, and ink corrections are unacceptable. Single space each part of the business letter and double space between parts.

The parts of a business letter

A typical business letter has these parts: heading, inside address, salutation, subject line, body, closing, notations, and an addressed envelope in which the letter is mailed. Your computer program may be able to help you format these parts automatically.

Heading

The **heading** includes the sender's address and the date of the letter. If you use letterhead stationery, you need only note the date. Otherwise, write your address (*without* your name).

Inside address

The **inside address** is simply the name and address of the reader to whom the letter will be sent. Readers are often pleased to be identified by their names, so when you write your job application letters, try to use the *names* of the persons responsible for new employee hirings. If you are unable to obtain the reader's name, then address the appropriate office or person by job title. For example:

Personnel Department

Director of Personnel

Customer Service

Write out the full name of the company—do not abbreviate. Spell all names correctly; if you are unsure of a spelling, check it. Do not guess.

Salutation

The conventional salutation, or greeting, is "Dear [Mr./Ms.] Last name:" (the formal greeting ends with a colon). If you are unsure of the gender of the reader—for example, if you are responding to a letter signed "S. H. Assad"—then write "Dear S. H. Assad." However, when gender is unknown or you are not writing to a particular individual, you may use "Dear Sir or Madam" or the name of the company, "Dear Major

Corporation." Another option is to omit the salutation entirely, as is frequently done in the simplified letter format (see p. 595).

Subject line

Although subject lines are common in memos, they are used less often in business letters. They may occasionally be seen in sequential letters about a project or in routine correspondence concerning orders and responses to orders. Subject lines such as the following also appear in sales letters:

YOU MAY HAVE ALREADY WON!

Body

The **body** of the letter conveys your message and should be brief and arranged in relatively short paragraphs for easy reading. The text is single spaced with double spacing between paragraphs. Begin the first sentence of each paragraph at the left margin if you are using the block format (see the sample letter on pp. 593-594). If instead you are using the modified block format, use indented paragraphs with the first sentence of each paragraph indented five spaces (see p. 595). Conclude the body with an action statement or a request for information, depending upon your intent. (See the model on p. 594.)

Closing

The **closing** consists of the complimentary close and the writer's signature. The most common closing phrases are "Sincerely," "Sincerely yours," and "Yours truly." The phrase "Respectfully yours" shows a bit more deference and respect, whereas "Cordially" and "Best regards" are more informal. Note that the second word in a complimentary close is not capitalized and that the entire closing phrase is followed by a comma. Type your name about four spaces below the complimentary close, leaving enough space for your signature (see pp. 594 and 595 for samples of two closings). You may also type the company name, your job title, or both below your typed name. And although you type your full name, you may sign your letter with a nickname if your relationship with the reader warrants it.

In the simplified format, the closing is omitted if you have also omitted the salutation (see the sample letter of complaint in the simplified block format on p. 596). In the modified block format, the closing is indented (see p. 595), whereas in the block format it is positioned at the left margin (see p. 594).

Notations

Beneath the closing and flush with the left margin you may include **notations,** such as "Enclosures" (sometimes abbreviated "enc." or "encl.") to direct the reader to items enclosed with the letter. Typing "EAK:fb" indicates the initials of the writer (EAK) and typist or secretary (fb), and adding "cc:" (concurrent copy) notes circulation of copies (*pc*: for photocopy) followed by the names of the recipients of the copies.

Envelope

Type your name and address in block form in the upper left corner of the envelope, unless of course the return address is already printed there. The recipient's name and address should be typed in block form exactly as they appear in the letter beginning at the middle of the envelope, as shown.

Sample business letter envelope

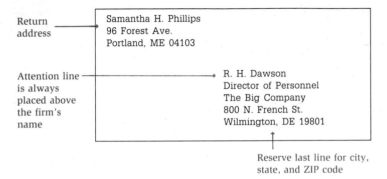

Return address → Samantha H. Phillips
96 Forest Ave.
Portland, ME 04103

Attention line is always placed above the firm's name → R. H. Dawson
Director of Personnel
The Big Company
800 N. French St.
Wilmington, DE 19801

Reserve last line for city, state, and ZIP code

Writing the business letter

As you write a business letter, imagine that you are the letter's reader. What would you as the reader need to know? How would you react to the letter?

When you write a letter to complain or to claim an adjustment for some error in service or in a faulty product, think about the remedy you seek and about the information the reader will need to meet your claim. Present yourself as someone credible, rational, deserving of the requested adjustment. Do not attack the reader. Announce your claim and then provide a narrative of the error. For a product, include such information as the product's name, model, serial number, and warranty information. Describe the requested action (e.g., specify whether you are requesting a refund, repair, or replacement). The model letter on p. 595 requests information. Note how the letter encourages a response through its specific questions and pleasant tone. A response letter in any situation should be written with the request in hand.

Sample business letters

Job application letter in block format

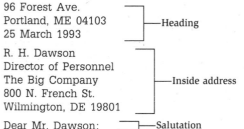

96 Forest Ave.
Portland, ME 04103
25 March 1993 ─── Heading

R. H. Dawson
Director of Personnel
The Big Company ─── Inside address
800 N. French St.
Wilmington, DE 19801

Dear Mr. Dawson: ─── Salutation

Single-spaced text

Paragraphs are not indented

From both Professor Lucia Gomez at the University of Southern Maine and your advertisement in the 15 March issue of the Wilmington News Journal, I have learned of your opening for an entry-level accountant. I am writing to apply for that position.

As my resume shows, I will receive a degree in accounting in June. My course work has concentrated on the financial management of large multinationals like The Big Company. Each course required extensive case analyses and practical problem solving. My high grade point average indicates my strengths in those skills necessary to do well in your position.

─── Body

In addition, through my work with POM Recoveries and the Publisher's Clearing House, I have gained experience in the day-to-day operation of a small and a large operation. For much of my work I was given an assignment that I completed largely on my own. I also learned and demonstrated skills with computerized accounting systems. Thus, I am confident that I can be the "knowledgeable self-starter" your advertisement seeks. A position with The Big Company especially interests me because of your recent acquisition of Steitman AG and the potential for learning about

German accounting practices as I apply my knowledge of the German language and culture.

[Double space between paragraphs]

I will be visiting Delaware during my spring break, 17-22 April, and will gladly meet with you any time during that period for an interview. If these dates are not suitable, please let me know and I'll make other arrangements for a time convenient to The Big Company.

I look forward to talking with you.

Sincerely,

S. Phillips ———Closing

Samantha H. Phillips

Enc. ☐—Notation

Letter requesting information in modified block format

Notice how the writer of this sample letter requests information, provides as much specific detail as possible, and ends the body of the letter with a summary request for information.

> 1111 Carriage House Drive, Apt. 27
> Tallahassee, FL 32306
> September 14, 1993

Indented heading

Angelo Piscatelli
Department of Entomology
Florida State University
Tallahassee, FL 32306

Dear Professor Piscatelli:

I saw a strange-looking insect in my garden yesterday. It was slender but large for an insect—about an inch long. It was a rather violent green, had greenish gossamer wings, and a tiny head with prominent black eyes. It appeared to be able to turn its head in a complete circle. As I watched the creature, it rose on its hind legs and folded its front legs. Could you identify it from this description?

Paragraphs indented 5 spaces

1. What is the name of the insect?
2. Is it destructive to plants?
3. If so, which plants?
4. What kind of spray should I use to destroy it, if necessary?

I would appreciate any information you can send me.

Sincerely yours,

Indented closing lined up with heading

Harvey Bergman

Harvey Bergman

Letter of complaint in the simplified format

Box 101D
Obden, PA 18102
May 18, 1993

Customer Service
Get Mugged, Inc.
12 Washington Lane
Chrystal Keys, MA 02161 ← Salutation omitted

I am writing about a problem with a recent order.

On May 1, I ordered 6 "Bunnies in Heaven" mugs from your catalog. The stock number is 45-66-77; the mugs appeared on page 10 of the catalog. On May 15, I received a package from you marked "1/2 dozen bunnies in heaven"; it contained, however, a combination of bunny mugs and "Moose in Maine" mugs. Moreover, the count was inaccurate. The case contained a total of 8 mugs: 4 bunnies and 4 moose.

In accordance with your guarantee, I am returning the moose mugs from the improperly packaged case to you. Please reimburse me for the postage costs and send me two more "Bunnies in Heaven" mugs. Thank you.

Graziella Lopez ← Closing phrase omitted

Graziella Lopez

56c Facsimile Transaction

A **facsimile transaction** or **fax** enables you to transmit written documents, photographs, drawings, and the like over telephone lines from a source (the sending machine) to a destination (the receiving machine) within minutes. The speed with which materials can be sent and received accounts for the wide use of faxes in the workplace.

To fax documents, whether memos, letters, or reports, prepare them as you would for mailing. The main difference will be the attachment of a facsimile cover sheet for the first page of the document. This cover sheet will contain important information including the date, the number of pages sent (this total should include your cover sheet), the name, address, and fax number of the recipient and then identical information for you, the sender. The format of cover sheets varies from business to business; for example, some cover sheets include an area for comments or messages, but all should contain the basic information just outlined.

56d The Resume

Your resume presents you as a potential employee. It must be concise, accurate, easy to read, and well designed. And it must be correct.

Start by making an inventory of your skills, education, and relevant experience. Note all of the jobs you have held, including their dates and responsibilities, as well as all paid positions, internships, and volunteer work. Also list major courses, academic achievements, and activities, especially offices held and leadership roles. Then select and arrange this information to provide a profile of yourself. Although the form of the resume may vary to suit individual tastes, most resumes conform to conventions in content and design.

The parts of a resume

The typical resume of a college student contains a stated objective, personal data, educational background, work experience, references, and other miscellaneous information. It is usually accompanied by a letter of application.

Objective

Although not all resumes include a statement of **objective,** some employers look for this indication of your career goal.

The objective can serve as a thesis supported by the evidence that is presented later in the resume. Avoid using a generic statement to cover several objectives. Instead, tailor the objective to be specific enough to state the position you are seeking.

Personal data

The **personal data** should include your name, address (home and school, if different), and phone number.

Educational background

The **education** section should list the schools you have attended since high school, starting with the most recent (reverse chronological order) and including dates of attendance and degrees received or expected. Major and minor fields of study should also be identified.

Work experience

In the **work experience** section you should list the jobs you have held, starting with the most recent. For each job, note the dates of employment, the title of your position, and the name and address of the company. Briefly describe your responsibilities. Avoid full sentences in the description; instead, use fragments beginning with action verbs, as in the model on page 600. Quantify your work wherever possible. Show independent work or a progression of responsibilities if that occurred.

References

Most prospective employers will expect you to provide **references,** the names of people who can vouch for you. You may keep a file of letters of reference at your college placement office; if so, note that on the resume. Because you may wish to select different references for different positions while keeping one resume for several possibilities, and because of a need to save space, you may elect not to name the references directly on the resume. Instead you may write, "References available on request."

Other information

Include mention of scholarships, awards, athletic activities, or other extracurricular participation in drama groups or clubs if you feel such information provides a better view of you as a potential employee. Such information also gives an interviewer a good opener for an interview. It is *your* resume. Just be brief and honest.

Formatting your resume

The format and appearance of your resume are almost as important as its content. The resume should be typed or printed on good-quality 8 1/2" × 11" bond paper and should be limited to one page. Consider preparing your resume on a computer, which allows you to experiment with various formats as well as font types and sizes and the use of boldface and italics for emphasis. Computers can also help you tailor your resume. For example, you can easily devise and insert different specific objective statements to match the different jobs you seek. However, do not get carried away with your options in type fonts. Finally, *proofread* the resume many times. One spelling error may very well send your resume to the reader's wastebasket. The model on page 600 shows one successful resume format.

Sample resume

SAMANTHA H. PHILLIPS

COLLEGE ADDRESS: 96 Forest Avenue
                            Portland, ME 04103
                            (201) 262-1155
                            (until June 1, 1993)

PERMANENT ADDRESS: 210 Waverly St.
                            Jericho, NY 11753
                            (513) 432-9655

OBJECTIVE: A position in internal auditing with a large multinational organization in which I can combine my accounting skills with my knowledge of different language and cultures.

EDUCATION: B. S. in accounting, University of Southern Maine, expected in 1993. Courses in managerial accounting, cost accounting, business law, finance, operations management, marketing. Earned 75% of college expenses.

ACTIVITIES: German Club, intramural soccer, and baseball

PERSONAL: Have traveled widely in the United States and Europe. Willing to relocate.

EMPLOYMENT EXPERIENCE

Summer, 1992   *POM Recoveries,* Syosset, NY. Posted financial statements on a computer.

Spring, 1992   *Publisher's Clearing House,* Port Washington, NY. Sorted checks, processed magazine orders, validated contest entry forms.

Summers, 1990–91   *Camp Thistle,* Rabbit Lake, NY. Organized games, taught swimming, supervised campers.

REFERENCES: Available upon request.

GLOSSARY OF USAGE

The items in this glossary reflect current usage among experienced writers. Use the glossary to check the appropriateness of your word choices.

A, An Use the article *a* before a consonant sound; use *an* before a vowel sound.

a receipt	a history	a one-liner	a unit	a B
an idea	an hour	an officer	an umbrella	an F

Aggravate *Aggravate* means "to make worse." In formal writing, avoid using *aggravate* with its informal meaning of "to annoy, irritate, or vex."

Agree To, Agree With Use *agree* with *to* when you mean "to grant or give approval." Use *agree* with *with* when you mean "to be in harmony," "to conform," or "to hold similar views."

The senator could not **agree to** the amendment.
The senator could not **agree with** his colleague on the need for the amendment.

Ain't In general, avoid this nonstandard contraction in your writing.

All Right Always write *all right* as two words, not as *alright*.

Allusion, Illusion An *allusion* is an indirect or casual reference to something. An *illusion* is a false or misleading perception or concept.

The poem is filled with many **allusions** to the Bible.
Five years in the theater stripped him of his **illusions** about the glamor of an actor's life.

A Lot Always write *a lot* as two words, not as *alot*. In general, avoid using *a lot* in formal writing.

A.M., P.M. *or* **AM, PM** *or* **a.m., p.m.** Use these abbreviations only with figures.

NOT: The lecture ends at eleven in the **A.M.**
BUT: The lecture ends at **11:00 A.M.**

Among, Between Use *among* with three or more people or objects. Use *between* with only two.

According to the will, the funds were to be divided equally **between** the two children.
He decided to leave his entire estate to his eldest son, rather than divide it **among** his six children.

Amount, Number *Amount* refers to mass or quantity. It is followed by the preposition *of* and a singular noun. *Number* refers to things that can be counted. It is followed by *of* and a plural noun.

The **amount** of time he spent completing the job was far greater than the reward he derived from it.
The **number** of domestic animals that have contracted rabies is alarming.

An *See* **a.**

And Etc.   The abbreviation *etc.* means "and other things" or "and so forth." Therefore, *and etc.* is redundant.

Anxious, Eager   *Anxious* means "worried, uneasy, uncertain." In formal writing, do not use *anxious* for *eager*, which means "expectant" or "desirous" but carries no implication of apprehension.

The doctor was **anxious** about her patient's condition.
Since we have heard so many good things about them, we are **eager** to meet our new neighbors.

Anyone, Any One   *Anyone* means "any person at all." It refers indefinitely to any person whatsoever. *Any one* refers to a specific, though unidentified, person or thing within a group. Similar cases are *everyone, every one* and *someone, some one.*

Anyone willing to work hard can get good grades.
Any one of these plans is acceptable.

Anyplace   *Anywhere* is preferred.
Anyways   *Anyway* is preferred.
Anywheres   *Anywhere* is preferred.
Arguement   This word is a variant British spelling of **argument.** *Argument* is the preferred form in the United States.
As   In general, use the stronger and clearer conjunctions *because, since,* and *while.*

NOT: We could no longer see the river from our terrace, **as** the new building blocked our view.
BUT: We could no longer see the river from our terrace **because** the new building blocked our view.

As, Like   *See* **like.**

Assure, Insure, Ensure   Although all three of these words have similar meanings, their usage varies. *Assure* is used in the sense of "to set the mind at ease." *Ensure* and *insure* are not used interchangeably in formal writing; only *insure* is used to mean "to guarantee persons or property against risk."

Awful   In general, use a more specific adjective such as *shocking, ugly, appalling,* or *great.* In formal writing, do not use *awfully* or *awful* as an intensifier meaning "very."

Awhile, A While   *Awhile* is an adverb meaning "for a short time." It is not preceded by the preposition *for.* A *while* is an article plus a noun. It is usually preceded by *for.*

> We asked our guests to stay **awhile.**
> They could stay for **a while** longer.

Bad, Badly   Use the adjective *bad* before nouns and after linking verbs. Use the adverb *badly* to modify verbs or adjectives.

> Several **bad** strawberries were hidden under the good ones.
> The students felt **bad** about the loss.
> The dancer performed **badly.**
> The book was **badly** written.

Being As, Being That   Use the more formal *because* or *since.*

> NOT: **Being as** the sketch was signed, it was valuable.
> BUT: **Because** the sketch was signed, it was valuable.
>
> NOT: **Being that** they needed money badly, they took a second mortgage on their home.
> BUT: **Because** they needed money badly, they took a second mortgage on their home.

Beside, Besides   *Beside* is a preposition that means "next to." When used as a preposition, *besides* means "in addition to" or "except for." When used as an adverb, *besides* means "in addition" or "furthermore."

She was buried **beside** her husband.
Besides mathematics, there are no required courses.
To keep warm, she wore a coat, a hat, and gloves—and a muffler **besides.**

Between   *See* **among.**

Between You and I   A common grammatical mistake. Write *between you and me.* (*You* and *me* are objects of the preposition *between.*)

Bring, Take   Use *bring* when you mean movement from a farther person or place toward a nearer one. Use *take* when you mean movement away from a nearer person or place toward a farther one.

Bring me the book I left in the bedroom.
Take this package to the post office.

Bunch   Do not use *bunch* to refer to a group of people.

Burst, Bursted, Bust, Busted   *Burst* is a verb that means "to come apart suddenly." Its past and past participle forms are both *burst*, not *bursted*. Bust, a verb meaning "to come apart suddenly" or "to break," is considered slang. Do not use it or its past form, *busted*, in formal writing.

Can, May   In formal writing, use *can* to indicate ability and *may* to indicate permission. In informal writing, you may use them interchangeably.

Can the defendant answer the question? (Is he or she able to?)
May the defendant answer the question? (Does he or she have permission to do so?)

Can't   In formal writing, avoid using *can't*, which is a contraction of *cannot.*

Can't Hardly, Can't Scarcely   Avoid these double negatives.
Use *can hardly* and *can scarcely* instead.

Center Around   Use *center on* instead.

Climactic, Climatic   *Climactic* refers to the climax, or highest
point of intensity. *Climatic* refers to the climate, or characteristic weather conditions.

Compare To, Compare With   Use *compare to* when referring
to the similarities between essentially unlike things. Use
compare with when referring to the similarities and differences between things of the same type.

> Hart Crane **compares** the sound of rain **to** "gently pitying laugh-
> ter."
>
> The professor **compared** a poem by Hart Crane **with** one by
> Edna St. Vincent Millay.

Contemptible, Contemptuous   *Contemptible* means "deserving
contempt." *Contemptuous* means "feeling contempt."

> She claimed that efforts to cut back funds for food programs for
> the poor were **contemptible.**
>
> She was **contemptuous** of people who ignored the suffering of
> others.

Continual, Continuous   *Continual* means "recurring regularly." *Continuous* means "occurring without interruption."

> He was kept awake by the **continual** dripping of the faucet.
>
> The nation was experiencing a period of **continuous** growth.

Convince, Persuade   *Convince*, which is often used with *of*,
means "to cause to believe." *Persuade*, which is often used
with an infinitive, means "to cause to do."

> The physicist **convinced** his colleague **of** the correctness of his
> methods.
>
> The doctor **persuaded** her patient **to undergo** therapy.

Could Of   Nonstandard. Use *could have*.

Criteria, Data, Phenomena   These words are plural and in formal writing take plural verbs. The singular forms are *criterion*, *datum*, and *phenomenon*.

Deal   As a word meaning "agreement," "bargain," or "business transaction," this word is informal and overused, as in "a done deal." It is also considered informal as (1) "a certain amount of," as in *a great deal of noise*, (2) "important, impressive," as in "*a big deal*" and "*to make a big deal (out) of,*" and (3) "cope," as in "*I can't deal with this.*"

Disinterested, Uninterested   *Disinterested* means "impartial." *Uninterested* means "indifferent" or "not interested."

> The jury paid special attention to the testimony of one **disinterested** witness.
> She did not finish the book, because she was **uninterested** in the subject.

Done   *Done* is the past participle of *do*. Do not use *done* as the past tense.

> **NOT:**   He always read the last page of a mystery first to find out who **done** it.
> **BUT:**   He always read the last page of a mystery first to find out who **did** it.

Don't   Avoid using *don't*, which is a contraction of *do not*, in formal writing. Never use *don't* as a contraction of *does not*.

Due To   In formal writing, avoid using *due to* to mean *because of*.

> **NOT:**   The shipment was delayed **due to** the bad weather.
> **BUT:**   The shipment was delayed **because of** the bad weather.
> **OR:**   The delay in the shipment **was due to** the bad weather.

Eager *See* **anxious.**

Ensure *See* **assure.**

Enthused In formal writing, use *enthusiastic.*

Etc. *See* **and etc.**

Everyday, Every Day Use *every day* as an adverb. Use *everyday* as an adjective.

> During training, he took vitamins **every day.**
> He needed an **everyday** suit.

Everyone, Every One *See* **anyone.**

Everywheres Nonstandard. Use *everywhere.*

Exam In formal writing, use *examination.*

Expect In formal writing, do not use *expect* to mean "to presume or suppose."

> **NOT:** I **expect** the performance went well.
> **BUT:** I **suppose** the performance went well.

Explicit, Implicit *Explicit* means "stated forthrightly." *Implicit* means "implied" or "suggested."

> The warning was **explicit:** Beware of the dog.
> Although he never said a word, his threat was **implicit** in his action.

Farther, Further In formal writing, use *farther* to refer to geographical distance. Use *further* to refer to time, quantity, or degree.

> We were **farther** from home than we had imagined.
> The court demanded **further** documentation of his expenses.

Fewer, Less Use *fewer* to refer to things that can be counted. Use *less* to refer to a collective quantity that cannot be counted.

This year **fewer** commuters are driving their cars to work.
In general, smaller cars use **less** fuel than larger cars.

Finalize   *Finalize* is an example of bureaucratic language. Do
not use it in place of *complete, conclude,* or *make final.*

Fine   *Fine* is informal and weak when used for the words
very well. In formal writing, use a more exact word.

Firstly, Secondly, Etc.   Use *first, second,* etc., instead.

Fix   In formal writing, avoid using *fix* to mean "predicament."

Flunk   *Flunk* is informal. In formal writing, use *fail.*

Folks   In formal writing, avoid using the informal word *folks*
for *parents, relatives,* or *family.*

Former, Latter   *Former* means "the first mentioned of two."
When three or more are mentioned, refer to the first mentioned as *first. Latter* means "the second mentioned of
two." When three or more are mentioned, refer to the last
mentioned as *last.*

Anita and Jayne are athletes: the **former** is a gymnast, the **latter**
a tennis player.
The judges sampled four pies—apple, plum, rhubarb, and apri-
cot—and gave the prize to the **last.**

Funny   In formal writing, avoid using *funny* for *odd* or *peculiar.*

Further   *See* **farther.**

Get   In formal writing, avoid using slang expressions beginning with *get: get even, get going, get on with it,* etc.

Good, Well   *Good* is an adjective. *Well* is usually an adverb,
but it can also be used as an adjective meaning "healthy."

She looks **good** in that color.
They work **well** together.
The baby looks **well** today.

Great   In formal writing, do not use *great* to mean "wonderful."

Had Ought, Hadn't Ought   Use *ought* and *ought not* instead.

Hanged, Hung   Use *hanged* as the past and past participle form when referring to a method of execution. Otherwise, use *hung.*

> In the Old West, horse thieves were **hanged.**
> The clothing was **hung** out to dry.

Has Got, Have Got   In formal writing, use simply *has* or *have.*

Herself, Himself   *See* **myself.**

Hisself   Nonstandard. Use *himself.*

Hopefully   *Hopefully* means "in a hopeful manner." Avoid using *hopefully* to mean "it is hoped" or "let us hope."

> **NOT:**   **Hopefully** it will not rain again this weekend.
> **BUT:**   **Let us hope** it will not rain again this weekend.

Illusion   *See* **allusion.**

Implicit   *See* **explicit.**

Imply, Infer   *Imply* means "to suggest or hint." *Infer* means "to draw a conclusion." A writer or speaker implies something; a reader or listener infers it.

> He **implied** that he knew someone had cheated.
> From his remark I **inferred** that he is worried about her.

In, Into   *In* indicates position. *Into* indicates direction of movement.

> When the sergeant came **into** the barracks, she found several of the new recruits still **in** bed.

Interesting Because it is overused, *interesting* has so many meanings that it has become an ambiguous word. In formal writing, explain why something is interesting rather than using the word.

Infer *See* **imply.**

In Regards To Use *in regard to* or *regarding* or *as regards.*

Insure *See* **assure.**

Into *See* **in.**

Irregardless Nonstandard. Use *regardless.*

Is When, Is Where Do not use these constructions in giving definitions.

> **NOT:** Improvisation **is when** actors perform without preparation.
>
> **BUT:** Improvisation **occurs when** actors perform without preparation.
>
> **OR:** Improvisation **is** a performance by actors without preparation.
>
> **NOT:** An aviary **is where** a large number of birds are housed.
>
> **BUT:** An aviary **is a place where** a large number of birds are housed.
>
> **OR:** An aviary **is** a house for a large number of birds.

Its, It's *Its* is the possessive case of the pronoun *it. It's* is a contraction of *it is* or *it has.* Avoid the contraction *it's* in formal writing.

> The cat was cleaning *its* paws.
> *It's* too late to submit an application.

Judgement This word is a variant British spelling of **judgment.** *Judgment* is the preferred spelling in the United States.

Kind Of, Sort Of   In formal writing, avoid using *kind of* and *sort of* as adverbs. Use instead the more formal words *rather* and *somewhat*.

> **NOT:**   His description was **kind of** sketchy.
> **BUT:**   His description was **rather** sketchy.
>
> **NOT:**   She left **sort of** abruptly.
> **BUT:**   She left **somewhat** abruptly.

Kind Of A, Sort Of A   When using these expressions to mean "type of," delete the *a*.

> What **kind of** fabric is this?
> What **sort of** person was he?

Lay   *See* **lie.**

Lead, Led   *Lead* is the present infinitive form of the verb. *Led* is the past tense and past participle form.

Learn, Teach   *Learn* means "to receive knowledge." *Teach* means "to give knowledge."

> We can **learn** from the mistakes of history.
> History can **teach** us many lessons.

Leave, Let   In formal writing, use the verb *leave* to mean "to depart (from)." Use the verb *let* to mean "to allow to."

> Paul Simon wrote about the many ways to **leave** a lover.
> The natives would not **let** themselves be photographed.

Less   *See* **fewer.**

Let   *See* **leave.**

Liable   *See* **likely.**

Lie, Lay   *Lie* is an intransitive verb that means "to recline." Its past and past participle forms are *lay* and *lain*. *Lay* is a transitive verb that means "to place." Its past and past participle forms are both *laid*. (See also pp. 222–223.)

Although he **lay** in bed for hours, he could not sleep.
Please **lay** the book on the table.
Then let it **lie** there.

Like   In formal writing, do not use *like* as a conjunction. Instead use *as, as if,* or *as though*.

NOT: The headlines claim that it looks **like** peace is at hand.
BUT: The headlines claim that it looks **as if** peace is at hand.

Likely, Liable   *Likely* indicates probability. *Liable* indicates responsibility or obligation.

The Kremlin asserted that changes in the makeup of the government were not **likely** to lead to changes in U. S.-Soviet relations.
The court determined that the driver of the truck was **liable** for all damages.

Lose, Loose   *Lose* is a verb. *Loose* is an adjective.

In what year did Nixon **lose** the election to Kennedy?
Loose talk can cause much trouble.

Lot   *See* **a lot.**
Lot Of, Lots Of   In formal writing, use *much, plenty of,* or *many* instead.
May   *See* **can.**
May Be, Maybe   *May be* is a verb phrase. *Maybe* is an adverb meaning "perhaps."

His findings **may be** accurate.
Maybe they will find a solution.

May Of, Might Of, Must Of   Use *may have*, *might have*, or *must have* instead.

More Importantly, Most Importantly   Use *more important* and *most important* instead.

Most   In formal writing, avoid using *most* to mean "almost."

> **NOT:**   The survey predicted that **most** everyone would vote.
> **BUT:**   The survey predicted that **almost** everyone would vote.

Myself, Yourself, Himself, Herself, Etc.   Pronouns ending in *-self* or *-selves* are reflexive or intensive. In formal writing, do not use them in place of *I, me, you, he, her,* and so on.

> **NOT:**   My friend and **myself** are campaigning actively.
> **BUT:**   My friend and **I** are campaigning actively.

No One   *No one* is a singular indefinite pronoun and therefore requires a singular verb.

> **No one** of the students **is** able to go today.

Nice   In formal writing, replace this weak word with a more exact one—*attractive, appealing, kind,* and so forth.

Not Hardly   Avoid this double negative. Use *hardly* instead.

Nowhere Near Enough   Colloquial. In formal writing, use *not nearly enough* instead.

> **NOT:**   The concessions the company made its employees were **nowhere near enough** to avoid a strike.
> **BUT:**   The concessions the company made its employees were **not nearly enough** to avoid a strike.

Nowheres   Nonstandard. Use *nowhere*.

Number   *See* **amount.**

Off Of   Use *off* without *of.*

> **NOT:**   During the tremor the paintings fell **off of** the wall.
> **BUT:**   During the tremor the paintings fell **off** the wall.

OK, O.K., Okay   Avoid these expressions in formal writing.

People, Persons   Use *people* to refer to a large group collectively. Use *persons* to emphasize the individuals within the group.

> The committee is investigating ways in which **people** avoid paying their full taxes.
> The group thought it was near agreement when several **persons** raised objections.

Old Fashion   This phrase is a shortened form of *old fashioned;* avoid using it in formal writing.

Percent, Percentage   Use *percent* after a specific number. Use *percentage* after a general adjective indicating size.

> The poll showed that 75 **percent** of Americans supported the President's foreign policy.
> The poll showed that a large **percentage** of Americans supported the President's foreign policy.

Persuade   *See* **convince.**
Phenomena   *See* **criteria.**
P.M.   *See* **A.M.**
Principal, Principle   *Principal* is a noun meaning "chief officer" or, in finance, "capital sum." As an adjective it means "major" or "main." *Principle* is used only as a noun and means "rule" or "fundamental truth."

> The **principal** spoke to all of the teachers today.
> The **principal** reason for doing so is not clear.
> She adheres to **principles** that are admirable.

Quote, Quotation   *Quote* is a verb. *Quotation* is a noun.

> During her speech she **quoted** from one of Blake's poems.
> She began her speech with a **quotation** from one of Blake's poems.

Raise, Rise   *Raise* is a transitive verb meaning "to lift." Its past and past participle forms are both *raised*. *Rise* is an intransitive verb meaning "to go up." Its past and past participle are *rose* and *risen*. (See also pp. 224–225.)

> Inflation is **raising** the cost of living.
> The cost of living is **rising.**

Real, Really   *Real* is an adjective. *Really* is an adverb.

> What is the **real** value of the dollar?
> Mortgage rates are **really** high this year.

Reason Is Because   Use *that* instead of *because* or rewrite the sentence.

> **NOT:**   The **reason** for the patient's lethargy **is because** his diet is inadequate.
> **BUT:**   The **reason** for the patient's lethargy **is that** his diet is inadequate.
> **OR:**   The **reason** for the patient's lethargy **is** an inadequate diet.
> **OR:**   The patient is lethargic because of an inadequate diet.

Respectably, Respectfully, Respectively   *Respectably* means "in a manner deserving respect." *Respectfully* means "in a manner showing respect." *Respectively* means "in the order given."

> The tenor performed his aria **respectably,** but his voice cracked during the duet.

The defendant **respectfully** asked permission to address the court.

Baghdad and Damascus are the capitals of Iraq and Syria, **respectively.**

Rise   *See* **raise.**

Sensual, Sensuous   Both of these adjectives mean "appealing to the senses," but *sensual* describes something that arouses physical appetites, while *sensuous* describes something that leads to aesthetic enjoyment.

The censors claimed that the dancing was too **sensual.**

The painter was praised for the **sensuous** quality of his still lifes.

Set, Sit   *Set* is a transitive verb that means "to put or place." Its past and past participle forms are both *set. Sit* is an intransitive verb that means "to be seated." Its past and past participle forms are both *sat.* (See also pp. 223–224.)

The stagehands **set** the chairs on a raised platform.

The actors will **sit** in the chairs during the rehearsal.

Shall, Will   The distinction between *shall* and *will* is fading. However, for strictly formal writing, use *shall* with first-person pronouns and *will* with second- and third-person pronouns to indicate simple futurity. Reverse the order to indicate determination, duty, or need.

SIMPLE FUTURITY

I **shall** see you at the theater.

He **will** meet us at the theater.

DETERMINATION

We **will** find a solution to this problem.

They **shall** not defeat us.

Should Of   Nonstandard. Use *should have.*
Sit   *See* **set.**
Someone, Some One   *See* **anyone.**
Sometime, Some Time   Use *sometime* as an adverb to mean "at an indefinite or unnamed time." Use *some time* after a preposition.

> The announcement will be made **sometime** next month.
> He has been retired for **some time** now.

Sort Of   *See* **kind of.**
Sort Of A   *See* **kind of a.**
Suppose To   *See* **use to.**
Sure, Surely   *Sure* is an adjective that means "certain." *Surely* is an adverb that means "undoubtedly" or "certainly."

> The expedition was **sure** to succeed.
> The expedition was **surely** a success.

Sure And, Try And   In formal writing, use *sure to* and *try to* instead.

> **NOT:**   Be **sure and** pay attention to the speaker's body language.
> **BUT:**   Be **sure to** pay attention to the speaker's body language.

Teach   *See* **learn.**
That, Which   Use *that* to introduce a restrictive clause. Use *which* to introduce either a restrictive or a nonrestrictive clause. (In order to maintain a clearer distinction between *which* and *that*, some writers use *which* to introduce only a nonrestrictive clause.)

> Is this the manuscript **that** he submitted yesterday?
> This contract, **which** is no longer valid, called for a 30 percent royalty.

Theirself, Theirselves   Nonstandard. Use *themselves*.
These Kind, Those Kind; These Sort, Those Sort   Since *kind*
and *sort* are singular, use singular adjectives: *this kind*,
that kind, *this sort*, *that sort*. For the plural use *these kinds*,
those kinds, *these sorts*, *those sorts*.
Thusly   Use *thus*.
Try And   *See* **sure and.**
Uninterested   *See* **disinterested.**
Unique   The word *unique* means "unequaled" or "unparal-
leled," a quality that is not capable of comparison.

> NOT: He has the **most unique** sense of humor I have encoun-
> tered.
> BUT: His sense of humor is **unique.**

Use To, Suppose To   The correct forms are *use**d** to* and *suppose**d** to*.

> NOT: In *My Dinner with André*, Wally **use to** be a Latin teacher.
> BUT: In *My Dinner with André*, Wally **used to** be a Latin
> teacher.

Wait For, Wait On   Use *wait for* to mean "await" or "attend
to." Use *wait on* to mean "serve."

> Many young actors **wait on** tables while they **wait for** the right
> role.

Ways   Use *way* to mean "distance."

> NOT: He lives only a short **ways** from London.
> BUT: He lives only a short **way** from London.

Well   *See* **good.**
When, Where   *See* **is when, is where.**

Where   Do not use *where* for *that.*

> **NOT:**   I read in the magazine **where** flood victims were receiving federal aid.
>
> **BUT:**   I read in the magazine **that** flood victims were receiving federal aid.

Do not use *where* for *in which.*

> **NOT:**   It is an agreement **where** everyone is happy.
>
> **BUT:**   It is an agreement **in which** everyone is happy.

Which, Who   Use *which* to refer to objects. Use *who* to refer to people. (*That* usually refers to objects but at times may be used to refer to people.)

> The book, **which** was written by Nat Hentoff, is called *Jazz Is.*
> Nat Hentoff, **who** wrote *Jazz Is,* contributes articles to many magazines.

Will   *See* **shall.**

-wise   Avoid using *-wise* as a noun suffix—*budgetwise, careerwise, marketwise.*

Without   Do not use *without* for *unless.*

> **NOT:**   The director could not act **without** the committee approved.
>
> **BUT:**   The director could not act **unless** the committee approved.
>
> **OR:**   The director could not act **without** the committee's approval.

Yourself   *See* **myself.**

GLOSSARY OF GRAMMATICAL TERMS

Absolute Phrase   A group of words containing a noun and a nonfinite, or incomplete, verb. It modifies the entire clause to which it is attached, instead of an individual word within the clause. (See also 6a; 10b.)

His energy depleted, the fighter conceded the bout.

Abstract Noun   *See* **noun.**

Acronym   A kind of abbreviation that creates a word from parts of words or initials without periods: *radar; CARE; ROM.*

Active Voice   *See* **voice.**

Adjective   A word that modifies, or describes, a noun or pronoun. An adjective tells what kind, how many, or which one. (See also 9d; 19.)

In **his latest** novel, **this prodigious** writer uses **several historical** studies to create **a realistic** portrait of **the** man often considered **our greatest** president—Abraham Lincoln.

Adjective Clause   A dependent clause that acts as an adjective and modifies a noun or pronoun. Usually, an adjective clause begins with a relative pronoun (*who, whose, whom, that,* or *which*). (See also 11b.)

The king of England **who broke with the Catholic Church** was Henry VIII.

Adverb   A word that modifies, or limits the meaning of, a verb, an adjective, or another adverb. An adverb tells *when, where, to what extent*, or *how*. (See also 9e; 19.)

This **extremely** absorbing book reports **quite successfully** the way computers **efficiently** function and **how** they will **most probably** affect our lives in the future.

Adverb Clause   A dependent clause that begins with a subordinating conjunction (*although, because, while*, etc.) and acts as an adverb in the sentence. (See also 11b.)

The museum was closed **because it was being renovated.**

Agreement   The correspondence in form between a verb and its subject or a pronoun and its antecedent to indicate person, number, and gender. (See also 16 and 17a.)

Each of these women **makes her** position understood.

Antecedent   The word or words to which a pronoun refers. A pronoun must agree with its antecedent in number and gender. (See also 9c and 17a.)

Jack pledged **his** support for the project.

Appositive   A noun or group of words acting as a noun that renames, identifies, or gives additional information about the preceding noun or pronoun. (See also 29d and 6a.)

Typhoid Mary, **the notorious carrier of typhoid fever,** died in 1938.

Article   The indefinite articles are *a* and *an*; the definite article is *the*. Articles are classified as adjectives. (See also 9d.)

Auxiliary Verb   A form of *be* or *have* used to form perfect tenses, progressive forms of tenses, and the passive voice. (See also 9b.)

> I **am** leaving.
> They **have** left.
> The money **had been** left in the safe.

Case   The structural function of a noun or a pronoun in a sentence. English has three cases—subjective, objective, and possessive. The subjective case indicates the subject of a verb or a subject complement:

> The **umpire** called a strike. The **umpire** was he.

The objective case indicates the direct or indirect object of a verb or the object of a preposition:

> Sampras returned the **serve** to Agassi. He returned it to **him.**
> Montana gave **me** an autographed **football.** I gave **it** to my
>   **IO**   **DO**   **DO**
> **nephew.**
>   **OP**

The possessive case indicates possession, description, or origin:

> The **team's** overall performance was disappointing. **Their** overall
> performance was disappointing.

Nouns and some pronouns have the same form in the subjective and the objective cases; an apostrophe and *s* or an apostrophe alone is added to form the possessive case: *in-*

vestor's, investors', anybody's. The pronouns *it* and *you* have special possessive forms: *its, your,* or *yours.* The following pronouns have different forms in all three cases.

SUBJECTIVE: I, he, she, we, they, who
OBJECTIVE: me, him, her, us, them, whom
POSSESSIVE: my, mine; his; her, hers; our, ours; their, theirs; whose

(See also 9a, 9c, 18, 38a.)

Clause A group of words with a subject and a predicate. A clause may be independent or dependent. An independent (main) clause is structurally independent and can stand by itself as a simple sentence:

The President honored the Unknown Soldier.

A dependent (subordinate) clause is not structurally independent and cannot stand by itself as a simple sentence. Therefore, it must be joined to or be part of an independent clause:

Although newspapers strive for accuracy, they sometimes make mistakes.

Dependent clauses, which can function as adjectives, adverbs, or nouns, usually begin with a subordinating conjunction or a relative pronoun. (See also 11.)

Collective Noun *See* **noun.**
Comma Splice An error that occurs when a comma is used to separate two independent clauses not joined by a conjunction. (See also 14a.)
Common Noun *See* **noun.**

Comparative, Superlative Forms of adjectives and adverbs used to make comparisons. The comparative form is used to compare two things; the superlative form is used to compare more than two. The comparative and superlative of most one-syllable adjectives and adverbs are formed by adding *-er* and *-est* to the base, or positive, form: *long, longer, longest.* The comparative and superlative of most longer adjectives and adverbs are formed by placing the words *more* and *most* before the positive form: *beautiful, more beautiful, most beautiful.* (See also 9d, 9e, and 19c.)

Complement A word or group of words that completes the meaning of a verb. The five types of complements are direct objects, indirect objects, objective complements, predicate nominatives, and predicate adjectives. (See also 8b and 8c.)

Complete Predicate *See* **predicate.**

Complete Sentence *See* **sentence.**

Complete Subject *See* **subject.**

Complex Sentence *See* **sentence.**

Compound A word or group of words that is made up of two or more parts but functions as a unit. Compound words consist of two or more words that may be written as one word, as a hyphenated word, or as separate words but that function as a single part of speech: *hairbrush, well-to-do, toaster oven.* A compound subject consists of two or more nouns or noun substitutes that take the same predicate:

Chemistry and **physics** were required courses.

A compound verb consists of two or more verbs that have the same subject:

The doctor **analyzed** the results of the tests and **made** a diagnosis.

(See also 9a, 16a, 29e, and 39.)

Compound-Complex Sentence   *See* **sentence.**
Compound Sentence   *See* **sentence.**
Compound Subject   *See* **subject.**
Concrete Noun   *See* **noun.**
Conjunction   A word or set of words that joins or relates other words, phrases, clauses, or sentences. There are three types of conjunctions: coordinating conjunctions, correlative conjunctions, and subordinating conjunctions. Coordinating conjunctions (*and, but, for, nor, or so,* and *yet*) join elements that have equal grammatical rank. Correlative conjunctions (*both . . . and, either . . . or, neither . . . nor, not only . . . but also, whether . . . or, just as . . . so*) function as coordinating conjunctions but are always used in pairs. Subordinating conjunctions (*after, as long as, because, if, since, so that, unless, until, while,* etc.) join subordinate, or dependent, clauses to main, or independent, clauses. (See also 9g.)
Conjunctive Adverb   An adverb that provides transition between independent clauses. (See also 9g.)

The movie received many excellent reviews; **consequently,** people across the country lined up to see it.

Coordinating Conjunction   *See* **conjunction.**
Correlative Conjunction   *See* **conjunction.**
Dangling Modifier   An introductory phrase that does not clearly and sensibly modify the noun or pronoun that follows it. (See also 23d.)
Degrees of Modifiers   *See* **comparative, superlative.**
Demonstrative Pronoun   *See* **pronoun.**
Dependent Clause   *See* **clause.**
Direct Object   *See* **object.**
Double Negative   A construction, considered unacceptable in standard modern English, that uses two negative words to make a negative statement. (See also 19d.)

Elliptical Clause   A clause in which a word is omitted but understood. (See also 11b and 18.)

He works harder than his partner [does].

Expletive   The word *there, here,* or *it* is used to fill the position before a verb of being but not to add meaning to the sentence. (See also 8a and 26d.)

There are several excellent reasons for taking this course. **Here** is one of them. **It** is wise to register early.

Faulty Parallelism   *See* **parallelism.**
Faulty Predication   *See* **predicate.**
Fragment   *See* **sentence fragment.**
Fused Sentence   Two independent clauses written without a coordinating conjunction or a punctuation mark between them. It is not the same as a comma splice. (See also 14b.)
Gender   The classification of nouns and pronouns as masculine (*man, he*), feminine (*woman, she*), or neuter (*skillet, it*). (See also 9a, 9c, and 17a.)
Gerund   *See* **verbal.**
Gerund Phrase   *See* **phrase.**
Imperative   *See* **mood.**
Indefinite Pronoun   *See* **pronoun.**
Independent Clause   *See* **clause.**
Indicative   *See* **mood.**
Indirect Object   *See* **object.**
Infinitive   *See* **verbal.**
Infinitive Phrase   *See* **phrase.**
Intensive Pronoun   *See* **pronoun.**
Interjection   A word that expresses emotion and has no grammatical connection to the sentence in which it appears. (See also 9h.)

Oh, how happy he was!
Wow, that was painful!

Interrogative Pronoun   *See* **pronoun.**

Intransitive Verb   *See* **verb.**

Inverted Word Order   A change in the normal English word order of subject-verb-complement. (See also 8a and 16h.)

sub.

In the doorway stood **Tom.**

Irregular Verb   A verb that does not form its past tense and past participle according to the regular pattern of adding *-ed* or *-d* to the present infinitive: *begin, began, begun; draw, drew, drawn; put, put, put.* (See also 15.)

Linking Verb   *See* **verb.**

Main Clause   *See* **clause.**

Misplaced Modifier   A modifier placed so that it seems to refer to a word other than the one intended. (See also 23e.)

Modal   A verb form used with a main verb to ask a question, to help express negation, to show future time, to emphasize, or to express such conditions as possibility, certainty, or obligation. The following words are modals: *do, does, did; can, could; may, might, must; will, shall; would, should,* and *ought to.* (See also 9b.)

Modifier   A word or group of words that limits the meaning of or makes more specific another word or group of words. The two kinds of modifiers are adjectives and adverbs. (See also 9d and 9e.)

Mood   The aspect of a verb that indicates the writer's attitude toward the action or condition expressed by the verb. In English there are three moods: the indicative, the imperative, and the subjunctive. The indicative expresses a factual statement or a question:

The weather **is** fine today. **Will** it **rain** tomorrow?

The imperative indicates a command or a request:

Buy your tickets today.
Please **be** quiet.

The subjunctive indicates a wish, an assumption, a recommendation, or something contrary to fact:

She wished she **were** home.
If she **were** mayor, she would eliminate waste from the city budget.

(See also 9b and 21c.)

Nominative Case   Another name for the subjective case.

Nonessential Element   A modifying phrase or clause that does not limit, qualify, or identify the noun it modifies. Since a nonessential element is not necessary to the meaning of the clause in which it appears, it is set off with commas. (See also 29d.)

Hurlyburly, **which was written by David Rabe,** conveys the confusion and aimlessness of modern American life.

Noun   A word that names a person, place, object, or idea. Proper nouns name particular people, places, objects, or ideas: *Gertrude Stein, Spain, Corvettes, Puritanism.* Common nouns name people, places, objects, and ideas in general, not in particular: *poet, country, cars, religion.* Concrete nouns name things that can be seen, touched, heard, smelled, or tasted: *portrait, mansion, chorus, garlic.* Abstract nouns name concepts, ideas, beliefs, and qualities: *honesty, consideration, fascism, monotheism.* Collective nouns refer to groups of people or things as though the group were a single unit: *committee, choir, navy, team.* (See also 9a, 16c, and 26b.)

Noun Clause   A dependent clause that acts as a noun in a sentence. It functions as a subject, an object, or a predicate nominative. (See also 11b.)

> **That an agreement would be reached before the strike deadline** seemed unlikely.

Noun Substitute   A pronoun, gerund, clause, or other group of words that functions as a noun in a sentence. (See also 9c, 9i, and 11b.)

Number   The quality of being singular or plural. (See 9a, 9b, 9c, and especially 16 and 17.)

Object   A noun or noun substitute that completes the meaning of or is affected by a transitive verb or a preposition. A direct object specifies the person, place, object, or idea that directly receives the action of a transitive verb:

The three heads of state *signed* the **treaty.**

An indirect object tells to whom or what or for whom or what the action of a transitive verb is performed:

They *gave* the **refugees** food and clothing.

An object of a preposition is the noun or noun substitute that the preposition relates to another part of the sentence:

The cat is sleeping *under* the **table.**

(See also 8, 9f, 10a, and 18.)

Objective Case   *See* **case.**

Objective Complement   A noun or adjective that completes the action of a transitive verb by modifying or renaming that verb's object. (See also 8c.)

Delilah cut his *hair* **short.**

History calls *Thomas More* a **martyr.**

Parallelism   Sentence elements that have the same grammatical structure. (See also 23c.)

They enjoy fish**ing,** hunt**ing,** and swimm**ing.**

Parenthetical Expression   An expression that comments on or gives additional information about the main part of a sentence. Since a parenthetical expression interrupts the thought of the sentence, it is set off by commas. (See also 29d.)

Music, **I believe,** is good for the soul.

Participial phrase   *See* **phrase.**

Participle   *See* **verbal.**

Parts of Speech   The eight groups into which words are traditionally classified based on their function in a sentence: noun, verb, adjective, adverb, pronoun, preposition, conjunction, and interjection. (See also 9.)

Passive Voice   *See* **voice.**

Past Participle   *See* **verbal.**

Personal Pronoun   *See* **pronoun.**

Phrase   A group of words lacking a subject and predicate that often functions as a single part of speech. (See also 10.)

Positive Degree   *See* **comparative, superlative.**

Possessive Case   *See* **case.**

Predicate   The part of a sentence that tells what the subject does or is. The simple predicate is the main verb, including any auxiliaries or modals:

The rice **was** lightly **flavored** with vinegar.

The complete predicate consists of the simple predicate and all the words that modify and complement it:

The rice **was lightly flavored with vinegar**.

(See also 8b.)

Predicate Adjective   An adjective that follows a linking verb and describes the subject of the verb. (See also 8c.)

Lestrade's solution was too **simplistic.**

Predicate Nominative   A noun or noun substitute that follows a linking verb and renames the subject of the verb. (See also 8c.)

The model for Nora Charles was **Lillian Hellman.**

Preposition   A function word used to show the relationship of a noun or pronoun to another part of the sentence. (See also 9f.)

Prepositional Phrase   A phrase consisting of a preposition, the object of the preposition, and all the words modifying this object. (See also 10a.)

The narrator **of the story** is a young man who lived **with the writer** and assisted him **in his work**.

Present Infinitive   *See* **verbal.**
Principle Parts   *See* **verb.**

Pronoun A word that stands for or takes the place of one or more nouns. A personal pronoun takes the place of a noun that names a person or thing: *I, me, my, mine; you, your, yours; he, him, his; she, her hers; it, its; we, us, our, ours; they, them, their, theirs.* A demonstrative pronoun points to someone or something: *this, that, these, those.* An indefinite pronoun does not take the place of a particular noun. It carries the idea of "all," "some," "any," or "none": *everyone, everything, somebody, many, anyone, anything, no one, nobody.* An interrogative pronoun is used to ask a question: *who, whom, whose, what, which.* A relative pronoun is used to form an adjective clause or a noun clause: *who, whose, whom, which, that, what, whoever, whomever, whichever, whatever.* An intensive pronoun is used for emphasis. It is formed by adding *-self* or *-selves* to the end of a personal pronoun. A reflexive pronoun, which has the same form as an intensive pronoun, is used to show that the subject is acting upon itself. (See also 9c, 17, and 18.)

Proper Adjective An adjective formed from a proper noun. (See also 46.)

Machiavellian scheme, **Byronic** disposition, **Parisian** dress

Proper Noun *See* **noun.**

Reflexive Pronoun *See* **pronoun.**

Regular Verb A verb whose past tense and past participle are formed by adding *-d* or *-ed* to the present infinitive: *analyze, analyzed, analyzed; detain, detained, detained.* (See also 9b; 15.)

Relative Pronoun *See* **pronoun.**

Restrictive Element A modifying phrase or clause that limits, identifies, or qualifies the idea expressed by the noun it modifies. Since a restrictive element is necessary for the basic meaning of the clause in which it appears, it is not set off with commas. (See also 29d.)

The woman **wearing the blue suit** just received a promotion.

Run-On Sentence   Two or more complete sentences incorrectly written as though they were one sentence. (See also 14.)

Sentence   A group of words with a subject and a predicate that expresses a complete thought. Sentences can be classified into four basic groups according to the number and kinds of clauses they contain. A simple sentence contains only one independent clause and no dependent clause:

> The relationship between the United States and Iraq needs to be improved.

A compound sentence contains two or more independent clauses but no dependent clause:

> The senator worked hard for passage of the bill, but his efforts proved futile.

A complex sentence contains one independent clause and one or more dependent clauses:

> Although the two nations were technically at peace, their secret services were fighting a covert war.

A compound-complex sentence contains two or more independent clauses and one or more dependent clauses:

> Voter confidence in the administration grew as interest rates went down; however, it quickly faded when interest rates started to rise.

(See also 8 and 12.)

Sentence Fragment   An incomplete sentence written as a complete sentence. (See also 13.)

Simple Predicate   *See* **predicate.**

Simple Sentence   *See* **sentence.**

Simple Subject   *See* **subject.**
Split Infinitive   Insertion of a modifier, usually an adverb, between the two elements of an infinitive phrase. Avoid splitting infinitives in formal writing.

He began **to excitedly speak.**

(See also 9i.)
Squinting Modifier   A modifier that, because of its placement, could refer to either the preceding or the following element in a sentence, resulting in ambiguity. (See also 23f.)
Style   The way in which words are arranged in written language as distinct from the ideas that the words express.
Subject   The part of a sentence that answers the question "who?" or "what?" in regard to the predicate, or verb. The simple subject is the main noun or noun substitute in the subject:

Women's **fashions** from the 1950s are becoming popular again.

The complete subject is the simple subject together with all the words that modify it.

Women's fashions from the 1950s are becoming popular again.

A compound subject consists of two or more words that take the same predicate.

Women's **fashions** and **hairstyles** from the 1950s are becoming popular again.

(See also 8a and 16a.)
Subjective Case   *See* **case.**
Subjective Complement   *See* **complement.**
Subjunctive   *See* **mood.**

Subordinate Clause   *See* **clause.**
Subordinating Conjunction   *See* **conjunction.**
Superlative Degree   *See* **comparative, superlative.**
Tense   The time expressed by the form of the verb. There are
    six tenses: (simple) present, present perfect, (simple) past,
    past perfect, (simple) future, future perfect. Each of the
    tenses has a progressive form that indicates continuing ac-
    tion. The present tense is used to write about events or
    conditions that are happening or existing now:

She **writes** a column for the local newspaper.

The present tense is also used to write about natural or scientific laws, timeless truths, events in literature, habitual
action, and (with an adverbial word or phrase) future time.
The present perfect tense is used to write about events that
occurred at some unspecified time in the past and about
events and continued actions that began in the past and
may still be continuing in the present:

She **has written** a series of articles about child abuse.

The past tense is used to write about events that occurred
and conditions that existed at a definite time in the past
and do not extend into the present:

The researcher **studied** voting trends in this district.

The past perfect tense is used to write about a past event
or condition that ended before another past event or condition began:

They **had studied** the effects of television on voting trends be-
    fore they made their proposals.

The future tense is used to write about events or conditions that have not yet begun:

They **will consider** her proposal.

The future perfect tense is used to write about a future event or condition that will end before another future event or condition begins or before a specified time in the future:

By next month, they **will have considered** all the proposals.

(See also 9b, 21c, and 22.)

Transitive Verb   *See* **verb.**

Verb   A word that expresses action or a state of being and has four principal parts or forms: present infinitive, past tense, past participle, and present participle. (See also 9b and 9i.) An action verb expresses action:

The ballerina **danced** beautifully.

A linking verb expresses a state of being or a condition. It connects the subject of the sentence to a word that identifies or describes it:

Vitamin C **may be** *effective* against the common cold.

A transitive verb is an action verb that takes an object:

The fleet **secures** the *coasts* against invasion.

An intransitive verb is any verb that does not take an object:

After deregulation of the industry, prices **soared.**

(See also 9b.)

Verb Phrase   A phrase made up of the infinitive, the present participle or the past participle plus one or more auxiliaries or modals:

> The candidate **will make** a speech tomorrow.
> Jesse Jackson **had proved** himself an effective negotiator.
> The gymnasts **have been practicing** regularly.

(See also 9b and 15.)

Verbal   A grammatical form that is based on a verb but that functions as a noun, an adjective, or an adverb, instead of as a verb, in a sentence. There are three types of verbals: participles, gerunds, and infinitives. The present participle and the past participle of most verbs can function as adjectives:

> One of the most memorable figures in *Alice in Wonderland* is the **grinning** Cheshire cat.
> The lawyer demanded a **written** contract.

A gerund is a verb form spelled the same way as the present participle but used as a noun in a sentence:

> **Walking** is good for your health.

The present infinitive and the present perfect infinitive form of a verb can function as a noun, as an adjective, or as an adverb:

> In *A Chorus Line*, the overriding ambition of each of the characters is **to dance.** Cassie was glad **to have gotten** the part.

(See also 9i.)

Verbal Phrase   A phrase consisting of a verbal and all its *complements* and *modifiers.* There are three types of verbal phrases: *participial phrases, gerund phrases,* and *infinitive phrases.* A participial phrase functions as an adjective in a sentence:

> The image of a garden **filled with poisonous flowers** dominates "Rappaccini's Daughter."

A gerund phrase functions as a noun in a sentence:

> **Exercising in the noonday sun** can be dangerous.

An infinitive phrase functions as a noun, an adjective, or an adverb:

> **To make the world safe for democracy** was one of Wilson's goals.

(See also 10b.)

Voice   The indication of whether the subject performs or receives the action of the verb. If the subject performs the action, the verb and the clause are in the *active voice:*

> Herman Melville **wrote** "Bartleby the Scrivener."

If the subject receives the action or is acted upon, the verb and the clause are in the *passive voice:*

> "Bartleby the Scrivener" **was written** by Herman Melville.

(See also 9b and 21d.)

Acknowledgments

Paula Gunn Allen, "The Sacred Hoop: Recovering the Feminine in American Indian Traditions." From *The Sacred Hoop* by Paula Gunn Allen. Copyright © 1986 by Paula Gunn Allen. Reprinted by permission of Beacon Press.

America: History and Life, entry for "John Adams' Opinion of Benjamin Franklin." Reprinted by permission of ABC-CLIO, Inc.

The American Heritage Dictionary, entries on "doubt" and "doubtful." Copyright © 1985 by Houghton Mifflin Company. Reprinted by permission from *The American Heritage Dictionary*, Second College Edition.

Eileen Biagi, "Career Achievement in Women." Reprinted by permission of the author.

John Jansen, "Comparable Worth: Equal Pay for Work Judged to Be of Equal Value." Reprinted by permission of the author.

Alison Jolly, "A New Science That Sees Animals as Conscious Beings." *Smithsonian Magazine*, March, 1983. Reprinted by permission of the author.

Brian Liptak, "Back Up, Bugs." Reprinted by permission of the author.

John McPhee, "Oranges." Excerpt from *Oranges*. Copyright © 1966, 1967 by John McPhee. Reprinted by permission of Farrar, Straus and Giroux, Inc.

Jennifer Neidenbach, "*Emma* and the Plight of the Spinster." Reprinted by permission of the author.

Robert M. Pirsig, *Zen and the Art of Motorcycle Maintenance*. Adapted from page 12, "You lost the frame . . . from immediate consciousness." Copyright © 1974 by Robert M. Pirsig. Reprinted by permission of William Morrow and Company, Inc.

Publication Manual of the American Psychological Association (3rd ed.), paraphrase of "Abstract" section used with permission of the publisher. Copyright © 1983 by the American Psychological Association. No part of this material may be reproduced in any form or by any means without the written permission of the APA.

Reader's Guide to Periodical Literature, © 1986 by the H. W. Wilson Company. Selection reproduced by permission of the publisher.

Caryl Rivers, "Rock Lyrics and Violence Against Women." Reprinted by permission of the author. Originally appeared in *The Boston Globe*.

Colleen Templin, Brian Molinari, Luis Villalta, Peter Charlton, and J. Stephen Headley, "Computer Design for 'Concentration.'" Reprinted by permission of the authors.

Index

ESL Index

This index refers to matters of sentence construction and usage of particular interest to students of English as a second language. The entries in the "Glossary of Usage" in this book are not indexed here.

British spellings, 427
Canadian spellings, 427
glossary of, 601–620
pronoun choices, 238–239
pronoun usage, 245
sexist language, avoiding, 237–239

V

Verb tense sequence, 273–277
  with clauses, 274–275
  with infinitives, 275–276
  with participles, 276–277
Verb tenses, 163–167. *See also* Verb
    tense sequence
  consistency in, 269–270
  defined, 163, 636
  for writing about literature, 555
  future perfect tense, 163, 167, 275,
    637
  future tense, 166
    defined, 636
  listing of, 636
  past perfect tense, 163, 166, 274
    defined, 636
  past tense, 163, 165–166, 217, 221,
    637
    defined, 163, 636
    events in literature, 636
    natural laws, 636
    scientific laws, 636
    timeless truths, 636
  present perfect tense, 163, 165
    defined, 163
  present tense, 164–165
    and habitual action, 636
    defined, 636
    events in literature, 636
    natural laws, 636
    scientific laws, 636
    timeless truths, 636
  progressive form of, 636
  shall, will
    determination, 617
    simple futurity, 617
  shifts in, 269–270
  simple future tense, 163
  simple past tense, 163

simple present tense, 163
writing about literature or history,
  270
Verbal phrases, 193–195
  absolute phrases, 194
  case of pronouns with, 249–251
  defined, 639
  gerund phrases, 194, 639
  infinitive phrases, 194–195, 639
  introductory comma after, 342
  participial phrases, 193–194, 639
Verbals, 189–191
  case of pronouns with, 249
  defined, 638
  gerunds, 189–190, 638
    pronouns preceding, 249
  infinitives, 190–191, 638
    present, 190–191
    present perfect, 190–191
    split, 191, 635
  introductory comma after, 342
  past participle, 190, 638
  present participle, 190, 638
Verbs
  action verbs, 111–112, 156–158,
    258–259, 637
  auxiliary verbs, 161–163, 207,
    623
  complete verbs, 207
  compound, 625
  defined, 156, 637
  finite verbs, 207
  intransitive verbs, 157–158, 637
  irregular verbs, 162, 217–221
    defined, 628
    listing of, 218–221
  linking verbs, 143, 151, 158–159,
    258–259, 632, 637
    listing of, 158–159
  modals, 161–163, 207
    defined, 162, 628
    listed, 162, 628
  mood, 168–170. *See also* Mood of
    verbs
    defined, 168, 628–629
    imperative mood, 168–169,
      628–629
    indicative mood, 168, 628–629

CONTENTS